NAKED THEATER & UNCENSORED HORROR

A Memoir by
Stuart Gordon

FAB PRESS

NAKED THEATER & UNCENSORED HORROR
A MEMOIR BY STUART GORDON

First edition published by FAB Press, 2023

FAB Press Ltd., 2 Farleigh, Ramsden Road
Godalming, Surrey, GU7 1QE, England, U.K.

www.fabpress.com

Managing Editor Gavin Baddeley
Page Layout, Typesetting and Design by Harvey Fenton
Cover Illustration by Jason Heeley
Index compiled by Francis Brewster

A CIP catalogue record for this book is available from the British Library

hardcover:
ISBN 978 1 913051 22 8
paperback:
ISBN 978 1 913051 23 5

Printed in the Czech Republic

To all the clowns who bring us God's greatest gifts:
laughter and joy.

PETER JACKSON

"Stuart Gordon not only made terrific movies, he also achieved a rare status – his work inspired many young filmmakers, resulting in a legacy much larger than his own body of work.

I am one of those filmmakers who was forever changed by seeing movies like *Re-Animator* and *From Beyond*. It's very possible that I wouldn't have made *Braindead* if it hadn't been for *Re-Animator*. Stuart's fearlessness and his delight in breaking cinematic taboos fueled my imagination at a critical time.

Several years ago, I was lucky enough to meet Stuart, and was touched by how gentle and modest he was. He was one of the good guys."

MICK GARRIS

"I first met Stuart Gordon at a *Fangoria* convention decades ago. I was with John Landis, George Romero and Tom Savini at the time, and it was pretty momentous, and may well have been when the first seeds were planted that led to our little dinner group, Masters of Horror. Already a huge fan of his work, I was struck by his dark humor, contrasted by a charming sweetness that was always present. When the Masters dinner gave birth to the *Masters of Horror* TV series, I knew that Stuart had to be a part of it.

During the production of his two episodes, I got to know him even better. He was a brilliant man who never let the years sand down the brash boldness of his filmmaking, his sense of cinematic exploration, or delighting in breaking taboos and boundaries. He was Santa with horns, a remarkable, funny, devilish and delightful man… with a sense of humor that sometimes would sneak up on you.

When we were filming his *The Black Cat* MoH episode, there is a scene where the eye of a black cat is being gouged out, and we were talking with the make-up effects guys from KNB about how to handle it. Stuart, without a trace of a smile, said we could just go to an animal shelter and do it for real. I didn't know what to think. He knew I was vegan, a member of PETA, and concerned about animals and their rights. He had a completely straight face as he made his suggestion, before it became quite clear that he was fucking with me.

I cherish his memory, and my fortune in being his friend. Stuart, I love you and miss you."

RICK BAKER

"Back in the '90s, I was a guest at the Sitges film festival. Stuart Gordon was a guest as well. I was very excited to meet him because *Re-Animator* is one of those films that I can watch over and over again and still enjoy it just as much each time as I did the first time. I really appreciated that despite the budgetary restrictions Stuart made a very entertaining film. Stuart was very approachable and friendly.

Not so much when I invited him to my shop-opening Halloween party. He came in a strait jacket foaming at the mouth and stayed in it, and stayed in character, all night long. That made me like him even more than before. I am so sad that we lost such a talented filmmaker and swell guy."

ROB ZOMBIE

"The '80s were definitely a jam-packed decade for horror films. Some amazing… some not so amazing. But without a doubt, nothing sliced through the crowded field like *Re-Animator*. I still clearly remember wandering into a New York City theater in 1985 with no knowledge as to what I was about to watch. Needless to say, I was floored. Scene after scene of shocking…yet hilarious insanity. Who was this director named Stuart Gordon? He must be crazy.

Many years later, I finally met the man responsible for this horrific masterpiece. It was strangely enough over lunch at an Italian restaurant on Cahuenga Boulevard in Hollywood. And as it turns out, this maniac director was actually a really nice, funny guy. In fact, Stuart was one of the first directors to graciously welcome me into this crazy world of horror directors. He made me feel right at home. For that, I will always be grateful. Rest in peace Stuart."

JOE MANTEGNA

"As one goes through their life, there are obviously countless individuals who will have an impact on that life, some more significant than others. Stuart Gordon was one of those individuals who had a tremendous impact on my life to the extent that he is among a handful of people who I can directly credit to having contributed greatly to not just the success I've had in my profession, but also served as a role model for friendship, marital relationships and parenthood."

"The older I get, the more clearly I remember things that never happened."

~ Mark Twain ~

CONTENTS

CONTENTS

A Message from the Family

During the filming of *Castle Freak*, our family stayed in the Italian castle where the movie was shot. Not only was the estate every bit as picturesque and charming as you might imagine, but it made Dad's commute to set relatively nonexistent and eased the sting of late-night filming. During one such night, just as our mother tucked our youngest sister into bed, there was a knock at the door. One of the film's PAs alerted us that they would be using the hallway just outside our room for a scene. "Please don't open your doors, and try not to make noise," she requested. But it wasn't long before there was noise — lots of it — in the form of blood-curdling screams and footsteps racing down our hallway followed by the more labored moans of the infamous "freak" following behind.

Just as the screams reached a terrifying crescendo, Dad's familiar voice boomed through the walls. "Cut!" he shouted. Minutes later the scene would play out again. On and on the sequence went until the noises outside our door were more routine than heart-racing, and the screams somehow began to lull us to sleep. Only a wall divided our family from the awesomely grotesque world just outside our door, and as always, Dad was the gatekeeper.

Growing up with a father who played make-believe for a living meant being accustomed to these unexpected moments — developing a zest for adventure and embracing the uniquely enchanting (and sometimes horrific) experiences that came with it. Life in our house was mostly typical: Friday Shabbat dinners, walking the dog, birthday parties… And sometimes not: Trips to far off places, Cirque du Soleil performers as house guests, recipes for fake blood…

Somehow Dad deftly straddled the line between director and family man in a way that enabled him to devote himself to everything and everyone. No one was ever deprived of his passion, brilliance, or humor — least of all his family. Whether he was crafting a complicated gory effect or helping his six-year-old transform into a "Bio-Mechanical-Warrior" for her school's Halloween parade, everyone got his best work. Dad always kept us close to his orbit no matter how involved he became in his projects. His work bag often housed our drawings and scribbles along with his scripts. He was a diehard sentimentalist and held onto just about every handmade gift we ever bestowed. "Treasures," he called them.

Dad also had a knack for finding the magic in seemingly mundane activities. It's true that the inspiration for *Honey, I Shrunk the Kids* stemmed from our love of *The Incredible Shrinking Woman*, but the concept for the script came about one evening when we pressed him for a bedtime story. There, sandwiched between our twin beds, Dad effortlessly spun the zany tale of a mad scientist who invents a machine that accidentally shrinks his own children as if it all just came to him. What started as an attempt to get two little girls to sleep somehow evolved into an epic film franchise (one intended for children this time). He was a gifted storyteller.

As this book documents, Dad's life was packed with shocking escapades, spectacular success, heartbreaking failures, lifelong friendships, and, of course, one epic love story. Some of it is almost too crazy to be believed, which is why nothing pleased him more than sharing his wild adventures with fresh ears. Dad loved holding court and reliving these fond memories. Dinners that started with Mom's chicken and dumplings often ended with a table piled high with books, music, or photos used to reference one thing or another, with the conversation lasting well into the night.

What a blessing it is to have these memories, told in Dad's own words, here for us to enjoy for generations. These are stories that deserve to be shared. His ongoing quest to overcome "the suits" in the name of art certainly provided us kids with endless entertainment and a hefty dose of pride. Only recently did it dawn on us just how impressive it is that he made a living in such a fickle industry without sacrificing his rebellious spirit. Still, there are so many details about the way Dad told a story that we will miss dearly — how his eyes grew wide before he delivered a punchline, his ability to quote Sir Winston Churchill and *The Producers* almost interchangeably for emphasis, the way a particular memory would strike him in such a fashion that his laugh would morph into a chortle.

Over the years, the door between Dad's world and our own opened wider and wider. We learned that he enjoyed what some would view as a lifetime of excitement before any of us children were even on the scene. We learned how special it was to have a father who remained true to his 11-year-old self even at the age of 72.

As his best friend and longtime collaborator Dennis Paoli writes in *The PS Book of Fantastic Fictioneers: A History of the Incredible*, "Stuart is a kid. At heart and at work. To credit his scripting and developing of the sci-fi fantasy *Honey, I Shrunk the Kids* is to recall his love for the movies he watched when he was young (and the Sunday comics: it was originally titled *The Teenie Weenies*). When Stuart directs, he is young, and his films have the energy — the inquisitive, transgressive, transcendent energy — of youth. And we are young watching them, impatient for them to begin, eager to be thrilled and surprised as we watch, delighted describing our favorite scenes to friends afterwards."

We learned that, while he loved horror, Dad lived fearlessly.

Our mother often likes to say that she "hitched her wagon" to Dad's star (he would surely say the same about her), but each of us feels quite privileged to have shared in the great adventure that was his life. Now we can all share in it together.

~ *Suzanna Gordon, Jillian Gordon, and Margaret Gordon-Carlile*

Prologue

I am often called Stuart "Re-Animator" Gordon. The middle name is the title of my best-known movie. It's based on a series of short stories by H.P. Lovecraft about a pair of medical students who develop a serum that can bring the dead back to life.

In 1984, after I'd been the artistic director of the Organic Theater Company in Chicago for fifteen years, my friend Bob Greenberg graciously gave me the opportunity to direct my first feature film. His generosity was not lost on me, and I accepted his kind offer on the condition that Bob would serve as my consigliore and guide me through the minefields of the motion picture industry.

Right after Thanksgiving and a week before we were to begin shooting, we had a meeting of the entire crew to hand out scripts and schedules. Bob suggested that I make a little speech to give them a sense of why I was making this movie. I wasn't sure what I would say as I tried to put into words what this film meant to me. Why had I chosen this story? What was the personal connection? And then it struck me. The movie was about conquering death. And who would I bring back to life if I could?

The answer was simple: my father.

Bernard L. Gordon died on December 24, 1961. He was 52. I was 14. He was handsome and so dark that his friends in high school had called him Sheik. As a teenager, he had studied drafting in the hopes of becoming an architect. But the Great Depression had killed that dream with its dearth of new construction, and Bernie needed to find immediate work to help feed his family, so he never did attend college.

A damaged heart, the result of contracting rheumatic fever as a child, had kept him out of the army during World War II. Wanting to do his part, he got a job working for Helene Curtis, who went from manufacturing shampoos and cosmetics to making shell casings for the war effort. They were so impressed with him that when peace finally came, they offered him a permanent position. Bernie soon became a production manager. My parents wed on October 27, 1946. My mother, Rosalie Sabath, married at the age of 36. Although an attractive blonde, her family somehow thought that she was destined to forever remain an old maid. In fact, her older brother Donald assumed that she would take care of their father Isidor, who had become a widower during the 1930s. My mother dutifully explained her situation to Bernie the night that he proposed. To her surprise and great relief, he told her that Isidor would be welcome to live with them.

So my father, mother, little brother David, Grandpa Isidor, and I all lived happily together in a little house on Keystone Avenue on the northwest side of Chicago. My folks let my grandfather sleep in the downstairs master bedroom, as climbing stairs was difficult for him. And my dad always insisted that Grandpa sit at the head of the table. That's the kind of man my father was.

Shortly after I entered high school, my father's heart condition worsened, and on Christmas Eve my mother came home from the hospital with my Uncle Donald. She looked pale and drawn. She called to David and me and we came to her and she hugged us. My father was dead.

It was snowing, and I remember looking out the window at the blueness and coldness of the evening sky. I felt numb. His funeral was a blur. Our rabbi spoke at his memorial, calling my dad a saint, a strange thing for a rabbi to say since my father was not an observant Jew. But he had always made sure that we followed his example and cared about our friends and family, doing for others whenever possible.

Sitting shiva, the parade of relatives and friends began. "Just let me know if there's anything we can do" became the most dreaded sentence in the English language. I escaped, spending as much time out of the house as I could. I didn't cry for over a year, until it finally began to sink in that my father was really gone forever. That I would never see him again. I've learned that this is how it is. When someone you love dies, you go into shock, which lasts for months. You can't believe it. It seems like he's gone on a trip and over time you slowly begin to realize that he isn't coming back. Ever.

I told my crew about the dreams I had in which my father was back with me, and how he sometimes looked as if he had crawled out of a grave. I still have these dreams. Often, he appears to me as he did when he was sick, looking haggard and frail. But I don't care, I'm so grateful to be with him again. It usually hits me during the dream that he's dead, but I don't want to mention it for fear that this will embarrass him and break the spell. I just hug him, holding him tight. I tell him that I love him, and he murmurs back that he loves me too, but I can barely hear him. "Dad, we've been given a second chance," I tell him, meaning that we could finally be together again and then I wake up. It always seems so real. "It's better to have a loved one back no matter how fucked up he or she may be than not to have them at all," I told my crew and I found I was getting a little choked up as I went on. They sat on the edges of their seats and you could hear a pin drop. They were starting to believe that this was a special project and suddenly we were all on the same page. Working in this new world of film was a huge change from my experiences as a member of a theater company. I was living in a strange city without my friends and family and I felt very much alone. I was also afraid. Here I was about to get my first chance to direct a real movie. What if I wasn't up to the task? I had had so many failures. Would this be another? And if it were a disaster, what would happen to me after my dream had died?

PART ONE

MADISON

CHAPTER 1

Carolyn

In September of 1965, I sat on a Greyhound bus with Dennis Paoli, my best friend from high school, bound for the University of Wisconsin in Madison to begin our freshman year. We were both eighteen years old: I, large and heavy-set, Dennis, short and exceedingly hairy. We both wore glasses. When the bus stopped to drop off passengers at a gas station in Beloit, on the Illinois/Wisconsin border, we noticed a "Help Wanted" sign in the station window. We were so nervous about starting college that we seriously discussed whether or not to get off the bus and apply for the job. Before we could decide, the bus door slammed shut and we were off to an unknown future. "There was only one job anyway," I said half-jokingly.

"You could always make spare change giving blow jobs in the toilet," Dennis replied.

I chose the University of Wisconsin in Madison because I heard it was a party school and was close enough to allow me to come home on weekends. My attempts to get into an Ivy League school had been a fiasco. Somehow, I had gotten through the preliminary screening process for Harvard and was invited to an interview by a group of alumni at the toney Standard Club. Wearing my tweediest sports coat, I seemed to be making a good impression until somehow the subject of censorship came up. "Is there censorship in America?" someone had asked. "Don't we have a free press?"

I took the bait. "Not really," I replied. "There are some things we aren't allowed to see." Like what? Don't we have magazines like *Playboy* that leave nothing to the imagination? "*Playboy* doesn't show everything," I said, and this is where I should have stopped.

The alums feigned surprise. "Really? What don't they show?" they asked.

And being an idiot, I continued, "They don't show public hair," I replied.

The alums looked at each other. One of them snorted. "Don't show *what*?"

"Public hair," I repeated.

Good-bye Harvard. Hello Madison.

Upon arrival at the university we checked into Ogg Hall West, one of the new high-rise dorms that had just been built to handle the glut of us baby-boomers. We were on the eighth floor and our room looked down on a vacant lot near the railroad tracks. Scenic.

We quickly met our neighbors. There was an assortment of locals from various Wisconsin small towns and some east coast guys from places like "Marston, New Jersey." We later learned he meant "Morristown," mangled by his thick Jersey accent. They asked us if we wanted to hit the bars, which surprised us since we were all underage. "This is the land of sky-blue waters," one of them informed us, quoting the Hamm's Beer ads. "You can drink all the beer you want, but you gotta have a beer card." This involved sending a copy of your birth certificate to the Wisconsin Secretary of State and usually took a couple of weeks.

The first day we had to report to the Field House, an enormous red brick building where basketball games were played. Folding chairs were set up on the court to accommodate the enormous class of 1965, the biggest in the history of the University of Wisconsin. But any pride or self-satisfaction in this was to be short-lived. "Look to your right," the University's Chancellor told us in his welcoming address, and we all did so. "Now look to your left. Neither of those people will be here by the time you graduate." A sobering moment indeed, until we later realized that it meant that absolutely no one would make it through to the end of the four years. Little did I realize that I would become one of those poor saps who didn't graduate.

I had no idea what to major in so I took general studies, which included anthropology and psychology as well as a drawing class, that I was sure I could ace. The anthro class involved reading a book entitled *Knowing the Gururumba*. Who the fuck wanted to know about the Gururumba, some obscure tribe in the highlands of New Guinea? Could there be anything more pointless? But I needed to stay in school. We were at war in Vietnam and if I flunked out, I'd be drafted on the spot and sent there to fight and most likely die or have my dick shot off in a war that was even more senseless than reading a book about the fucking Gururumba. So I studied their complicated kinship systems and funeral rites.

A few weeks into the course, my Aunt Eleanor's husband Ted died of a massive heart attack, and I went home for his funeral. While I watched the funeral proceedings I had come to know too well, I realized that our traditional funeral rituals were not that different from the Gururumba. For example, instead of covering the corpse's face with make-up to make him look alive as we did, the Gururumba painted the deceased a chalky white. Suddenly my anthro class started to make perfect sense to me. I realized that all people have the same needs and feelings and fears. Whether a member of a technically evolved society in America or a primitive tribe in New Guinea, people are people. And more importantly, I discovered that everything you learn is useful, no matter how obscure it might seem at the time. At some point in your life you will be called upon to put every bit of knowledge you've acquired to use.

I returned to Madison and found my beer card from the Wisconsin Secretary of State waiting for me in my mailbox. That evening Paoli and I and our new friends from Ogg West went out to put it to use. After several pitchers at the KK (Kollege Klub) we stumbled back to the dorm.

CAROLYN

Having come from Lane Technical High School, an all-boys vocational establishment, girls held a special place in our lustful boyhood hearts. Girls were like mythical creatures to us. Any time a reasonably good-looking female set foot in our lunchroom, everyone went nuts, pounding on the tables and whistling like they do in prison movies. Even sexy teachers caused an uproar. Intoxicated with our first beer buzz, we madly began dialing random phone numbers in the hope of finding a member of the female sex. All the campus numbers began 262 and then we dialed whatever numbers came into our drunken minds. When my turn came, I got lucky. A pleasant female voice answered: "Hello?" I motioned to the others. I got one! They crowded around the phone trying to hear. "Who is this?" she asked.

"Who's this?" I asked her back.

"I asked you first," she said sounding a little irritated.

"Well, I asked you second," was my lame reply.

"Who are you calling?" she wanted to know.

"You. Are you pretty? You sound beautiful."

She laughed. "Very beautiful," she told me, "A knock-out. And you sound really drunk."

I covered the mouthpiece. "She's beautiful!" I told the others. "What's your name?" I asked her.

"Carolyn."

"That's a pretty name. You sound nice."

"Ask her if we can come over," shouted Paoli and I did.

"They want to come over," I heard her say.

"She's talking to someone."

"Her roommate!" Paoli whispered. "Ask her what *she* looks like."

"Where do you live?"

"No, you can't come over. It's too late. We're in bed."

"They're in bed!" the guys hooted.

"Where?!" Paoli wanted to know.

"Call us again when it's not so late and you're sober."

And with that she hung up.

Shit! Where's her number? What number? You made it up. I wracked my brain trying to remember.

The next day, after a few dozen wrong numbers, I finally reconnected with Carolyn. We talked for hours. I had never met a girl so easy to talk to. I found out that her last name was Purdy, that she was studying to become a nurse and that she came from Janesville, Wisconsin, where her father was a doctor. We told each other about ourselves and our families and our friends, our hopes, and our dreams. This went on for weeks on the phone.

One day I suggested that it was time we should finally meet. I had an assignment in my art class to draw some Victorian houses on the corner of Pinckney and Gilman. I asked her to meet me there after class. I sketched the buildings and waited. It started getting dark. No Carolyn. When I got back to my dorm room, I called her. What happened? It turned out she had talked to her sister who had advised her not to go. After all, she didn't know me as we had never been properly introduced. I laughed. This sounded more Victorian than the buildings on Pinckney and Gilman. "How do you do, my name is Stuart Gordon," I told her. "And you are…?" We picked another time and place to meet the next day. But this time, I decided that two can play at this game. So I didn't show up.

That evening I called her and apologized for standing her up. "I guess I had it coming," she told me.

"Alright," I said. "Come on downstairs. I'm in the lobby of your dorm."

I waited what seemed like several hours, but was really just a few minutes, and finally I heard her voice behind me, "Stuart?" I turned around and there was the most beautiful girl I had ever seen. Enormous sparkling jade-green eyes that turned into crescent moons when she smiled, and what a terrific smile! She wore a tennis sweater and a pair of wheat jeans over a perfect figure. I couldn't speak. And neither could she. After weeks of wonderful endless chatter, we were suddenly both completely speechless.

Carolyn later told me that she had thought that I was a juvenile delinquent because I wore a leather motorcycle jacket, engineer boots and had long sideburns. She believed that I was a diamond in the rough that with some work could be cleaned up and civilized – a back-alley hood that she could help go straight. The result turned out to be exactly the opposite. I corrupted her.

I thought that Carolyn must come from a rich family, her father being a doctor and so on. Her grace, wit, modesty and natural ability to put people at ease contributed to this perception. I instantly knew she was the one for me.

The rest of the semester flew by. I was in love. I begged her to marry me. She laughed. "We hardly know each other." Every evening we ended up kissing goodnight with the throngs of other lovers at her dorm's back door. There was a 10:30 curfew during the week and a 12:30 AM curfew on Friday and Saturday nights.

We clutched each other tightly in the midst of a hundred other couples, until the lights blinked and Miss Bone, the tall skinny, spinsterish house mother, opened the door and called out "One minute!" Then the girls had to say their goodbyes and go inside. I would rush back to my dorm, and Carolyn and I were on the phone into the wee hours.

Over winter break, Carolyn's parents separated.

Not wishing to spend Christmas with her mother and younger brother now that her father had left, Carolyn stayed by herself in the now deserted dorm through the winter break. But the phone lines between Madison and Chicago hummed with activity. I learned that Carolyn had a steady boyfriend in Janesville who went to Northwestern University, and I made up my mind that I would take her away from him or die trying.

Summer came and I made visits to Janesville to see her, and she visited me in Chicago. That summer of '66 became unforgettable when Martin Luther King decided to lead Civil Rights marches through Chicago neighborhoods, picketing for open housing. "There's no racism in Chicago," Mayor Richard J. Daley told him.

"Then there shouldn't be any trouble, should there?" was Dr. King's reply.

One Sunday afternoon, my friend Ron Berman picked me up in his VW bug and we drove to a church on Chicago's south side to join the civil rights marchers. We were asked to provide transportation for two other marchers, a middle-aged black couple who were veterans of King's marches in Selma and Birmingham. They described some of the hair-raising episodes they had endured: snarling dogs, fire hoses and rocks and even Molotov cocktails thrown at the protestors. "But nothing like that will happen here," I offered nervously. "This is Chicago."

"We'll see," the black man responded. "In the south at least you know where you stand. Anything is possible here." When we arrived in Evergreen Park, we found the streets lined with angry white neighbors. Many carried signs: "Niggers go home!" A cordon of baton wielding Chicago police kept them on the sidewalks and at a safe distance from the marchers. As we assembled to begin the march, the mob erupted in screamed taunts. Rocks, bricks and bottles were thrown. A bare-chested man roared past on a motorcycle waving a Confederate flag. I couldn't believe my eyes. We might as well have been in Alabama. We marched down the street singing "We Shall Overcome" as the rocks and bricks landed at our feet and bottles shattered on the pavement. Often the line would be forced to stop, and we covered our heads as the police struggled to keep the mob from tearing us apart. One officer went down, his head bleeding from a rock. But we kept marching. When we got to the end of the gauntlet, we stumbled to our car and headed back to the church, where the other returning marchers described similar reactions in Cicero and Gage Park. "It was worse than Selma," they told us. Dr. King had been hit by a brick but kept on marching.

"I've been hit so many times, I'm immune to it," he was later quoted as saying.

Mayor Daley used to make a speech in which he said that the neighborhoods of Chicago were like a beautiful patchwork quilt. Rainbow colors, side by side.

What he didn't say was that if you happened to leave your neighborhood and venture into another, you might get your skull cracked open by a baseball bat. "These aren't neighborhoods, they're ghettos," King said.

As Ron and I drove home, still badly shaken, we talked about the rednecks on the south side. Chicago has always been a divided city, Northside and Southside, Cubs and White Sox. But a couple of weeks later I watched my own neighbors transform into howling racists as King marched through my neighborhood. To see my usually kindly neighborhood women, some holding their babies and small children, shrieking the foulest insults imaginable made me realize how hard it is to live in America if you're not white; how strong and poisonous the hatred can be that everyday people carry around inside themselves, and how little it takes to make it explode.

And I learned what true bravery is: I didn't have it. I had marched once and had ended up shaking like a leaf, never to join King again. He and his followers had stood up to the ugly face of racism again and again and didn't quit until laws and attitudes were changed. I also learned the most disturbing lesson of all: that deep down, no matter what we say, we are all racists. Every one of us.

I counted the days until school started again and Carolyn and I could be together, but when I got back to Madison, she informed me that she didn't want to see me anymore. Why? I wanted to know. She said that she really needed to concentrate on her studies without me distracting her. I suspected that her boyfriend in Janesville was somehow behind this and tried to talk her out of it. But she was having none of it – or me. My heart was broken.

I tried calling her, in an attempt to continue our wonderful conversations, I even tried the dreaded "Can't we just be friends?" but to no avail. My life was going nowhere. I knew that next year I would have to declare a major and I had absolutely no idea what I wanted to do. Then I remembered the 8mm movies that I had made for fun (and no profit) with my friends as a teenager, and decided to enroll in the film class. In those days there was only one course, mostly for grad students, and sadly it was already full. So I decided to take a beginners acting class instead, thinking that learning about acting was something that could be helpful making films.

My teacher was Bob Buzecky, an instructor from New York who had performed on and off Broadway. He was a devotee of Stanislavsky's Method. During the following weeks he taught us about objectives, super objectives, given circumstances, and beats.

Beats is a term for units of action that had come from one of Stanislavsky's Russian apostles who was describing the process of breaking down a scene. "Is like eating a turkey," she began. "You cannot eat whole turkey in one bite so you must cut him up in little beats." She meant to say "bits" but, because of her accent, it became "beats" ever since, for all time.

I learned that acting always begins with yourself. You must believe that the story's events or given circumstances are really happening to you. You aren't pretending to be someone else. It's you up there and you must be ready to reveal yourself with complete honesty. This is why good acting is so difficult.

I also was introduced to visiting celebrities. George Stevens, the great film director of *Giant*, talked to us about his decision to use the sound effect of a howitzer for the first gunshot in his classic western *Shane*. "I wanted the audience to feel the power of a gun," he told our class. I actually shook hands with the amazing comedian Harold Lloyd, who showed us that he was missing his right thumb and index finger due to a mistimed gag in one of his silent films. When you see him clinging to the side of a building hundreds of feet above the pavement in *Safety Last!*, he is wearing a prosthetic glove to cover their loss.[1]

* * *

One day as I was coming down Bascom Hill, I ran into Carolyn who was with a group of her sorority sisters from Alpha Phi. I stopped to say hello and she actually seemed happy to see me. We talked about the fact that the TV series *The Fugitive* was having its final episode on Friday and that Dr. David Kimble would finally confront the one-armed man who had murdered his wife. "Why don't you come over and watch it with me and my roommates?" I offered. "In fact, I'll even make dinner for you."

"You can cook?"

"Sure," I told her. "I'm a terrific cook."

The fact is that I'm not much of a cook at all. Fried eggs and burgers are about it for me. But that night I called my mom and got some advice. When Carolyn showed up that Friday night, I served her what we called "Gordon Steak," a thick chuck steak tenderized within an inch of its life with MSG. This delight was accompanied by frozen French fries heated up on a cookie sheet, and green bean casserole (canned beans in mushroom soup with canned fried onions forming a crust on the top) all things that my mother assured me were so simple to prepare that even I couldn't screw them up. I had even gotten a bottle of wine and some candles to create a romantic atmosphere.

"Where are your roommates?" Carolyn asked when she arrived, looking around nervously.

"They went to the movies," I told her, failing to mention that I had paid them off to get lost for the evening. She seemed to like the meal and after

---

1 NOTE: Existing sources maintain that the accident occurred with a prop bomb during a photo shoot. Perhaps Mr. Lloyd decided to embellish his recollection in relating it to the students.

dinner as we sat on the couch and watched *The Fugitive*, I don't remember if Dr. Kimble ever found the one-armed man because we ended up in each other's arms kissing passionately. It turned out she had broken up with her boyfriend. Ah Bliss. I ended up trying to pull her into bed with me even though I was burning up with a 104-degree fever. But that was nothing compared to the heat I felt for her.

As the weeks went by our relationship intensified and I pleaded with her to marry me, or at the very least consummate our lust. She was worried about my roommates hearing our lovemaking and so I hatched a plan to find some privacy. I discovered that there was a dusty attic above our apartment and in it I found an old mattress leaning up against a wall. One afternoon, while my roommates were at class, I led Carolyn up the stairs to the attic and showed her the secret bedroom I had created. As sunlight streamed in through the one window and created leafy patterns on the mattress, our bodies entwined amidst the dancing dust mites.

Although I have to admit that the first few times were very brief, due to over-excitement on my part, Carolyn was patient and encouraging and together we learned the best way to express our love for each other. We made love constantly and how we managed to pass our final exams is still a complete mystery. Youth believes that they are the first people on Earth to discover sex, and if I had practiced the clarinet as much, I'd be Benny Goodman.

1967 was called "The Summer of Love" and I can personally attest that it was.

CHAPTER 2

Taking Sides

There was another new love in my life: THEATER. That fall I declared myself a theater major, and it was a requirement of Advanced Acting that everyone had to appear in a play, so I auditioned for a production of *Marat/Sade* by German playwright Peter Weiss. The full title (which tells it all) is: *The Persecution and Assassination of Jean Paul Marat as Performed by the Inmates of the Asylum of Charenton Under the Direction of the Marquis de Sade.*

Unlike most plays, the audience of *Marat/Sade* actually plays a part in the proceedings. They are the invited guests to the mad house, there to watch the wild antics of the lunatics. The audience soon senses that things can go horribly wrong as the patients, directed by fellow inmate de Sade, seem barely controlled by the club wielding nuns (played by men) and could leap into the audience to rape and pillage the spectators at any moment (which is how the play concludes). This was a revelation to me, as I had always thought of theater as bad movies: watching tiny figures overacting from the second balcony distanced further by the invisible "fourth wall." Little did I realize that this play would provide a glimpse into the future, events that were about to take place in our own country that would change my life for all time. What I did realize was that this play introduced me to the raw power of theater. "The most important thing," says Weiss' Marat, "is to pull yourself up by your own hair, to turn yourself inside out and see the whole world with fresh eyes." And that's exactly what his play did to me.

Marat/Sade had its English language premiere in 1965 at the Royal Shakespeare Company under the direction of the visionary Peter Brook. Now it was being directed at the University of Wisconsin by Professor Ed Amor, newly hired by the department in the hope that he would bring avant-garde theater to Madison. Besides utilizing the alienation techniques of Brecht and the Theater of Cruelty of Artaud, the play would also feature nudity (a first for the college). Ed Amor seemed young and hip. In his late thirties, slim and graceful, he wore his longish black hair combed straight back and often had a sweater draped over his shoulders Italian style.

We were asked to sing at the audition as the play is a musical with a rousing score by Richard Peaslee. My voice isn't great, but I can carry a tune, and the song got enough laughs to get me cast as an inmate. I decided to play the part as if I had a lobotomy, wearing a bloody bandage around my head. I stumbled around like Boris Karloff's Mummy, with a palsied hand. And I decided to drool. A lot.

I made friends with the other cast members: flower child Lois Danzig and Ina Jaffe, who played the guitar and had a Joan Baez-like voice and repertoire. She was very cool (and still is) a petite beauty with long dark hair, always wearing black, who didn't have the time of day for me.

All the major roles were played by graduate students, one of whom complained that my drooling was upstaging her song. Maybe it was, because I was drooling from the top of a twenty- foot platform and each strand of spittle hit the stage floor with a resounding "Plop! Plop! Plop!"

I met the charismatic Richard Fire: tall, rail-thin and very intense. He was Marat, who sat in his bathtub until the end of the first act when he rose naked (his back to the audience with a sock covering his dick). I guess Richard wore the sock to protect the virginal eyes of the female cast members, which didn't make a lot of sense as Richard ended up sleeping with almost all of them. I don't think I ever spoke to Richard during the entire production.

Ten days before the play opened, an event occurred in Madison that rocked the once quiet college town. On October 18th, 1967, a peaceful sit-in protesting the presence of recruiters for Dow Chemical was forcefully broken up by the Madison Police Department. Striding in wearing helmets and carrying baseball bat-sized clubs, they attacked the protestors, injuring 74 students (among them Paul Soglin, who six years later would be elected mayor of Madison). The reason for the sit-in was that Dow Chemical was manufacturing napalm, a jellied gasoline that our Air Force was using to bomb civilians in Vietnam, literally burning off their skins. But the over-reaction of the powers-that-be showed their very real fear of what they perceived as the beginning of a very real revolution.

The brutality of the police polarized the student body, radicalizing thousands, among them my darling Carolyn who, like many others, was tear gassed on her way to class. The old university of beer suppers and panty raids was changing into a political hotbed. A war at home. And *Marat/Sade* with its themes of revolution and madness was amazingly on target. When the nuns began to beat the inmates with clubs, you could hear the audience gasping with recognition and anger.

I was now completely obsessed with the power of theater. I found myself performing in student productions. I also decided that directing was where it was at. I knew that if I directed, I could be sure to get my ideas before an audience. For better or worse.

Every spring there was a play writing contest, and the winner would have his play produced in the little 150-seat Play Circle Theater. I was taking a creative writing class with Professor Richard Knowles in the English department, and when I asked him if I could write a play instead of a short story, he replied, "Why not?" So I went to work. The ideas from *Marat/Sade* were swirling around in my head and I knew I wanted the piece to involve audience participation.

There was a television game show that was popular at the time called *Let's Make a Deal* in which Monty Hall, the emcee, would tempt the contestants with a handful of cash or whatever was behind Door #3. He reminded me of Satan himself. I came up with the idea of a game show that would take this concept a bit further: make the contestants do embarrassing things for money, escalating from humiliation to beatings, torture, rape and ultimately murder. I saw it as a condemnation of capitalism and the "anything for a buck" attitude that we embrace as a society.

I decided to see how far I could push this, to make an audience believe that they were in real physical danger. Of course, causing genuine harm to audience members would be criminal and could end up with me doing twenty-five to life. But what if the audience members seemingly being harmed were actually actors, planted in the audience?

I named the master-of ceremonies Monty, after the devilish Mr. Hall, and he was assisted by Wanda, a beautiful, imposing dominatrix (a term I had yet to learn in those innocent days). A group of large muscular ushers carried out Monty's orders and the play began with them chaining the doors shut (with breakaway chains). I assumed that the audience would sit quietly, as they had for *Marat/Sade*, and my play ended with Monty bawling out the audience for allowing these unspeakable crimes to take place. I saw it as a condemnation of apathy. I named the play *The Game Show.*

The day of the first performance I decided to turn up the heat in the Play Circle as high as it would go in order to make the audience sweat even before things got tense, and they were given fake playbills listing imaginary characters and performers. The show began with an unseen voice announcing that half the parts would be played by understudies, and the audience, clutching their colored tickets, looked at each other wondering "what have we gotten ourselves into?" Then their attention turned to the auditorium doors as they heard the sound of chains sliding into place and watched as they were "locked in the theater" as enormous padlocks were clicked shut. Then with a burst of show-bizzy music, Monty took the stage and Wanda spun the color-wheel and we were off. The yellow ticket holders were herded into the contestant section down front, many looking back helplessly as they were separated from their dates, but it all seemed in good fun. The show began with a woman being offered money for a run in her stocking and since she had none, Monty encouraged her to tear her stocking herself. Which she gladly did. Then two male contestants were offered even more money if they would kiss each other on the lips. When they finally complied, they were humiliated as "fags" and dragged offstage. During intermission the audience was forced to stay in their seats and remain silent while the ushers roamed the aisles with large billy clubs, confronting anyone who spoke or tried to leave. As I sat taking notes, my legal pad was ripped out of my hands by one of the ushers and torn to pieces. Even I wasn't safe. I felt like Frankenstein. I had created a monster.

Act Two began with a contestant being whipped with a belt. This, of course, was a plant with hidden padding on his back, but the audience was clearly terrified. And when a woman contestant was forced to remove an item of clothing every time she made a mistake in repeating a loyalty oath, the show reached a whole new level. As her "husband" is beaten by the ushers for trying to rescue her, the woman is forced to remove her bra and tries to cover herself with her hands. But the imposing Wanda grabs the woman by her wrists and exposes her bare breasts to the audience while the victim sobs and screams for help. At this moment the entire audience leapt to its feet and charged the stage, attacking the performers. And they weren't throwing fake punches. The performance turned into a very real riot, with the actors trying to save themselves by running into the wings only to be dragged back onstage to be kicked and beaten by the enraged audience.

I don't remember how we restored order, but the crowd stormed the locked doors, easily snapping the break-away chains. Everyone was extremely shaken up. The audience stayed in the lobby hugging each other, some shaking, others crying, all of them traumatized. The actors were in even worse shape. This wasn't the way it was supposed to have happened. The audience was supposed to just sit there, only to be scolded for their apathy by Monty's final speech. But something much more exciting had occurred.

I assured the actors that this wouldn't happen again. Their safety was paramount. We'd tone down the show. We wouldn't lock the doors. But the next day there was a rave review in the *Daily Cardinal* by someone named bury st. edmund (all in lower case). He called the show revolutionary and said it was the most exciting piece of theater he had ever witnessed. Within hours, all remaining tickets were sold out. Since they were free, I'm not sure "sold out" is the correct term, but many ended up being scalped for exorbitant fees.

When I arrived at the theater for the matinee, the cast had had a change of heart. They wanted to do the show as we had the night before. But we needed to come up with a way to save them from the audience's rage if they rioted again. We devised a plan for an old song and dance man to appear onstage dressed in a skeleton suit singing "Ain't We Got Fun?" Our hope was that this would distract the audience long enough for our cast to escape their clutches and retreat backstage. My old buddy Dennis Paoli was drafted to play this extremely important role.

Sure enough the audience rose up again at exactly the same moment. It was as if they were following a scripted stage direction: "The audience riots."

Dennis sprang into action, "In the morning, In the evening, Ain't we got fun?" he sang. The audience stopped in mid attack, their jaws dropping, not knowing what to think, as the ushers quickly pushed them out of the theater.

I was so excited that I ran up to Carolyn, who had attended the performance, and couldn't stop talking about how brilliant I was until I realized she was looking at me like I had lost my mind… or my soul. "I don't know who you are anymore," she said, her eyes welling with tears. How could I do such a thing to a trusting audience? What kind of a person was I to put people through that? She compared *The Game Show* to yelling "Fire!" in a crowded theater and told me she didn't want to see me again. I was crushed. She even refused to talk to me when I called. But the show was the talk of the town and I was invited to hang out with Lawrence D. Cohen, the student film critic of the *Daily Cardinal* and his very cool friends: the Madison "in crowd." Larry was an undergraduate from Glencoe, Illinois who was the same age as me but seemed much older and wiser. Larry had a large third floor apartment in the same building as the Orpheum Theater on State Street and it was the closest thing that Madison had to a real salon.

I finally met the mysterious bury st. edmund, who turned out to be one Lenny Kleinfeld from Brooklyn. Caustic, cynical, profane and hilarious, Lenny and I soon became fast friends.

André De Shields was frequently there. A muscular black man with an Afro and a dancer's body, André was the first openly gay man I had ever met. I had first seen him at an audition for a show to be directed by Paul Gray, an *avant garde* theater artist who had worked with R.G. Davis of the San Francisco Mime Troupe and was a visiting artist in Madison. Gray was going to direct what he referred to as an "artistic assemblage" and asked André what he was going to do for his audition. André replied that he was going to sing "Stormy Monday." André spoke with perfect enunciation and almost an English accent, which I guess Paul Gray assumed was nervousness. "You don't need to be uptight, André" he told him. A long pause as André looked Paul Gray up and down, and replied, "I'm always uptight, Mr. Gray." Then he proceeded to belt out an amazing rendition of the blues song. That made such an impression that I always think of André' whenever I hear "Stormy Monday."

One day, I was summoned to the office of John Ezell, the chairman of the Theater Department. Because of him, Madison was known as the best school in the country for design and technical theater and his disciples went off into the world to design world class productions on and off Broadway.

I was nervous and didn't know what to expect, but Professor Ezell immediately put me at ease. "Call me John," he began. He told me how much he had enjoyed *The Game Show* and then asked me if I would be interested in a summer program dedicated to producing experimental theater. Of course,

I was. And he went on to say that we would do five productions, and the students who participated in them would receive college credit. Too good to be true. "I'd love to be a part of this," I told him. "What do you want me to do?" "I want you to run it," he answered. My jaw must have hit the floor, because he immediately cautioned me that there wasn't much money, but that there also would be no interference. Then he said my favorite words in the English language, "You can do whatever you want."

As I was leaving his office, my feet barely touching the floor, John turned to me and said, "Now this is just a thought, but do you think it would be possible to do a production of *Peter Pan* without flying harnesses?" I shrugged. *Peter Pan*? "I don't know," I told him, "Let me think about it."

When I told Larry Cohen about it, he offered to be my dramaturge. What should we name the program? We decided on "Screw Theater" because our plays would screw themselves into the audience's brain. Like a plague. Very Artaud. And we liked the pun too. Fuck the establishment. We immediately started coming up with ideas for our five productions.

We were sitting around Larry's dining room table brainstorming on the evening of June 5th, 1968. Lenny and Ina were sitting on the couch watching the election returns from the California primary. It was near midnight in Los Angeles and 2:00 AM in Madison, and it looked like Bobby Kennedy had beaten Eugene McCarthy – and was about to take the stage at the Ambassador Hotel. We huddled around the small black and white TV.

President Lyndon Johnson had chosen not to run for re-election. His escalation of the war in Vietnam and the mounting American death toll had made him extremely unpopular. Bobby Kennedy was our hope for real change, and for ending the hated war in 'Nam. The crowd at the Ambassador were chanting "Bobby! Bobby!" as he addressed his jubilant backers.

"I'm gonna work for him this summer," said Ina.

"Me too," said Lenny as he put his arm around her. Larry and I looked at each other. Yeah, right.

The crowd began chanting, "We want Bobby! We want Bobby!" And we chanted with them. It was the power of live television.

Suddenly there was the sound of screams and the chanting fell apart. There is a sense of panic onscreen as the crowd starts moving toward the exits. Voices were shouting, "Please stay back!"

We looked at each other. What was happening? An unidentified man approached the podium. "Would a doctor come right here?! We need a doctor here!" Larry started shaking his head, "No, no, no."

"Everyone please clear the room in an orderly fashion. Can you please clear the room so we can get medical aid to the Senator." Now we knew. We stared at the small TV in shock.

"They've shot him," said Lenny. "The motherfuckers have killed him."

The details began to emerge. As Kennedy was exiting through the kitchen, a young Palestinian named Sirhan Sirhan had approached Bobby with a .22 pistol and fired several shots into him. We saw Kennedy lying on the floor in a pool of blood, his head being held by a Latino busboy as he stared into space.

He died the next day.

We had just watched Bobby Kennedy assassinated on live television. It's hard to explain to someone who hasn't lived through the sixties what that was like. The closest thing to it in today's world was seeing the attack on the World Trade Center on September 11th, 2001. That event traumatized the country and escalated conflict in the Middle East. Now imagine if an event like that happened every other month, and you can begin to get an idea what 1968 was like.

Two months before Bobby was shot down in Los Angeles, Martin Luther King had been killed by a sniper's bullet in Memphis. As a result, the whole country erupted in riots coast to coast. JFK had been murdered in '63 and now, five years later, Dr. King and Bobby were both wiped out. It seemed as if all the good guys were getting killed off one by one; that the powers-that-be were putting out hits on anyone they perceived as a danger to their status quo.

A war was taking place on the streets of America. A revolution was being fought. As strait-jacketed Jacques Roux shouted in *Marat/Sade*, "When will you learn to take sides? When will you learn to stand up?"

Screw Theater

Screw Theater's first production was an adaptation of Shakespeare's *Titus Andronicus* entitled *Vis*, which means "force" or "strength" in Latin. It also forms the root of the word *violence*, and *Titus* may be the most violent play ever written, with rape, mutilations, murder and cannibalism graphically portrayed onstage. We decided to present it in a post-Apocalyptic style with our actors wearing tattered rags, and it was performed in the burned-out ruins of a university building that had recently been destroyed by fire. The audience sat on the edge of a blackened pit. But what made the show even more audacious was that I decided to cut all of Shakespeare's poetic language.

Could Shakespeare's story of a Roman general's revenge on the barbarian queen whose sons have raped and mutilated his daughter be told with grunts and growls in place of the bard's elegant and eloquent poetry? That was our experiment. With a company made up of my theater class friends (among them André De Shields as Aaron, the duplicitous slave) we began rehearsals. To stage the violence, we created gallons of fake blood. One of our inventions was washable blood, a combination of baby shampoo and red food coloring that would not permanently stain the costumes. The only drawback was that on opening night it started to drizzle, and all the bloody dead bodies began to foam up, much to the delight of the audience. The stage became so slippery, it's amazing that no one was seriously hurt. The show played to large enthusiastic audiences and rave reviews, which made it all worthwhile.

Something truly surprising occurred. After weeks of not hearing from her, Carolyn called and said she had to speak to me. She arrived at my apartment that evening, her eyes red from crying. She didn't want to tell me what was going on with my roommates around, so we went for a walk. "What is it?" I asked her. "What's wrong?"

"I love you," she sobbed. "I mean I'm in love with you." She was referring to the many discussions we'd had in which she had told me that she loved me but wasn't "in love with me" which meant that it wasn't serious, that she couldn't commit to spending the rest of her life with me. "I don't see us growing old together," she had said. But now she was saying something else. "I want to marry you," she told me. I must have looked shocked because she burst into tears. "Oh no, I knew it was too late. You don't want to marry me anymore." She started to rush off, but I grabbed her and pulled her into my arms. "Of course I want to marry you. I love you." She looked up into my eyes, not sure if I meant it. "I'm in love with you," I insisted. Now I was crying too. We hugged each other tight. We were back together. This time for good.

CHAPTER 3

What had changed her mind? "I just realized that I couldn't live without you," she told me. "I realized that I want to be a part of your life and go where you go. I want to be with you. Forever."

When I told my mother that we wanted to get married, she suggested that we should live together for a while. "What's the big rush?" she asked. Carolyn and I found two apartments in the same building on Henry Street, one right above the other. I (officially) lived alone and she had a female roommate, but we spent every minute we could together at my place. The only time she was upstairs in her apartment was when her dad visited.

We decided that we should tell her father that we wanted to get married, and that I should formally ask his permission. We invited him to Sunday dinner at Hoffman House, an upscale steak house in Madison. Dr. Purdy seemed nice enough: tall and thin, his reddish hair graying at the temples. He looked very much the kindly small-town doctor. We ordered a round of drinks. Beers for Carolyn and me and an Old Fashioned for the good doctor.

"I want to marry your daughter," I told him, getting right to the point. He looked at me, a little shocked. "I love her." There was a long pause.

"We love each other," Carolyn added, taking my arm.

"When were you thinking about doing this? Getting married, I mean?"

"Next year after we graduate," I answered.

He looked very relieved and took a big swallow of his Old Fashioned. "So, there's no rush," he said smiling.

Carolyn looked at him, shocked. "Dad!"

"A father has to ask these kinds of questions, Honey." He turned back to me. "So how do you plan on supporting yourselves?" I told him that I wanted to be a professional theater director. He nodded, thinking, "And what does that line of work pay, if I may ask?"

I hemmed and hawed, said something about getting a teaching certificate to fall back on, something my mother had urged me to do.

"He might direct movies someday," Carolyn added. "He's very talented." Dr. Purdy took this all in. Still very non-committal.

"I love your daughter," I blurted out. "With all my heart. And I promise to take good care of her."

He looked at Carolyn. She smiled and nodded. Another long pause. He raised his glass. "Then let's drink to the wedding," he said. We laughed, all of us very relieved, and clinked our beer steins with his glass. Now it was official.

Dr. Purdy later asked Carolyn if we were "shacking up" and then before she could answer said, "I don't even want to know!"

Peter Pan

In August of 1968 the Democratic National Convention began in Chicago. Abbie Hoffman and his Yippies had announced that a "Festival of Life" would take place simultaneously in Grant and Lincoln Parks. As a result, students from all over the country flocked to Chicago to protest against the war in Vietnam in the hope they could influence the Democratic Party to end it. Hoffman's antics were highly theatrical. He had dumped burning dollar bills onto the floor of the New York Stock Exchange, causing a riot. On August 23rd at the Chicago Civic Center his cohort Jerry Rubin and activist folk singer Phil Ochs had nominated a pig, aptly named Pigasus, for President of the United States. They all were quickly arrested, including the pig.

We decided to postpone our fifth Screw Theater production and head for Chicago. Upon arrival, Carolyn, Dennis and I borrowed my mother's car and headed to Lincoln Park, where rock and roll bands played as shirtless hippies and Yippies snake danced through the park and Allen Ginsberg recited his poetry. As evening approached, the Chicago Police Department moved in and cleared the park, imposing an 11:00 PM curfew. The anti-war forces knew that this was a violation of Freedom of Assembly and were determined to resist the next night's curfew. They were joined by 200 clergy men and women who had brought a 12-foot cross as a rallying point. There was a crowd of two thousand and we were part of it. Black Panther founder Bobby Seale made a speech in which he told us that "now you know what it's like to be niggers" and exhorted the crowd to use whatever means necessary to defend ourselves, but the organizers of the protest urged the crowd to remain non-violent. They suggested that we wet handkerchiefs to protect our eyes from the tear gas the police had used the night before and would certainly use again. Carolyn, Dennis and I looked at each other. Who carried handkerchiefs? I asked Carolyn if she wanted to leave but she bravely shook her head. Then someone started singing "We Shall Overcome" and we joined in.

A voice cut in on a bullhorn, "This is the Chicago Police. You must clear the park immediately!" But we continued to sing. Then a bank of blinding lights came on. We could see that they were mounted on army trucks surrounding the park. "Link arms!" the organizers of the protest told us, and we did. The engines of the trucks started, and we could see that there was a line of several hundred helmeted policemen wearing gas masks and carrying batons marching in front of the trucks as they closed in on us from all sides. There was no way to leave if we had wanted to. The clergymen circled their cross, praying as a cloud of tear gas was released, backlit by the lights on the advancing trucks.

CHAPTER 4

The glowing gas moved toward us. "Stay together!" the organizers shouted through their bullhorns. "Don't fight back!" The gas began to sting our eyes as the wind carried it toward us. And I looked at the cross and saw it topple to the ground as the clergymen were attacked by the club swinging police. And then everyone started to run. I grabbed Carolyn and we took off toward the street, running past policemen who were mercilessly beating protestors, men and women, curled up in the fetal position on the ground in vain attempts to protect themselves. Heads were cracked. Blood flowed, but miraculously we were untouched. We ran into the street where squad cars skidded to stops and more cops jumped out. Rocks shattered a police car's windshield and canisters of tear gas landed at our feet. A protestor grabbed the smoking can and hurled it back at the cops. Our eyes were burning, we could hardly see, but we ran on. A group of Yippies surrounded a squad car and began rocking it as the cops tumbled out. We ran into Wells Street. Where was Dennis? Somehow, we found my mother's car and made it back to our house, where she comforted us, putting wet towels over our burning eyes. God bless her. She couldn't believe what was happening. The city was a war zone.

The next evening we picked up Dennis, who had gotten home the night before after being nearly blinded by tear gas, and the three of us were back with the protestors. Tonight we were on Michigan Avenue near the Hilton Hotel where the delegates were staying. That day they had rejected a peace plank for the Democratic Party platform. We moved shoulder to shoulder with the angry crowd, packed together, surrounded by gas mask-wearing National Guardsmen carrying rifles with fixed bayonets.

This time the media and news crews were there, and the crowd chanted "The whole world is watching! The whole world is watching!" And they were. In fact, Dan Rather was beaten by the cops and as a result, his coverage of the war protests changed dramatically. Inside the Convention Center, Connecticut Senator Abraham Ribicoff, during his nomination speech for George McGovern, condemned the "Gestapo tactics on the streets of Chicago." Mayor Daley was caught on camera screaming words that lip readers later surmised were: "Fuck you, you Jew son of a bitch! You lousy motherfucker! Go home!"

We made a run for it and ended up on State Street where we escaped into Flo's Pies, an open-all-night restaurant. There we were greeted by a truly mindboggling sight: hippies and Yippies sitting peacefully drinking coffee and eating pie in the same restaurant with tables of uniformed Chicago cops. There were even delegates from the convention wearing their state badges around their necks. One lady delegate came over to our table and asked us if the cops had been hurting us. We nodded but couldn't really get into it with her as the next table was full of cops. We all paid our checks and went back into the fray to continue protesting and getting the shit kicked out of us. It reminded me of those old Warner Bros. cartoons where the wolves and sheepdogs pleasantly greet each other as they punch in at the start of their shifts at the meadow.

The convention ended with the nomination of Hubert H. Humphrey, Johnson's Vice President, to head the Democratic Party's Presidential ticket with Edmund Muskie as his Vice Presidential nominee. We had thought Humphrey might have a chance of unseating Richard Nixon, but the oppressive tactics of the over 30,000 police, army, and guardsmen against 10,000 protestors destroyed any possible positive spin. In his acceptance speech for the nomination, Humphrey said, "And may America tonight resolve that never, never again shall we see what we have seen." A national investigative committee headed by Dan Walker branded the events of the convention a "police riot," causing Mayor Daley to respond in his inimitable style that "The policeman isn't there to create disorder, the policeman is there to preserve disorder."

The powerful events of that week did have one positive effect. I was suddenly struck with a vision of pure inspiration. I now knew how to produce *Peter Pan* without a single flying harness. I realized that without changing a word of J.M. Barrie's script, I could turn his play into an allegory about the Chicago Democratic Convention. Wendy and her brothers would be straight Midwestern middle class kids (like Carolyn and myself) who are radicalized (taught to fly) by Peter Pan and his Lost Boys, who would be portrayed as Abbie Hoffman and his tie-dyed Yippies. Captain Hook would become Mayor Daley and his pirates would be the riot-helmeted Chicago Police Department. Tiger Lily and the Indians would become Bobby Seale and the Black Panthers, and Tinkerbell, Peter's fairy companion, would be his gay lover. Flying without harnesses would be accomplished simply by having the Darling children drop tabs of LSD. The next question was how to portray the acid trip onstage. Lois Danzig knew just the people to help us: the members of the Kamphalous Light Show. Lois and her husband Michael introduced me to their friends Jerry Fortier and his girlfriend Kathy who were their partners in this psychedelic adventure in mixed media. Combining slides and movies with pulsating liquids projected on army surplus parachutes or billowing clouds of Patchouli oil-fragranced smoke, they created magic, and were surreal sorcerers of the sixties.

Rehearsals began immediately with the idea that the play would open at the beginning of the fall semester. Handsome Frank Hilgenberg played Peter with his shoulder length blond hair and walrus mustache. Lois was Wendy and Fred Stone and Michael Wilmington played her brothers. André was Tiger Lily, although he really wanted to play Tinkerbell, but Howard Waxman ended up as bisexual Peter's jealous lover. Dennis Paoli played both Lost Boy twins as a schizophrenic talking to himself.

We realized that we needed a few more black actors to play the other Black Panthers, but in those days, André was the only African American actor in the theater department. One day, as we were hanging out in the Rathskeller in the Student Union, Lois noticed a table full of black students, many wearing Black Panther style berets. Before anyone could stop her, she ran over to their table.

"Hey, do any of you spade cats want to be in a play?"

In a flash they were all on their feet, towering over her. "What did you call us?" We rushed over to save her, and André explained that this little honky just didn't know what she was saying.

"Yes, I did," Lois insisted. "Spade cats – like in jazz clubs. It's hip."

The leader of the group was in her face. "It ain't hip. If you're going to talk to us you need to address us with respect."

"Hey, I didn't call you niggers or jigs..." André moved between her and the angry group and made Lois apologize and soon her tiny hand was engulfed in a black power hand grip. "I don't like being called a honky," she whispered to André. "I'm a person." André shrugged and turned to the other brothers, "We're doing a play," he explained. In a few minutes, and a few tokes, he convinced them to join the cast. We rehearsed in the Play Circle each night after the last movie audience had left, which meant pulling all-nighters. During one dance rehearsal, Lois just couldn't contain herself. "This is bullshit!" she shouted from her seat in the audience and the dancers stopped. She jumped onto the stage and walked over to them pointing to their white tights. "Stuie, this is all wrong!" (She was one of the only people in my life I allowed to call me Stuie). "They don't look like mermaids in these leotards!" And then she pulled her madras print mini-dress over her head and walked into the lightshow projections stark naked, as she never wore underwear. The patterns moved beautifully across her tiny taut figure. "Isn't this better?" she asked. Speechless, I could only nod. In that instant it was decided that the dancers would perform nude. One or two dropped out of the show that evening, but it became a point of honor for the others and most of them ended up staying. I found myself begging Carolyn to take the place of a departed dancer. She had taken some ballet lessons as a teenager and moved gracefully, although she had never been on stage before. "But won't we get into trouble?" she very sensibly wanted to know. "Of course not," I confidently told her in words that would come back to haunt me for the rest of my life. "This isn't a go-go club. It's art." "Besides," I told her, "No one will be looking at your face." We opened on Monday, September 23rd, 1968 for what was scheduled as the first of three free performances. The SRO audience was hugely enthusiastic, and the next morning Carolyn and I were awakened by Dennis calling from the Student Union. There was a rave review in the *Daily Cardinal* but what really excited him was an article in The Wisconsin State Journal about our production under the headline "Naked *Peter Pan*." The article was written by a stringer from the Associated Press and was picked up by papers all over the country, including *The New York Times* who found the combination of a beloved children's story and naked co-eds irresistible. My elation was short-lived as the next phone call was from Bill Dawson, head of the Union Theater, which included the smaller Play Circle. He wanted to see me in his office immediately.

Dawson, a heavy-set middle-aged man with a graying crew cut and ever-present flannel shirt, was apoplectic, which turned his normally ruddy face a bright purple. James Boll, the Dane County district attorney, had also seen the newspaper articles and had called Chancellor Young of the University, informing him that if the show weren't closed immediately, he would close it himself and arrest everyone responsible. Bill had just gotten off the phone with the Chancellor, who had instructed him to shut down our show. "Why?" I wanted to know. Dawson rolled his eyes, "Because it's obscene!" "But it's not obscene," I insisted. "In fact, the dance symbolizes innocence." This raised Bill's bushy eyebrows. "You know, like in the Garden of Eden."

"These girls are stark naked!" he sputtered. I wouldn't back down. "Besides, how does the D.A. know it's obscene? He hasn't even seen it." I paused for a second, knowing that neither had Dawson. "It's a violation of free speech," I continued, my revolutionary zeal still fresh from battling cops in Chicago.

There was a long pause. "Michael!" he called to his assistant Michael Goldberg in the outer office. "Get Chancellor Young on the phone!" Then he turned to me. "I'll get back to you," and the meeting was over. Soon I was informed that on the following Monday we would be giving a command performance for the D.A. so that he could determine if the play was indeed obscene. I met with the cast and informed them. Their response was that the powers-that-be would almost certainly find the play objectionable and ban us from performing it again. So, what was the point? Forbidding us to perform our play without a court of law determining that it was obscene was a violation of free speech, I told them. So we should not abide by their decision to close our show even if it meant defying the district attorney and the university. "But we'll be arrested!" someone said nervously.

"So we'll be arrested," I responded. The room exploded with voices. Some were in favor of my plan. Others thought it was insane. Finally, cast member Michael Wilmington (who would become the film critic for the *Chicago Tribune* and later the *Los Angeles Times*) took the floor and said something I will never forget. "It seems to me that the issues are pretty clear cut," he began. "In fact, it couldn't be any more black and white." Now he had everyone's attention. You could hear a pin drop. "As we get older, we're going to find that everything is just going to become different shades of gray. Things will never be this clear again. Never. We'll have jobs and kids and mortgages, a lot more responsibilities and a lot more to lose." He paused. Everyone was hanging on his every word. “If you can’t take a stand when you’re young and idealistic, when will you ever be able to do it?” Someone called for a vote, and the uproar began again. I tried to quiet the room and get everyone’s attention. “This is a personal decision,” I told them. “There shouldn’t be any group pressure. Just call me with your decisions.” The meeting broke up and soon my phone was ringing off the hook. Almost all of the dancers quit. It was just Carolyn and one other girl left. So André became the third dancer making up in spice what had been lost in numbers. Several of the non-dancing cast members also left the show saying that their parents were pressuring them and would pull them out of school. Ten out of our cast of thirty had quit. The most surprising drop-out was the ultra-cool Lenny Kleinfeld, Mr. bury st. edmund himself. It turned out his father was a New York City policeman and he could be fired if his son were to get himself arrested. I told them all that I understood, and that there would be no hard feelings. I turned to Carolyn. What should we do? “Isn’t there an old saying?” she asked. “Something about the show going on?”

I hugged her. “You don’t have to do this,” I told her. But she was adamant. “Hey, I signed up for the whole trip. Wherever it takes us. And just for the record, so far it’s been pretty entertaining.”

“But what about your parents?” I knew that her father had been in a nasty custody battle with her mother for her brother Roger, who was still a minor.

“This isn’t about them. It’s about us. If we don’t do this, we’ll be kicking ourselves for the rest of our lives.” She put her arms around my neck. “I love you,” she said, “No matter what. I want to be with you. Is that so hard to understand?” We clung to each other for a long time.

Neverland

The performance of *Peter Pan* for the District Attorney was taking place on Monday September 30th. I had spoken to my mother about our decision to defy the authorities and perform our show even if they banned it, which we knew they would. She had put me in touch with Elmer Gertz, a legendary attorney famous for defending Grove Press, the publishers of Henry Miller's *Tropic of Cancer*, against obscenity charges in the early 1960s. How she knew Mr. Gertz is something of a mystery, although since he was also from a Lithuanian Jewish family and attended both my father's high school Crane Tech and my mother's University of Chicago there were many possible explanations. Mr. Gertz urged me not to do it, saying that the legal defense would be difficult and expensive and was this *really* worth it? Being an idealistic idiot, I told him it was. My mother begged me to reconsider. She argued that this could ruin both Carolyn's and my own life. I could end up going to prison for five years. And for what? I reminded her that all of my life she had taught me to stand up for what I thought was right. There was a long pause. "I lied," she told me. The day of the performance arrived and the lobby of the Play circle was filled with members of the press and local television crews, who were all denied entrance to the actual show. I had discovered that the Associated Press stringer was a friend of mine who had taken photos of the dance sequence during the initial performance. As he showed me these photos (stunning even in black and white) I begged him not to print them as they would aid the authorities in identifying the other dancers. Amazingly, he agreed. I never saw them again and over the years I wished I had asked him for copies.

James Boll arrived and was whisked into the theater, as was Madison Police Chief Wilbur Emery, University Police Chief Ralph Hanson, and City Attorney Ed Conrad. As they say in the biz, it was a rough crowd. Jonathan Curvin, head of the Theater Department and its faculty, including my teachers Ed Amor and Bob Buzecky, filled an entire row. Even John Ezell, the patron of Screw Theater and the one who had suggested we perform *Peter Pan* without flying harnesses, was there. Bill Dawson took the stage and welcomed all the visiting guests and thanked them for taking time out of their busy schedules to attend. Then he explained that neither he "nor any of the officers of the Union Theater Committee had any prior knowledge of the content of our play and that they had never given approval for it to be performed."

"Thanks a lot, Bill," I thought.

"We leave it to you to judge its merit, pro or con," he concluded. "And now without further ado, on with the show."

CHAPTER 5

As soon as the play was over, Boll emerged from the theater and announced, "After viewing this performance, I have determined that it is definitely obscene and has no redeeming value whatsoever. It is therefore officially banned. Any attempts to perform it in the city of Madison or Dane County will be punishable by arrest." He was barraged by questions from the press and was in the process of answering them when I entered the lobby. Suddenly the reporters were all around me. What was my reaction to the District Attorney's decision? "My mother liked it," I told them. It turned out that James Boll was up for re-election as District Attorney, and he clearly recognized a media-op when he saw one. The reporters asked if we would abide by the D.A.'s ruling. "The cast is united in our belief that his banning of our play is a violation of our civil rights," I told them. So what were we going to do about it? "Come back at 7:45 tomorrow evening and find out," I replied.

When we arrived the next day around six in the evening, the lobby was again packed with students and reporters. Lois ran up to me, her face a mask of anguish. "We're locked out!" she cried. "We can't get in to do the show!" Bill Dawson's assistant and my friend Michael Goldberg stood in front of the locked doors looking very conflicted. "I'm only following Bill's orders," he told us. We hooted. Only following orders! That's what the Nazis had said at the Nuremberg trials. Lois was furious. "Our lightshow equipment is in there!" she shrieked. "That's our property! You have no right…"

Cast member Michael Wilmington took me aside. His friend Joe McBride ran the student Film Society and there was a meeting in B10 Commerce tonight. "I bet they'd rather see *Peter Pan* instead of the Buster Keaton movie that's scheduled," he whispered.

The Film Society had taken a vote and decided to let us use their lecture hall. It held over 600 seats, four times the size of the Play Circle.

When we entered the lecture hall, I saw that it was lit with institutional style fluorescent lights. We didn't have any theater lights or a dimmer board to run them. But Jerry Fortier was setting up the large overhead projector on a folding table stacked on top of another folding table in the rear of the hall. "Stuart! Look at this!" He flicked on the projector and it covered the shallow lecture room stage with light. Then he threw colored gels on it and the light turned blue then yellow then red. "Check this out." He put a piece of paper with a cut-out circle onto the overhead and created a follow spot effect. "Jerry, you're a genius!" I hugged him and with that we opened the doors, and the audience came pouring in. In five minutes, the hall was filled to overflowing and there were still hundreds of people clamoring to be let in. I huddled with the cast. Would they be up for doing a second show if we weren't busted after the first one? "Hey, we were supposed to do three performances in the first place," answered André. "I say they owe us two more." And so I went out and told the crowd that filled the square surrounding the Commerce building that they'd all get in to see the second show if we were around to perform it. The crowd applauded and suddenly I saw a helmeted figure pushing through them toward me. "Oh shit," I thought. "Here come the cops!" But the helmet came off and there stood Lenny Kleinfeld! "I couldn't let you do the show without me," he stated, grinning ear to ear.

"But what about your dad?" I asked.

"Fuck him," was Lenny's concise reply.

Someone ran up to me holding an army blanket. "We've got these to cover the dancers when the pigs show up," he told me. "And it might be possible for them to make a dash out of one of the side exit doors to get away." He looked me in the eye. "So can you." We hugged each other. "Hey you fruits," Dennis called to us. "We got a show to do!" I looked at the others. They nodded or gave a thumbs up. I looked to Carolyn. "The show must go on," she said, smiling at me. I went on stage and was hit with Jerry's makeshift follow spot. "I want to thank the Film Society for letting us use their space tonight." The crowd applauded. They knew that the society, Joe McBride (who later achieved fame as a film scholar and author) and Michael Wilmington could also get into trouble for aiding and abetting. I took a page from my recent experiences in Chicago, "In the event that the police show up, please keep things peaceful and non-violent." I took a deep breath. There was no turning back. And now, without further ado, I give you *Peter Pan*!"

The audience was huge and appreciative. There was a charge in the air. We were all breaking the law together. During the dance sequence I kept looking toward the back doors of the lecture hall expecting the police to come barging in at any minute. But they didn't. Carolyn hugged me after she, André and Judy Anderson, the other dancer, came off stage. She was glowing with excitement. She never looked more beautiful, and I was never prouder of her.

The first act ended with Captain Hook and the pirates closing in on Wendy and the Lost Boys. It was staged like the scene we had witnessed in Lincoln Park with the silhouetted riot-helmeted policemen moving toward the protestors through glowing back-lit white smoke. The entire audience immediately got the reference and began chanting "The whole world is watching! The whole world is watching!" It gave me goosebumps and reminded me that nudity was not the only reason that the authorities were clamping down on our production. The political statement that we were making upset them just as much, if not more. The performance ended with a standing ovation. We took our bows, looking at each other amazed that the police had not shut us down. The audience cleared the hall, and their seats were immediately filled with the next group. The second show proceeded without a hitch and after it was over, the adrenaline that had been powering us all evening suddenly left our systems, leaving us exhausted and feeling a strong sense of anti-climax. We were all too beat even to have a beer together. We hugged each other, said our goodbyes and went our separate ways. Carolyn and I walked down Bascom Hill together, the crisp, clear autumn sky filled with shining stars. We weren't sure what the morning would bring, but we felt good. We had stood up for what we believed in, and as Michael Wilmington had said, things would never be this clear-cut again. At 9:00 AM there was a pounding at our apartment door, and Carolyn and I jumped out of bed sure that the cops were about to break in Gestapo style and drag us off to jail. "Who is it?" I called out. A gruff voice replied, "Jack Van Metre from the ACLU." I unlocked the door and peeked out. There stood a disheveled, pockmarked middle-aged man in a worn-out trench coat. "May I come in?" he asked.

Unbeknownst to me, my mother had contacted the American Civil Liberties Union as soon as Boll had declared our production obscene and now Madison was buzzing about our two outlaw performances. Van Metre told us that I'd probably be arrested either later that day or the next. "What's the delay?" I wanted to know. "What's the big rush?" he replied with a grin. "They can't find anyone to come forward and sign a complaint. How many people saw it last night?" "Over 1,200." This seemed to please him. "Well, they need someone to say that it's obscene and that they were personally offended," Van Metre explained, lighting a cigarette. "Obscenity is all about community standards, so it has to be an ordinary citizen."

The next day Jonathan Curvin and the entire faculty of the Theater Department released a statement to the press saying that they did not believe the play to be obscene. But it also said that the show was not produced under their supervision so they couldn't be blamed for it. Two birds, one stone. No waiting. Then Boll took University Police Chief Ralph Hanson off the case because, "As of late Friday, three days after I had outlawed *Peter Pan*, he did not have one person who could identify either of the two nudes and he refused to sign a complaint against the producer of the play whom we know." He turned the case over to the Franz Haas, Dane County Sheriff. "A real dick," according to Van Metre, never one to mince words. So, on October 7th, a week after the outlaw performances, Van Metre and I stood before Judge Buenzli, who I remember as a small man with a slightly bemused expression. District Attorney Boll and City Attorney Conrad wanted me to name the dancers, but I replied "No comment," as I had been coached by my attorney.

I had received a call from the District Attorney's office on Friday telling me to report at the court for my arraignment, which gave me a chance to get my hair cut (also per Van Metre's instructions). I was never officially arrested or booked. My bail was discussed: "Your honor," Van Metre began, "Mr. Gordon has an excellent school record, with no previous arrests and very strong ties to the community. In fact, his friends and family have raised $1,500 to be made available." This was the first time I had heard this. It turned out that Professor Bart Friedman of the English Department and his wife Sheila had gone so far as to put up their house up as collateral. This still astounds me. Judge Buenzli waved his hand, "I don't think a cash bail is necessary, Mr. Van Metre. He's known for nearly two weeks that he might face a charge. At least he should have, because the whole state of Wisconsin knew it, and he appeared voluntarily today." He pounded his gavel. "Gentlemen, I'll see you in court."

* * *

One evening Carolyn and I were about to go out to dinner when the phone rang. She answered it and suddenly went pale and, her voice shaking, quickly said "no comment" before hanging up. It was someone from the *Capital Times* wanting to know what her reaction was to being identified as one of the nude dancers. It turned out the reporter's wife was from Janesville and had come with him to one of the performances in B10 Commerce where she had recognized Carolyn. She later called to apologize, saying that she hadn't meant to get her into trouble. "I guess someone *was* looking at my face," Carolyn told me, not knowing whether to laugh or to cry.

The next day we were both in Van Metre's office being introduced to Jack Olson. He was handsome and clean-cut with blond hair. He wore a blue blazer, and he didn't seem much older than we were. He would represent Carolyn.

"Why can't you?" I asked Van Metre.

"Because they're trying you separately, the pricks," he replied. "But don't let Jack's looks throw you. He's been around the block a couple of times."

"You're both named Jack?" Carolyn wanted to know.

"Yeah," grinned Van Metre. "A pair of Jacks. Not a bad hand."

Legally Carolyn had to formally request that Jack Olson represent her. When he agreed, she laughed and said, "I feel like we're going steady." But Van Metre quickly put an end to the "love-in." "Are you two living together?" he wanted to know. We hemmed and hawed. This clearly upset the Jacks. "The prosecution is going to do everything they can to convince the jury that what you did was immoral," Van Metre said sternly. "Living together out of wedlock is not going to help you." Carolyn was arraigned before Judge Mittelstadt, Jack Olson at her side. Mittelstadt asked her if she was one of the "famous *Peter Pan* Dancing Girls." "No comment," was her reply. Mittelstadt pushed on, "Miss Purdy, did you or did you not dance before God and all of his children without a stitch of clothing?"

"No comment," Carolyn repeated.

"This court would be much more lenient if you were to give us the name of the other dancer." Carolyn looked him right in the eye. "No comment," she said again. While she was being pilloried in Mittelstadt's court, I had been summoned to a tribunal of the faculty of the Theater Department. We met in Chairman Curvin's office where Ed Amor read me the riot act while the other faculty members, including John Ezell, sat quietly. My productions would have to be more carefully supervised, I was told. The script for any show I intended to direct would have to be reviewed by the department and approved before I could begin production. All auditions and rehearsals would be overseen by a member of the faculty, and any staging or business that was found to be offensive would be cut. I looked to John Ezell, but he said nothing and lowered his eyes. "So now you've become the censors," I said. "How dare you!" exploded Curvin, the usually dignified elder statesman of the department. "We all signed the statement endorsing your tawdry little play. But I will be damned if we will let it happen again." He rose and approached me, his face turning a bright red in his fury as he waved his finger in my face. "Do you realize how many gifts and grants the university has lost thanks to you? Hundreds of thousands of dollars! And this department is taking the blame. You have embarrassed us for the last time!"

It seemed that things couldn't get much worse, but of course they did. That weekend Carolyn's father arrived at her Henry Street apartment and announced that he was pulling her out of school and taking her home. I attempted to apologize but Dr. Purdy would have none of it. He felt that I had not only ruined the reputation of his daughter but his own as well. Worse than that I had lied to him. I had tricked him into giving us his blessings while all the time I was planning to make a fool of him. I tried to explain that nothing could be further from the truth, but he turned to Carolyn. "Do I have to pack your suitcase for you?"

I stepped between him and his daughter. "She's not going," I told him. We were nose to nose.

"Get out of my way," he said.

"I think you better leave," I said. I was so furious that I was afraid it would get physical.

"If anybody leaves, it's going to be you," Dr. Purdy responded. "I can't believe that your mother…"

"Don't talk about my mother!" I snapped.

He realized he had hit a nerve and pushed on. "If I was your father…" "You're not my father, thank God!" I shouted. My father, of course, had died when I was fourteen and he held a special place in my heart. There was no way I would let anyone invoke him against me. "Now get the hell out of here!" I screamed at him. "No. You get the hell out!" Now he was shouting too.

Carolyn had had enough. "Stop it both of you!" she screamed. "This is my apartment! Both of you have to leave."

Dr. Purdy tried to mollify her, "Now Cottie…" he began ("Cottie Wump" was his baby name for her). But Carolyn was furious. "Get out!" she shouted.

"You heard her," I said, thinking I was backing her up. Carolyn wheeled on me. "You too! Out!" And before I knew it both Dr. Purdy and myself were out in the hallway, the door slammed in our faces. We looked at each other, neither knowing what to say or do next. And then Dr. Purdy stomped down the stairs and was gone. I knocked at the door. "Go away!" Carolyn shouted. "Where should I go?" "I don't care!" It took a while and a lot of pleading and apologizing, but I finally got her to open the door. Tears were pouring down her face, which always shocks me because she so seldom cries. "What are we going to do?" she sobbed. I held her in my arms, not knowing what to say. Then it hit me. "Let's get married," I suggested. She looked at me like I had lost my mind.

"That's your answer for everything," she said.

"No, I'm serious," I told her. "It solves all of our problems. They don't want us living together anyway, but if we're married…" She was thinking about it. "The only thing we have is each other," I pleaded. "We can't let them break us apart." We kissed. "And besides if we're married, we can't be made to testify against each other." The next thing I was back in the hallway and the door slammed in my face. The trial dates had been set for December 4th for Carolyn and December 6th for me. But just before Thanksgiving we were called and told to come to Van Metre's office right away. When we got there both he and Jack Olson were grinning like cats who had swallowed a pair of canaries. "Remember when I told you I was going to check out that Roger Mott fellow, the one who had filed the complaint against you?"

"He never saw the show!" I exclaimed, thinking I had guessed the cause of their jubilance.

"No, he saw it," Van Metre said. "But it turns out he has an arrest record himself. He's…"

"A convicted child molester," Olson blurted out so excited he couldn't let Van Metre finish the sentence. "So much for community standards!" he crowed.

They were sure that the D.A. would have to drop the charges, but on November 21st it was announced that Roger Mott was withdrawing his charges because he had "received abuse." A new version of the complaint had been signed by Madison Police Chief Wilbur Emery, who claimed he had sent plain clothes cops to the second performance in the Commerce Building. So our trials were still on. Carolyn and I each spent Thanksgiving with our families: she with her dad in Janesville, and me with my mom and brother in Chicago. We let them know that we planned to get married. My mother and brother were ecstatic. Dr. Purdy not so much.

December 4th arrived, and we steeled ourselves for the inquisition. Our attorneys had prepared us for the sort of character assassination we should expect. So in our most straight clothes, my hair cut even shorter, we proceeded to Van Metre's office. We were told he was on the phone when we got there, so we nervously waited in his reception room. He came out a few minutes later, beaming. The D.A. had withdrawn the charges. Van Metre was convinced that Boll had been using the immense publicity from our case to get himself re-elected. Now that he had been, he didn't need us any longer. He did point out that he had only withdrawn the charges, not dropped them, and they could be reinstated at any future time. We held a press conference. And the picture of Carolyn and myself that ran in the next day's papers was the happiest we have ever looked. The relief is tangible and Carolyn is glowing, looking at my beaming face with what can only be described as adoration.

We had been changed by the adventures of the last few months and would never be quite the same again. We had met each other as children and now we had grown up. Although we were both only twenty-one years old, we had grown up together. The wedding took place on December 20th in the Frank Lloyd Wright-designed First Unitarian Church. Carolyn made her own wedding dress, a beautiful Victorian design with a high button collar, out of ivory satin. We stayed up almost all the preceding night baking our wedding cake. We had wanted to make a spherical cake – why, I can't remember, except we thought it would be cool. It didn't work out, so we ended up making a more conventional cake, which Carolyn decorated with real flowers, something she continues to do with our children's birthday cakes to this day. The church was filled with our friends, although some had to go home for winter break. My brother David was my best man. My mom and brother had made the trip, as had Carolyn's brother Roger and sister Marilyn, who was there as Carolyn's matron of honor with her husband George and two-year-old daughter Lisa, who cried because she wanted to be a flower girl. Even my Aunt Eleanor and cousin Gene were there. And believe it or not, Dr. Purdy came to walk his daughter down the aisle, although he told Carolyn that he would not stand at the altar with us or answer the question "Who gives this bride in marriage?" The only person who didn't show up was the bride. It was an hour past the time the service was scheduled to start, and Carolyn hadn't arrived at the church yet. Max Gabler, the minister, was asking me if we should reschedule. I didn't know what to tell him. I had called her apartment on a pay phone and hadn't gotten an answer. I was about to make an announcement to the audience when Carolyn finally arrived. Our friend Gary Mechanic had been late picking her up because it was snowing and the traffic had been bumper to bumper. We scrambled and got things going quickly. It started off smoothly, but her dad stepped on her dress's train, and it came partially undone as she walked down the aisle. Her sister rushed to re-attach it as we were taking our vows. I don't remember any of this. I only know that Carolyn looked radiant as she walked to join me at the altar. We read Shakespeare's 116th Sonnet. It seemed appropriate:

> Let us not to the marriage of true minds
> Admit impediments. Love is not love
> Which alters when it alteration finds,
> Or bends with the remover to remove:
> O, no! it is an ever-fixed mark,
> That looks on tempests and is never shaken;
> It is the star to every wandering bark,
> Whose worth's unknown, although his height be taken.
> Love's not Time's fool, though rosy lips and cheeks
> Within his bending sickle's compass come;
> Love alters not with his brief hours and weeks
> But bears it out even to the edge of doom.
> If this be error and upon me proved,
> I never writ, nor no man ever loved.

Our reception, fittingly, was at the Student Union, where many of our adventures had begun. We ran up the steps for photographs (almost none of which turned out – the ones that did are dark and gothic looking) but we ended up in a joyous snowball fight with our friends and family in the beautiful, pristine, freshly fallen snow. Dennis and André and a few other friends entertained by lip-syncing to the Vanilla Fudge's "You Keep Me Hangin' On," the significance of which still escapes me.

That evening Carolyn and I dined at Madison's one and only Chinese restaurant in the Capital Square as the snow continued to fall, and then went to a late screening of the film adaptation of Terry Southern's scandalous *Candy* starring Marlon Brando among others. It put us to sleep. We came back to my (now our) apartment on Gilman Street and unwrapped the wedding presents. We had received three or four fondue sets, which must have been *the* gift to give in 1968. There was also a note from André that he would come to our apartment and cook us a meal, which he did a few nights later, the best sweet and sour pork I have ever tasted. We crumpled up the wrapping paper and burned it in the small fireplace in our bedroom. It made a beautiful glow until we realized that we had thrown our wedding checks and marriage license into the fire as well. Frantically we tried to pull them out, saving the license which still has burned edges (giving it an antique look like the Magna Carta) and a few of the checks. We then fell blissfully asleep in each other's arms.

CHAPTER 6

Down on the Farm

Having missed most of my classes during the fall semester because of all the legal maneuvering, I started my senior year again in the winter semester of 1969. Ed Amor had agreed to be my advisor for what was called Advanced Directing. Considering I had never taken a beginning directing class, I thought I was doing pretty well. My project was an adaptation of Shakespeare's *Hamlet* but following in the blasphemous tradition of *Vis* I decided to rewrite the Bard's dialogue and do the play as a Western. I called it *El Sinore* after the prince's Danish castle Elsinore. The king was a Texas land baron, Ophelia the pretty schoolmarm, her brother Laertes became trigger-happy Laredo, the traveling players were a medicine show, and Polonius looked and sounded just like Gabby Hayes. Hamlet (renamed Ben) had been studying "back east" and returned for his father's funeral. He later straps on a six-gun to avenge him. His famous soliloquy became, "It's a simple question. To live or to die – Yup."

Since cowboy movies were the inspiration, it made perfect sense that the audience should be on bleachers that could move up to the actors for close-ups and farther back for wide shots. During the climactic duel – which, in our production, was a knife fight – the bleachers revolved in one direction as the duelers circled in the opposite direction. Surprisingly, no one lost their lunch. To have the space necessary to accommodate the rolling bleachers, we got permission to do the play in the enormous cafeteria of the Ogg, Sellery, and Witte dormitories, which happened to be named Gordon Hall. So it was meant to be.

The show was well received, and I realize now that it was the first of many productions that would make use of a cinematic approach. I was making movies without film.

* * *

In February the New York-based Living Theater came to town and performed *Paradise Now* at the same Unitarian Church where Carolyn and I had been married in December. The legendary group had been performing their shows all over the world to great acclaim and controversy and had achieved the status of rock stars. The play began with the members of the company, which included its brilliant founders, the skeletal Julian Beck and his wife Judith Malina, moving through the audience chanting, "I am not allowed to travel without a passport. I am not allowed to smoke marijuana." They started screaming in frustration and pulling off their clothes, ending up in only jock straps and bikini tops and collapsing to the ground in a heap of bodies that looked like the recent My Lai massacre.[2] The actors lay motionless for what must have been at least five minutes, infuriating the audience. Altercations broke out and I saw someone spit directly into Julian Beck's face. His response was to hug the offender, pressing his nearly nude body against him telling him that he loved him, totally freaking the guy out.

Members of the audience began removing their clothes, but not stopping with underpants and bras. Soon entirely naked people made up almost half of the audience. District Attorney Boll's fear that Madison would have naked people running around "throughout the community" had become a reality. Max Gabler, the minister who had married us, was beside himself, "I can't let this go on," he told me, tearing his hair in panic. I tried to calm him down, assuring him that no one would be hurt, and that to call in the police could create a violent riot. Wisely he allowed the show to continue. Strangely, no charges were brought against The Living Theater, as they kept themselves clothed (scantily) while the audience got naked. I wished I had thought of that.

The performance had inspired me, reminding me of what I wanted to do with my life. I wrote dozens of letters to all of the regional theaters in America looking for work as a director. I received a couple of form letters telling me they would keep my resume on file, but one day a letter showed up from the Milwaukee Rep, which told me that, in their opinion, there were two ways to become a working theater director: A) You could pay your dues toiling in the box office and over the years slowly working your way up the ladder until they finally let you direct a small workshop production, or B) You could start your own theater company and begin directing immediately. If your company manages to survive the first year, it has a pretty good chance of continuing and you are on your way.

Needless to say, I chose Plan B. I gathered a group of actors and designers in the large upstairs gallery room that belonged to The Co-op, a hippie grocery co-operative and bookstore on Broom Street that provided us with a name – The Broom Street Theater. We soon learned that The Co-op was planning on moving to Mifflin Street (where it would become the famous Mifflin Street Co-op), so we would have to find another performance space. As we put together our first production, we were on the hunt for a theater. We found a large open space on the second floor of an office building on the corner of Johnson and Gorham, just off State Street, which is the University's main drag. It had high fifteen-foot ceilings and a minimum of support beams, so the sight lines were good and with some work it could be turned into a usable theater.

---

2 On March 16th, 1968, soldiers of the U.S. Army Americal Division under the command of Lt. William Calley killed between 347 and 504 unarmed South Vietnamese civilians.

The problem was that it had no ventilation system or air-conditioning, both essential for obtaining a theater license. We found that the system we needed would cost about $4,000. Carolyn and I decided to use the money we had received as wedding presents (and hadn't burned up) to make a down payment. Probably not the brightest of moves, since we were only renting the space. We rehearsed and built the theater at the same time, leaving little time for studying.

The play we chose to open the theater would be Aristophanes' *Lysistrata*, an ancient Greek comedy (400 B.C.) in which a group of women stop the Peloponnesian War by withholding sex from their warrior husbands. My plan was to do it as a cross between the conventional Greek tragedy style and a tawdry burlesque show, not unlike the ones Dennis and I saw in downtown Chicago when we cut high school. The girls would be wearing skimpy G-strings and pasties, but – we hoped – covered enough to avoid another obscenity bust. Our rehearsals were often quite physical, inspired by Polish experimental theater guru Grotowski, they involved strenuous warm-up exercises and what was then called "sensitivity training." These included "trust" exercises in which an actor would fall backwards with his eyes closed knowing he would be caught by the other cast members.

One concentration exercise involved maintaining a Zen-like "ommmm" with your eyes closed while the other members of the ensemble tried to break your concentration and make you stop. Tickling usually did the trick but I remember one game in which the actor could not be distracted. He was tickled and pinched but continued *omm*ming. The other actors began to undress him but still he chanted. Finally, he was completely naked, and the actors lifted him up and carried him around the rehearsal room, but they still couldn't break his concentration.

"Open the window," someone said. "Let's hang him outside by his feet." They thought that this would stop the ommmming but it didn't. His naked body was lowered out of the second story window over a bustling State Street. Luckily no one looked up and he continued blissfully, "ommmmmmmm." We pulled him back in and told him he could open his eyes. He had won the game. Grinning, he sat up and began putting on his clothes.

Everything was coming together – with the exception of our occupancy license. Although our theater had passed all the requirements of the Building Department, the Madison City Council withheld our request for a license because my character was "in dispute." Apparently, there were still bad feelings about the obscenity charges being withdrawn for *Peter Pan*. I was able to get Carolyn's attorney Jack Olson to come to my defense and argue that, since I had never been convicted of a crime, my character remained unsullied.

Cast member Nancy Jallings ended up saving the day. It turned out that she had made friends with a local councilman while dancing topless at the

Bunny Hop and he was madly in lust with her. She convinced him to pressure the other council members to give us the license. And they did. We opened a week later.

Lysistrata was a smash – probably because at least half of the tickets ended up being bought by the Madison Police Department. They sat taking notes at every performance and even sent nuns, priests, and ministers with the hope that they would be offended enough to sign formal complaints. Fortunately, no one did. Nevertheless, things were not happy at Broom Street Theater. To say that many of the members of the company were questioning my leadership is putting it mildly. Shouldn't everyone have an equal share in creating company policy? And shouldn't they be choosing the shows and who should be directing them? I had no problem with the idea of other projects being done by other directors, but something akin to a mutiny was taking place. Suddenly neither Carolyn nor I had any control of a theater that we had started and financed with our charred wedding checks. It became very emotional, and I'm sure I said many things I shouldn't (the proof being that I honestly can't remember any of them). Finally, I contacted our attorney, Jack Olson, and asked him to step in, as our meetings had become so acrimonious. He saw that things were beyond anyone's control, including his. He explained to me that since Broom Street had been set up as a collective, I had no control over what the group decided to do, which by now involved tossing me and Carolyn out. "It would be different if this were your theater and you had hired the actors and technicians," he told me. "But it's not, and you didn't."

So Carolyn and I left Broom Street Theater.

June rolled around and my fellow classmates were graduating. Larry (Lawrence D.) Cohen was going back to New York to break into the movie business, but before he shut down his salon above the Orpheum Theater, he gave us his antique wooden dining room table, where so many wonderful discussions had taken place and our outrageous plans had been hatched. We still have it and continue putting it to good use: having more discussions, hatching more plans, and eating Carolyn's wonderful meals. Larry did achieve his dream of making movies, writing the screenplay for Brian De Palma's *Carrie* (1976). With the film's enormous success, he became the go-to guy for Stephen King adaptations and wrote the TV mini-series *It*. When we saw him after a lapse of many years he was fit and even muscular (and no longer smoking!) living happily with composer Michael Gore. But he still called me "Kiddo."

On July 20th, 1969, man first set foot on the moon. There should be a work of art to commemorate the triumph of Apollo 11, I thought. Suddenly it hit me that it should be a dance. For after all wasn't that first step on the dusty lunar surface the beginning of a new cosmic dance? I went to the university dance department and suggested that we create a modern dance celebrating the moon landing. They embraced the idea (as long as the dancers kept their leotards on).

I enlisted the members of the Khamphalous to join me and create a lightshow on an enormous weather balloon, which could transform from the earth to the moon as well as a thousand psychedelic mandalas in between. The score would be live rock music, played by Oz, Madison's most popular group, led by the talented Jack Lee. The scenario again took inspiration from Kubrick's *2001: A Space Odyssey* and maybe Stravinsky's "The Rite of Spring" ballet. The dancers began crawling around on the stage floor as primordial sludge, eventually rising up and stepping from the sea to the land, then becoming men fighting battles, taking to the air and finally walking upon the moon. The incredible moonwalk dance was performed by Larry Sommers, a professional dancer and instructor in the department. The piece lasted about 20 minutes and was performed in the huge Main Stage Theater in the Student Union. It brought the audience to their feet.

Don't Panic, It's Organic

One day I got a phone call from a gentleman with the unforgettable name of Ferdie Mattioli. He owned American TV, a big electronics and appliance store on the Beltline. He had been following the *Peter Pan* debacle and its aftermath and considered me "a creative guy." He wanted to advertise on late night television. I started to tell him that I wasn't interested in doing advertising. I was an artist and – he cut me off. "No, not just commercials," he told me. He had his own show on TV, but it needed a make-over. Would I be interested in helping him put it together?

The idea of my own television show instantly captivated me as Ferdie, being a consummate salesman, knew it would. We started throwing around ideas. His show was called *Ferdie's Inferno* and showed cheesy horror movies on Fridays at midnight on Channel 15. Every city had similar shows; in Chicago it was called *Shock Theater*. Being forbidden to watch scary movies when I was a child, I couldn't watch it unless, of course, my folks were going out for the evening. And then I became a secret fan, watching the great Karloff and Lugosi in *Son of Frankenstein* (which was the model for Mel Brooks' *Young Frankenstein*) and enjoying the cornball antics of beatnik-like host Marvin (ventriloquist Terry Bennett in a black turtleneck and thick glasses) and his fictional sponsor Happy Harry's Coffins: "To carry you off in."

Ferdie liked the horror movie idea, but he wanted to get rid of all the cornball antics. "That's why I came to you," Ferdie told me, "because you're supposed to be creative."

We devised a show that would be about the supernatural. If it were done today it would be called a reality show. Our plan was to have real people who had dabbled in the occult or had experienced strange, unexplainable happenings and would be willing to talk about them.

We started the new television show, I can't remember what it was called, but it wasn't *Ferdie's Inferno*, probably something like *Into the Unknown*. The show started with a kaleidoscopic projection that we borrowed from Khamphalous. Then there was a half-hour talk show style discussion about the occult followed by a horror movie. We also did the commercials, but the only one I can remember was one in which we smashed up a TV set with a sledgehammer. Not sure what the point of that was.

When Ferdie discovered that I didn't have a color TV to watch the show, he generously let me borrow a large 27-inch set. We did a few more episodes, but Ferdie got sick, I think it was cancer, and his brother Lenny took over the day-to-day business of American TV. He wasn't crazy about our show and decided to go back to the old format, and changed the title to *Lenny's Inferno*. I never did return the TV set and, as a result, learned a hard lesson about karma. But more about that later.

* * *

I had decided not to enroll for the fall session at Madison. I had been reading Peter Brook's inspiring book *The Empty Space* and felt that it was time for me to earn my living as a professional director of theater. Carolyn and I talked about starting another company, and this time it wouldn't be a collective; it would be our theater and we would hire the actors. We wanted to create a theater that would pay us enough for our work onstage that we wouldn't need to get other part-time jobs to pay the rent. No waiting tables or driving cabs. We wanted to be able to devote all of our time and energy to the creation of mind-blowing theater. We named our new venture The Organic Theater Company, clearly inspired by The Living Theater, but also based on Stanislavsky's statement that "Theater is an organic process."

We got permission to stage our first production in the basement of the United Methodist Church on University Avenue. Again inspired by Peter Brook, I chose Shakespeare's *Richard III* as our first production. The gimmick was that there were no gimmicks, and for the first time I would use Shakespeare's words as he wrote them. I was fascinated by Richard, possibly the theater's first anti-hero, who is so charismatic and cunning that the audience can't wait to see what he will do next.

I rounded up a new group of actors, as my previous ensemble had either graduated or taken part in the Broom Street Mutiny. Cecil O'Neal was a Theater Department grad student who had helped me out during *Peter Pan* by playing a pirate in the outlaw performances in the Commerce Building after so many original cast members had dropped out. Considering how extreme our past productions had been, *Richard III* was a relatively tame affair: no nudity or bloodletting. The production opened to good reviews and decent audiences, and we settled into our three-week run. But on the Monday morning after our premiere, the city building department showed up and told us that the auditorium was not permitted for public performances. When I asked what the problem was, I was told that the floor would have to be lowered six inches. "You mean the stage?" I asked them.

"No," they told me, "The entire auditorium." If we didn't comply, we would have to close our show immediately.

Again, I called Jack Olson. This was clearly harassment from the Madison powers-that-be, still smarting from *Peter Pan* and *Lysistrata* but since they couldn't bust us for obscenity, they were using the building department to do their dirty work. Jack told us that there wasn't much we could do about it. So we scrambled, looking for another performing space. We spent every week hauling our scenery from place to place and resetting the lights, as if the show were on tour. It was a hassle, but we somehow completed the run.

Carolyn and I spent Thanksgiving in Chicago with my mother and brother. That weekend we went to see a production of *Grimm's Fairy Tales* directed by Paul Sills. Paul was the founder of the legendary Compass Players that gave starts to the careers of Mike Nichols, Elaine May, Shelley Berman, and Barbara Harris, whom Paul had married. After that, he had created The Second City, then left Second City a few years later because he had become bored with what had become a highly successful formula, walking away from a gold mine of his own creation.

Now he had created a new theater form: 'Story Theater,' in which the actors each narrated for their own characters as they mimed the actions and also spoke the dialogue. His first Story Theater production had been *The American Revolution*, which was performed for free at Second City during the Chicago Democratic Convention. Tear gassed and beaten protestors were able to regain their strength and idealism by watching a show that compared their activism to our founding fathers.

Paul had turned an old factory on Lincoln Avenue into a theater that he named The Body Politic. The building included The Oxford Pub, a bar and grill where audiences and performers could hang out or grab a bite before and after shows. The upstairs space was rented out to various political arts groups like Rising Up Angry, a collective of pissed-off redneck poets. But Lincoln Avenue was still very much an industrial area in those days, with a tool and die company right next to Paul's new theater.

The night we attended Story Theater we sat on crude plywood benches painted in bright primary colors and watched his young company create magic before our eyes. Accompanied only by a single guitarist who played songs by The Beatles and Bob Dylan, we were enthralled as the small cast of seven transformed themselves into princesses, dwarves, robber bridegrooms on prancing horses, and even barnyard animals – chickens, geese, and ducks – using only a few hats and scarves to supplement their costumes.

Afterwards we went backstage to congratulate the actors and met Paul Sills himself. He was in his forties with frizzy light brown hair and intense blue eyes that seemed to be able to see right into your soul. He had heard about *Peter Pan* and even *The Game Show* and, as I told him about our recent problems in Madison, he nodded. "You should move your theater to Chicago," he told me. "They'll leave you alone here. Right now, it's just us and the Kingston Mines across the street," he continued, referring to the other experimental theater that occupied a converted trolley barn a block away in Lincoln Park. "If there's three of us, we'll have a scene."

Carolyn and I left, inspired. Paul Sills always had that effect on me. He even offered to help us find a performing space. On the drive back to my mother's house, we agreed that he was absolutely right. We had outgrown Madison, and Chicago offered a large and hungry audience who had been forced to subsist on touring Broadway shows with second tier casts and dinner theater in the suburbs. As Paul had said, we could be part of a scene; an exciting new kind of theater, offering Chicago audiences world premieres instead of tired old fare.

When we returned to Madison, we called a meeting of the company and told them about the idea of moving The Organic to Chicago. Some loved the idea, but others had doubts or were unable to leave, having jobs or classes that they couldn't just abandon. But Cecil O'Neal and his wife Cookie were onboard, and so was broad-shouldered actor Tim Malish. A few days later Bob Engel approached me. He had heard about our plan to move the company to Chicago and wanted to know if he could join us. Overjoyed, I hugged him. Now there were six of us, all sharing the same dream.

PART TWO

CHICAGO

CHAPTER 8

A Gift from God

One evening Paul Sills called and told me that he had found a performing space for our theater company, and we could have it rent free! "It's the Holy Covenant Methodist Church." A church?! Do they know the kind of theater that we do? Nudity? Blood? Profanity? "They're very progressive," Paul told me. "You should come down and meet their pastor."

Reverend Jim Reed was a tall, gentle man in his forties with a warm smile. He showed me the main sanctuary, which had high arched ceilings with massive wooden beams and beautiful stained-glass windows. Rows of pews faced the raised altar. He explained that he wanted us to help them unbolt the pews so they could be moved around, and as long as we returned them facing the altar in time for Sunday morning services, we could arrange the seating however we wanted. I started to explain to him about our shows and that they may not be suitable, but he cut me off. Paul Sills had told him about *Peter Pan* and our travails in Madison, and he promised that they would not censor our shows or interfere with them in any way. "We see your coming to Holy Covenant as a gift from God," Reverend Reed told me to my amazement.

In January of 1970, Carolyn and I loaded our belongings, which amounted mainly to secondhand furniture and some artwork, into a rented truck and drove to Chicago. It was freezing cold as we moved into our newly rented apartment. We had found a place on Burling Street near Fullerton. Our landlady was a kindly little old lady named Elsie Rossberger. Roger Ebert lived across the tree-lined street and, as we headed to rehearsal each morning, we would sometimes see him on his way to the *Sun-Times* where he worked as a film critic. He had gotten the job because he had been one of the few critics to appreciate *Bonnie and Clyde*, which the old guard had disparaged. Buoyed by the film's success, he had established himself as a "new wave" cineaste and, as they say, the rest is history. But we became friends, and he often attended our shows, even writing about them from time to time, though as a film critic, theater was somewhat out of his bounds.

We had decided that our first show at the Holy Covenant should be an adaptation of George Orwell's *Animal Farm*. I was still smarting from the debacle of being ousted from Broom Street Theater, and Orwell's story about a revolution going awry hit a nerve. We held auditions and cast three talented local actresses: Amy Benesch, a brunette with a forceful presence and wonderful sense of humor; Lisa Roger, curvaceous and sexy with curly black hair; and Drew Shiflett, who was the beautiful blonde daughter of Jim Shiflett, an ordained minister and friend of Paul Sills. Jim was tall with a full beard and always reminded me of *Moby Dick*'s Captain Ahab. He also happened to own the Body Politic building. We also cast a tall, thin, balding fellow who called himself Euclid Harque Life. Euclid looked just like the famous da Vinci drawing of the four-armed man in the circle. Originally named Gerald Kirschbaum, Euclid had changed his name when he decided not to follow his father's career path as an investment banker, dropping out to become an actor. He proved to be an inspired character man with an off-kilter sense of humor. In other words, he fit right in.

The deal we offered the troupe was simple: every member of the company would have a role in each of our shows and a vote in company decisions. All would help build the sets and costumes, distribute flyers and posters, and even sweep and mop the floors, and we would share equally in whatever we took in at the box office after expenses, with one share going to the theater itself. Our original goal was to provide a minimum of $55 a week. We offered meals for fifty cents per person per meal while we rehearsed our first show.

Our first task had been to unbolt the pews from the floor. We decided to stage the show in the round, ringed by the bench-like seats. In Grotowsky-esque fashion, the costumes were tights and leotards that we spattered and spotted with brown and black paint to approximate the coats of pigs and horses. A trip to an army surplus store inspired the idea of a wall of camouflage netting to cage the animals as their society became more totalitarian and repressive. Level after level of netting would be raised until the audience could barely see the actors. Our lighting instruments were floodlights in coffee cans with colored gel taped over the ends, and we bought a six-dimmer lighting board on credit. The $1,800 to start our venture was loaned to me by my mother, probably the person least able to be so generous, but that was always her way, God bless her. We finally did pay her back a few years later, only to borrow it back. We sent out press releases to a list provided by Paul Sills, and my old friend Ron Berman (now a doctor) took the production stills that we sent to the papers. When opening night arrived, however, only one critic showed up. He was Richard Christiansen from the *Chicago Daily News*. Thin and angular with large glasses and an eternal twinkle in his eye, he sat there taking notes during the show and quickly left after our curtain call. Did he like it? We soon found out that he did, as his rave review welcomed our new company to the city and said that we were presenting an exciting new type of theater. He proved to be a real friend of the theater, reviewing almost every show we ever did.

The phones started ringing off the hook and our tickets, which we bought on a roll like they have at carnivals, began selling out. We did six performances a week, Wednesday through Sunday, with two shows on Saturday night, 7:30 and 10:30. After our final performance on Sunday, we would divide up the money into equal piles on the floor like a pirate band with their booty. Amazingly, we were able to exist without taking other jobs and could devote our full time and energy to our art. We were now professionals, earning our livelihood (barely) by our work onstage. The move to Chicago was paying off. It felt great.

For our next show we decided to adapt Homer's *Odyssey*. We staged a nearly wordless production. The opening image was of the Trojan Horse, formed Living Theater-style of the leotard clad actors' bodies. The horse broke apart with screaming soldiers ravaging Troy. Cecil O'Neal was Odysseus looking every bit like the Greek hero with his muscular body and flowing blond hair, and Euclid played the towering Cyclops sitting on Tim Malish's powerful shoulders. The production was visually stunning, and our new friend, *Daily News* critic Richard Christiansen, described us as "one of Chicago's most interesting 'theaters of poverty.'" He continued, "Beginning first with an adaptation of George Orwell's *Animal Farm* and now with a new version of *The Odyssey* director Stuart Gordon, 22, has put his young cast through productions that stress sensual involvement over verbal byplay, that delight in a communal spirit between actors and audience, and that rely on the players' physical versatility rather than elaborate props and settings for their imagination." He closed the review with "It would be worth your while to drop in on *The Odyssey*. It is cheap ($2.50), it is fun, and it is, with thanks to Homer, a pretty good story." God bless you, Richard Christiansen.

Summer was fast approaching, and the Holy Covenant Church wasn't air-conditioned. We bought electric fans to cool the theater, but they were too noisy to leave on during the show, and our sweating spectators ended up fanning themselves with our programs. The crowds started falling off. The temperatures were rising as we headed into Chicago's muggy July. Then, as if by some divine intervention, I got another call from Paul Sills. He was taking his Story Theater production to the Mark Taper Forum in Los Angeles and wanted to know if we'd be interested in renting the Body Politic for the summer. We would be filling Sill's inspired shoes, anointed as his heir-apparent, performing in his fabled space which, praise the gods, happened to be air-conditioned! Our production was saved. We said goodbye and thanked the Holy Covenant Church and moved into the Body Politic on Lincoln Avenue.

* * *

We did good business at the Body Politic playing *Odyssey* through the summer and into the fall.

That fall we began rehearsals of our next show. It was inspired by Tarot cards that had become all the rage. I had what I thought was a brilliant idea. We could create a scene portraying each card of the Major Arcana: The Lovers, The Devil, The Wheel of Fortune, and so on. Then we'd shuffle the cards and let the audience pick them one by one to tell their own fortune. As there are 22 cards in the deck and only 12 are drawn to tell a fortune, every show would be different. Bald headed, skeletal Euclid was the Magician who dealt the cards. Cecil stood at the door seating the audience according to their astrological signs in one of the four elemental sections: air; earth; water; fire. The fact that we would separate audience members who had arrived as couples to the theater didn't deter us.

Opening night all the critics were there to see how this new company measured up to Paul Sill's vaunted Story Theater troupe. The theater was packed and, as the cards were chosen, it soon became apparent that our fate had been decided for us. All of the most depressing and doomed cards came up one by one: The Devil with its enslaved lovers; The Tower, which shows a tall, imposing structure hit by lightning and a figure plummeting to his death. Years later I couldn't help thinking of this card as I watched the horrifying images of 9/11 play out on our TV screen. And at last, The Final Outcome: Death. We didn't have to wait for the reviews to know that our show was deader than a doornail. We knew we had to go back into rehearsal ASAP. And this time we decided we'd better do a comedy.

CHAPTER 9

The Best of All Possible Worlds

That cataclysmic Tarot reading wasn't done with us yet. One night, Carolyn and I were awakened by Lefty, our feisty West Highland White Terrier, barking furiously in the living room. Carolyn rushed in just in time to see a leg quickly withdrawing from the open window facing the street. The next day I nailed the large window shut.

That evening we were eating a late dinner when we heard someone knocking at our door. "Who is it?" I asked. "Our car broke down," a voice answered. "Can we use your phone to call for help?" Foolishly I opened the door to find two street thugs. One was pointing a pistol at me. "We're coming in," he said. The first thing they did was to make us lock Lefty in our bedroom. Clearly the leg we saw exiting the window the night before belonged to one of these guys. Carolyn held Phoebe, our other dog, in her arms. Then they told me to lie down on the living room floor with my hands behind my back. "Don't hurt her," I begged them as they tied me up and then gagged me with a torn-up pillowcase.

"If you do what we tell you, we ain't hurtin' nobody," was the reply. I have never been as scared as I was that night. They wanted the large color TV that we had "borrowed" from Ferdie Mattioli in Madison. (Karma's a bitch, ain't it?) We stupidly had it sitting in our living room window where it could be seen from the street, and it had obviously attracted the attention of the robbers. They told Carolyn to unplug it. "I'm not helping you," she fiercely told them. "If you want it, you'll have to do it yourselves." I braced myself for them to slap her or worse, but they simply unplugged the set. Then they had her empty her purse and took the fifty dollars they found inside. All the while I was secretly working my hands free as they turned and headed for the door, the bigger one lugging our TV set. The guy with the gun whipped around, I held onto the pillowcase tie to look like I was still trussed up. He waved the pistol in our direction. "Don't try to follow us or call the police," he warned. "Or you be dead." And they were gone.

Carolyn ran to me and helped me free myself. We crawled to the window and peeked out. Shit! The gunman was right outside, and he pointed the gun at my face. I quickly ducked down behind the window ledge, gasping for breath. "They're still out there," I whispered to Carolyn. When I got the nerve to look again, they were gone.

"Those motherfuckers," Carolyn said, her anger clearly overpowering her fear. I, on the other hand, was shaking. "Call the police," she told me.

It didn't seem that things could get much worse, and maybe that's why the phrase "This is the best of all possible worlds" jumped into my head.

It's the key phrase from Voltaire's comic novel *Candide* (subtitled "Optimism"). We decided to stage the piece in a broad and colorful *commedia del'arte* style with the actors in whiteface. Bob Engel was perfect as the innocent Candide, wearing an oversized baby blue Pierrot costume with a white ruff around his neck and enormous floppy sleeves that covered his hands. Euclid played Pangloss and assorted villains, while Cecil, in a striped harlequin outfit, was the Grand Inquisitor. Amy Benesch played the Old Woman with one buttock (her story involved being shipwrecked and she and the few starving survivors in her lifeboat end up dining on her posterior). Carolyn played a number of roles. Lisa Rogers had decided to leave the company and take a position working at the United Nations. One of our rehearsals was interrupted by FBI agents, showing up unannounced, to do a background check on her. Her replacement was Simone Deely, a beautiful blonde actress who had been classically trained in her native Canada. Married and with a small son Mathew who she sometimes brought to rehearsal, Simone was talented but a bit clueless. She sometimes reminded me of a young Margaret Dumont, and we were the Marx Brothers. She played Cunégonde and, in one scene in which she was being assaulted by a Jewish moneylender played by Euclid, he pulled an enormous Kosher salami out of his pants and chased her around. During one rehearsal he must have forgotten the sausage and instead pulled out his penis. Shocked, Simone stared at it exclaiming, "Euclid, what is that?!"

Candide proved to be our biggest success yet, selling out thanks to rave reviews and terrific word of mouth.

We ran through the holidays and our salaries now far exceeded the $55 per week of our original guarantee to the company. As we began 1971, we received a call from Michael Butler. Michael was the wealthy playboy son of the Chicago-based Butler Aviation family.

It turned out that Butler had produced an Off-Broadway musical based on the Tarot, and it was playing to mixed reviews and half-filled houses. He wanted me to take a look at the show with the idea of re-making it into a success. I confess I was amazed, as our production of *Tarot Cards* had been a complete disaster. But maybe the success of *Candide* had turned things around, at least in his mind. I agreed to go to New York to see the show and travel arrangements were quickly set up. I persuaded him to allow Carolyn to accompany me for what would be my first trip to the Big Apple. They even put us up at the Plaza Hotel.

The idea of bringing *Candide* to New York stayed with me and so, before leaving for the city, I sent a letter to Joe Papp. He had just opened his Public Theater on Lafayette Street and was bringing productions from all over the world to perform there. To my great surprise and delight he quickly got back to me and said he was sending his right-hand man, Bernie Gersten, to see our show. Bernie loved *Candide* and we went out for drinks with him at the Oxford Pub next door to celebrate. He invited me to meet with him and Joe to work out the terms when we arrived in New York.

I'll never forget the first time I ever saw Times Square: a garish combination of bright lights and tawdry signage: porno theaters, massage parlors, Nathan's, the streets overflowing with garbage, packed with people moving hurriedly in what almost seemed like a sped-up film. They used to call Chicago "the city that works" and now I understood why. Yet Chicago seemed downright orderly compared to New York, but Manhattan has a wild energy that Chicago will never have. Wide-eyed, Carolyn and I were carried along by the crush of people, all in a hurry. We felt like country mice in the big city for the first time, dealing with fast-talking hustlers who all had half-baked scams. Nothing seemed finished and so we decided that if Chicago was the city that worked, the motto of New York should be, "You get the idea."

We went to see Michael Butler's Tarot musical at The Circle in the Square which, despite its famous pedigree, turned out to be a dumpy little theater in the Village. We were totally underwhelmed by the musical. It had the same problems that our own Tarot show did, plus a score of forgettable songs sung by a cast that was trying way too hard to please. But we loved the Plaza Hotel, although our tiny room overlooked a dank view of heating ducts and pipes. The lobby looked the same as it had in *North By Northwest* and we kept expecting to run into Cary Grant. We ordered room service for the first time and had breakfast in bed, although there was barely room for the service cart, let alone the waiter, in our teensy little room.

The next day we met with Joe Papp and Bernie Gersten at the Public Theater. Papp had struck a deal with the City of New York to rent him the enormous four-storey Astor Street Library for one dollar a year. Small of stature but with an enormous personality, Joe Papp immediately bowled us over. Often called Napoleonic, Papp was well into his campaign to conquer the world of not-for-profit theater. His tie loosened, his sleeves rolled up, wearing a vest but no jacket, he quickly worked out the deal for us to bring *Candide* to the Public the following month as Bernie – tall, thin and dryly witty – took notes and asked pertinent questions. We couldn't get a word in edgewise. Joe took us out for lunch after making our deal, which involved us working for next to nothing until the play could catch on. But he wanted us to bring the show to the Public ASAP. It was April and the waiter proudly let us know that the first strawberries of the season were available for dessert, so we all ordered them. Joe picked up one of the enormous red berries and held it up dramatically. "Remember this moment," he said, looking us in the eye, and so we never forgot it. It wasn't until many years later watching Bergman's film *Wild Strawberries* that I realized that Joe had been quoting the famous line from the film.

When word got out that we had made a deal with Joe Papp to bring *Candide* to New York, Michael Butler was furious. "We paid for the trip, so you were there on our nickel and had no right to meet with Papp," Butler's rep scolded me. "But you didn't want to bring our show to New York," I reminded him. He was still pissed and told me not to ever expect any more help from Michael Butler.

We loaded our set (the stage was made of large wooden cable spools) into a rented truck that David and Jonathan drove to New York while the rest of us made our way after them by plane or car. Carolyn and I had been told that Bernie Gersten had the keys to an apartment we could use in Manhattan.

The next day we were shown our theater on the fourth floor of the Public. It was named Martinson Hall after a donor, and had yet to be renovated. The walls and ceiling were covered with peeling paint and the floor was littered with garbage. "We can fit about 200 people in here," we were told, but when the company saw it, their faces clearly said, "What a dump!"

"You get the idea," I thought. But when the world hands you a lemon, etc. I had an idea: "We'll put up a banner over the door that says, 'This is the best of all possible worlds.'" Everyone laughed. A perfect illustration of Voltaire's theme. We made a trip to the garment district and got some cheap yellow fabric. Our plan was to create a broken-down circus tent feeling. The night before our first preview, we stayed late and distressed the fabric with tea, and then black paint, but the cloth still looked shiny and new. Exhausted, everyone left but Carolyn and me. I then had another brilliant idea: we could burn the edges of the cloth panels to distress them further. Unfortunately, the fabric had not been fireproofed and was already hanging on ropes from the ceiling, and since fire always burns upwards, the cheap synthetic cloth ignited, quickly becoming a blazing bonfire. The enormous flames were leaping up to the ceiling and of course there was no sprinkler system in place. Carolyn and I rushed to pull them down, stomping on the fire madly to put it out. We never called for help, more afraid that our New York engagement would be cancelled than that we would end up burning down the Public Theater.

Thank God we were able to put out the fire and open the windows to let out the thick, and probably poisonous, black smoke. No night watchman ever showed up and so, covered with soot and looking pretty distressed ourselves, Carolyn and I slipped out of the theater.

The previews went well, and it looked like we would soon have our first New York hit. But we were soon to learn that sometimes there's more drama in the lobby than on the stage. On opening night, Joe Papp got into a shouting match with the eminent *Times* critic Walter Kerr ten minutes before our show was to begin. "Get out!" Joe screamed at Kerr, having banned him from the Public due to a string of bad reviews.

"I bought a ticket!" countered Kerr, the older man not giving an inch to Papp's bullying.

"Well, they shouldn't have sold you one," shouted Papp.

"But they did!" exclaimed Kerr, holding up his ticket for all to see. Joe grabbed the ticket and tore it up.

"You're no friend to this theater!" sputtered Papp.

"I'm a critic," responded Kerr "I don't have to be a friend!" The audience watched in amusement as Papp was finally forced to relent and seat Kerr. But watching the two giants of the American Theater duking it out reminded me of Godzilla versus King Kong.

"It's good press," Bernie assured me. "It'll be all over tomorrow's news." But Kerr's response was to pan our show (surprise, surprise) putting it down as amateurish work from the hinterlands. Clive Barnes wrote in the *New York Times*: "If what this town needs is a fair-to-good children's show for fair-to-good dirty children, it may have found one in *Candide*." Luckily, many of the other reviews were better, tickets were selling, and it looked like the show could actually have a run. But a few days later I was called in to see Bernie. "We're closing the show," he told me, never being one to beat around the bush.

"But audiences love it," I reminded him.

"Doesn't matter," he said waving off my protests, "It's the fire department. We don't have an occupancy permit for the space and they say it's a fire trap." I bit my tongue, as we had already discovered this fact ourselves, but it was so ironic that it could only be more karma, or God as the great cosmic practical joker.

But… I had a plan. While at the Public we had watched one of their shows, *Subject to Fits*, a brilliant adaptation by Robert Montgomery of Dostoevsky's *The Idiot.* The elegant production with well-spoken actors in period clothes gave me an idea: a play based on the tragic all-too-short life of Edgar Allan Poe and his mysterious death in the streets of Baltimore in 1849. Richard Fire, the talented actor who played the lead role of Marat at the University of Wisconsin, had come to see *Candide* at the Public and we had gone out for drinks after the show. Richard made it clear that he would be interested in joining our company on the condition that we would bring more shows to New York. Richard's nervous presence seemed ideal for Poe, and André De Shields, now also living in New York, agreed to join the company. He would be fantastic as the Raven.

We headed back to Chicago to find the rest of the actors to fill out our new company. One day, out of the blue, I got a call from Frank Hilgenberg. It was an awkward call – we hadn't spoken to each other since the Broom Street Theater Mutiny – but he was looking for work and, as I told Carolyn, he is one of the best actors I had ever directed. So I invited him to play John Allan, Poe's abusive father. It turned out there was a catch. "I'd like to bring my girlfriend, Jory," Frank told me. "She's a dynamite actress."

Jory, it turned out, was a long-legged beautiful brunette with a turned-up nose. She was also a vegetarian who never shaved her legs (or anything else). I remember long discussions with her about bowel movements. "Vegetarian shit always floats," she once told me. Frank was right, she was a good actress. She would play Poe's southern belle fiancé Elmira Royster.

The play, titled simply *Poe*, focused on the last days of the poet's life in which he had virtually disappeared on the eve of his second wedding. He had stopped in Baltimore to gather up his personal possessions on his way to Richmond where his childhood sweetheart, now a wealthy widow, waited for him. Two days later he was found unconscious on the Baltimore streets without identification and wearing someone else's clothing. Raving, never fully regaining consciousness, he died at the age of forty in a pauper's hospital. Six people attended his funeral.

Our play would take place in his feverish mind, a phantasmagorical collage that would interweave his nightmarish tales and poetry with his own life story, a story that was just as bizarre and tortured as his fiction. Working with playwright Stephen Most, we fashioned a script whose structure was inspired by Poe's story "A Descent into the Maelstrom" and created a downward spiral that built speed like a whirlpool. The play begins with Poe mugged and robbed on the streets of Baltimore and ends with the Raven lifting up the dying Poe and enclosing him tenderly in his black wings as the writer exclaims his actual final words, "Lord, help my poor soul!"

During rehearsals, we were paid a visit from a representative of Actors Equity. He was concerned because André, a member of the union, was working for a non-union company, namely us. André had brought the highest level of professionalism to our company that I had ever experienced, and he set an example that inspired us all to strive for his high standards. Now his own union was insisting that he leave the show. André was having none of it. "You should be helping me find work, not denying me work," André angrily told him. "If you can find me an Equity job I'll take it, but until you do, I'm staying here." Chastened, the rep left, not sure what to say. A few days later, however, I received a call from his superior telling me that they had discovered that Richard Fire was also a member of Equity and that I would have to pay both actors Equity minimum as well as make contribution to the health and pension fund. When I responded that it would be unfair to the other company members, the caller snorted and explained that, after all, they were not professional actors. This infuriated me and I told him that all the members of our company made their living acting and so indeed they were professionals in the true sense of the word. He would not be moved from this position, telling me that both André and Richard would be heavily fined if they stayed with our show without an Equity contract, and that I needed to face the fact that eventually the entire company would need to go Equity as well. After thinking about it long and hard, my solution was to raise the minimum company salary from the original $55 to the Equity minimum, which was $100. Everyone would be paid the same, which pissed off the union. Eventually, as the rep had predicted, the entire company became members of Actors Equity.

The show opened in the fall of 1971 and received good reviews and decent houses but was not the huge hit we had hoped for.

To Walk As a God

Back during those tumultuous Madison days, theater critic Lenny Kleinfeld introduced me to the joys of Marvel Comics. Although best known as the home of Spider-Man and the Fantastic Four, Marvel also drew me to the darker mystical world of Doctor Strange and the Norse mythological realm of the Mighty Thor.

Superhero comics had been banned to me when I was a teenager. This was probably due to Dr. Fredric Wertham's 1954 book *Seduction of the Innocent*, in which he made the case that violent comic books were a major cause of juvenile delinquency. These brightly colored, action-packed stories that Lenny introduced me to were fresh and full of wonders. Marvel, under the inspired editorship of Stan "The Man" Lee and his brilliant artist partners Jack Kirby and Steve Ditko, were taking comic books to a new and more human level. Their heroes were not just the square-jawed archetypes that filled the pages of their rivals' books. The Marvel heroes were flawed, often uncertain, and usually completely unappreciated.

These comic books seemed like ready-made scenarios for the stage, telling their stories visually with tons of fast-paced action. We contacted Marvel to get permission to put their characters onstage but were quickly turned down. Disappointed at first but too excited by the concept to throw in the towel, we realized that we would have to create our own characters from scratch.

One evening the story suddenly popped into my head like the light bulb in a comic book thought-bubble. It was inspired by Freud's ideas of Id (the primitive need for immediate gratification above all) and Super-Ego (the opposing need for law and order) that together form the conscious Ego (or Self). My story was about a hopeless schizophrenic locked in a padded cell at an asylum until one day his dual personality completely splits apart, leaving only his Super-Ego behind. Seemingly cured, he becomes a successful bank teller and is engaged to marry his boss's beautiful daughter when he is suddenly whisked away to the Fifth Dimension. There he meets the wise old man who tells him that he is actually Lord Cumulus, Defender of the Universe, and that he must destroy the evil Chaos, Prince of Madness. He is trained for cosmic combat by an Amazon warrior who shows him how to use his powers, but when he finally confronts Chaos, he discovers that his enemy is in fact his own Id, the amoral side of himself. "I am you, brother!" Chaos shrieks at Cumulus. Later, when faced with a foe more powerful than either Cumulus or Chaos, they would have to join forces to form Ego, the ultimate superhero. The theater piece would be told in serial form in seven episodes and, like the comic books, each part would end with a cliffhanger so the audiences would have to come back again and again to find out what happens next.

But who would write this? We needed someone familiar with the florid over-the-top dialogue that fills comic books. Then another light bulb popped on. Of course! It was so obvious! The man who had turned me on to comic books in the first place, Lenny Kleinfeld, aka the ultra-cool bury st. edmund.

Inspired, we started naming the characters in my sketchy outline. Lenny had read the *Epic of Gilgamesh* and some of the names of the characters from that ancient Sumerian myth found their way into our story. The wise old man became Lugulbanda, who also simply called himself Knowledge. His Amazon warrior became Sargon, named after the famous hero of the Saga. We decided that Chaos needed a henchman and created Symax, his fawning purple ape. For the evil seductress, we came up with a four-armed insect sorceress that we named Valaria (inspired by malaria).

Casting was easy: blond muscular Cecil clearly would play Lord Cumulus and his bank teller alter ego David Carson. Carolyn would double as David's girlfriend Mary Louise and the glittering Valaria. Richard Fire would be the wise old Lugulbanda, Cordis [Heard] Fejer became Sargon, Mistress of War and Bill Norris was Symax and the bank president. Tom Towles, new to the company, would play Prince Chaos. Tommy, like Cordis, had been a member of Paul Sills' Story Theater where he was unforgettable as the Superfly-like Foxy Loxy, the sly rogue who disposes of Chicken Little and his friends. Tall and slim, sporting an Afro, a wide grin and a booming laugh, Tommy was a larger-than-life character onstage and off. Born to a black father and a light-skinned mother, Tommy was what might have been referred to in another time as "high yellow" and he was always confusing street blacks by calling them "brother."

We named the show *Warp*, after the multidimensional travel that enables our hero to enter the fifth dimension or "level" as Lenny called it. The first episode was entitled (in true Marvel style) "My Battlefield, My Body," inspired by the warring elements within the schizophrenic protagonist. We quickly realized that, since it had taken so long to create the first installment, we would only produce three episodes instead of the originally planned seven.

We began rehearsals in October of 1971. We built the set ourselves: a series of disk-like platforms, under the guidance of our designer Beverly Sobieski, who I unsuccessfully tried to convince to drop her first name entirely and become simply "Sobieski." We covered the platforms with Ensolite®, a thick rubber padding that would allow the actors to hurl themselves around like cosmic superheroes without killing themselves. The Ensolite was covered in shiny metallic blue vinyl provided free by Ina's father Max, who ran a luggage company. Once again Cecil's wife, Cookie Gluck, created the costumes, this time out of elastic macramé, and the gossamer silk butterfly wings she built for

Valaria, the insect sorceress, were truly stunning when hit with black light. Many of the costumes left the actors' bare bottoms exposed, and this became part of the distinctive look of *Warp*. I had thought it a bold design choice until Cookie confided that she just didn't know how to create bottoms for the costumes.

As we had no money, found objects were the name of the game; a corkscrew became a ray gun and the Cosmic Cube, the story's much sought after McGuffin, was simply a clear plastic cube. "Energy spears" were chromed exhaust pipes. The robotic Faceless Ones wore orange jumpsuits and long black rubber gloves used by farmers for artificially impregnating cows. The actors' faces were covered with metal baking sieves giving them a fencing master look.

We began previews in December and soon discovered that the audience found our show funny. What I had embraced with the almost religious fervor of an acid trip, our initial audiences were finding ludicrous. We decided to play into this, and the actors improvised some line changes that were quickly incorporated into the script. Richard made Lugulbanda absent-minded, the idea being that he knows so much that he has forgotten half of it. Like Marvel, we gave our characters quirks as well as senses of humor. This allowed the audience to laugh but also enjoy the super-powered heroics. *Warp*, which we billed as "The World's First Epic Adventure Play in Serial Form," opened at the Body Politic Theater in mid-December and became our biggest hit ever. We packed in audiences who came to see the show again and again. During the day Lenny and I worked on the next episode, which came together much quicker as we now knew our characters and could play to the strengths of our company. Episode Two, "Unleashed! Unchained!" opened in March of 1972 and the two episodes ran in rotating rep with both One and Two playing on Saturday nights. We found that many audience members bought tickets to both shows and made it a four-hour evening at our theater. *Warp* was sold out for weeks in advance. This was five years before the creation of *Star Wars*, and audiences loved the science fiction world and its unforgettable characters who were now performing superhuman feats before their astonished eyes. The actors were getting recognized on the streets ("Aren't you Lord Cumulus?") and we felt like we truly were walking as gods.

Many of the actors, in an effort to sport heavily muscled physiques like the comic book heroes, began to work out on a weight bench that was kept backstage at the Body Politic. And of course, they tried to top each other with the huge amounts of weight they were able to press, to the point that one black day Cecil O'Neal badly injured his back.

That night Bill Norris (looking like Woody Allen) gamely put on Lord Cumulus' superhero costume. But it was clear from the subdued audience reaction and Cecil's doctor, who told us the next day that his patient would need months to recover, that we had to face the music and find another actor to replace him. This was especially hard for me as Cecil (besides Carolyn and myself) was the only other company member who had been with us from the very beginning, pulling up stakes and making the precarious move from Madison during that February three years earlier to take his chances in Chicago.

But actress Cordis Fejer had an idea. “I can call my brother,” she told us. “He’d be a great Lord Cumulus.” So a few days later John Heard (yes, THE John Heard) arrived from Washington DC where he had been performing at the Arena Stage. Tall, blond and handsome, John reminded me of a young Errol Flynn, and had Flynn’s self-deprecating sense of humor.

Work on the third episode stopped while we rehearsed John into the first two episodes. The only wrinkle was that John had a love scene with the character played by his sister, and as the entire cast watched, they clinched for a passionate kiss. “I’ve been wanting to do that all of my life!” John exclaimed, cracking us all up and diffusing the tension. But I knew it was hard for Cecil, watching the role he had created, that had been making him a star, taken over by another actor, and knowing that John would reap the benefits.

Episode Three, “To Die... Alive!” opened in late August of 1972 and the reviews were good thanks to a brilliant finale in which our heroes finally confront the all-powerful He Who Dreams only to discover that he is a burned-out remnant, a decrepit skeleton played to perfection by André De Shields.

“How can we save you?” asks Cumulus.

“You do not save He Who Dreams, you become him!” is the god’s response. The two superheroes, Cumulus and Chaos, realize that they must join together to form Ego one last time, but this time for eternity. Thus, as the title states, they must die… alive, sacrificing their identities for the sake of saving the universe. They heroically do so, and the young, newly formed Ego is horrified looking at the hideous visage of He Who Dreams, who intones some of the most wonderful lines ever written by bury st. edmund, Lenny Kleinfeld, or anyone else: “Yes, yes this is the swindle. This twisted wreckage of your former splendor is all the thanks you can expect – the price we pay for the privilege of being!” As I write this now, at the end of my sixth decade, with tears running down my cheeks, I am amazed that Lenny, then in his mid-twenties when he wrote these words, understood so perfectly the feeling you get each day when you look at your wrinkled, balding, decimated self in a mirror. How can I walk like a god, when I’m up to my chin in shit?

* * *

Warp was a phenomenon. People had to wait months for tickets, and they were often scalped for hundreds of dollars. We were approached by producers who wanted to bring the show to New York. Among them was Tony D’Amato, who had been an associate producer of *Grease*. He felt that we should close the show by the end of 1972 and open off-Broadway the following February. The budget was $300,000, with a quarter of a million to remount the show and advertise it and $50,000 to be kept as a reserve to keep the show running. It seemed like a good plan, although in retrospect we were fools not to have kept the Chicago production going. I was so full of myself in those heady days and asked, "Would the Rolling Stones replace themselves?" Of course not. We were stars. Superstars. To further complicate things, after making several trips to New York, we couldn't find a suitable off-Broadway theater. One day Tony had interesting news: the Shuberts had offered him the Ambassador Theatre for the same price as an off-Broadway house. With 1,100 seats sitting on the Great White Way, it was a huge leap from our 200-seat Body Politic. Nevertheless, Paul Sills had played there with his Story Theater production a year before, and if he could do it…

We started talking about a poster for the show. My brother David and I had created the posters for the performances at the Body Politic and they were our attempts to ape the style of the great Marvel comic book artists. But now we could actually hire one of them to do our poster, and in our minds, there was only one choice: Neal Adams. Would he do a poster for *Warp*? Of course he would. I later learned that Neal never turned down any offer of work as he had a large growing family to provide for. But he'd have to see the show first, so we flew him to Chicago where he watched all three episodes, making wonderful sketches all the while. Before his return to New York, he dropped a bombshell on us, though: What would we think if he redesigned the show?

"Costumes?" I asked, not sure what he meant.

"Yeah; costumes, sets, props, everything." My jaw must have dropped, because Neal, on a roll like a runaway train, continued. "I can do it, because everything I draw can actually work." I never attempted to sort this out with him, wondering if he meant the contraptions on Batman's utility belt or Iron Man's flying boots. They really worked? All I remember was grinning and shaking hands. *Warp* looking like a Neal Adams comic! How can you say no to that?

Around this time, I got a call from John Belushi. I had met John while he was performing at Second City, and he frequently came to catch our shows. He was calling to offer me a job directing him and some of his friends in a show called *Lemmings* for the *National Lampoon*. The show was going to play off-Broadway in New York and, among the other performers, were names I didn't recognize at the time: Chevy Chase and Christopher Guest. I explained that I was in the middle of planning *Warp*'s New York premier. "Can't you do both?" John wanted to know. I felt I couldn't split my focus and declined. Looking back, it's obvious that this was the show that put John on the map, in a big way (partly due to his dead-on impersonation of Joe Cocker) and was the beginning of the company that would become *Saturday Night Live.* I sometimes wonder how different my life would have been if I had accepted Belushi's amazing invitation.

We decided to close *Warp* in Chicago on the one-year anniversary of its opening. As a farewell celebration, we would do all three episodes in one night and, to make it even better, we would serve the entire audience a six-course meal, one course between each of the six acts. We called it the Warpathon and charged the then-unthinkable price of $100 a ticket.

We all gave our landlords notice. After all, we were going to New York to become rich and famous and would no longer need our Chicago apartments. We told Jim Shiflett, who now ran the Body Politic, that we wouldn't be coming back to the theater. During the Christmas/New Year vacation Carolyn and I booked a trip to Grand Cayman Island in the Caribbean so we could finally take the honeymoon we had never had. It would be a good way to relax before we began putting together the New York production.

The next thing we knew, we were in New York.

Betty Lee Hunt, the famous Broadway press agent, was hired by Tony D'Amato because she had repped *Grease*. Tall with red curly hair and a husky voice, she reminded me of a cross between Ethel Merman and Bea Arthur. She could hold her own in a roomful of men, chain smoking as she cut through the bullshit, taking charge and no prisoners. She advised us to buy a double page ad in *The New York Times* to announce the opening of our show, to "put it on the map." Lenny, dusting off his advertising chops and using the new logo that Neal had designed with Cumulus and Chaos shooting mind blasts through the word *Warp*, headlined the piece "HIT OR MYTH?" This was followed by a dozen quotes from the many rave reviews we had received in Chicago. Why Betty Lee Hunt had allowed this is still a mystery to me. She must have known that if there's anything New York critics hate it's being told that other critics in lesser-known places (i.e. other than New York) loved your show. It's like waving a red flag at a bull.

Opening day arrived: February 14th, 1973, Valentine's Day. Betty Lee Hunt had arranged for several local television crews to tape interviews and show snippets of our show on the evening news, but there had been a snafu and many of our actors were not yet at the theater, including Carolyn, so I asked one of the new understudies to put on Carolyn's Valaria costume. She was an immediate sensation as the skimpy costume and the beautiful cape became the centerpiece of the coverage. When Carolyn arrived and discovered this, she was furious. I tried to apologize and calm her down, but it was too late. "What should I have done?" I asked her, "They needed to film something."

"Make them wait until I got here!" was her response. She was right, but it wasn't the best way to go into a big opening night.

The theater was packed and many of our friends and family had come from Chicago to share the moment: my mother was there wishing us well. "Is there anything I can do to help?" she wanted to know. I hugged her and told her to "Just love the show." And then it was showtime. The audience response was tremendous. Eleven hundred people laughing at our jokes and cheering on the super heroics. We were on a roll and couldn't lose. But during the final battle as Bill Norris' Symax was getting mind-blasted off the stage, he seemed to fall in a funny way; like a marionette whose strings have been cut. And then he wasn't there for the curtain call. The audience was on its feet, a standing ovation, but I had this feeling that something was terribly wrong. When I got backstage the cast were gathered around Bill, who was lying on the stage floor. "I caught my arm on the platform," Bill told me. "I think it's broken." He looked up at me with tears in his eyes, "I'm sorry," he said softly.

"Don't worry," I told him. "You'll be fine. You probably just twisted it."

I encouraged him to go to the emergency room and have it checked out. "Come to the party when you're done," I urged him. "I'm sure it'll be going on well into the night."

The party was being held in the ballroom of some hotel. We originally had planned on having the party at Sardi's, but I had urged Tony to put the money on stage.

The party was just getting started when the first review came in. It was from Clive Barnes of the all-important *New York Times*. Richard Fire read it to the crowd. It began by listing Goethe's three questions of criticism: What is the artist trying to do? Did he succeed at doing it? Was it worth doing? They are putting a comic book on stage. Did they succeed? Yes. Was it worth doing? "We live in a junk world," Barnes stated, "And this is junk art. Beautifully cooked – but junk."

The crowd was silent and then began to boo. "Fuck him!" someone shouted. But the room had suddenly grown cold and, as the other daily papers and television reviews (featuring Carolyn's understudy in the Valaria costume) came in, it got colder. It's hard to believe that anyone would put down comic books now that every other blockbuster movie is based on them, but this was in 1973 and *Star Wars* was four years away.

"Apparently they read a lot of comic books in the Midwest," one of the reviews stated, not satisfied to just trash the play, but also the entire heartland of our country. Another review accused us of packing the audience with busloads that we had brought over the Appalachian Mountains to New York City. People were leaving the party in droves. The evening had become a disaster. The Saint Valentine's Day Massacre. Richard Fire was on his knees at my feet weeping. "What did we do wrong?" he asked, "What did we do?"

The critic from the *Chicago Reader* and his wife pulled me aside, "I spent a lot of money to come here to cover this," he began. "Out of our own pockets!" his wife jumped in, "What are we supposed to do now?"

"I'm sorry," is all I could say.

The show closed at the end of the week. I still run into people who tell me that they saw it on Broadway. If everyone who told me this had actually shown up, we would have had lines around the block.

King Tut's Tomb

Carolyn, David, and I crawled back to Chicago with our tails between our legs. The Organic Company had once again been splintered by another New York disaster. André decided to stay in Manhattan and found a new home for himself and his amazing talent in New York City. He would go on to play the title role as *The Wiz* in the original Broadway production and later star in *Ain't Misbehavin'* and *The Full Monty*, establishing himself as a legend of the Broadway stage, winning a Tony for *Hadestown* in 2019.

Richard and Tommy also stayed in the Big Apple, as did John Heard, who was now working with Joe Papp at the Public Theater playing roles that, in a few short years, would lead to the movies and stardom.

We stayed with my mother, having given up our apartment, and there was something both reassuring and depressing about going back to the little house on Chicago's northwest side where I had grown up.

These were bleak times. Richard Nixon had just been inaugurated for his second term after a landslide victory. Inflation was out of control. Soaring gas prices, due to oil shortages, were so severe that drivers were forced to go to the gas stations on alternate days. Rising food prices had prompted meat boycotts.

I kept waiting for a letter from Joe Papp inviting me back to New York to direct something at the Public Theater but, of course, it never came. I've learned that when you're watching the mail or waiting for the phone to ring (or now waiting for an email), you're in deep trouble. No one is going to ride in on a white horse to save your ass. The only one who can save you is you.

I'm not sure how this came about, but I was hired by *Oui* magazine (a men's magazine created by *Playboy*'s Hugh Hefner to compete with the more explicit *Penthouse*) to interview Marcel Marceau, the internationally famous mime who was performing his show at the Auditorium Theater. I met with him in his dressing room after watching his amazing performance. Marceau had just turned 50 and looked much older without the white-face and wig that he wore as Bip, his famous alter-ego, but he was energetic and his English was excellent. He seemed interested when I told him that I was a theater director, and soon the story of the *Warp* debacle was pouring out of me. I told him how difficult it had been to get myself back on my feet and he nodded sympathetically.

"Sometimes you just have to let life pull you down," he told me. This shocked me and I asked him what he meant. "It's like the ocean when a big wave hits you and forces you under water. If you fight too hard you will only exhaust yourself and you will certainly drown. But if you let the wave have its way, and go with it, you can ultimately float back to the surface." I told him this sounded very Zen-like, and he confided that he was a student of Aikido, a Japanese martial art that was entirely defensive. "You use your opponents' negative energy against them," he explained. I left feeling a great deal better about things. I had been in the presence of a true master.

The months went by, and spring came.

One day David brought me a copy of a play by Ray Bradbury called *The Wonderful Ice Cream Suit*. It was the story of a group of down-and-out Mexican-Americans who each puts up his last ten bucks so they can buy a beautiful vanilla white suit. As they are all the same size, they plan to take turns wearing it and, after purchasing it, they're so excited that they decide to each try on the suit for an hour on this "fine Saturday evening." Each one discovers to his amazement and delight that his dreams come true while wearing the suit. Is the suit magic? Or do the clothes really make the man? The script is funny and heartwarming in its simple theme that sharing can create lasting friendships.

Like Gomez, the play's hustling ringleader who hatches the plan to buy the magical suit, it was up to me to find the five skeletons who would fit the play. Bill Norris and Cordis Fejer were back in Chicago ready to rejoin Carolyn and myself in the new enterprise. But who would play the Mexicans? I immediately thought of Joe Mantegna. André De Shields had introduced us when they worked together in the Chicago production of *Hair*. Tall, dark, and handsome (his family is Sicilian after all), Joe, with his great sense of humor, was constantly surrounded by his many friends. He was like a young version of *The Godfather* with his lovely girlfriend Arlene Vrhel, whom he met in high school in Cicero. She had also performed with André in *Hair*. They would often invite the *Warp* cast to their apartment on Cornelia to drink "Dago-red" wine and eat delicious homemade pasta in a secret family red sauce that took hours to prepare, which they always called "gravy." We all got along well, but would Joey be ready to join our ragtag company after playing the big downtown houses for big downtown pay? I showed him the script and asked him to look at the role of Gomez, the outrageous con man. "I love it," he told me the next day. "But who's playing the other Mexicans?" I shrugged. He suggested Bruce Taylor, a talented black actor with whom he had worked in *Hair*. Taylor ended up being cast as Dominguez, the handsome Latin lover. Bill Norris was friends with a great physical comedian named Mike Saad. "He'd be perfect for Vamenos," the dirtbag the group begrudgingly accepts as their fifth and final member. Muscular and compact with a wild Afro of black curls, a braying laugh, and an I'll-try-anything attitude, Mike was brilliant in the role.

Lenny invited Carolyn and me to see his wife Ina in a production at Candlelight, a suburban dinner theater. They had a new artistic director who, choosing not to produce the usual fare of musical comedies, was presenting an *avant garde* piece by a Polish playwright. The show was stolen by a wildly comic actor in the role of the play's crackpot inventor. He was a young man named Dennis Franz. Tall with wild hair and a bushy mustache, Dennis was shy and quiet offstage, but seemed genuinely excited when I asked him to audition for *Ice Cream Suit*. He became Villanazul, the intellectual poet of the group.

That left only one more Mexican, and I ended up casting an actual Mexican-American, Joseph Martinez. Small, thin and well spoken, he surprised us by speaking no Spanish. He was, however, an excellent fight choreographer, excelling in fencing. He became the innocent young lover who is unnoticed by the beautiful girl in the window of the house next door until he puts on the gleaming white suit. The character, as it turns out, is also named Martinez. Perfect.

Fully cast, we began rehearsals that summer with the opening set for mid-September. Would we be able to attract an audience? Would our fans brave the trip to our out-of-the-way location on Beacon Street in rundown Uptown? Our preview houses were sparse, but the audiences seemed to enjoy the show, and *Ice Cream Suit* opened to ecstatic reviews. Chicago was happy to have us back. Our New York debacle was forgotten. Amazingly, the crowds came. The play, an extended one act, ran only an hour and fifteen minutes, but no one ever complained that it was too short, or that it was not original. The audience embraced the play, and we were back in business. Like the suit that makes friends of strangers, Bradbury's play made lifelong friends of the members of our new company.

CHAPTER 12

Pirates and Singles' Bars

The Wonderful Ice Cream Suit was a hit, but it wasn't *Warp*, and after a few weeks we realized that we should start planning our next show. The fact that Joseph Martinez was a gifted fight choreographer and fencer seemed to suggest that whatever we did next should involve sword fighting, so I put him in charge of teaching the company how to use sabers while I read as many Jacobean revenge tragedies as I could get my hands on. Revenge seemed to be in the air. President Richard Nixon was in the throes of the Watergate scandal for authorizing a sleazy break-in to steal secrets from the Democratic Party Headquarters, an act that seemed even more infuriating (and unnecessary) after his landslide re-election. The country wanted blood.

Searching for a project that reflected this, we had readings of *The Changeling* and *The White Devil*, but the company felt that these plays, although filled with betrayals and murders, were far too talky without enough action. One night, Carolyn and I were watching Errol Flynn and Olivia de Havilland in *Captain Blood* on late night TV and the idea of a pirate play struck me. As far as I knew, there were no pirate plays with the possible exception of *The Pirates of Penzance* – not much sword-fighting there. What would be the plot? I found inspiration in the definitive 18th century book *A General History of the Pyrates*. There they all were: the infamous Blackbeard, whose grave we had visited in Grand Cayman; the misunderstood Captain Kidd; and the forgotten Calico Jack Rackham and his two women pirate shipmates, Anne Bonny and Mary Read. Both women had separately passed themselves off as men until Anne made a pass at Mary and discovered the truth. When Rackham's ship was attacked by a British man-of-war, the men cowered below decks while the two women reportedly fought like demons. All were captured and condemned to swing from the gallows, and Anne famously told Rackham, "Had you fought like a man you wouldn't be hanged like a dog." Both women "pleaded their bellies" (pregnancy) and were spared. There are many legends about where they ended up, but my favorite has them living together in Louisiana, where they raised their children.

I also learned that pirates were incredibly democratic, with each man receiving an equal share of the booty, and that the only time the captain was in charge was during battles. This somehow mirrored the way the Organic Theater was run, and brought to mind those days when we had dumped the box office contents on the floor at the end of each week's performances and divided it equally amongst us. I distinctly remember that the plot for our pirate story hit me while Carolyn and I were having a late dinner after the show at

The International House of Pancakes. What if Olivia de Havilland transformed into Errol Flynn? As the idea took shape it went something like this: a young noblewoman is kidnapped by pirates. The handsome captain falls in love with her much to the disgust of a tough female pirate who secretly yearns for the pirate chief herself. But when the captain is murdered, the young woman proves to be more ruthless than the rest of the crew and, with the help of the woman pirate, takes command of the ship. The title? *Bloody Bess*.

When I sprang this scenario on the company they were excited and we immediately started casting the characters: Cordis would be the young kidnapped Bess, Carolyn the tough as nails female pirate, Bruce would play an African pirate formerly a slave, Joseph Martinez the dashing captain, and Joe would be Calico Jack Rackham, the first mate. Bill Norris would get the Lionel Atwill part as the effete pirate hunter. He took me aside and asked if he could write the script with his friend John Ostrander, showing me a few scenes that they had written together. I was impressed. While the cast trained to be proficient with saber and dagger, Bill and John wrote the script.

I learned from fight-master Martinez that fights are like dances and that the person who seems to be receiving the abuse is the one controlling the fight and doing most of the work. It's all about eye contact and secret nods to let the other actor know you are ready. Joseph also pointed out that in most swordfights on stage it appears as if the actors are aiming at each other's swords when in reality they would be aiming at their opponent's body. For this reason, it became crucial for the actors to have enough control that they could stop the blow if necessary before it makes contact. If someone gets hurt, you're doing it wrong.

Bloody Bess: A Tale of Piracy and Revenge opened on February 20th, 1974 to good but not outstanding reviews. The show was criticized as melodramatic and its feminist message was all but ignored, although audiences seemed to love the spectacle. But life has a way of imitating life. The month we opened *Bess*, the granddaughter of William Randolph Hearst was kidnapped by a radical terrorist group that called itself the Symbionese Liberation Army (SLA). They demanded that five million dollars' worth of food be given free to feed the poor people of Oakland, and the Hearsts had carried out their demand. But the kidnapped girl, Patty Hearst, was not freed. On April 3rd the world was rocked when Patty announced that she had joined the SLA, and pictures of her holding an assault weapon in front of their hydra-headed flag appeared in the media. She took part in their bank robberies and was finally captured in the apartment she shared with the group. During her trial her defense pleaded that she had been a classic victim of the Stockholm Syndrome, in which the captive identifies with her captors. She was ultimately pardoned by President Jimmy Carter. Suddenly *Bloody Bess* was seen as a show ripped from the headlines, an analogy to the Patty Hearst story, even though our production had opened six weeks before the news events occurred. Zeitgeist, anyone?

The shows were dangerous. Sword blades broke and went flying, and at one performance a rope accidentally wrapped around an audience member's neck and, when the actor grabbed it to swing onto the stage, the poor spectator was yanked out of his seat and came with him. Luckily for all concerned no one was seriously injured (or sued). Bruce Taylor had a very emotional scene holding the severed heart of his foe in his bloody hand. It was an actual pig's heart (that had to be replaced every week) and during one performance there was someone in the last row talking. This annoyed Bruce so much that instead of throwing the heart into the wings as rehearsed, he threw it at the offending audience member, very hard, just missing his head but leaving a red heart shaped mark on the back wall that could still be seen years later. Mike Saad, who shaved off the thick curly locks that had worked so well as Vamenos in *Ice Cream Suit*, played the Greek, the muscular helmsman of our pirate ship (ironically christened the "Gods Love"). His character had to swing from a rope onto the stage into the midst of a swarm of sword fighting pirates and soldiers. Each night he barely missed being hit with a blade by a fraction of an inch and narrowly avoided impaling Carolyn with his first sword thrust. When she mentioned this to him, his response was, "Don't worry, Luv. I've got everything under control." But one evening he showed up wearing his new contact lenses and, when he swung onto the stage, he screamed like a girl and stood frozen, shaking like a leaf for several beats in the fray. "Oh my God!" He told the cast later, "I had no idea I was coming so close. I could have been killed!"

A few weeks into the run Eric Loeb approached me with some good news and bad news. In these situations, I always ask for the bad news first, and he told me that British director Pip Simmons had contacted him, and he and Laura would be leaving to join Pip's company in Amsterdam to work on three shows that they would be touring in repertory throughout Europe. The good news? He had spoken with Ritsaert ten Cate, the impresario of the Mickery Theater, and told him about *Bloody Bess*, and Ritsaert was coming to see the show with the idea of bringing it to Amsterdam.

Ritsaert arrived a couple of weeks later. He reminded me of a Dutch Benjamin Franklin, slightly balding but with a long shoulder length fringe of hair that reached his shoulders. His face was incredibly pale, almost chalk white with large bags under his Basset Hound eyes, and although it now turns out he was only ten years older than the rest of us, he seemed very much our elder. He watched the show stone-faced, without a single reaction. I assumed he hated it, but after the play was over, he spoke to Eric who told us that he had liked the show and was inviting us to perform it at the Mickery that fall. And with that he was gone.

Ritsaert had been born to a wealthy Dutch family and although he had studied economics in college, he decided to spend his life nurturing the arts, specifically experimental theater. He had turned his farm in Loenersloot, on the outskirts of Amsterdam, into a performing space which he named the Mickery after his first wife. And in 1972 he had bought an old cinema on the Rozengracht in Amsterdam and turned it into a black box experimental theater with the same name. It soon became one of the most famous centers for *avant garde* theater in the world.

Unfortunately, it became clear that *Bloody Bess* would not be able to run until we left for our first European tour in September. We needed another show and needed it right away. During this time, I was being harassed by a young local playwright who seemed to have written a new script every other day. His name was David Mamet. He was my age but acted like he was a businessman in his fifties. His conversation was peppered with colorful obscenities. "Call me Dave," he'd tell us, but nobody ever did. He was always "David" or usually just "Mamet." "Read this one, it's going to win the Pulitzer Prize!" Mamet, constantly puffing on a huge cigar, would boast. I'd just laugh, not realizing that in a few years he actually *would* win the Pulitzer Prize. But he wouldn't win it with *these* plays. The first one he showed me was called *Lakeboat* and was based on his own experiences working on a cargo ship on the Great Lakes during a summer vacation from his classes at Goddard College. It was filled with vivid characters and wonderful dialogue, but absolutely no story. "That's what Mike Nichols told me," Mamet replied when I told him my criticisms, "He said great characters, now write them a play."

That was the problem with David's writing in those days. No story. Lenny Kleinfeld described early Mamet this way: "Act One he wakes up. Act Two he puts on his socks." But the dialogue was divine. Mamet's characters talked like real people because David would sit in a booth at his favorite coffee shop ("The Laugh-Inn" at the Lincoln Hotel where he lived) and listen in on conversations going on at the nearby tables while secretly he took notes. Sometimes he would read us exchanges he had overheard. One of my favorites was, "That pisses me off. That pisses the fuck off outta me." Mamet is now famous for the brilliant ways he uses profanity in his scripts, but I can tell you that most of it was due to his great ear and how he could capture the way that Chicagoans talked and continue to talk today. Every other word is *fuck*.

David had written a script with a title that could sell a shitload of tickets: *Sexual Perversity in Chicago*. The play was a series of two-character scenes in which they talked about nothing but sex. Two waitresses, two cops, two investment bankers and so on. It had hilarious dialogue, but guess what, no story. I kept looking at his many scripts and one day while reading something called *Danny Shapiro and His Search for the Mystery Princess*, there it was: an actual plot. The story was about a love affair in which a couple meet, fall in love, and ultimately break up; the oldest story in the world, boy meets girl, boy gets girl, boy loses girl – but this one ended tragically without the two getting back together. Suddenly it hit me. You could call *this* play *Sexual Perversity in Chicago*, the perversity being the failure of these two characters to become a loving couple and live happily ever after. And you could give each of them a jealous friend urging the two lovers to break up who could speak the bitingly funny dialogue from Mamet's original script.

David, sensing the possibility of an actual professional production of his work, did a quick (and brilliant) rewrite and we were off to the races. Carolyn could play the mystery princess, Deborah Solomon, and Eric Loeb could be Danny Shapiro. But who would play the two jaded older friends? Joe Mantegna did a read-through as Bernie Litko, Danny Shapiro's foul-mouthed co-worker, my hope being that he would instantly fall in love with this cynical character who had all the good lines. Joe loved the script but, unfortunately, after the meager wages at Organic, Joe needed the paycheck from understudying a touring production of *Lenny*, so it was not to be. And Cordis was taking the summer off to supervise the remodeling of an apartment building that she had just bought. I needed two older actors to play these roles and remembered enjoying performances by Warren Casey and Roberta Custer at the Kingston Mines Theater. Warren, then in his late thirties, was a wonderful actor who, with Jim Jacobs, had written the musical *Grease*, which had by now become a huge hit on Broadway. Warren was raking in the dough and living in a beautiful town house in the Gold Coast near Michigan Avenue and the iconic Water Tower. He loved the script (how could he not?) and signed on to play Bernie. His nasal New York accent added just the right combination of superiority and boorishness.

During rehearsals David continued to revise the script, bringing in sheaves of new pages that he had pounded out the night before on his old Underwood typewriter. (He still uses it to this day, refusing to touch a word processor or computer of any kind.) At one point, Carolyn, frustrated that her lines kept changing, held up one of the pages and asked Mamet "What is this?" Without hesitation, David replied, "It's good writing." But he also said the greatest thing I've ever heard a playwright say to an actor: "These are just the words," he told her, "You can do whatever you want while you say them." And it's true that with Mamet, and real life in general, the scene is often not about what's being said.

A great deal of the play is set in singles bars and so I took Mamet and the entire cast to Mothers, a Rush Street singles bar, as research. It was a bit dispiriting as we guys found that the women there would have nothing to do with us, while Carolyn and Roberta were the belles of the ball, not able to drink all the free cocktails sent their way by the admiring throng. David spent much of the evening writing down things he was overhearing, which included a guy claiming to be the pilot of a "Jumbo jet" in order to impress a woman he was trying to pick up. Of course, the line ended up in the play. Mamet and I had our disagreements. I wanted the actors to appear nude in the after-sex scene, and Mamet felt it wasn't necessary. In fact, he suggested to me that the dialogue was so good it could stand on its own, and that the whole play should be performed with the actors wearing black turtlenecks sitting on stools. I felt that with a title like *Sexual Perversity* you'd better have at least a little visual titillation.

We opened in June and the reviews were decidedly mixed. The run was moderately successful, allowing us to make it through the summer, and David asked me if I would consider making him our playwright in residence. I was taken aback. "You mean we would only produce your plays?" I asked him. He nodded.

"Let me think about it," I replied, not knowing what to say. At the time I couldn't imagine doing only David Mamet plays and now I kick myself that I ended up turning him down. I told him I'd like to continue working with him and maybe do one of his shows each season. I could see the disappointment on his face. Plays were pouring out of Mamet in those days like water from a fountain, and as much as I loved his writing, I wanted to be free to do other things. Stupid. Stupid. Stupid.

A year later he brought us a new script he was working on and we did the first reading of it after a show, sitting in the seats of our theater. It was *American Buffalo*, and I've never witnessed a better or funnier production. Joe Mantegna read the role of manic Teach, who hatches the plan to steal a valuable coin collection. The great Jack Wallace read Donnie, the owner of the rundown pawn shop where the play is set, and Brian Hickey was Bobby, the half-witted junkie. I should have scooped it up on the spot but again missed the fast-moving train that was David Mamet. *Sexual Perversity* had been produced off-Broadway in New York and not only did David forget to give us our agreed upon cut of the royalties, but the press release also failed to mention that Organic had originated the play in Chicago. But it was the beginning of a long and fruitful collaboration between David and Joe Mantegna, who would join forces on *Glengarry Glen Ross*, which would go on to win that Pulitzer Prize for David and a Tony Award for Joe.

CHAPTER 13

Innocents Abroad

When Eric Loeb left for Europe to join Pip Simmons' company, I replaced him with the equally talented David Rasche. Blond and blue-eyed with Robert Redford good looks, David had made quite an impression when I saw him at Second City. He was incredibly funny, but the word was that he and the director (the famous improv guru Del Close) did not get along. I had heard a story that Del, who carried a miniature tape recorder with him to make notes during the shows, had recorded himself laughing his ass off, barely able to speak. "David, you bastard," he could be heard as he gasped for breath between guffaws, "I'm laughing but I'm hating myself for it."

Rasche was terrific in our show. He had initially balked at doing the nude scene in *Sexual Perversity*, but with some coaxing had finally agreed to it. Now he needed to be worked into the productions that we were taking to Amsterdam, replacing Joseph Martinez in *Bloody Bess* and *The Wonderful Ice Cream Suit*. He easily took over the role of the French pirate captain Levoiseur, but could he be believable as a Latino in *Ice Cream Suit?* We found a washable black rinse for his hair and with brownish make-up to darken his skin he almost looked Mexican if you didn't notice his piercing blue eyes.

We celebrated Organic's fifth birthday by performing the three shows (*Bloody Bess*, *Ice Cream Suit* and *Sexual Perversity*) in repertory before we left for our European tour. We almost killed ourselves with the nightly scene shifts and lighting adjustments, as our actors were also the backstage crew. But we were young and excited to be heading off for what we knew would be a great adventure.

And so, in October of 1974, we boarded a plane to Amsterdam. We had all gotten our passports and had packed the metal touring trunks with our props and costumes the night before. Joe Mantegna hated flying, and he and Arlene showed up with sleeping pills to get them through the twelve-hour flight. We were a large group: the nine actors, John Paoletti and Mary Griswold our set designers, Geoffrey Bushor our lighting designer, my brother David and me.

Our plane landed at seven in the morning at Schiphol Airport just outside of Amsterdam, where a van picked us up and brought us directly to the Mickery Theater. It was located on the Rozengracht, not far from the house in which Anne Frank and her family had hidden from the SS. The Nazis seemed very much a real presence in Amsterdam in those days, as they had been occupying the city only thirty years earlier. We soon learned that the Germans had used the central post office as their headquarters, and the train station to fill the boxcars with Jews who were sent to the concentration camps. I inadvertently insulted our hosts when I remarked that Dutch was similar to the German I had studied in high school. "It's nothing like German," I was told, and the subtext was: "So don't even try to speak it."

Eric Loeb was waiting for us at the theater. He had several "stucks" (pronounced shtooks) for us to smoke. These were hand rolled mixtures of tobacco and hashish, which took a little getting used to. There was almost no marijuana in Europe in those days, but hash, most of it from Morocco, was plentiful. It came in a variety of colors: golden, smelling like curry, that would crumble if you heated it with a match, or dark and hard that you had to shave with a knife. Some was black and opiated and would quickly put you into a wonderful dream-filled sleep. Although hash was not technically legal in those days, it was allowed to be sold in small quantities in specific places (such as the drawbridge in front of the Melkweg [Milky Way] a music club where Lois and Michael Danzig and Kathy and Jerry Fortier did lightshows).

We had a quick meeting in the coffee bar of the Mickery. Ritsaert was there, and he introduced us to Peter Schneider, his chief administrator, who sported a goatee. The show would open in a few days at the Mickery for a two-week run, Peter explained. If it were successfully received, a tour would be set up that would include the rest of Holland as well as possible appearances in Belgium and Germany.

We were then taken to the nearby Hotel Washington, where we would be staying while in Amsterdam. On our walk to the hotel, we noticed how clean the city was, no graffiti or garbage. In fact, we would often see older women on their hands and knees scrubbing the sidewalks. Every gleaming spotless window seemed to have a beautiful lace curtain, and the buildings looked like they were out of fairy tale storybooks. We walked over picturesque little bridges that spanned the many canals, passing herring stands where you could buy a fresh fish cut into bite-size pieces that you would eat with a toothpick, and chip stands that served French fries covered with mayonnaise.

The hotel was a five-story walk up, and the small lobby had a bust of George Washington on display. It was run by Russell, a gay American expatriate and his Dutch boyfriend Hans. They owned a pair of overweight Welsh Corgis. Breakfast was served until ten and we usually were among the last to drag ourselves into the little second floor dining room where we would be served delicious coffee, rolls, hard boiled eggs and slices of ham and cheese.

The room that Carolyn and I shared was on the fourth floor, and we had a view that overlooked the rooftops of Amsterdam with the towers of the Rijksmuseum in the distance. The skies were usually very dramatic: billowing grey and white clouds with patches of bright blue peeking through that reminded me of the paintings by the Dutch masters.

As we recovered from our jet lag, we began setting up the show. When I reminded Ritsaert that we had put a warning in our program cautioning the audience not to move during the swordfights, he shrugged. "Life is dangerous," he told me. "You walk down the street you can be hit by a bus." So there were no warnings; in fact, there were no programs.

We soon met some of the other companies who shared the main stage space with us. Miguel Pinero, the Puerto Rican playwright, was there with *Short Eyes*: his play about an imprisoned pedophile who is persecuted by his fellow inmates. Pinero had written the play while in prison himself for armed robbery and had cast his fellow inmates to perform the play. Joe Papp had seen a small production in a church and moved it to off-Broadway where it had won an Obie.

The Mickery had to provide a doctor who would give shots of heroin to many of the members of Pinero's company after each performance. The drug was legal in Holland and Ritsaert and his staff feared that the addicted actors might overdose on the pure uncut heroin that was readily available in Amsterdam. Pinero's ex-con actors were a rough and scary bunch, and I remember one of them screaming at the Mickery's staff who had started speaking Flemish in front of him (which they often did when they didn't want us to understand what was being discussed). "Don't talk that Dutch shit!" the actor exploded, "It sounds like you're going to spit on me!"

There was also a Scottish socialist theater called 7:84 whose name was derived from the fact that 7% of the population of Great Britain owned 84% of the wealth. They would make jokes about the Queen and her husband "Phil the Greek" but got offended when we started making disparaging comments about the Royals. "You're bloody Americans, what the fuck do you know about it?" they told us.

The Mickery's 200 seats were filled for our first performance of *Bloody Bess* and as the show played, we were met by a total lack of audience reaction: no laughter, no applause, just an intense silence. I went backstage at intermission. The cast was very dispirited. "I guess we'll be heading back to Chicago tomorrow," Roberta Custer gloomily predicted.

I urged them to just play their objectives, my go-to note when things aren't going well. "Yeah, fuck-'em," Joe translated.

So, we finished the show and as we took our curtain call the entire audience sprang to their feet in a thunderous standing ovation. The actors' jaws dropped in amazement, quickly turning to enormous grins. I should have realized from the total silence during the performance that the audience was listening very carefully. Maybe they needed to concentrate on translating the dialogue, but why hadn't they responded to the fights the way our American audiences had with whoops and cheers? We soon learned that this was the

Dutch way: a reserved coolness. And I began to feel like we were in an old '50s science fiction film in which a dying alien race needs to import creatures from other planets to vicariously experience emotions.

Our reviews were rave, or so we were told since they were in Dutch, and using my primitive German I could sort of get the general idea. The Amsterdam run was quickly sold out and the Mickery told us that we would be taking the show on the road. Our first performances would be one-night stands in the outlying cities and towns: Groningen, Enschede, Delft, Utrecht, Haarlem, Den Haag and Rotterdam. The Mickery provided two vans: one for the cast and one for the costumes and props.

The theaters we played on our tour of the Netherlands ranged from little storefront spaces to huge performing arts centers, and in these enormous theaters, Carolyn's swordfight on the balcony rail was often thirty feet from the ground with no safety nets of any kind. But thankfully there was not one single injury.

Sometimes our hotels left a bit to be desired. I remember one that had no heat and when I went to the front desk to complain that our room was freezing, the clerk asked me if the water was running. Taken aback, I told him that it was. "Then it is not freezing," he told me in the maddening matter-of-fact Dutch style. Carolyn, David and I slept together with our clothes on that night to stay warm under the damp sheets.

We returned to Amsterdam while the next leg of our tour was being set up, and we spent time exploring the city. The red light district with its brightly-lit picture windows, in which you could see hookers of all shapes and styles, from those who looked like wholesome blonde kindergarten teachers to the dark-haired dominatrix decked out in black leather holding whips and spike-studded dildos. We went to the Cosmos, a co-ed bathhouse and spa with saunas and showers where everyone walked around totally naked, and the women were so beautiful that I didn't dare lie on my back because my hard-on would quickly belie my nonchalant demeanor.

The entire cast and crew spent an afternoon at Zandvoort, a nudist beach just outside the city, and although we had all seen each other in various states of undress every day in our dressing rooms, the reality of hanging out (literally) completely naked made us more than a bit self-conscious.

Sex and nudity seemed to be everywhere. Advertisements often featured naked couples, and I started to realize that Europe was an alternate reality, not hampered by the American Puritanism that had already cracked down on Carolyn and me back in those dark "Peter Pan" days. It made me see that things didn't have to be the way they are in the States. There were no victimless crimes in Holland. And I know now that America is one of the most heavily censored countries on Earth, bleeping language on *South Park* and cutting nude scenes from televised films. And all drugs were available in Amsterdam as long as you bought and used them in the right neighborhoods. Everything was allowed as long as it was kept in its proper place.

The second leg of our tour began in Brussels, where we played Theatre 140, run by a wonderful man named Jo Deckmine. Short and intense with wild black hair, he spoke French with a voice that reminded me of Charles Aznavour (who Carolyn and I would get to meet thirty years later.) Besides presenting theater, a ton of rock bands had played at Theatre 140 including Pink Floyd and The Who. It was a small house and there were no showers in the dressing rooms, so Jo had to furnish washtubs of hot water that he boiled on the stove of his nearby apartment so the cast could wash off the Texas Dirt (which is what it actually was) that we used to give our pirates sunbaked tan bodies.

We stayed in the Hotel Cecile, whose narrow staircases were filled with hookers and their johns tramping up and down all night. I remember taking pictures of the view out of our room that overlooked nothing but a brick wall and rusted pipes and gutters. Très charmant.

One night after the show we went to a fairly upscale restaurant, and some Belgians at a nearby table started making racist comments about Bruce. When we complained, the manager and his waitstaff just shrugged. But when the bigots started hassling Taylor, our entire table stood up. With all our sword fighting and stage combat we were in the best shape of our lives and more than ready to kick their Belgian asses. The offenders quickly backed off and, needless to say, we left the waiters no tips.

The next stop was Duisburg in Germany, where we played in a theater where the ceiling was so low that we couldn't hoist poor Patrick Williams high enough to get the bucket under his head to catch the blood when we slit his throat. David Rasche informed us that the stagehands were complaining about us, not realizing that he spoke German (until he told them to go fuck themselves auf Deutsch.) And he later discovered that the Germans and the Dutch couldn't understand our English if we used black slang, so from then on, we all spoke jive just to get even.

We returned to Amsterdam before heading to Hamburg, and the day before we were to leave, Carolyn and I visited the Anne Frank House. It was a very emotional experience and brought home the reality of the Holocaust in a very personal and devastating way. How could human beings be capable of such horror, killing women and children and then going home for dinner with their own families? The experience colored our trip to Germany the next day. Was everyone over forty that we met a former Nazi?

The actors had brought wads of hash with them and when we crossed the border, German customs officers boarded the train and began checking everyone's papers like a scene out of *The Great Escape.* We freaked out and

Bruce quickly took his hash and jammed it in an empty cigarette pack and tossed it on the floor of our compartment. This way if they found it, they couldn't prove it was his. But it was completely ignored by the German officers, a brilliant ruse right out of Poe's *The Purloined Letter.*

None of us was prepared for the size and scope of Hamburg, Germany's great port city. We were playing at the majestic Schauspielhaus and when we arrived at the imposing domed edifice of this enormous repertory theater, we couldn't believe our eyes. It turned out that our show was assigned to the Malersaal, the smaller second stage behind the main building. It held 350 audience members and unlike the elegant Schauspielhaus had an industrial look, with its curved trusses and brick walls.

Our dressing rooms and green room were connected to the backstage of the main theater, and the German actors from the other shows would be in their elaborate costumes and make-up. As it was rotating repertory, that changed every night and we never knew what to expect. One night they would be dressed for an S&M inspired production of *Twelfth Night*, the next a sophisticated Noël Coward drama, but we were not prepared when we walked in one night and found them all in Nazi uniforms. Sieg heil!

Bloody Bess was a huge hit there, selling out nightly, and unlike the Dutch audiences, the Germans were boisterous and cheered loudly. They especially seemed to love the bloodshed and often they would throw bouquets of flowers to the actors during the curtain calls.

Carolyn and I were fascinated by Hamburg. It had been heavily bombed during the war and several ruined buildings still stood. The one that captured my imagination was the steeple of a huge church that towered above the rubble. It looked like something straight out of the writings of H.P. Lovecraft.

One night a good looking Asian fellow and his entourage asked to meet the company after the show. He was an American singer named Chris Yim, who had become a rock star in Germany as a member of The Les Humphries Singers. He invited us to join him for a tour of the Reeperbahn (pronounced "raperbon"), Hamburg's infamous red light district. With his shoulder length black hair and mustache, Chris was instantly recognized wherever he went, and people begged to be photographed with him or asked for his autograph.

He took us to the Club Salambo, which he told us had once been the Star-Club where The Beatles had played before becoming superstars. Now it was Hamburg's most outrageous sex club. As we walked in our jaws dropped. Onstage was a chorus line of naked men with a naked girl kneeling before each of them giving them blow jobs. As Joe Mantegna later pointed out it seemed as if the guys were so bored that they were checking out the women in the audience. Not one of them climaxed and Chris pointed out that it would be difficult for them to do the three shows a night if they had.

The show at times seemed to have been directed by Mel Brooks with a topless Josephine trying to get Napoleon's penis to stand at attention, slapping it, twisting it, biting it and so on. But the act I remember most vividly involved a naked woman writhing on the top of a coffin and Dracula, wearing nothing but a cape, climbing on top of her to make love. As they build to a crescendo, she wrapped her legs around him and he began flapping his cape like an enormous bat and up they both went, an actual flying fuck.

After the tour, we went back to Amsterdam and some of the company decided to stay on and, using the cheap rail passes, explore Europe. Joe and Arlene went to Paris where they were married at the Eiffel Tower. Carolyn and I decided that before returning to freezing cold Chicago, we wanted to go somewhere warm. We looked at a map and saw that the furthest south we could go would be down the boot of Italy, to Sicily. So, using the money we had saved from our meager per diems, we bought tickets and headed off on a personal adventure. Just the two of us.

We fell asleep in our railroad compartment and awoke to see the sun rising majestically over the snow-covered Swiss Alps. Stunning mountain views were ours as the train entered Italy. We spent the day going down the boot, looking out the windows at picturesque villages, vineyards and the occasional castle.

The next morning, we entered Rome and were told that the train wouldn't be leaving for a couple of hours. We could see the Colosseum in the distance and decided to run over and take a look. I'll never forget the sun rising over the ancient home of the Circus Maximus as we stood there alone with the hundreds of feral cats that had long ago taken the place of the lions.

We ate a meal of pasta and vino at the train station and discovered that even the simplest meal in Italy, at the most unassuming restaurant, could be a delight for the senses. We bought some bread, cheese, and wine to take with us on the train, and even this humble fare was more flavorful than the Dutch meals we had been eating for the last several weeks. We were falling in love with Italy.

Reaching Napoli, we were told that the entire train would be put on a boat to take us to Sicily. It was an amazing feat of engineering in which the tracks were carefully lined up with those on the ferry. And as we crossed the water, we looked at a map of Sicily and tried to figure out where we should go. We chose Siracusa, mainly because I liked the musical *The Boys from Syracuse.*

The climate was warm, and we could see oranges growing on trees in the orchards we passed. When we arrived in Siracusa, we walked from the train station through the dusty streets, shielding our eyes from the bright sunlight. We found a little hotel and the large woman who ran it pointed at her wedding ring. Were we married? We showed her our rings and she begrudgingly let us have a room. The only thing on the whitewashed walls was a large crucifix.

We took a nap and when we woke up, I decided to count our money and discovered that we only had a few guilders left. I had stupidly underestimated the costs of our journey and now panicked. Carolyn calmed me down. "There's nothing to worry about," she told me. "We're here and we have enough money for our dinner and a few things for the train ride back to Amsterdam. So let's enjoy this day," our one day in Siracusa.

It turned out coming to Siracusa couldn't have been a better decision. The city had been home to the Greeks and then the ancient Romans and during the Napoleonic wars, the French. We visited the ancient Greek amphitheater, the largest in the world. It could hold an audience in the thousands, but there was no one there but the two of us. I asked Carolyn to stand on the stage and I climbed to the last row of seats at least 200 yards away. When she spoke, I could hear every word. "Now whisper" I called to her. And I'll be damned if I couldn't hear those too. The acoustics were perfect. And not a bad seat in the house. Amazing.

We visited the Tomb of Archimedes, the famous Greek scientist famous for running naked through the streets crying "Eureka!" But the most amazing thing we saw on this wonderful day was the Ear of Dionysius: an enormous 100-foot-tall opening in the side of a mountain that looked more like a giant vagina. People would stand at the mouth of the cave and ask questions, and answers would reputedly come echoing out of the depths. Very theatrical. Upon closer inspection we discovered a spot hidden at the top of the opening (the clitoris?) where a lookout could observe the questioner through a small peephole without being seen themselves. Ancient magic tricks and special effects.

The next day we got on the train and headed back to Amsterdam. But if I had one day to live over again like Emily Webb does in *Our Town*, this would be the one. To be young, footloose, and fancy-free with my sweet wife in a timeless place surrounded by astonishing beauty; it's as close to heaven as I ever got.

above:
Age 8, riding the merry-go-round at Knott's Berry Farm in California.

left:
Off to a Scouts meeting with Dad, December 1957.

above:
With my brother David (left) and my mother Rosalie, January 1961.

top right:
Filming one of my early 8mm shorts in Chicago during the summer of 1966.

right:
With best friend and future collaborator Dennis Paoli (left), 1966.

below:
Getting booked for obscenity in October of 1968. Defense attorney Jack Van Metre on right.

right:
Carolyn and me on our wedding day, December 20, 1968.

opposite page:
With Dennis performing a sketch with our satire group The Human Race.

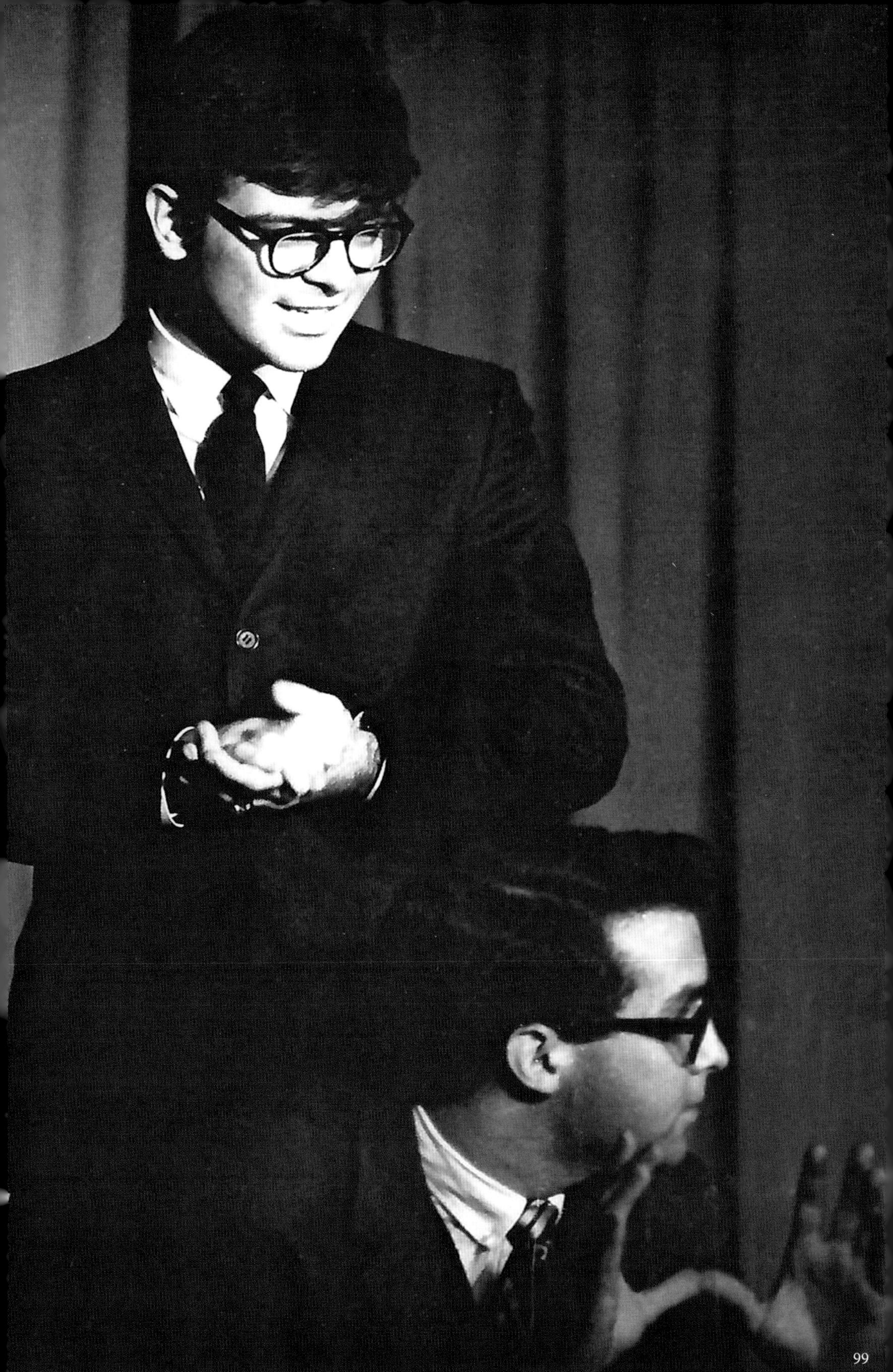

This spread: The Human Race Players.
The large picture at the top of this page features (left to right):
Me, Gary Mechanic, Marsha "Moose" Kolodny, and Dennis Paoli.

above: The Organic Theater Company. *Row 1—seated on the floor, left to right:* Stuart Oken, Jack Wallace, Joseph Martinez, Ian Patrick Williams, Geoffrey Bushor, Ina Jaffe, Tom Towles. *Row 2—leaning on sign, left to right:* William J. Norris (in golf cap & glasses), Cordis Heard, Carolyn Purdy-Gordon, Arlene (Vrhel) Mantegna, Keith Szarabajka, Jonathan Pearthree. *Row 3—left to right:* Richard Fire, me, Joe Mantegna, Dennis Franz, Mike Saad. *Row 4—left to right:* Brian Hickey, Roberta Custer, Mary Griswold, Meshach Taylor, Michael Stoneall.

opposite lower left, opposite lower right, and above: Flyers for Organic Theater Company productions.

THE ORGANIC THEATER COMPANY PRESENTS

"This drama of human characters is so sweet, sad, understanding, and utterly believable that it just about knocked me out with pleasure"
Richard Christiansen, Chicago Daily News

"A remarkably concise and painfully funny picture of the single-swingle lifestyle. It is the kind of show that asks the question 'who could ask for anything more?'"
After Dark Magazine

"A funny and feeling burlesque of a sad, inert lifestyle we all know and love"
Jonathan Abarbanel, Chicago Express

"Sexual Perversity in Chicago is that rare and wonderful phenomenon --an evening of promises fulfilled"
Terry Curtis Fox, The Reader

"Hilarious, deadpan observations"
Marvin Mirsky, WBBM Radio

A New Play By DAVID MAMET

Directed By STUART GORDON

Previews Begin June 7th / Opens June 19th

Leo A. Lerner Theatre / Uptown Center Hull House

4520 N. Beacon / Chicago 60640

Wednesday Thru Sunday / Tickets $2 - $5

For Reservations Call (312) 271-2436

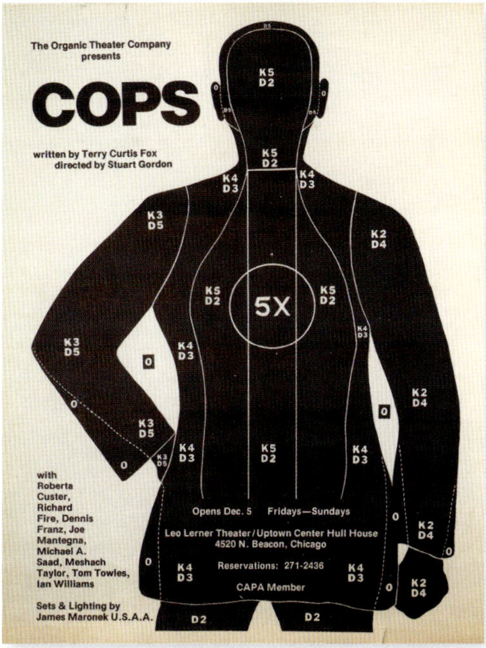

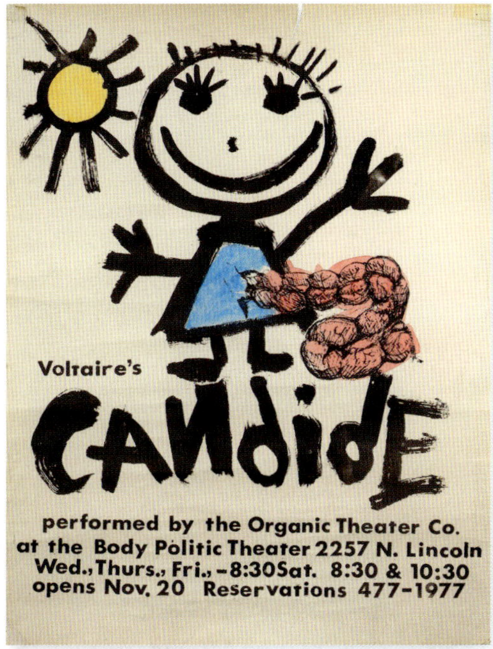

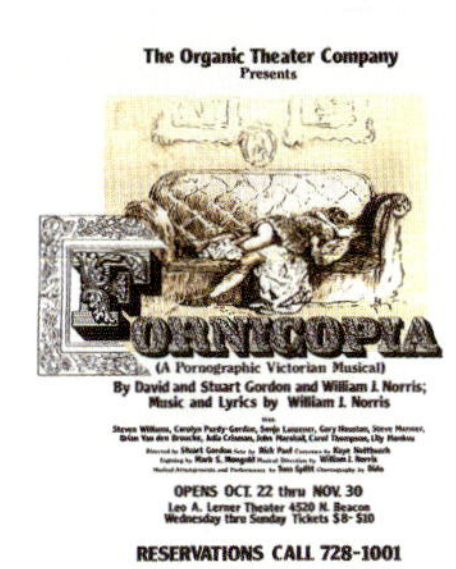

opposite and this page:
Flyers for Organic Theater Company productions.

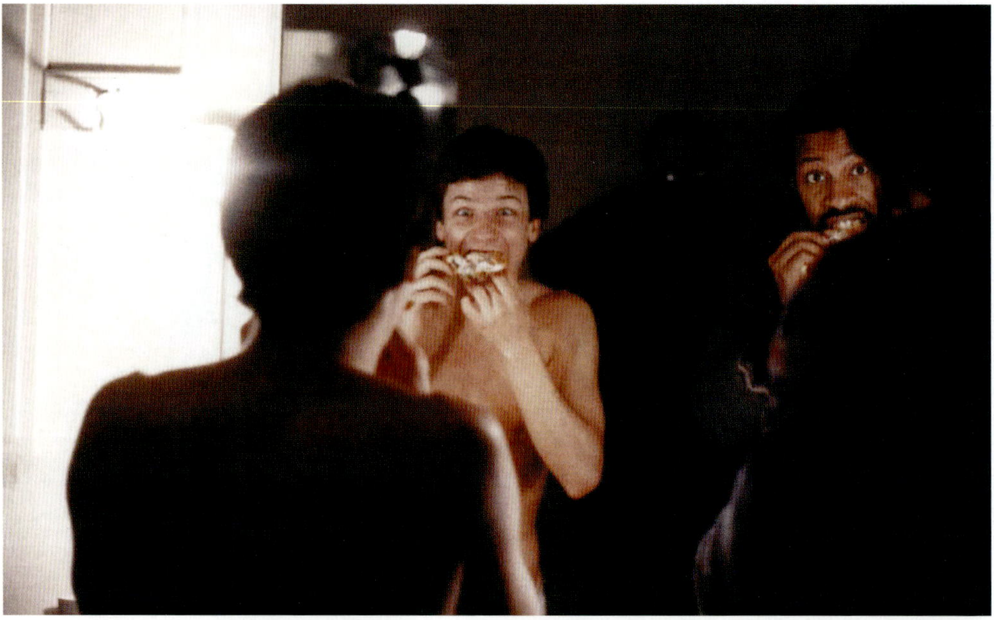

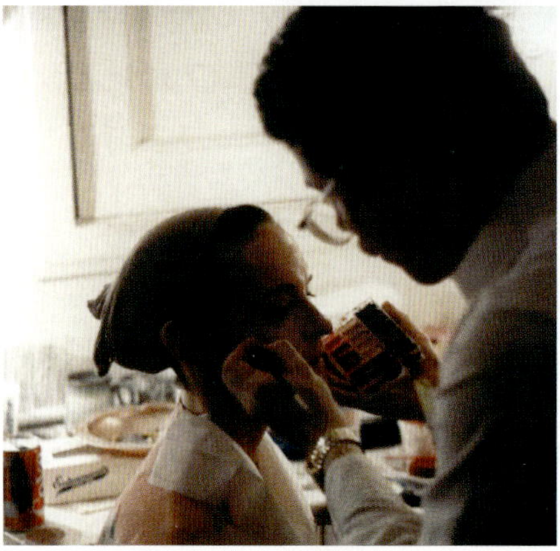

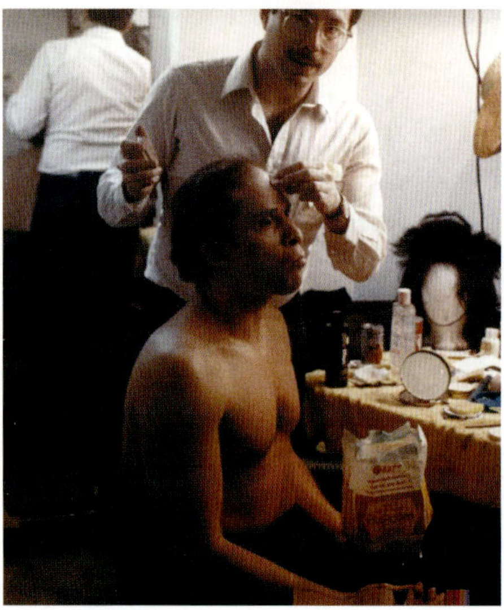

above: Cecil O'Neal as Lord Cumulus in *Warp.*

top: John Cameron Mitchell and Meshach Taylor backstage during *Adventures of Huckleberry Finn.*

center left: Carolyn, *Adventures of Huckleberry Finn.*

lower left: Tom Towles, *Adventures of Huckleberry Finn.*

THE WORLD'S FIRST SCIENCE FICTION EPIC ADVENTURE PLAY IN SERIAL FORM
WARP
AMBASSADOR THEATRE
49th St. West of B'way. 265-1855 OR TICKETRON
"PHANTASMAGORICAL"
—PLAYBOY
STARTS JAN. 30th

above: Tom Towles as Chaos and William Norris as Symax in *Warp*.
right: John Heard, Richard Fire and Tom Towles in *Warp*.
opposite: Lora Staley as Sargon (left), and Carolyn Purdy-Gordon as Valaria in *Warp*.

THE ORGANIC THEATER PRESENTS
WARP!
BY THE SEVEN MOONS OF MITRA CUMULUS KILL HER NOW!!
DAVID, I LOVE YOU!
I KNOW IT ISN'T THE REAL MARY LOUISE, BUT I CANT DO IT!
SPECIAL ORIGIN #1
THE WORLD'S FIRST SCIENCE FICTION EPIC ADVENTURE PLAY IN SERIAL FORM
ENTITLED
MY BATTLEFIELD, MY BODY

PLAYBILL
MAGAZINE
AMBASSADOR THEATRE
WARP
BY THE SEVEN MOONS OF MITRA, CUMULUS, KILL HER NOW!
OH DAVID, I LOVE YOU!
I... I KNOW IT'S NOT THE REAL MARY LOUISE, BUT I CAN'T DO IT!
WARP ONE: "My Battlefield, My Body"

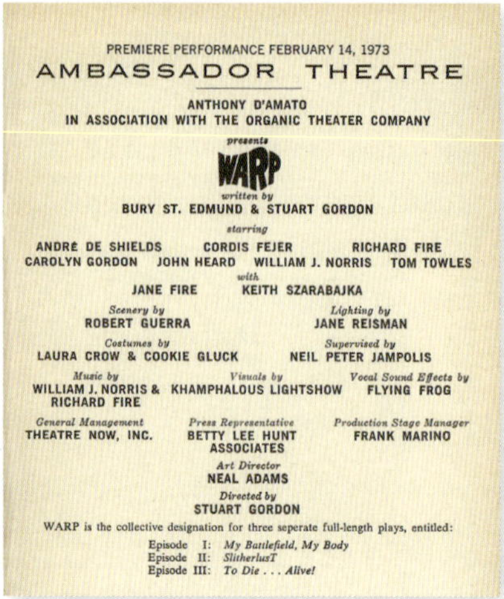

PREMIERE PERFORMANCE FEBRUARY 14, 1973

AMBASSADOR THEATRE

ANTHONY D'AMATO
IN ASSOCIATION WITH THE ORGANIC THEATER COMPANY

presents

WARP

written by
BURY ST. EDMUND & STUART GORDON

starring
ANDRÉ DE SHIELDS   CORDIS FEJER   RICHARD FIRE
CAROLYN GORDON   JOHN HEARD   WILLIAM J. NORRIS   TOM TOWLES

with
JANE FIRE   KEITH SZARABAJKA

Scenery by ROBERT GUERRA   *Lighting by* JANE REISMAN

Costumes by LAURA CROW & COOKIE GLUCK   *Supervised by* NEIL PETER JAMPOLIS

Music by WILLIAM J. NORRIS & RICHARD FIRE   *Visuals by* KHAMPHALOUS LIGHTSHOW   *Vocal Sound Effects by* FLYING FROG

General Management THEATRE NOW, INC.   *Press Representative* BETTY LEE HUNT ASSOCIATES   *Production Stage Manager* FRANK MARINO

Art Director
NEAL ADAMS

Directed by
STUART GORDON

WARP is the collective designation for three seperate full-length plays, entitled:

Episode I: *My Battlefield, My Body*
Episode II: *SlitherlusT*
Episode III: *To Die . . . Alive!*

this page:
Flyers and program notes for *Warp*, *Warp II*, and *Warp III*.

opposite top left:
André De Shields as Xander the Unconquerable in *Warp II* at the Body Politic, Chicago 1971.

opposite top right:
William J. Norris as Symax in *Warp*.

opposite bottom:
Carolyn as Mary Louise and Richard Fire as Dr. Scharzenegger during the first scene of *Warp*.

The Wonderful Ice Cream Suit. above, from left: Meshach Taylor, Joseph Martinez, Dennis Franz, and Joe Mantegna. *lower right, from left:* Meshach Taylor, Joseph Martinez, Joe Mantegna, and Dennis Franz.

CHAPTER 14

Down the River

During our "honeymoon" in Grand Cayman, Carolyn had read Mark Twain's *Adventures of Huckleberry Finn* for her lit class at the University of Illinois, where she completed her bachelor's degree. She loved Twain's novel, and I started reading it myself during the European tour. The book was a revelation. Hilarious, scary and shocking, it was clearly not the children's story I had expected. Huck was an uneducated white trash kid in a very violent world who finds himself helping a runaway slave to freedom in pre-Civil War Missouri. As slavery was legal in those days, he knows he is committing a serious crime by stealing someone else's property, and he feels guilty about it. "If I had a yaller dog that didn't know no more than a person's conscience does," he tells the reader, "I'd pison him."

The book has likely been banned in America more than any other work of fiction, and I always assumed it was because of the repeated use of the word *nigger*. After reading the book, it was clear to me that what caused the real controversy was the notion that laws, accepted by our entire society and taught to our children could, like slavery, be completely immoral, horribly dehumanizing and just plain wrong. Twain himself described his book as a battle between a "good heart and a deformed conscience."

"Alright then, I'll go to hell!" Huck finally declares.

I also realized that the book, often branded as racist, is in fact a powerful diatribe against racism and that its use of the N-word reflected the language of the time in which the story is set. In fact, the slave Jim is the most moral character in the entire book. I also realized that no one had ever done justice in adapting this story, often turning it into a companion piece to *The Adventures of Tom Sawyer*, which Twain had intended as a nostalgic view of his own childhood to be read by children. Like the Widow Douglas who adopts Huck and attempts to civilize him, other adaptors cleaned up the novel, cut out the controversy, and sanded off all the rough edges. I knew this would be our next play. Or to be more accurate, our next two plays.

Trying to jam the events of a four-hundred-page book into a single evening's entertainment had forced other adaptors to cut some of the best material, such as the sequence in which Huck lives with the Grangerford clan and finds himself in the middle of a blood feud which results in the deaths of the entire family. I discovered that Twain had written the book in two parts. He had become bogged down about halfway through after Huck and Jim mistakenly rafted past Cairo, Illinois in a fog and missed their chance to go north on the Ohio River to freedom. Couldn't they just leave the raft and hike back?

It took Twain a number of years to solve this dilemma by introducing two inspired rogues: the self-crowned King and his disreputable companion, the Duke. These carpetbaggers keep Huck and Jim prisoners on their own raft and force them to continue the journey south down the Mississippi further into slave country.

Following Twain's lead, this seemed like the perfect place to begin the second play. We had been able to get audiences to come back to see all three episodes of *Warp*, so couldn't we do the same with an American classic like *Huck Finn*? I took out a box of crayons and began marking up the book: yellow for dialogue, green for action, and orange for Huck's often hilarious narration. It took me a while to convince Meshach Taylor to play Jim. (Upon returning to Chicago, Bruce had changed his first name to Meshach after the biblical martyr whose faith in God allows him to survive being thrown into the fiery furnace.) Meshach had always thought that the character of Jim was an "Uncle Tom" due to the NAACP's crusade to ban the book from school reading lists. "Just read it before you decide," I begged him. And thank God he did, because it turned out to be one of the most amazingly heartfelt performances of his entire career.

And who better to play Huck's drunken white trash father than Jack Wallace? I had wanted to work with Jack since seeing him starring in a production at the Kingston Mines Theater, which he performed bare-chested and was an unstoppable force of nature, rough-hewn and raw. Jack had been a professional boxer and an armed robber, doing time at Joliet Prison. When released, he became a roofer and was in the process of putting a new roof on an apartment building when he noticed a steady stream of people going into the church across the street. During his lunch break he decided to investigate and discovered that they were all auditioning for a play. Jack ended up reading for a role and was cast.

Soon he was in rehearsal for the role of Pap Finn, who ends up kidnapping his own son and locking him up in his rundown cabin in the woods. He wants to get his hands on the gold that Huck received as a reward at the end of *Tom Sawyer*. One day during rehearsal Jack took me aside. "I been thinking about this kid," he began. I was already confused, which kid was he talking about? "Huck," he impatiently explained. "He's got all this money and he can't even give his dad a few bucks so he don't have to sleep with the hogs?" I was astonished. This was an actor truly identifying with the character he was playing. Instead of seeing Pap as a monster who at one point even tries to murder Huck in a drunken rage, Jack was looking at the story through the old man's eyes and feeling his pain. As a result, his portrayal was brilliant, giving the character dimension and real humanity.

I cast Joe Mantegna as the Duke and Bill Norris as the King. They worked together beautifully, creating a comic duo that could give Laurel and Hardy a run for their money and perfectly illustrating the maxim that the second liar always wins. Carolyn and Roberta Custer would play the many women that Huck and Jim encounter on their travels down the river. Roberta was the kindly Widow Douglas who adopts Huck, and later she played hysterical Aunt Sally who is driven to distraction when Huck and Tom Sawyer plan Jim's escape from her farm. Carolyn played Jim's owner, the spindly Bible-thumping Miss Watson, as well as Judith Loftus, the woman who sees through the boy's disguise when he shows up at her house dressed as a girl. Ian Patrick Williams, our utility outfielder, played a variety of characters, including the town doctor who becomes the story's *deus ex machina* and unravels the plot's convoluted outcome. For this role Pat wore a white suit, wig, and mustache to become the spitting image of Mark Twain himself. And Keith Szarabajka, who had more than proven himself by going on as Lord Cumulus for John Heard on Broadway, would be an ideal Tom Sawyer, as well as a score of townsfolk and river rats.

Who to play the title role? I put in a call to Brian Hickey, who had been living in New York since playing Candide in our production at the Public Theater. I felt that the same wide-eyed innocence that had served Voltaire's hero so well could be an equally good fit for Twain's. Watching Brian make this massive role his own was one of the great joys of the production.

There were no scripts printed for the rehearsals. Instead, everyone bought a copy of the book and we used Twain's own words as our text. My goal of being faithful to the book's narrative resulted in a first act that initially ran over three hours at our first run-through, so we ended up hacking and slashing entire chapters. Still, the total running time was almost five hours for the two parts.

Adventures of Huckleberry Finn, Part 1 opened in February of 1975 and received mixed reviews – a rave by Richard Christiansen, "A rare and memorable piece of theater that pays honest, glorious homage to one of the great works of American literature" and a pan by Glenna Syse in the *Sun-Times*, "Gordon's Twain flops in telling." When the second part opened two months later, both Christiansen and Syse reversed themselves. Glenna now wrote, "This one is a corker. A finger-lickin', back-slapping, rip-snorting, spine tingling, rib-tickling, jim-dandy show" and appreciative audiences filled our theater for the entire run.

The success of *Huck Finn* brought an invitation from William Woodman, the new artistic director of the Goodman Theatre, for me to direct *Chemin de Fer*, a French farce by Georges Feydeau, as the final show in the 1974-75 season. Bill Woodman was a New York-based director who presented the world premiere of Brian Friel's *The Freedom of the City* during his first season in Chicago, and it became the first Goodman production to be taken to Broadway. Bill Woodman had brought young Gregory Mosher from New York to serve as his assistant. I think they had met while Bill was teaching at Juilliard. Tall, thin and prematurely balding, Greg had that "lean and hungry" look and, a few years later, would take Woodman's job away from him. One of the first things Mosher did was set up a second stage at the Goodman that could present more adventurous fare. His first production was David Mamet's *American Buffalo*, the same play that we had first read after a performance at the Leo Lerner a year before.

Mamet would later admit he sold the screen rights to *Perversity* "for about $12 and a mess of porridge." The film, produced by Stuart Oken (more about him later) and Jason Brett, changed its provocative title to *About Last Night...* and starred Demi Moore in the role originated by Carolyn. It was remade in 2014 with a primarily black cast.

But back to *Huck Finn*. Ritsaert ten Cate of the Mickery invited us to bring the show to Amsterdam in the fall of 1975, and Eric Loeb recommended the show to his friends Joan and Peter Oliver who ran the Oval House, an experimental theater in London. The idea of performing an American classic for British audiences seemed like an opportunity not to be missed. Things seemed to be going our way, but I've come to learn that this is usually the prelude to the shit hitting the fan. One night after the show my brother David told me that we needed to talk. It turned out that he felt that the two of us made such a good team that we should share the role of artistic director of the company. I tried to let him know how much I valued his contributions to our shows and had even given him the title of Assistant Director, but I felt that he was over-reaching. A few days later my brother announced that he was leaving the Organic Theater. I tried to talk him out of it to no avail. "I'm tired of living in your shadow," he told me. "I need to make my own mark." David was not the first to leave the theater, but his decision to go cut extremely deep. I agonized about changing my mind and sharing control with him, but in the end, we said our goodbyes and Carolyn, the company, and I took off to Amsterdam for our second European tour.

Dutch audiences struggled to understand our show's Southern dialects. Jim's moving speeches and Huck's humorous asides were lost on them. Ritsaert called me to his office and in his typical Dutch uncle no-bullshit style told me that they could not set up an international tour of *Huck Finn*. He wanted to send us back to Chicago immediately. "Don't worry, I'll bring you back with your next show," he promised. I explained to him that we had a London engagement in a couple of weeks and that we couldn't cancel it. Ritsaert was not happy with this, but finally agreed to let us stay if we would cover our own expenses. Ritsaert never invited us back to the Mickery again.

When I explained our dilemma to the company, many saw it as an opportunity to go sightseeing. Carolyn and I decided to spend a week in Paris.

We stayed in the Montparnasse district in a picturesque little hotel. On our first morning we were awakened by knocking at the door and we thought that the breakfast service was ending as it did at ten every morning at our Dutch hotel. "We're coming! We're coming!" we yelled through the door as we hurriedly pulled on our clothes. And as we stepped into the hallway, we discovered a tray with coffee and croissants sitting on the floor. They had brought us breakfast in bed. Vive la France!

Unlike the stereotype, no Parisian was ever rude to us. If you just made an effort to speak French, they bent over backwards to be helpful. In fact, Carolyn's French got very good. "I could live here," she told me. I nodded, knowing that the only way I could survive would be with her constantly at my side as a translator. We headed off from Holland to London, booking passage on a ship to cross the English Channel (no Chunnel in those days). Our only concern was transporting our firearms into the UK, as this was strictly forbidden, a situation exacerbated by the Troubles in Northern Ireland. As our guns were antique replica flintlocks and old-fashioned six-shooters, we decided to take the chance. The guns were kept in a long, flat wooden box that was kept padlocked, and before boarding the ship Carolyn and I decided to check that they had been safely packed. We opened the box in a parking lot near the pier and discovered to our horror that every gun was fully loaded with black powder and percussion caps, ready to be fired. Hiding behind parked cars to block the view from any passers-by (and especially the police), we hurriedly unloaded them all before boarding. The ship left from Hoek van Holland and would land in Harwich the next morning, so we spent the evening in a windowless cabin below decks sharing the small room with Roberta Custer. I remember falling asleep to the rocking and groaning of the old ship, feeling like I was Jim Hawkins in *Treasure Island* about to have my first great adventure on English soil.

We landed and went immediately to Customs where we were asked if we had anything to declare as large signs forbidding the bringing of firearms into the country stared us in the face. We innocently shook our heads and our passports and manifests were stamped and we were quickly passed through to board a train that would take us into London. As we lugged our trunks of costumes, one of the customs men asked if he could give us a hand. Before we could answer, he picked up the gun box and threw it over his shoulder. We all looked nervously at each other and followed him toward the train platform when suddenly the box slipped from his shoulder and fell onto the concrete floor. We all gasped, expecting it to break apart spilling weapons everywhere, but luckily it held together, and the customs guy apologized for his clumsiness.

We were met at the station by Joan and Peter Oliver. Peter was tall and thin with balding gray hair and a goatee, and Joan was petite and blonde.

They seemed to be opposites in every respect: Peter was very erudite and Joan was very Cockney, but both were extremely welcoming, and they immediately took us to the Oval House Theatre, which was named after nearby Kennington Oval, the famous cricket ground. They had started the theater as an activity to replace football at a nearby boy's club. It was so successful that it soon became the center of what was to be called "The Fringe," giving Athol Fugard, David Hare, Steven Berkoff, Mike Figgis, and Salman Rushdie their starts. The South London neighborhood was rundown and reminded us of our home in equally rundown Uptown. The theater, which was set up in an old storefront, reminded me a bit of the Body Politic, very rough-hewn and thrown together. When we walked into the theater itself, however, we received quite a shock. The entire room was covered with a mixture of flour and coal dust. "That's from last night's show," Peter sheepishly explained. "They promised they'd clean it up." I asked when they would do so, but it soon became obvious that the only way it would be cleaned up was if we did it ourselves, so we all rolled up our sleeves and went to work.

The company's spirits were low; any hope for a big, classy London premiere was completely dashed. A large sign on a nearby pub proclaimed "Take Courage" in big red and gold letters and so we did. We soon discovered that Courage was a local brew. We opened our show the next night for a five-performance run and had large appreciative audiences but, unfortunately, only one critic showed up. He gave us an excellent review, but we weren't the smash hit that we had hoped to be. Maybe *Adventures of Huckleberry Finn* is such an American story that it really couldn't connect with European audiences. *Bloody Bess* and her pirate crew were easy for them to relate to because as a German audience member once told me, "Pirates are our folk heroes, like your cowboys are to you."

CHAPTER 15

Great or Good?

My mother turned 65 in May of 1975 and was forced by her union to retire from her job as an English teacher. She was much beloved by her colleagues and students at Roosevelt High School and was given a big party as the semester ended in June. I still run into her former students from time to time and they always tell me how much my mother changed their lives and gave each of them the courage to pursue their heart's desire. I always smile and nod, knowing that she did exactly the same thing for me. She had allowed me to drop out of college and start an experimental theater company, not the most stable of occupations, and she never gave me any grief about it, backing my decision 100% as well as putting up her own money to help me get started. I doubt I would be as supportive if one of my kids had done the same thing. But my mother provided unconditional love, long before the term became a cliché.

I'm not sure how this came about, but it was around this time that I was contacted to stage and direct a fight scene for a movie. The film was *The Last Affair*, and I learned that it was initially intended to be a porno film produced by a group of Chicago investors. Things had gone terribly wrong filming the sex scenes, and the investors decided to add a fight scene in an attempt to save the film. After all, action is action. I gathered a group of my Organic actors to play the brawlers, among them Dennis Franz and Richard Fire as well as Jack Wallace and Ron Dean, who starred in the film. We shot it in a bar in Old Town. "What is the fight about?" I asked the director. He just shrugged. "Beats me," was his reply. So I got a chance to stage and shoot my first scene for a film, in 35mm no less.

I knew where to place the camera to make the punches look real and it probably came out all right, but I never saw the completed film, which is just as well as it received some of the worst reviews in cinema history. The producers had rented a local theater on Rush Street to premiere it and Roger Ebert attended. "An appallingly bad movie," he pronounced, and as for my work, "The fight has no apparent purpose in the film." No shit. I was credited as "Choreographer – action scenes." I'm glad they added the last two words.

Around this time, we were approached by two bright young men, Stuart Oken and Michael Stoneall. 24-year-old Stuart Oken was short, intense and very serious. He had served a year as business manager of the Drury Lane Theater. 25-year-old Michael Stoneall, a large easy-going guy with a wide grin and a nervous giggle, had been the general manager of Pheasant Run Dinner Theater. They explained that they were huge fans of Organic and although they believed that our work was top-notch artistically, they felt that we could be taking greater advantage of our recent success if the company had equally excellent business management. This struck a nerve, as I have never thought of myself as much of a businessman. In fact, to this day I often forget that, besides being a director and writer, I am also a producer. When Organic began, we were happy just to be paid enough to avoid waiting tables and driving cabs so we could devote all of our time to creating theater. Stuart Glicken, who had been my youth group advisor at Temple Beth Israel, had become a successful real estate lawyer. He graciously filed the paperwork that transformed Organic into a not-for-profit corporation. I was the president, Carolyn was the treasurer, and Stuart was the secretary. We tightly held legal control as we did not want to repeat our mistake at Broom Street and allow the possibility of the theater being taken away from us. But now, six years later, the actors often complained that they were not receiving the kind of money that they deserved, and our company meetings often turned into bitch sessions, "If we're so good, how come we aren't rich?" I suggested that Stuart Oken and Michael Stoneall should make a presentation to the entire company explaining how they could improve things for us fiscally. They showed up with graphs and charts and the company was so impressed that the two were hired immediately. They were given the same deal that we all had: a guaranteed minimum salary (which, if memory serves, was then about $150 a week) and an equal share of the profits. With their help, we all hoped that there would be a little more gravy for our biscuits. I was relieved that I could focus on my role as artistic director and someone else could take the blame for our financial shortcomings.

We had been receiving small grants from the Illinois Arts Council and the NEA, but they were never generous enough to pay the bills, so ticket sales were always the only way to keep the wolf from our door. Thanks to the work of Oken and Stoneall, the grants became more significant, raising the company to the level of an emerging regional theater. They helped us negotiate a Midwestern tour of *Huckleberry Finn*, funded by the Illinois Arts Council for America's bi-centennial celebration, and it was such a great success that it was followed by a Western States Tour through Idaho, Nevada and Utah, sponsored by the National Endowment for the Arts. Organic was now more than thirty members strong and able to produce two shows at the same time. Thus, while half the company was on tour with *Huck Finn*, we began rehearsals on our next show, *Switch Bitch*, based on the short stories by Roald Dahl.

Almost everyone knows that Dahl is the author of wonderful children's books like *Charlie and the Chocolate Factory* and *James and the Giant Peach*. What many don't remember is that before writing these charming fables, Mr. Dahl wrote some of the most devilishly disturbing stories since Edgar Allan Poe. His trademark was the surprise ending that would pull the rug out from under the reader and leave him flat on his ass gasping for breath. Roald Dahl wrote unforgettable classic episodes for *Alfred Hitchcock Presents*, which is where I first discovered his "Lamb to the Slaughter," in which a housewife kills her husband by cracking his skull with a frozen leg of lamb, then cooks it and feeds the murder weapon to the investigating police officers. Or "Man from the South," the famous story in which a weird little man (Peter Lorre) bets a Las Vegas gambler (Steve McQueen) that, if he can't light his Zippo ten times in a row, he must forfeit the little finger on his left hand. But my favorite Dahl stories were in *Switch Bitch*. Every story was not only suspenseful as hell but also incredibly sexy. Somehow I was able to get permission to adapt three of these stories to the stage, and the show pulled an enthusiastic audience from the day it opened (June 18th, 1976), partially due to its terrific title but also to an especially perverse little story by Mr. Dahl called "The Great Switcheroo." The tale centered on a pair of next-door neighbors who each have the hots for the other man's wife. Since they can't convince their spouses to try wife-swapping, they decide to switch beds in the middle of the night and have their way with their neighbor's wife without their own wives knowing it. To pull this off they must use the same aftershave lotion, get identical haircuts and imitate each other's lovemaking style. The result is edge-of-your-seat suspense with an almost Job-like retribution.

One day I got a note from Patricia Neal, then the wife of Roald Dahl, saying that she was coming to Chicago and wanted to see our show. Meeting her was quite a thrill as Ms. Neal was a real live movie star, and the first one I had ever met. Tall, leggy, and incredibly beautiful, she starred in dozens of films including *The Day the Earth Stood Still*, in which she recited the famous line, "Klaatu barada nikto," that saves our planet. She also won an Academy Award® as the slatternly housekeeper who is almost raped by Paul Newman in *Hud*.

"Roald must see this!" she enthused after the show in her famous husky voice, "He'll absolutely love it." She and I went out to dinner after the show. It was a Saturday night and we had two performances, so Carolyn wasn't able to join us, as she was onstage for the second show. I took Patricia Neal to a Chinese restaurant on Lincoln Avenue and, amazingly, all the Chinese waiters immediately recognized her, and the entire kitchen staff swarmed our table asking for autographs. We ended up having our picture taken with them all, and I got the impression that this happened to her all the time. After we finished dinner, Pat asked me where I lived. I told her that Carolyn and I had moved into an apartment building in Uptown. It looked like a wreck from the street but the fourth-floor apartment was beautiful with large picture windows from which you could get a view of the lake (if you stood on a chair) and watch hookers giving blow jobs in the parking lot across the street (I didn't tell her this).

"May I see it?" she asked.

I was taken aback. "Now?" She smiled and nodded. Was she coming on to me?

I felt like I was walking down the street with the Statue of Liberty as passersby stared at her, their mouths hanging open in amazement. I was seeing the power of a movie star firsthand, and it was exhilarating. I took her up to the fourth floor in the elevator that always smelled like cabbage soup and showed her our place. She seemed amused by our waterbed and sat on it, bouncing gently on the waves. If this was my cue, I missed it, honoring my marriage vows and also thinking that the last angry husband in the world you wanted coming after you was Roald Dahl. After having a glass of wine together, I called a cab to take her back to her hotel.

A few weeks later she contacted me to let me know that her husband would indeed be accompanying her to the play that Saturday. Roald Dahl was a tall, balding man in his fifties who stood ramrod straight (he had been an RAF pilot in the war) and, as I watched him watching our show, he never even cracked a smile. "'Switcheroo' has some possibilities," he dryly told me afterward. "We should get together for dinner to discuss it."

"We'll invite them to our apartment!" Carolyn declared. We were both flying high with the idea that this legendary author and his glamorous movie star wife would be sitting at our table and eating my wife's wonderful cooking. Then Carolyn started to laugh. "We'll serve them leg of lamb!"

The Dahls arrived on time and, as they entered our apartment Roald walked straight to the table and pointed to the glasses of ice water. "These will have to go," he declared like a visiting monarch. Carolyn and I, his trembling servants, quickly grabbed the glasses and whisked them away.

"Don't mind him," Patricia Neal whispered to Carolyn, "He has bad teeth. The ice hurts them." Then she noticed the leg of lamb sitting on the counter waiting to be carved. "Oh Roald! (she pronounced his name Rooeld) Look!" Dahl looked at the meat and turned back to her perplexed and confused. "It's leg of lamb!" she explained. Then he got it. But still no smile. "Oh, quite," he sniffed.

The ice had been broken (or at least removed) and the dinner conversation was strange and funny. "You don't mind if I smoke?" Roald asked after the meal. Carolyn offered him one of her cigarettes, but he shook his head.

"He rolls his own," Pat explained.

"Saltpeter," Dahl began. "It's used in making gunpowder and they put it in factory-made cigarettes so they never go out and you have to keep buying more." Then he leaned forward as if imparting an important secret. "And saltpeter is also put into the inmates' food at prisons. It inhibits the sex drive."

Pat Neal laughed her low wonderful laugh. "It's never stopped me," she told us, winking at her husband and squeezing his arm.

Patricia Neal had suffered a terrible stroke ten years before we met her. She had been in a coma and when she awoke three weeks later was half paralyzed. She was told she would never walk or talk again. But Roald had brought her back from the dead, coaxing and haranguing her and just plain loving her until she defied the doctors' dire predictions and recovered. The story was so inspirational that a TV movie starring Glenda Jackson as Pat and Dirk Bogarde as Roald was made in 1981. But Mr. Dahl did not want to discuss Pat's stroke, feeling it violated his and his wife's privacy. They agreed to do a few local news and talk shows to help us promote our show and, although we had briefed the newscasters not to bring up Pat's stroke, that was always the first thing they asked them. Roald seemed genuinely excited about "Switcheroo" and told us that he would like to do a rewrite on our script with the idea of bringing the show to London. I was flying high.

My favorite moment with Roald Dahl occurred while driving him to the airport as he headed home to England. I asked him what he was working on. He launched into a story that would become his next book, *My Uncle Oswald*, and, if it's possible to be on the edge of your seat while driving, I absolutely was. I suddenly had this amazing realization that the great Roald Dahl was telling *me* a story yet to be written, and I felt as lucky as if I had won one of Willy Wonka's golden tickets. Roald later put me in touch with Bernard Sandler, his producing partner. I soon discovered that they had no intention of bringing our company to London and that he and Mr. Dahl were pulling a great switcheroo of their own. "I can't let you do that," I told Sandler.

"Why not?" he wanted to know, amazed that a shaggy unkempt hippie was not in awe of his classy oh-so-English demeanor.

"Because it's our script," I explained.

"But it's Roald's story," reminded Sandler.

"Yes, he wrote a story and we turned it into a play." In fact, the show's funniest scene, in which the two men explain their lovemaking techniques to each other, was only referred to in the story but had to be entirely improvised for our production by Dennis Franz and Richard Fire, who played the two husbands. The fact that we had a copyright on our adaptation meant that neither side could do anything without the other's permission, and thus a stalemate was created. As a result, the play was never produced again, and I had made an enemy of one of my favorite writers.

Even sadder, Dahl, famous for his surprise twist endings, pulled one on the wonderful Patricia Neal several years later when it was revealed that he had been having an affair with her best friend, causing the couple to divorce after 30 years of marriage.

Should've Kicked Him

A representative from New York-based Herbert Barrett Management came to check out Organic at the invitation of our business manager Stuart Oken. Barrett, who represented mainly classical musicians and created *Great Performances* for PBS, already repped John Houseman's esteemed "The Acting Company," and Oken believed that we could regularly tour the country with yearly trips to New York as they did. The talent scout turned out to be a round little man in his seventies named Joe Lippman who absolutely loved our work. We began discussing an East Coast Tour.

When I was working with David Mamet on *Sexual Perversity*, I suggested the idea of writing something about the Chicago Police Department. This was the result of a recent scandal in which the cops had shot an unarmed man and claimed he had pulled a gun on them. (Some things unfortunately never change.) I felt that David could give us a shocking exposé of these corrupt policemen. A few months later he told me that he had decided to collaborate with *Chicago Reader* critic Terry Curtis Fox and that they were now developing the project together. It was simply named *Cops*. For reasons I never learned, David and Terry soon had a falling out and David left the project, giving all rights to Fox. The unfinished script was only about 45 pages long, but those few pages showed tremendous promise. Taking place in a greasy spoon restaurant at 2:00 in the morning, we are introduced to a couple of plainclothes cops who shake down the café's owner for free food and bad bets on the Bears. When the cops recognize an armed robber who enters the establishment, all hell breaks loose, and a gunfight ensues. A waitress and a uniformed cop are killed and the shooter is pinned down behind the counter, taking the owner hostage. The dialogue is prime Mamet, but the action must be attributed to Fox as David in those days supposedly felt there was little need for it.

We had a reading of the incomplete script with the company; Joe Mantegna and Dennis Franz desperately wanted to play the cops. The question was how to finish the script, as Mamet had no intention on coming back to the project. Joe suggested that maybe we could help Terry Fox finish the script by allowing the company to assist in expanding it. Joe also brought in his friend, Officer Ken South, and his partner, who were plainclothes cops, to serve as technical advisors. The play ends with the police officers blowing away the cop-killer after he surrenders and drops his gun, so we never showed our technical advisors the complete script, but instead asked them questions about procedures and their own personal experiences. Several of their stories made it into the play, including one in which a uniformed cop gets himself locked in the back seat of his own squad car while fucking a hooker and his partner sends out an officer in distress alert as a joke.

We also learned that a cop always carries at least three guns: his police-issued revolver, his own piece (usually an enormous .357 Magnum), and an unregistered Saturday Night Special. The latter was "a drop piece" to be thrown down next to the body of an unarmed victim. The moment of truth came when we finally invited our technical advisors to a dress rehearsal to make sure that we were on the right track. We were worried that they might be infuriated to the point of raiding our homes for drugs and so we all cleaned up our apartments before the rehearsal. They laughed at many of the lines, recognizing their own stories, and, when we reached the ending with the cops killing the unarmed perp, they grew very quiet. "So, what did you think?" I asked them.

"Should've kicked him," Ken South replied.

I was confused. "Kick who?" I asked.

"The guy," South impatiently explained.

"But he's already dead," I stammered.

"So what? They should dance a fucking fandango on his face so that when they haul his ass out of there everyone in the neighborhood can see what happens to a cop killer."

We added the kicking (and the fandango line) as Ken suggested.

When the play opened, half the audience was made up of police officers and their reactions could be chilling. They usually laughed when the onstage cop tells the perp, "Give yourself up. We won't hurt you." It also became clear that the audiences – cops and civilians alike – regarded the cops as heroes. It didn't matter that we showed them shaking down the restaurant owner or harassing the waitress; when the shit started flying, they had to put themselves on the line and deal with it. Whereas any sane person would flee as quickly as possible, the policeman has to stay to the bitter end. I also learned that dramatizing someone's life is the highest compliment that can be paid, and that no matter how negative the portrayal may be, the subject will usually love it.

This was the most naturalistic show we had ever done. During the run of the play a casting director for Brian De Palma's film *The Fury*, which was shooting in Chicago, caught the show. Dennis Franz was soon cast as a policeman in that film, which led to a life as an onscreen police officer in *Hill Street Blues* and *NYPD Blue*. Some say that *Cops* led the way to these series and others like *The Wire* and *The Shield* that show policemen as flawed, deeply troubled people.

The Shape of Things to Come

"After turning out successful show after successful show, why hasn't the theater grown?" asked our new business manager, Stuart Oken, in a January 16th, 1976 article in the *Chicago Tribune*. "The answer is we need to become more marketable. We need a wider audience, a bigger space, a better location. And we can do that by getting out of Uptown."

It was clear that the economics of a 144-seat theater couldn't make money even in the best of times, and I drove our business managers crazy by refusing to raise ticket prices, as our mantra was that theater was not just for the wealthy. I still believe that live theater shouldn't cost much more than a ticket to the movies. In fact, I still get the heebie-jeebies when I see Theater spelled "Theatre." It makes it seem like it's putting on airs and is only for the elite and effete. I always believed that a theater is not a building, it's people who create the art and resisted the edifice complex. But, like the rest of the company, I was swept up in the excitement of finding a new home for our theater. So I ultimately endorsed a plan to acquire the large, luxurious Ivanhoe Theater adjacent to the venerable restaurant of the same name on north Clark Street. Without a true board of directors to fundraise, we were unable to find the money for this ambitious move so eventually Stuart Oken, and later Michael Stoneall, lost patience and left Organic in frustration. I tried to encourage Stuart to stay but he had plans of his own. He wanted to open a 300-seat theater, and he even bet me that his dream would become a reality before we would find our new home. He won the bet in 1978, building the Apollo Theater on Lincoln Avenue from scratch with his partner Jason Brett. Their first hit was a new production of *Sexual Perversity in Chicago* starring Jim Belushi. It would be a lie to say that I didn't feel a bit betrayed.

Rebecca Ditzler replaced Stuart and Michael as our new Managing Director and arranged a $250,000 Challenge Grant from the Ford Foundation if we could raise matching funds.

This seems like a fitting place to mention that in March of 1977 Carolyn discovered that she was pregnant. We were both turning thirty and were now ready to assume the responsibilities of raising a child. We knew this would change our lives, but what we didn't know was how much we would enjoy it.

The departure of Oken and Stoneall and the fiasco of failing to move the theater to the Ivanhoe left me with an overpowering desire to find a larger performing space. Now, with the quarter of a million-dollar Challenge grant, it seemed possible. I started exploring the neighborhood looking for our new home. Most of the buildings had been used for industrial purposes (like The

Body Politic) and had pillars interrupting the sight lines or low ceilings that would not allow room to hang lights. But one day I discovered a large building on the corner of Clark Street and Buckingham Place that intrigued me. It had a concrete sign over the entrance that read "Buckingham Theater" and after some checking I found that it had been built in 1914 and used as a movie theater until 1954, when a fire had shut it down. I finally found the realtor who repped the property and he opened it for me. The theater had been gutted after the fire and now there were only scorched bare brick walls and a dirt floor, but I immediately realized that this space was exactly what I was looking for. Massive iron trusses, supported by the walls, arched forty feet above the ground, and there was not a single pillar to interrupt our patrons' sight lines. It would take a tremendous amount of work to renovate, but the bare bones of an amazing theater were clearly there, and my imagination was sent spinning. The front of the building on Clark Street had street-level shops, and the second floor housed a karate school. When I showed the building to Stuart Glicken, by now a successful real estate lawyer, he immediately saw that we could rent out the shops to pay the mortgage and use the second floor for our administrative offices. Stuart told me that we would need to find a parking lot for our patrons' cars in order to get an occupancy permit.

Although this seems absurd today, he was worried about the neighborhood itself. Now Wrigleyville, as the area is called due to its proximity to the friendly confines of the Chicago Cubs, is one of the City's most desired and expensive neighborhoods, but back then it was a rough area with graffiti-covered buildings and tenement apartments. When I showed the Buckingham to the folks from the Ford Foundation, their eyes lit up. They excitedly told me that creating a theater on north Clark Street would be ideal in proving their thesis for urban development that theaters were economic catalysts for the revitalization of neighborhoods, attracting restaurants and stores and ultimately gentrified apartments and homes.

The building cost $240,000 if memory serves, and we needed $90,000 as a down payment. Where to find the money? I had become friends with Hope Abelson, Chicago's greatest patroness of the arts. Small and slender, with tremendous energy, Hope (then in her mid-sixties) did not suffer fools gladly and had a reputation as something of a dragon lady. She once told me that donating to the arts was the closest thing to royalty in the United States. If this is true, Hope Abelson was a queen. What made her especially amazing was that, unlike the other wealthy donors who funded big snooty institutions like the Lyric Opera or Chicago Symphony, Hope loved the new struggling *avant-garde* companies, especially theater and dance. She didn't want to meet with the bean counters or development execs; it was the artists she loved, and she wasn't hesitant about sharing her opinions with them, good or bad.

She had worked as a producer in New York and helped bring Tennessee Williams' *Camino Real* to Broadway. She loved theater so much that she once said, "If I were on a desert island, I would make a flea circus." Hope told me that, as a young woman, she had acted in summer stock and this was how she met her husband, Lester. Lester, short and bald with coke-bottle glasses, had founded Barton Brands, a liquor distribution company, and he absolutely adored his wife, so he dutifully accompanied her to every theatrical opening.

I have always been a big fan of the work of Kurt Vonnegut Jr., and my favorite book of his is *The Sirens of Titan*. The story follows the adventures of Malachi Constant, who begins the story as the richest man in the world and ends up on an inter-planetary journey that takes him through most of our solar system. Along the way he encounters bizarre alien creatures, a man and his dog who have become unstuck in time and space, and a religion called the Church of God the Utterly Indifferent. Vonnegut wrote it as a science fiction version of his experiences serving in the Second World War, but most readers were unable to make the connection, so he wrote a second book, *Slaughterhouse-Five*, that spelled it all out for them. In *Sirens*, Vonnegut rails about being used for purposes he despises, but by the end he states that, "The worst thing that can possibly happen to anybody is not to be used for anything by anybody." The book spoke to me. I found it hilarious and profound. I contacted the publisher about getting the rights to adapt it for the stage. To my great joy, I was finally told that Vonnegut had granted us permission on the condition that he would have approval of the final script. I welcomed his involvement and hoped that I would get the chance to meet him. I sent him my first draft of the script and got some notes back along with him telling me that he would be in Chicago to receive an award just as our show was about to open and he would like to be present at the last week of rehearsals. Meeting him surpassed all of my expectations. Tall, with his distinctive mop of curls and his Mark Twain mustache, he was warm and funny. After watching a run-through of *Sirens*, he told me one of the best things I've ever heard a writer say: "I think you have to pretend that I've been dead for ten years." What he meant was that our adaptation was too faithful to his novel. "I wrote a book; you're doing a play. Cut and combine characters, lose some locations. You have to be ruthless."

He sat down with me and made suggestions that we would have thought far too daring, but of course he was absolutely right. He was pleased that I had realized that his time-traveling character, Winston Niles Rumfoord, was his version of Franklin Delano Roosevelt. Dennis Franz gave a spot-on impersonation of the famous wartime president with Carolyn playing Rumfoord's wife as Eleanor Roosevelt, sporting false buck teeth and an upper-class accent.

"Everyone thinks that World War II was the just and righteous war," Vonnegut told me, "But there is no such thing. All wars are bad." When I mentioned the Vietnam War, which had finally ended in 1975, he told me "If you didn't serve, you really can't criticize it." He had lived through the horrors of warfare first-hand, and I hadn't, and so his observations on the futility of war had the genuine power of both personal experience and personal sacrifice.

We had traveled down the length of the Mississippi on a bare stage, but now we were traveling from Earth to Mars to Titan, the largest of Saturn's moons. How to accomplish this? Designer Jim Maronek solved the problem by creating a wonderfully imaginative set. It was a cyclorama made of elasticized white plastic rope that formed a screen upon which we could project the various interplanetary locales. The actors could literally enter through the screen by pushing aside the stretched ropes. Simple, elegant, and effective, but a bitch to build. Roberta Custer fell off a ladder during construction and had to be taken to the emergency room.

Rehearsals were not going smoothly. Tom Towles, who was playing Salo, the alien robot that explains it all at the end of the piece, was having a hell of a time memorizing his lines. He had just had dental surgery and was flying pretty high on pain medications of all sorts. As we got closer to opening night, it was clear that in his present condition he simply couldn't play the role. I should have talked to Tommy privately, but thinking he would be relieved, I stupidly announced that Richard Fire would be taking over the role. Tommy went berserk. I had humiliated him, and all of his frustration came pouring out in a furious tirade in which he referred to me as "Fat Boy," among other expletives. Tommy stormed out of the theater. I called him that evening and apologized but he would have none of it. It would be over three years until we spoke to each other again.

The show opened April 7th, 1977 to very mixed reviews. Linda Winer began her review in the *Chicago Tribune* thusly: "It may be of some consolation to Stuart Gordon and the Organic Theater Company to remember the Kurt Vonnegut, Jr. character who said, 'God never wrote a good play in his life.' That probably includes stage adaptations of early Vonnegut novels." The headline in the *Sun-Times* review called the show a "Case of cosmic confusion." But Richard Christiansen, God bless him, called the show "The Organic's *2001*" and ended his review by saying that, like Kubrick's film, "It may be some kind of masterpiece."

We ran the show in rotating rep with *Cops*, which played on Wednesdays and Thursdays, while *Sirens* performed on the weekends, an exhausting experiment that audiences and critics alike never quite seemed to completely appreciate. Eventually it became clear that we couldn't continue to pay the salaries of the company, so we all decided to go on unemployment while we planned our next production. Carolyn and I went on food stamps for a while but found the process so degrading and demoralizing that we didn't do it for long. Things were pretty bleak, and we needed to come up with a sure-fire hit or the Organic could go down the tubes.

As we often did in those days, we had a company meeting to discuss new ideas. Joe Mantegna had the floor and began with, "Doesn't it kill you that we can't pull an audience, when right down the street there are lines around the block to see a team that hasn't won a World Series since 1908?" He was of course referring to the Chicago Cubs in nearby Wrigley Field. He went on to talk about the die-hard fans he saw in the bleachers when he went to the ballpark. "There's a bunch of gamblers who will bet on anything: whether a pigeon will cross the third base line. There's a pair of blind guys who want to be play by play announcers. There are the left field bleacher bums who believe the fans can affect the outcome of the game and taunt the opposing outfielders, getting them so pissed off that they end up climbing the vines." He had our full attention. "Maybe the show follows a group of fans through a season starting with complete optimism and ending in total heartbreaking defeat. But at the end they all say, 'Wait until next year.'"

We couldn't wait to accompany Joe to the ball game and, sure enough, everything he had told us was completely true. The group he had described sat together in the center field bleachers; calling them colorful doesn't begin to do them justice. One of the most vocal was Zoz, an overweight older guy with a huge nose who constantly puffed on a cigar while clutching a handful of bills as he made one bad bet after another. He lost hundreds of dollars at each game, blaming it on the wind, or the heat, or the sun in the fielder's eyes. The blind guys were there with their transistor radios pressed up to their ears giving their own versions of the play-by-play. Around them were beautiful girls in bikini tops sunning themselves, seemingly unaware that a baseball game was even going on.

We knew we had an amazing cast of characters. Each of the actors chose one to play: Dennis Franz would be Zoz (we changed his name to Zig). Carolyn, whose pregnancy was beginning to show, covered the little bulge with a housedress as Rose, Zig's long-suffering wife, who appears at the park to finally stop his idiotic gambling. Mike Saad would play the blind play-by-play announcer; Roberta Custer would be a buxom sunbathing blonde beauty in a Farah Fawcett wig; and Keith Szarabajka would play one of the left field Bleacher Bums. Richard Fire became a disenchanted fan that now makes a fortune betting against the Cubs. We named him Marv, but Richard played him like Satan. Joe chose to be Mr. Decker, inspired by the real Mr. Becker who ran a nearby dress shop but would escape to the bleachers every summer afternoon. He would show up in a jacket and tie but by the seventh inning stretch he would end up bare-chested, wearing his shirt wrapped around his head like a turban. Finally, Patrick Williams was Richie, the slob that no one could stand. He idolizes Decker but ends up as the pawn of the malevolent Marv.

We came to game after game with little hidden tape recorders to capture dialogue. Each actor followed around his real-life model. As part of our research, we met with Jack Brickhouse, the famous announcer from WGN. Jack was the voice of the Cubs in those pre-Harry Caray days, and he was a large, good natured, red-headed Irishman. He talked about his long love affair with the team and told us his ultimate wish/dream in which both the Cubs and the White Sox get into a subway World Series, "And it goes to seven games and it's all tied up in the 23rd inning when they bring Ernie Banks out of retirement and he hits a grand slam home run to win the game." There were tears in his eyes (and ours too) as he finished, and we all knew that this wonderful speech would have to be the ending of our play.

For those of you who are not fans of our national pastime, or Chicagoans, I should tell you that Ernie Banks, whose nickname was Mr. Cub, was the star of the team for nineteen seasons (from 1953-1971), often singlehandedly winning the game. His mantra was "Let's play two!" and I often quote him when feeling frisky. I remember seeing him appear in the bleachers after he retired and immediately being surrounded by adoring fans. Carolyn magically got him to sign her program. "Let that pregnant lady through!" Banks had called to the fans surrounding him, and they had parted like the Red Sea. Ernie died in 2015 and the Cubs players wore his number 14 on their uniforms' sleeves in the playoffs.

I had transcribed all the improvs and was assembling the script, but it just wasn't coming together, and I was beginning to feel like we were never going to end up with anything remotely producible. Carolyn suggested that I get in touch with my old friend Dennis Paoli. Besides being a gifted writer and immensely funny, Dennis just happens to be one of the biggest Cubs fans on Earth. He had moved to New York, and I called him there, explaining what we were doing. I copied my pages and sent them to him. We spent many late nights on the phone, running up the long-distance bills, working on the script. Finally, he came to Chicago and, with the help of the entire company, we shaped a workable scenario. The through-line – or, as I prefer to call it, "the clothesline" – was a baseball game. We decided it should be against the Cubs' arch-rivals, the dreaded St. Louis Cardinals. We wanted a typically heartbreaking game with the Cards beating the pants off the Cubs in the early innings and then the Cubs rallying and taking the lead, only to ultimately lose the game in the final inning.

"Shouldn't they win?" I asked.

"Wouldn't be realistic," Paoli responded with a laugh, "and there's almost seventy years of history to back me up." (In 2016 the Chicago Cubs beat the Cleveland Indians to win the World Series, breaking a 108-year losing streak.)

Bleacher Bums opened on August 2nd, 1977 and was an immediate hit. The show played to sold out houses until we closed it at the end of baseball season as, once more, the Cubs managed to fall from first place and out of the playoffs, confirming the truth in Marv's line, "Nobody ever went broke betting against the Cubs after the fourth of July." We could have run the show much longer, but our New York-based manager, Herbert Barrett, had booked us a tour of the West Coast. Our tour covered the entire state, with performances at Berkeley and UCLA as well as regional art centers in La Mirada and La Jolla. We played in large auditoriums that could hold over a thousand people and we filled them with cheering audiences, a welcome change from the box office famine we had experienced in our home theater in Uptown earlier that year.

But the best thing that happened was the night we were told that Ray Bradbury was in the audience at UCLA for our performance of *The Wonderful Ice Cream Suit*. That night we got a standing ovation and we brought Ray onstage with us to take a bow. He was tall with a mane of silver hair and his trademark horn-rimmed glasses, and he hugged us all warmly. "I want to put on the suit!" he announced to the audience. The actors looked at each other. Is he kidding? Ray was already shedding his sports coat, so they surrounded him, and he stripped down to his skivvies. I cued the flamenco music and, in a flash, there he was – America's greatest fantasy writer wearing the gleaming white suit of his own story. Everyone went nuts. He told us afterwards that this was the best production of the play he had ever seen, including his own. He invited us over to his house on Cheviot Drive, which was filled with mementos from his stories and plays. He wanted to talk about the idea of bringing the show to New York. His production had played there during a newspaper strike in 1965 and he had lost all of his investors' money, which continued to haunt him. Maybe our production could lift the curse. He promised to contact us after we got back to Chicago. After all, once you've seen someone in their underwear, you're friends for life.

While in Los Angeles, I also had the chance to get reacquainted with my friend Bob Greenberg. I had met Bob when he was an actor at Kingston Mines. He had moved to Hollywood to make movies and had joined forces with John Carpenter and writer Dan O'Bannon at the film school of USC. They made a short student film called *Dark Star*, a science-fiction comedy about a spaced-out crew of astronauts whose job is to destroy unstable planets. It had been such a success that a producer had found financing to expand it into a feature. Bob did the special effects. In the meantime, O'Bannon had developed another script for the group's next project, which they intended to do as another low budget affair with Carpenter directing. Its title? *Alien*. Twentieth Century-Fox, encouraged by the success of *Star Wars* (which had opened to enormous box office grosses in the summer of 1977), bought the script and planned to produce it as a big budget film.

Bob brought me to the Fox lot where they had been developing *Alien* in a prefab office/trailer for over two years. The walls were covered with some of the most spectacular drawings I have ever seen, by artists such as Moebius, Chris Voss, and Ron Cobb, who had served as a production designer on *Dark Star*. But the project was floundering, as the powers-that-be had decided that John Carpenter wasn't ready to direct a big studio film, so they were in "development hell," trapped in the little office full of great ideas, but with no place to go. Eventually Ridley Scott, a British director of commercials and one feature film (*The Duellists*), would be hired, O'Bannon would show him disturbing alien concepts by surrealist H.R. Giger, and cinematic history would be made.

Bob also gave me a tour of the studio lot. "Just follow me and act like you know where you're going," he told me; excellent advice which I still follow to this day. It was my first time on a studio backlot. He showed me the New York street and the tropical lagoon where miniature ten-foot-long battleships used in *Tora! Tora! Tora!* still floated. I was in heaven, seeing firsthand how the magic of the movies was created. I always get excited whenever I'm on a studio lot; they are places of wonder that stir me with the promise of infinite possibilities. Bob must have picked up on this.

"You should be making movies," he told me.

I realize now that this was one of those prophetic moments where your future life's path is shown to you in unforgettable detail, not realizing that Bob Greenberg, who I only viewed as a casual friend, would be the one to make my wildest dream come true.

Suzanna

We had just returned from our west coast tour, and Carolyn was looking very pregnant. They always talk about how pregnant women glow, and it's absolutely true.

The baby was due in mid-December so, when Dennis Paoli asked if he could stay with us while he visited his folks at Thanksgiving, we said no problem. "Just don't have the baby when I'm there," he admonished us half joking, and we promised we wouldn't. We spent Thanksgiving at my mother's new high-rise apartment on Hawthorne Street and my grandmother Bessie (my father's mother) was invited as well. Carolyn and I picked her up in our new AMC Pacer. Bessie had generously insisted on giving us the money to buy the car. "Use it in good health," she told us. It seemed only right that Grandma Bessie should be chauffeured from her nursing home in style to my mom's Thanksgiving feast. After dinner, on the way home from dropping off my grandmother, we got a flat tire. Carolyn insisted on getting out of the car while I jacked it up because she was afraid her extra weight would make my job more difficult. I could see she was shivering and urged her to get back inside, but it was too late; the next thing we knew, she was going into labor.

By six in the morning, her contractions were ten minutes apart. We woke up Dennis to let him know we were heading to the hospital and asked him if he would walk and feed our dogs, Lefty and Phoebe. "Shit!" he exclaimed in true Paoli style, "You promised!" I told him I was sorry, and he laughed. "Go, go, go!" he cried, pointing to the door, and we were off.

At the hospital, I went into my coach routine while Carolyn's contractions sped up to five minutes apart, then two. She barely had time to catch her breath between them. "I don't think this is a good idea," she told me, "let's go home." I laughed, which made her furious. By then my Uncle Donald had arrived. He was our obstetrician and told us that this would be his last delivery before he retired. We were very honored, as he was now the head of a hospital ("A little hospital," my Aunt Sylvia would say dismissively). Tall, with the trademark blue eyes and blond hair that he had inherited from his mother's Viennese side, appropriately named the Weisskopfs (white heads), Donald was a distinguished, good-looking man with an easygoing manner. His very presence was calming. We knew we were in good hands.

We were brought into the delivery room. I put on a scrub suit and surgical mask, as did my uncle. I had my trusty Nikon to record this momentous event for posterity (and to have something to do). By now the transitions were less than a minute apart and Carolyn was in intense pain. "I want the drugs!" she screamed, "Give me the drugs!"

"It's too late," my uncle told her. "They won't do any good."

"You unscrupulous scoundrel!" Carolyn shrieked. Those words have become a family joke ever since. The cervix has to stretch to ten centimeters before the baby's head can begin to emerge. This is called "crowning," and it is the first glimpse you have of the infant, although all that's visible is the top of the head. My uncle seemed worried by what he saw. He asked the nurse for the forceps. This scared me, as I immediately thought of my father's younger brother Eddie. He had been a forceps delivery and the doctor had damaged Eddie's head, causing him to have a permanent limp, a withered arm, and appear slow-witted. "Is it really necessary?" I asked my uncle. "We have to turn the baby, or it could suffocate going through the birth canal," he replied as he inserted the steel instrument and began gently turning. "There," he said as he handed the nurse the forceps, "That's better." Now Carolyn could push, and with a series of deep groans, she sat up and pushed as hard as she could. In a moment I saw the baby coming out. "I win my bet," my uncle said, "It's a girl," then he lifted the infant, tapped the bottoms of her feet, and she immediately began to cry. "Good lungs," he said as he snipped the umbilical cord and handed the child to a nurse to have the baby's nose and mouth suctioned. The little face was red, but the rest of her body was blue-grey; she looked like she was made out of clay. As she cried, her chest gradually turned pink, and then the pinkness spread to her arms and legs. It was like watching a miracle unfold before my eyes. The Bible says that God created man from clay, and here it was, happening right in front of me – the wonder of creation. I felt that I was in the holy presence of a force greater than Man, that at that very moment, God was there in the delivery room with us, blessing us. I prayed for the first time in years. In my heart I promised Him that, in thanks for this blessing, I would worship Him again and forever praise His holy name.

My father's family were non-believers. This is because my grandfather Sam had been a yeshiva student in Lithuania until the day a pogrom had forced the rabbi and his students to take refuge in the temple. "God will protect us," the rabbi told his terrified students, and they believed him until the Cossacks rode their horses right into the temple and horse-whipped all of them. When the next pogrom broke out, he took a large two-by-four, pounded big spikes through it, and waited in an alley for a Cossack to ride by. Then he jumped out, knocked the rider from his horse, and beat him bloody. The next day he left for America.

The Gordons still had big family dinners on Friday nights, and that was where my father first met my mother. Her family were Reform Jews who had helped found their temple in Oak Park. When I was born, my parents agreed that it would be my choice if I wanted a Jewish education or not, so one evening when I was about five years old, my mother took me on the bus (because my father refused to set foot in a temple). It was Simchas Torah Eve, and I was given a paper flag to wave and an apple to eat as we marched around the synagogue, singing. I became a practicing Jew and our family joined the temple. But I had fallen away since leaving for college – until this miraculous moment, the birth of our still-unnamed child.

The baby was sponged off and then placed on Carolyn's chest so she could see her. "She's beautiful," she whispered, tears in her eyes.

"Good going, kiddo," my uncle said patting Carolyn's knee. It was 11:28 PM, November 25th, 1977.

The tag on our infant's ankle read "Baby girl – Gordon" and the nurses told us that we would have to give her a name before we could bring her home. We named her Suzanna, after Shakespeare's first born, and because her name began with an S like mine. But we added the Z so we could call her Zan as a nickname.

As we placed Suzanna in her crib, I had a moment of panic. We had been taught everything in our Lamaze class about how to birth a baby, but I didn't know the first thing about taking care of one. I asked Carolyn if she knew how to care for a baby and she laughed. "Don't worry," she told me, "I've been preparing for this moment all my life." She soon proved to be an absolutely wonderful mother, and Suzanna proved to be an amazingly happy baby: cooing and smiling and so good-natured that I nicknamed her "Suzanna Sunshine." Even when she awoke us in the middle of the night or early in the morning, she was always so happy to see us that we just had to smile.

They say that new babies bring good luck, and in March we began our east coast tour. Herbert Barrett had booked us into the Annenberg Center in Philadelphia. We also had set up a run of *Bleacher Bums* at the Performing Garage in New York City. I had met Richard Schechner, the artistic director of The Performance Group, while a member of the board of the TCG. Short and intense, with a head of dark curls, Richard had visited Organic where he saw a performance of *Cops* and liked it so much, he asked if he could produce it in New York. We worked out a deal in which we would allow him to produce *Cops* if he would let us present one of our plays in their second space on Wooster Street in the Soho district.

We were greeted by Dr. Sidney Bloom, who ran the Drama Guild that produced a season at the Zellerbach Theater in the Annenberg Center. We presented *Ice Cream Suit* to appreciative crowds and filled the houses during our run, but one day Dr. Bloom asked us about *Bleacher Bums*. Could we do a performance in Philadelphia? Why not? We had the costumes and a newly built portable set of risers. But would an east coast audience appreciate a play that was essentially a love letter to the Chicago Cubs? We decided to present the show as an experiment to see if the rest of America would appreciate *Bleacher Bums*.

The answer turned out to be an emphatic YES! Jack Wallace replaced Joe Mantegna as Mr. Decker because Joe had been cast in a musical version of Studs Terkel's *Working*, which had been produced at the Goodman Theater prior to a Broadway run. It was too bad that Joe, who had conceived the idea of *Bleacher Bums*, wasn't there for its east coast premier. As a tip of the hat to our new friend, when Keith Szarabajka's cheerleader heckles the Cardinal center fielder about his bad teeth, we gave a new name to the dentist: "Dr. Bloom says you owe him twenty-eight hundred dollars! He says you got the worst root canals in the National League!" Dr. Bloom has lived in our play ever since.

The next stop was the Performing Garage, whose name says it all. It was an actual garage before becoming a theater. It's a large, amorphous space that, at the time, had two theaters carved out. The first held Schechner's production of *Cops*. Among the actors were Spalding Gray and Willem Dafoe, both in their twenties. We set up our bleachers across the room from *Cops* and, as there was no sound separation, we planned to have our performances begin after *Cops* came down. I again hired Betty Lee Hunt to be our press agent, and she was able to fill our opening night with critics repping the major publications as well as TV and radio stations. As we were performing off-off-Broadway, the reviews trickled in over the next few days, but it soon became clear that we had a full-blown hit on our hands. We got a lot of celebrities coming to see us. I'll never forget the night that John Belushi dropped in. He got there late, and there was standing room only so, instead of standing, he paced, laughing loudly when amused. About halfway through the show, I felt an arm around my neck strangling me. It was Belushi, and he had me in a choke hold, his lips to my ear, "If the Cubs lose, I'll kill you!" he hissed.

* * *

We headed back to Chicago but, as usual with our New York endeavors, we ended up losing some key company members. Joe Mantegna's production of *Working* had also closed after a brief run on Broadway, and he and Arlene decided to move to Los Angeles that Fall to see if he could make it in film and television. Dennis Franz also left Organic and headed west, as did Meshach Taylor. Keith Szarabajka stayed in New York. We had kept this amazing group of actors together for five years, the longest of any Organic company, and watching them grow and flourish has been among my greatest pleasures. But nothing is forever, and these wonderful actors, and now good friends, needed to take their shots at fame and fortune in Hollywood and I'm happy to say that they all succeeded. Once again, we needed to put together a new company. We did pick up a new business manager, with Rick Obadiah making the move from New York to Chicago.

Carolyn, Suzanna, and I finally moved out of Uptown. Things had been getting progressively worse in our ramshackle apartment on Buena Vista Street. The neighborhood had gotten so bad that one day while walking our dogs I saw a pimp holding his hooker by her hair and bashing her head repeatedly against the hood of a parked car. "Stop it!" I yelled, moving toward them, unable to quiet my outrage. The hooker raised her bloody face from the car's hood and began screaming at me, "Get away! He'll kill you! Get away!" Badly shaken, I retreated. This poor girl was more frightened for me than herself.

We moved into a second-floor apartment on tree-lined Seminary Avenue near Belmont and Clark, a couple of blocks from the Buckingham Theater, which still sat there, an empty shell. We had to fish or cut bait. At thirty-one I had crossed the line and become the enemy the '60s counterculture always warned us about. "Don't trust anyone over thirty," we used to say. I was no longer an infant terrible, I was just plain terrible, and I knew that it was time to try something new. But what?

CHAPTER 19

Something New

We had been approached by Patterson Denny of our local PBS station, WTTW, about doing a television version of *Bleacher Bums*. Spurred on by the excellent New York notices, he felt that, if done properly, it could be picked up by the nationally broadcast *Great Performances*. Pat had been the original director for *Sneak Previews*, the WTTW show that had launched the TV careers of film critics Roger Ebert and Gene Siskel. Pat felt that we should not simply videotape a performance of the play. A theater audience could use their imaginations to believe that they were in a ballpark, but Pat and his production designer, Mickey Lowenstein, who had created the movie theater set for *Sneak Previews*, felt that a television audience would need a more realistic setting. There had to be a way of suggesting a crowd. Pat and Mickey came up with an excellent design idea that included the silhouette of the famous scoreboard with additional rows of ballpark fans behind our actors.

That March, our company and thirty-five extras spent two weeks rehearsing and five days shooting *Bums* for television, for which Joe and Dennis returned from Los Angeles and joined the rest of the original cast. We did have to soften the swearing a little bit, and Pat suggested adding a brief preface in which Greg, the blind play-by-play announcer, gives a quick history of the Cubs and their woeful attempts to win their first series since 1908, as it was Pat's hope (and mine) that the show would be televised nationally to an audience who wouldn't be as familiar with the Cubs' misfortunes as the local fans.

It was around this time that my old friend, and now consigliore, Stuart Glicken told me in no uncertain terms that we needed to create a real board of directors if we expected funding institutions to give us the kind of grants that would enable us to finally renovate the Buckingham Theater. "You have to show that you have the community's support," he advised. After our inability to match our $250,000 Ford Foundation Challenge Grant, I had to listen. One of the first people he introduced me to was Julius Braun, who owned a bottle-making company on the Chicago River. Tall and thin, in his mid-seventies, Julius was a real character. Practically bald with a pointed goatee, he reminded me of Don Quixote. "Ah, the sweet smell of bullshit," he would say if he thought you were flattering him. Julius's son, Zev Braun, was a well-known movie and television producer in Hollywood, and his younger son David and I soon became good friends.

When Stuart Glicken told Julius that I was worried about handing over the reins of our theater to a board of directors, Julius found this funny and asked me why I was so afraid to do so. I told him about what had happened at Broom Street when the company had thrown me out of my own theater, and he laughed. "These people on the board don't know a damn thing about how to do theater," he told me. "They'd be insane to get rid of you. You need to have more faith in yourself." I finally agreed, not realizing that what Julius was telling me also had that familiar sweet smell. He became the first member of our new board.

Stu Glicken invited several of his business associates to join our board. They included an insurance salesman, real estate developers, and the vice president of the Albany Park Bank in the neighborhood where I grew up. Stu had invited the prospective board members to see one of our shows and, for most of them, it was their first time at our theater. At our first board meeting, it became clear that, as Julius had predicted, they had little idea of how theater was produced.

"You know what you should produce?" one of them asked me. "What?" I responded, all ears. He leaned forward as if to tell me a great secret: "A hit."

"Good idea," I responded, having a hard time not laughing. I wasn't sure if he was kidding or not, but when it became clear that he was serious, I responded, "We think all of our shows have the potential to become hits."

The Little Sister kicked off our subscription series in April of 1979. Joe Mantegna would have been perfect for the role of Marlowe, Chandler's hardboiled, wisecracking detective made famous by Hollywood icon Humphrey Bogart. But Joe had just headed to Los Angeles, so I ended up casting an actor named Mike Genovese to play the part. Although he was quite good in the role, he turned out to be a nightmare for me and the Organic Theater. He seemed perpetually pissed off and refused to take part in the warm-up exercises the company always did an hour before each show. He wouldn't show up until half hour call, per Actors' Equity rules. Genovese fractured the ensemble that had been the key to our success over the years. I should have replaced him, although this wouldn't have gone down well with Actors' Equity. I was so depressed that I cowardly ended up avoiding this show as much as possible, leaving poor Carolyn at Genovese's mercy. After the six-week run of *The Little Sister*, I have never been so glad to see an actor leave the company. I should have seen that this in-fighting was killing our work. The secret of success is having everyone on the same wavelength, working together to create the same show. That's why there are so many bad plays and films – because you have dozens of egos all pulling in different directions. Our greatest hits were always the result of a strong ensemble where everyone respected the others' talents and ideas. The company was always greater than the sum of its parts.

My pain was somewhat assuaged when *Bleacher Bums* premiered on local Chicago television May 15th, 1979. In an article written for the *Tribune*'s *TV Week*, our old friend Richard Christiansen quotes me as saying, "Wouldn't it be wonderful if all the great plays done here in Chicago could have a life and an audience beyond their original stage runs?" What I really meant was wouldn't it be wonderful if Organic (and I) could get a foothold in television. The show was a huge success and did get shown nationally on *Great Performances* as Pat Denny, WTTW, and I had hoped. We ended up getting nominated for a local Emmy for the best original show.

Carolyn and I went to the award show assuming we would surely lose. I bought an antique tailcoat for the occasion and Carolyn wore a beautiful black dress and we drank champagne and kidded around until we heard our names being read as the winners of the prize. Amazed and in shock, the actors and I stumbled to the stage where we were each given a miniature Emmy. Carolyn still believes that the only time you ever win an award is when you're sure you won't.

Finally, it was time to remount *Warp*. We held open auditions and half the city's actors showed up. Lora Staley, a strong shapely brunette, was quickly cast as Sargon, but Cumulus seemed more problematic. It came down to two actors: Bruce Young, a muscular black actor, and John Malkovich (yes, THAT John Malkovich). John was a member of the newly arrived Steppenwolf Theater Company, which had been performing at a church in Highland Park, a Chicago suburb. The ensemble which, unlike Organic, did not yet produce original work, was getting wonderful reviews for their unique acting style. Their company included Gary Sinise, Jeff Perry, Laurie Metcalf, Joan Allen and Terry Kinney, all of whom have since made their marks in film and television.

I ended up casting Bruce Young over John Malkovich. Although John looked nothing like a superhero, he is such a good actor that he could convince you that he was able to leap tall buildings in a single bound. I became friends with John and helped him move Steppenwolf to the Jane Addams Center on Broadway Avenue. Chicago was now bustling with dozens of storefront theaters. It was a heady time to be working in Chicago. We were all hanging out together: William H. Macy, Bill Murray, William Petersen, George Wendt, Shelley Long, Harold Ramis, trying to top each other with the most outrageous theater anyone had ever seen.

Audiences again flocked to *Warp*. Bruce "Moose" Young was terrific as David Carson/Lord Cumulus, and no one seemed to mind the colorblind casting. In fact, I think it encouraged black audiences to embrace the show. The chemistry between the new members of the company and the old timers seemed to work just fine.

The seventies were ending. Tom Wolfe had called them the "Me decade" and our new president Jimmy Carter had said that America was in "a malaise." We were still in an energy crisis with the price of gasoline skyrocketing,

American diplomats were being held as hostages in Iran, and Three Mile Island had just melted down in Pennsylvania. The Soviets had invaded Afghanistan, and Great Britain had just elected Margaret Thatcher.

But we had survived our first ten years in Chicago. Gone were the days of dividing up the money on Sunday nights. Our yearly budget was now over $250,000 and we were just completing our first subscription series. Rick Obadiah started putting together a brochure for our next season that encouraged our patrons to "meet the challenge of the eighties." The real question was, could we?

CHAPTER 20

The Buckingham

I had discovered Anthony Burgess's great book about William Shakespeare, *Nothing Like the Sun*, and found that it spoke to me. Burgess showed me a Shakespeare more concerned about filling the seats of his theater than becoming the world's greatest playwright. "I know it's no good," he says as he hands his players scripts to the newly written *Hamlet*, "but we need something on the boards by Christmas." The book presented a man who was writing roles for the members of his company that played to their strengths, just as Lenny and I had done when we wrote the three episodes of *Warp* for our Organic actors. Its sequence that really hit a nerve was the one in which the landlord of Shakespeare's theater, The Rose, raises the rent so severely that it makes it impossible for them to continue. "If you don't like it, take your things and leave!" the hard-nosed landlord tells them. The company meets, just as Organic frequently did, to discuss their options. One of the members of Shakespeare's company tells the group that his family owns farmland on the other side of the Thames. Couldn't they build a theater there?

"With what?" the company wants to know. But Shakespeare has an idea: "He said to take our things and go, didn't he? As far as I'm concerned, this theater is one of our things." So a plan is hatched in which The Rose is dismantled while the landlord is away for the summer and secretly moved across the river. There it is reassembled as The Globe.

This story gave me an idea. It was 1981, we still had no luck with matching our $250,000 Ford Foundation Challenge Grant, time was running out, and soon the offer would be withdrawn. But what if we were to use the building itself as a match for the funds? If we were smart, we could build a bare bones theater and get it open. As in Shakespeare's plan, we would do the renovations quickly and in secret without building permits. We would open the theater that spring, suddenly appearing out of nowhere as if by magic. I tried this idea out on Stuart Glicken and his eyes twinkled. "It could work," he said. "But if you decide to do it, we never had this conversation."

Stu got our friends at the Ford Foundation to agree to our plan, and their money was ours. The first step was to put in a concrete floor. We knew that the large concrete trucks would alert the building inspectors, so we waited until the weekend when we knew they weren't on duty. A large ramp leading from the lobby into the theater was created for handicap access, and I remember holding Suzanna's hand as she roller skated down it during those early weeks of construction. All the work was done in secret: electrical, carpentry, and plumbing. But how would we install the ventilation system?

The ventilation unit was the size of a box car and needed a huge crane to lift it into place. We chose another Sunday and prayed that the neighbors, seeing that gigantic unit lifted from the bed of a semi trailer and hoisted 300 feet into the air and onto our roof, wouldn't blow our cover.

We hired our theater carpenters to put up dry wall that created dressing rooms and bathrooms. We bought theater seats from a movie house that went out of business, and my friend Chris Walberg generously gave the Buckingham's façade a sandblasting that made the bricks shine like new.

We said our goodbyes to Brooks Miller and the Hull House staff and moved out of the Uptown Center and allocated one of the storefront spaces in the Buckingham building to be used as an office, quickly renting out the others. The last thing we did was to paint "Organic Theater Company" in big letters across the front of the building against a fiery rainbow pattern to announce our occupancy.

Our opening play at the Buckingham? *The King Must Die*, based on the great novel by Mary Renault, telling the true story behind the legend of Theseus and the Minotaur. I had discovered that the movie rights had been sold to Twentieth Century-Fox in 1958 but, as is often the case, the sale did not include the live theater rights. I wrote Mary Renault, "Your book is an account of a true hero for an audience desperately in need of heroes – a positive statement which says that the world can be changed for the better if the leaders take responsibility for the people they lead." Like Kurt Vonnegut before her, she gave us permission to adapt her book if she could have approval of the final script. I asked Bill Norris to work with me on the adaptation, and we received extensive notes from Mary Renault on our first draft. Eventually, we had an approved script. I never met or even spoke to her, which I regret to this day, but just the fact that I was able to collaborate with this brilliant author was an incredible thrill.

The show opened for previews on May 6th, 1981, and the next day the city inspectors showed up. Stu Glicken (God bless him) met with the mayor's office and somehow convinced the powers-that-be not to close our show. We had built the theater to code and they finally allowed us to stay open while we worked toward obtaining our occupancy permit. The head of the Electrical Department in the Building Code offices, however, insisted that he had to be present on opening night and would sit in the first row in the event that he saw sparks flying. "If that happens, I'll have to immediately evacuate the theater," he solemnly told us. Well sparks did fly, but not the electrical kind, for the inspector was bowled over by our topless bull-dancing actresses less than five feet away from where he was sitting. He loved the show so much that he came back with friends several times. They always sat in the first row, and we always comped them. Let's hear it for the Chicago Building Department!

The show opened to the public on May 20th, and Richard Christiansen began his *Tribune* review by quoting Orson Welles' famous line that a movie studio "is the biggest electric train set any boy ever had!" He continued, "The spacious new theater carved out of the old Buckingham movie house is indeed a great toy for Gordon, and if he and his company have not quite created *Citizen Kane*, they have at least produced their *Ten Commandments* or *Samson and Delilah*." *Sun-Times* critic Glenna Syse also gave a rave review to the new theater: "Now as a theater space with 300 seats, the rebuilt theater works. It cajoles the ear and it interests the eye. The audience comes at the stage from all angles and many levels. It has adaptability, height and motion going for it and in this production, most notably it gives you the feeling you are sitting in a bull-ring." So far so good. But then she continues, "Trouble is, I don't think Mary Renault…is much of a matador…*The King Must Die* lives, but as a theater piece it has a terminal disease."

I knew that without the support of both major dailies, our chances for box office survival were minimal at best. Maybe I was crazy, but I did something that I had never done before: I called Glenna Syse to complain about her review. She began the conversation very sweetly, "Go ahead," she cooed, "Vent."

"It's clear from the review that you're not a fan of Mary Renault," I began.

"No, I'm not," she confirmed.

"Then you should have excused yourself and let someone else who was unbiased review the show."

There was a long pause.

And then the soothing Glenna became a shrieking harpy, "How dare you tell me what I can and cannot review!" she screamed at me before slamming down the phone, ending the conversation. So much for venting. As a result, I don't think Glenna, the head critic for the *Chicago Sun-Times* ever reviewed another show at Organic.

Our next play was a musical version of William Kotzwinkle's brilliantly satiric book, *Dr. Rat*. Richard Fire and June Shellene had been hard at work on the songs and script for over a year, and I related to the story of a group of laboratory animals rebelling against their scientist captors. Dr. Rat is an insane lab rat that has been experimented on so many times that he now identifies with his tormentors and believes he is a scientist too. Stockholm syndrome anyone? Richard Fire seemed like the perfect candidate to play him. The show reminded me of *Marat/Sade* in many ways, with the lab animals being very much like the mental patients in Peter Weiss' play, so I decided to go a step or two beyond Peter Brook's staging. I locked the audience in cages so that they would feel like trapped animals. When the revolution begins and the actors are freed, they would open the audience's cages as well. "Come on!" they would urge the patrons, "Come and join our revolution!" I assumed that some would leave their cells, and some wouldn't. But I was happily surprised when as many as a hundred audience members per performance joined the cast onstage. They were given army helmets and taught to march and even joined in with some of the songs. The greatest moment was at the end of the play when the animals discover that their revolution has spread throughout the world and all the creatures on Earth have joined forces to free themselves from enslavement by humanity. This infuriates Dr. Rat, and he (wearing a protective gas mask) opens up canisters of poison gas and kills all the rebelling lab animals. The animals gasp and fall to the floor, painfully coughing and crawling until they die. What made this moment so powerful was that the audience members who were onstage "died" as well, convulsing and twitching until they too ceased to move. The effect of a hundred bodies lying motionless onstage was devastating. It reminded me of the horrifying pictures of the Jonestown Massacre that had happened three years earlier in Guyana.

But we still failed to fill our new theater, and I was getting nervous. We were running out of money and Nick Rabkin, our new managing director, informed me that we only had enough money for one more production. If that show didn't work, we would have to close the doors of our freshly-opened theater.

However, these worries were eclipsed toward the end of 1981 when Carolyn and I discovered that we were expecting of our second child.

CHAPTER 21

Jillian

My old friend Ron Berman was now a doctor and had spent much of his residency working in hospital emergency rooms. He had some hilarious stories of the unbelievable things he had witnessed (such as having to remove a light bulb from a patient's anus without breaking it), and if you could figure out a way to link these events into a single evening, you would have a hell of a show. Ron and I put together a list of his best stories and pitched it to the company. They loved the idea and had been working on it as a group for over a year, improvising scenes much in the same way we had created *Bleacher Bums*.

The main conflict in our drama involved an uptight emergency room specialist (Gary Houston) dealing with a moonlighting ENT specialist (Richard Fire) who is trying to grab some sleep through his 48-hour shift. Of course, everything that can go wrong does, with heart attacks, gunshot wounds, and unexpected births. The two docs are forced to work together and ultimately learn to respect each other.

Lily Monkus, our colorful office assistant, surprised everyone with her ability to play Joan Thor, the unflappable head nurse. Ron Berman had us all learn to administer CPR, as we had to make it look realistic in our show. We practiced on a Resusci Anne doll, a manikin torso of a young blonde woman that was modeled after the real daughter of the creator of the device. She had died because no one with her knew how to administer CPR when she suffered a medical emergency. Resusci Anne lets you know if you are doing the technique properly by beeping, and she even breathes after you have "saved" her. Thank God I learned CPR, as I was called upon to use it in a real emergency not long after. But more about that later.

We started rehearsals in December and had so little money that designer Rick Paul used leftover plasterboard from the construction of the theater to build our set.

As opening night approached, Carolyn reached term in her pregnancy. But there was a complication. X-rays showed that the baby was upside down. This meant that unless the baby shifted at the last minute, it would have to be born by Caesarian section. To complicate things even more, my Uncle Donald had retired and could not be present for the delivery. He had recommended a colleague who seemed very personable when we met with him but, after a couple of visits, he let us know that it was very likely that he wouldn't be present if the baby weren't born during his regular 9-5 office hours. "What happens then?" Carolyn asked.

"One of my associates will handle it," was his off-handed response. We asked if another doctor could be our OBGYN, as we felt it was important to build a relationship so that the doctor knew us, and we felt confident that we were in good hands. My uncle's love and tender care had spoiled us.

Carolyn became the patient of Dr. Nada Jazbek, who was Yugoslavian. After a meeting with her, though, we started having doubts. An intense, unsmiling woman, she did not project the warm and cozy bedside manner we had so appreciated with my uncle. Carolyn's dad suggested that if his daughter was going to have a C-section, she should ask the doctor to use a Pfannenstiel incision. This is sometimes called a bikini cut and is a horizontal incision just above the pubis. "What, you are go-go dancer?" was Jazbec's response, irritated that Carolyn even knew the medical term. Jazbec grudgingly agreed on the condition that, if the baby was in distress, she would use the traditional vertical incision (from the bellybutton to the groin).

Everything always happens at once. When I got home after the afternoon rehearsal to get dressed for opening night, I discovered that Carolyn had gone into labor. I scrambled to let everyone know that, for the first time in our lives, neither of us would be present for an opening night. Instead, we were at a real hospital for a completely different kind of opening. It was Groundhog Day, February 2nd, 1982. 2/2/82. Lots of twos for a second child.

I thought that I would be with my wife while she was giving birth, but Jazbek saw me with my camera and told me that I was not allowed in the operating room. Carolyn and I looked at each other. "I'll be alright," Carolyn said as she was wheeled into surgery. I watched through a little window in the door but really couldn't see much of anything as the surgical draping hid Carolyn's face from me. A few minutes later I heard a baby crying.

Jazbek came out. "Is girl," she said. "You go in now." I started snapping pictures of my beautiful brand-new daughter, and Jazbek pointed to some bloody surgical towels. "Here, take a picture of this," she said, smirking. Serbian humor. Unlike Suzanna's birth four years earlier, Carolyn was barely conscious and unable to say much, but she did manage a brave smile before they whisked her and the baby to the recovery room. I later learned that our baby had been born with her umbilical cord wrapped around her neck twice, and this would certainly have ended badly if we had attempted natural childbirth. I thanked God that both Carolyn and our new baby were alive and well.

I spent most of the night at the hospital waiting for Carolyn and the baby to be admitted to their room on the maternity floor, where they would be staying for the next few days. When I finally got to see them, they both seemed completely exhausted. I kissed my wife goodbye and headed off to pick up Suzanna, who had spent the night with my mother, and to walk Lefty and Phoebe. On the way, I stopped at a newsstand and picked up the early morning editions and hurriedly found the reviews. My heart sank as I read them. They were both pans. Even our old friend Richard Christiansen had hated *E/R*, calling the show a television sitcom. I was crushed.

The next morning, I brought my mother and now big sister Suzanna to see Carolyn and our new daughter, who we named Jillian Bess Gordon, the Bess after my grandmother Bessie. Carolyn sensed that something was wrong, and when my mom took Suzanna to get her a snack from the hospital cafeteria, I showed her the reviews. "We're finished," I told my wife as tears started running down my cheeks. Carolyn, who was in real pain from major abdominal surgery, comforted me. "You always told me babies were lucky," she said. But I knew in my heart of hearts that things were pretty hopeless. Here we were with another mouth to feed and our new theater was going down the tubes.

But amazingly the audiences kept coming. The hospital staff that filled the previews had started a word-of-mouth buzz and in spite of the bad reviews, our houses were full and the audiences appreciative. We soon realized that we had a full-blown hit on our hands. The theater was saved! Our new daughter Jill had provided a double blessing. We kept the show running for a year and cancelled plans for a revival of *Bloody Bess*, which was part of our subscription season. In the theater, closing a hit show is considered a crime against God, so we felt compelled to keep *E/R* running, refunding the subscribers' money.

Nevertheless, I was getting antsy. Shouldn't we be developing more new work? Nick Rabkin had the solution. "Let's move the show," he suggested. A deal was made to bring *E/R* to the Forum Theater in the northern suburb of Summit. Would suburban audiences support our scruffy, bloody show set in a Chicago emergency room? Indeed they did, and the show ran for over two years to packed houses. Soon Organic was out of debt for the first time in its thirteen-year history. Our board was ecstatic; no need for them to fundraise. I had finally taken their suggestion and produced a hit.

Jill turned out to be a cyclone of energy, walking at nine months, idolizing her big sister, and doing her best to catch up with her. She had been born with a lazy left eye, a trait she had probably inherited from her namesake Bessie. Her great grandmother had had surgery to correct it back in the 1920s, and it was only partially successful, but Jill avoided surgery by wearing an eye patch and, ultimately, thick glasses. With her large brown eyes, it made her look like a baby owl, but she never complained. We were able to take a picture of Grandma Bessie holding her new great-grandchild, and I used it to make a drawing that I presented to her on her 90th birthday. My Aunt Eleanor could never be sure how old Bessie really was because she had been lying about her age for years. "She might be ninety-five for all I know," Eleanor had said.

Bessie constantly complained about how terrible her life had become and often talked about killing herself. When she was staying at my Aunt Eleanor's high-rise on Lake Shore Drive, a neighbor saw her trying to climb over the balcony rail of her apartment, which was on the twenty-somethingth floor. He had called the police and when they arrived, Bessie had gone back inside to get a babushka. She told them that it was too cold out there on the balcony to commit suicide.

After that, she had been put into an assisted living complex, and when I would visit her, she would always tell me how miserable she was and that she couldn't wait to die. This broke my heart, and one day I told her that if she really felt that way I would hold a pillow over her face and help her leave this world. Her eyes grew large with fright, and I realized that no one really wants to die, no matter what.

Bessie died an unassisted death six months after Jill's birth. A few months later, her namesake learned to talk, and one night she climbed out of her crib and walked into the living room where Carolyn and I were watching television. Jill announced to us that she was "A Messenger from God." I asked her what the message was, but without answering, she turned and went back to bed. Was she sleep-walking? We were amazed, but never doubted her. Jill could be very mischievous and, once, Carolyn sat her down and said, "Jill, I know that somewhere inside you there is a sweet and wonderful little girl just waiting to come out." Jill looked horrified, and her voice trembling, asked, "Who is she?"

Meanwhile, *E/R* was playing to capacity houses at the Forum Theater and I was finally able to continue producing new work at the Buckingham. For the first time in the theater's history, we had money in the bank. I began work with author Joe Haldeman to adapt his Nebula award-winning science fiction book *The Forever War* for the stage. The story concerns a war between Earth and the mysterious alien Taurans, so named as they seem to come from a planet within the constellation of Taurus. Since our soldiers have to travel light years to engage the enemy, they experience time dilation and find that hundreds of years have transpired when they finally return to Earth. The hero lives through the entire war, which lasts over a thousand years.

Author Joe Haldeman was a Vietnam veteran who had been badly wounded by a "Bouncing Betty," a land mine that pops out of the ground before it explodes at waist height. Joe had almost been cut in half, and he returned to the states badly damaged. Luckily, his high school sweetheart Gay stayed at his side, helping him make the difficult adjustment back to civilian life. Joe had written a book about his experiences in 'Nam entitled *War Year*, but no one wanted to hear, let alone read, about the atrocities of that dirty pointless war. Joe regrouped and decided to retell the story in science fiction terms and the result was *The Forever War*. The last section of the book is about an Alamo-like siege in which Mandella, our hero, commands a base on a distant world under attack by a massive Tauran invasion force. Since most of it takes place in an underground bunker, it occurred to me that this could be done live as a play onstage.

Joe Haldeman wrote the adaptation himself. Bruce Young played Mandella, Carolyn played the company doctor who is attracted to Mandella, and Gary Houston played a mutinous underling. We bought a dozen television monitors to show views of the topside battle as well as play communications from the orbiting star fleet. The talented designer Steve Jones created early computer graphics for the displays. *The Forever War* opened October 19th, 1983 to mixed reviews and closed by the end of the year. The show did decent business, but by now our board of directors gauged success by *E/R* standards so anything less was a flop in their eyes. I tried to convince them that *E/R* was an anomaly, the biggest hit by far in our thirteen-year history, and it was absurd to expect every show to equal its success.

The board held a meeting to which I was not invited and decided that the theater should not spend any more money on new projects. "Our losses are a result of producing untested plays," they told me. "The answer is to no longer produce new shows." This was like a knife through my heart and went against the very essence of the company's mission to create original work. I told the board it was like an oil company deciding not to drill new wells. But they would not back down.

The board demanded a voice in the selection of new plays and insisted that they be invited to readings of new scripts and that they would have to approve all new productions. And future plays would have to be done in workshop productions in our tiny fifty-seat storefront space, as the cost of advertising and marketing new shows was prohibitively expensive. I found this especially galling, as we had built the Buckingham specifically to be able to sell enough seats to make our shows financially viable. But I had no choice except to go along with the new rules. Even my old friend Stuart Glicken sided with the board.

I now realized that the creation of the board had been a huge mistake. We had thought that they would help with fundraising, and their existence did encourage foundations to give us larger grants. As a body, however, they had done very little in terms of raising money or even selling subscriptions. The goals of the theater that Carolyn and I had formed were lost on them; none of them (with the exception of Stuart Glicken) would have ever created Organic in the first place. It had been started by young artists with nothing to lose and everything to gain, dividing up our weekly take into equal shares on the floor after our Sunday evening show. Now I was being sidelined by my own board, prevented from doing what I truly loved.

Hollywood Beckons

The board, in an attempt to ameliorate my bad feelings, offered me a raise in salary. I would no longer receive the same salary as the other members of the company, but significantly more. I had mixed feelings about this. It's true that, unlike the actors, Carolyn and I had children to raise, but this would effectively destroy the "all for one and one for all" ethos of the company and smacked of the line from *Animal Farm*: "All animals are equal, but some animals are more equal than others."

"You need to be able to buy a house," Stuart Glicken argued in an effort to make me accept the board's generosity. Looking back, I realize that this was a key moment, and what I should have done was turn down their offer and go about the business of replacing my board. Instead, I accepted this bribe, and Carolyn and I soon began house hunting. There was nothing that we could afford, even with our newly improved financial situation.

It was around this time that we were approached by Hollywood producers who wanted to turn *E/R* into a television show. I had made a videotape of the show and sent it to David Braun, the son of our "sweet smell of bullshit" board member Julius. David's brother Zev was immediately interested. We also somehow got a copy to Norman Lear and he sent bright young Eve Brandstein, an assistant-turned-producer, to see our show.

We were amazed at how quickly things came together. Lear would create what was known as a back-door pilot, in which the characters of an existing series would visit our emergency room. In this case it would be a two-part installment of Lear's successful series *The Jeffersons*. Ron, Carolyn, and I were flown to Los Angeles to meet the writer/producers. We were put up at the Beverly Garland Hotel, which was a Holiday Inn owned by the famous B-movie star of some of Roger Corman's best known films such as *It Conquered the World*. When you got your morning wake-up call, it was Beverly Garland's recorded voice that greeted you. We were taken to dinner at The Palm, a large trendy restaurant on Santa Monica Boulevard whose sawdust-covered floor and murals of celebrity caricatures let you know that this was the center of the Hollywood universe. We all ordered three-pound lobsters as we met the writing team that would turn our little play into network television. We were introduced to Saul Turteltaub and Bernie Orenstein. Both in their mid-fifties, Saul was tall and angular, and Bernie was short and round. They had been a writing team for so long that they finished each other's sentences. They had started on *That Girl*, the Marlo Thomas comedy in the sixties, and worked together on *Sanford and Son* in the seventies. They had a lot of ideas about adapting *E/R* to television, the main one being that the emergency specialist should become a woman. This would create a battle of the sexes between her and the slacker, Dr. Sheinfeld (we had borrowed his name from Lenny Kleinfeld), and there could be a hint of attraction between the two feuding doctors. We thought this was inspired. "Would they become an item?" I wanted to know.

"Not until the series is cancelled," Saul quickly replied, knowing that comedy, like drama, is based on conflict.

My job on the series was officially a "consultant." I was to be on the set to watch how the director, Peter Bonerz, did his job and was promised an episode to direct myself if we got picked up as a series. Peter was a Second City alum who had grown up in Milwaukee. He had been a regular on *The Bob Newhart Show* playing Bob's neurotic dentist. Now he was a successful sitcom director working for Norman Lear. Friendly and funny, he offered to show me the ropes, allowing me to watch him at work on the set and in the control room trailer where he called the show. "Go Camera One! Get ready Camera Three… Go Camera Three!"

The show would be taped before a live studio audience with four cameras, much in the same way that Pat Denny and I had shot *Bleacher Bums* for WTTW. Each episode would be rehearsed for a week, starting with a table read, then blocking the actors and setting up which camera would cover each moment. Then it would be taped twice before live audiences and pickups could be shot the next day as needed.

Elliott Gould was cast as the moonlighting Dr. Howard Sheinfeld, and Marcia Strassman, who had been a star of the series *Welcome Back, Kotter*, was cast as Dr. Eve Sheridan. They chose veteran actresses Lynne Moody and Conchata Ferrell (best known now as Berta the housekeeper on *Two and a Half Men*) to play our *E/R* nurses. The biggest surprise was their decision to cast two of Organic's actors in recurring roles: Shuko Akune as Maria the receptionist and Bruce (Moose) Young as her boyfriend, Fred the Chicago cop. Tall and striking, Shuko had joined our company during *Dr. Rat*. Her real name is Shirley and before becoming a company member, she had received excellent reviews in a production of *Josephine the Mouse Singer*. Thus, she graduated from being a mouse to a rat. Tommy Towles found out that Shirley's mother had called her Shuko as a nickname and he urged her to adopt it as her stage name. And the rest, as they say, is history. She was hilarious as the *E/R* receptionist who, we discovered during our emergency room research, often performed triage (deciding which patients should be seen first) even though she usually has absolutely no real medical training. The normally demure Shuko would scream, "Stay behind the white line!" to great comic effect.

The pilot, a two-part episode of *The Jeffersons*, had series star Sherman Hemsley visiting his niece Julie (Lynne Moody), an emergency room nurse.

He ends up having to wait while the sequences from our play fill up the majority of the 45-minute playing time. The banter between the two docs had been turned into sitcom-ese by head writers and executive producers Saul and Bernie.

One day I made a suggestion for a line change to maintain the reality of emergency room protocol only to have Saul take out a rubber stamp from his desk drawer and stamp my script. The stamp read "Who gives a shit?" I was now beginning to understand my role as a consultant on the television show.

Carolyn, Ron, and I had the best times hanging with Elliott Gould. I had loved him in *M*A*S*H*, *Bob & Carol & Ted & Alice*, and the under-appreciated *The Night They Raided Minsky's*. Elliott was in movie jail, a place that film people are sent after appearing in a bomb or two, and he was now making his debut on network television. This didn't seem to bother him – after all, work is work – and he was very down-to-earth, funny, and accessible, never playing the big star that he still is. In fact, he did his best to calm down Marcia Strassman.

A few months later, the pilots aired, and we watched the shows back home in Chicago. There was a theme song sung by Lou Rawls. The iffy jokes had been "sweetened" with canned laughter. It was all very slick. We were told that the network liked it and the overnight ratings had been quite good. CBS was ordering eleven episodes.

But there would be a few changes. Not surprisingly, the network had asked that Marcia Strassman be replaced by Mary McDonnell (who would be nominated for an Oscar® in 1991 for her wonderful performance in *Dances with Wolves*) and I was being bought out of my contractual right to direct one of the episodes. This stung a bit, and it made me wonder if this was Peter Bonerz's doing, as he ended up directing every episode of the show. Most likely, though, it was due to me making a pest out of myself during the shooting of the pilot. I was already being branded as "difficult." This was my first experience with the fact that movie studios and television networks would rather hire a dependable, easy-going player than a difficult one, no matter how brilliant. In films, the studios will put up with a diva actor or director as long as he or she is making them money, but as soon as that ceases to be the case, he or she is quickly given the boot. I was tossed out of *E/R* the television series, but Ron Berman carried on as the show's medical consultant and the Organic author/actors, including Carolyn, all got their chance to perform on the series. I was left to take care of the kids while she spent ten days in LA playing a woman who had been accidently shot in the arm and was treated by a new charismatic member of the cast named George Clooney. George had been brought in after a few weeks when the network felt the show needed younger characters to compete with *Who's the Boss?*, which was winning the timeslot on rival ABC. Clooney played Nurse Thor's nephew, Ace, an intern at the hospital. The son of Los Angeles television announcer Nick Clooney, George had all the women on the series swooning, and it was clear even then that he was a young man on his way up. Carolyn has told me that he was extremely nice and a pleasure to work with and we had both watched his meteoric rise to superstardom with great satisfaction. A few years later, when he was cast in a second show entitled *ER* (created by Michael Crichton and Steven Spielberg), George Clooney was the only one to mention our original series of the same name.

It always amazed me how similar the two shows were. Both were set in a Chicago hospital, but when I considered suing, my lawyer reminded me that I hadn't invented emergency rooms. As I had learned from the Tony D'Amato *Warp* lawsuits, whoever has the most money usually wins.

There is an old maxim that everything happens at once. While we were in the throes of production on the *E/R* TV series, something else was quickly taking shape. Every summer Carolyn and the kids and I would rent a cabin on scenic little Forest Lake in the Kettle Moraine area of southern Wisconsin. Our old lightshow friends Kathy and Jerry Fortier, who had by then moved to Milwaukee, had put us on to the cabin and for the next several years we vacationed there for two weeks of pure heaven – swimming, fishing, and hiking. We would sometimes invite family and friends and members of the company to join us, and one year, Carolyn's brother Roger was there with his girlfriend Laurie Anderson (not the singer).

One evening in the summer of 1983, as we were sitting around a barbecue on the shore of the beautiful lake, I remember getting into a conversation with them about how bored I was with all the vampire movies that were constantly being produced in those days. "Why doesn't someone make a Frankenstein movie?" I asked.

"Have you ever read *Herbert West—Reanimator*?" Laurie wanted to know. "It's by H.P. Lovecraft." Although I had read a great deal of Lovecraft, I had never heard of that particular story. "It's about medical students who bring the dead back to life," Laurie told me. "You should check it out." I was intrigued. When we got back to Chicago, I started hitting the bookstores looking for this story but couldn't locate it anywhere. Finally, on a visit to the local library, I found it listed in the card catalogue. It turned out that the only copy of this story was in the Special Collections of the big central library downtown. I was told that I would have to fill out a postcard requesting to read the story, which I did, and months later I received a reply telling me that although I could not check the book out, I would be permitted to come to the old library on Randolph Street and read the story there.

When I arrived, it was like the Thatcher memorial library scene from *Citizen Kane*. I was led to a large table in an upstairs reading room. The librarian then opened a tin box and placed the book in front of me, but unlike the large tome in Orson Welles' film, it was a worn little wreck of a book, its spine held together with masking tape. As I opened it and turned the pages, the pulpy paper literally began to crumble in my hands. I quickly asked the librarian if I could Xerox the story. Although she was clearly not happy about this, she agreed. I brought the copies home and that night finally read the story.

It turned out that there were actually six stories, each no more than five pages long. Lovecraft had written them in 1922 as a serial for a pulp magazine called *Home Brew*. He also hated the stories. Why? Because he had been paid to write them. Over the years, as I learned more about the short sad life of the author, I would better understand this, discovering that he viewed himself as an amateur writer and that the definition of amateur means doing something for pleasure. Since he had been paid to write *Herbert West*, it became, in his mind a "work-for-hire." He had received filthy lucre ($20) and from then on, he spoke disparagingly about the *Herbert West* stories, if he spoke of them at all. Yet I found the tales themselves to be exceptional. Unlike much of Lovecraft's slow internalized ramblings, these were fast-moving and action packed. They were also incredibly shocking. They told the story of young medical student, Herbert West, and his unnamed assistant/narrator and their catastrophic experiments reanimating the dead. Each story usually ended with West shrugging and saying, "I guess he just wasn't fresh enough." The tales follow the two med students from the turn of the century to the 1920s, a twenty-year span, their experiments becoming more outlandish as they go along. At one point, West reanimates both the head and body of a fellow scientist only to have the decapitated monstrosity pursue him, carrying his own head in a hatbox with holes cut out for his eyes. It was ghastly and hilarious at the same time, and I felt as if I had struck gold.

My initial thought was to do it as a serial, like the stories, and I teamed up with Bill Norris to write the first episode as a half-hour program based on Lovecraft's opening tale. Like the story, the episode was set at the turn of the twentieth century and involved the med students digging up a recently buried corpse and attempting to bring it back to life in a deserted farmhouse. Bill's caustic sense of humor was a perfect match for Herbert West, and the character ended up with all the best lines. I sent it to Pat Denny at WTTW and waited for his reaction. He quickly got back to me telling me that Ronald Reagan's attack on public television had decimated their budget, and as much as he liked the story, he knew that they would never do it there. The idea of *Herbert West—Reanimator* premiering on public television now seems totally nuts. What the hell was I thinking? Because of our success on television, however, first with *Bleacher Bums* and now *E/R*, I somehow couldn't imagine the project as a film. We were told that half hours were only for sitcoms, and if we wanted to sell it as a pilot it would need to be an hour long. When I relayed this to Bill, he told me that he didn't have the time to keep working on it. I think he realized that this project really had no future on network television and there was no cable TV back then. Today, with the success of such horror-based shows as *The Walking Dead*, our idea might have worked but, as Carolyn likes to tell me, I'm always fifteen minutes ahead of my time.

I contacted my old friend Dennis Paoli. Luckily, he and his wife Heidi were in town visiting Dennis' family for Thanksgiving. We met at a restaurant and discussed the idea of his helping me adapt our script into an hour-long format for television. "We can add the second Lovecraft story," I suggested. Dennis was intrigued and so was Heidi. "I have a good feeling about this," I remember her saying. After Dennis read the Lovecraft stories and our half hour adaptation, he had some questions. "Why are we setting this in the past?" he wanted to know. "It would be much more immediate if set in the present day, and cheaper too." I quickly agreed. Today I'm always taking heat from Lovecraft purists who believe that his stories need to be set in the era he wrote them; the 1920s and '30s. I firmly believe there is no reason to do so. The concepts are not dated, they're just as fresh and disturbing as the day he wrote them; in fact, even now, Lovecraft still seems way ahead of his time.

The other suggestion that Dennis had was that we needed to add a girl. One of the oddest things about Lovecraft's already odd tales is their almost total lack of female characters. So Meg Halsey was born, the beautiful daughter of the medical school dean and girlfriend of the story's narrator, whom we named Dan Cain. In Lovecraft's second story, Dean Halsey dies and is reanimated; in our version, his daughter Meg is on the case believing (correctly) that her boyfriend and his strange new roommate Herbert West are to blame. An hour-long script was created, and I sent it to my only Hollywood friend, Bob Greenberg. "I like it," he told me, "But it should be a movie."

This knocked me back on my heels.

"What about television?" I wanted to know.

"No one is going to put this on television," Greenberg replied. "But horror movies are always in demand. In fact, no matter how badly they turn out, the investors always get their money back." I found this a bit insulting but appreciated Greenberg's frankness. He went on to remind me that many prominent directors had begun their careers with horror. Francis Ford Coppola's first film, *Dementia 13*, had been done for Roger Corman. We were at the beginning of the VHS home video craze and horror movies were jumping off the shelves of the new video rental stores that were popping up on every corner. "You need to expand the script to ninety minutes," was Greenberg's final suggestion. Disheartened, I put the project on hold.

I soon got a call from a very excited Greenberg, "I showed your script to a producer, and he wants to do it," he said. Then he added the phrase that every prospective filmmaker always yearns to hear, "And he's got money!"

The producer was Brian Yuzna. He had placed an ad in *Daily Variety* looking for a director, and Bob had applied for the job. Brian had raised a budget of $800,000 from his friends and relatives in North Carolina to make a film, but they weren't happy with the script they had and so, rather than return the money, Brian had asked Bob if he knew of any other projects. Bob showed him Dennis' and my script, now entitled simply *Reanimator*.

"So you'll direct it?" I asked Bob.

"I can if you want," was his answer, "But I'm ready to step aside if you want to direct." And then he added, "But I want to be there as a producer, and I think you'll be grateful for my help. You've never directed a movie, and Brian has never produced one." I immediately agreed and was already beyond grateful. Whoever heard of someone with a chance to direct his first feature film offering to step aside for a friend? Soon I was on the phone with Brian Yuzna. A bright loquacious man, he told me how much he had enjoyed the script. Of course, it would need to be expanded. "We can add the third story" I said, explaining that Lovecraft wrote the original story in six installments.

"No," Brian responded, "Throw in all the stories."

This shocked me. "But what if we want to do a sequel?" I asked.

"There won't be a sequel unless you knock the audience on their asses," he told me. "So we need to throw in everything and the kitchen sink."

"Okay. . ."

"And one more thing," Brian added, "I think we need to add a hyphen in the title after the *Re-* so it doesn't look like *Rean imator*." And so the re-spelled *Re-Animator* was now becoming a reality.

Dennis and I immediately went back to work on the script. We added a character that we named Dr. Hill, based on Lovecraft's decapitated scientist who West brings back to life by injecting both the severed head and headless body with his reagent. Of course, headless Hill would have to kidnap the girlfriend. But what would he do with her after he has her?

One night I got a long-distance call from New York. I knew it was Dennis as we did most of our work on the phone late at night when the long-distance rates were lower. He was laughing uncontrollably.

"I think I just wrote the world's first visual pun," he told me.

CHAPTER 23

Merkins

Brian Yuzna came to Chicago to see *E/R* and we finally met in person. Brian was tall and thin with longish hair and a mustache. He reminded me of a young Ted Turner. "Well, you certainly can direct actors," he told me after the show. The unspoken half of his sentence was, "But can you direct a movie?" Thank God he took the leap of faith and hired me to direct *Re-Animator*. My fee was $10,000, which seemed like a small fortune compared to what I was making at the theater (even with the raise). Brian also gave me 2% of the profits. Our script was purchased for $5,000, which was split three ways between Dennis, Bill Norris, and me. We also got 1.5% of the profits.

"Don't expect to see any profits," Bob Greenberg counseled me. "You always have to give away your first movie." In the spring of 1984, I was flown to Los Angeles to meet with Brian and the first members of our crew, which Bob Greenberg was assembling. I stayed with Brian in his rental home on the top of Lookout Mountain in Laurel Canyon. It had clearly been a bachelor's pad as the walls were bright red and the furniture was black leather. Brian was living there with his beautiful wife Cathy, who reminded me of actress Andie MacDowell, and their two kids: his son Conan was seven, and his daughter Zoe, who was four. They ran around playing while we discussed the movie, and Brian didn't seem to mind that our conversation often included talk of decapitation and the re-animated dead.

I was soon introduced to Tony Doublin. He had been working with Bob as a partner in Magic Lantern, his special effects company, and was a master of practical effects, which meant effects that can be done live on a stage while shooting, as opposed to optical effects, which are done in post-production. Ninety-nine percent of our effects were practical as we really couldn't afford opticals. Most involved figuring out ways to deal with the fact that Dr. Hill walked around carrying his own head for the film's final half hour. Tony was a diamond in the rough – craggy with a booming laugh. He proved himself to be invaluable as he had done every possible effect in the many low-budget movies he had worked on and could dream up even more. We decided early on to avoid the obvious solution of building fake shoulders on an actor to make him appear headless as this would result in his arms looking too long and his legs too short. Instead, Tony came up with what he called the "Fozzy the Bear" solution, named after Jim Henson's Muppet character, in which the actor would stick his head through a fake torso and could still use his own arms to make it appear he was holding his own head.

We went through the whole script discussing each effect, and Bob Greenberg told me that storyboards would be needed ASAP to make it clear how each effect would be shot. Finally, my art school training would pay off as I told the group that I could do them myself. I also showed Tony an idea for Herbert West's re-animating reagent. It was a chemical called luminol and I had seen it at an Ace Hardware store in Chicago. It was a tube of liquid with a glass capsule inside that, when broken, would cause the liquid to glow a bright chartreuse green. It was designed to be used as a flare if you had a blow-out on the road. I gave one to Tony and he immediately activated it. "I'll have to check this out and see how it photographs," he said, "But it's pretty cool."

I returned to Chicago jazzed. I had already begun researching the world in which the film took place – the hospital morgue. I started out by contacting the medical school at the University of Illinois and set up an appointment to meet with the head of the Pathology Department, but as soon as I mentioned I was working on a horror film, I was quickly shown the door. I mentioned this to Ron Berman, and he advised me to go to the Cook County Morgue and the other local hospitals and speak directly to the pathologists themselves. "Will they talk to me?" I asked him.

"They'll talk to anyone," he replied, "They're the loneliest guys in the world."

The next thing I knew, I was meeting Dr. Robert Stein, the medical examiner of the Cook County Morgue. He was a small grandfatherly man in his early seventies who had a reputation for being blunt and direct. Above his desk was a plaque which read, "Let conversation cease, let laughter flee. This is the place where death delights to help the living." It was also the place that had the worst smell I had ever experienced in my life. The sickly-sweet smell of death permeated every square inch of the place. When I told Stein that I was working on a horror movie, he suggested that I shoot the film at the morgue. "You can even use the bodies," he told me, "as long as you don't show their faces." I smiled weakly, the idea of spending weeks in that stench boggling my mind.

"Let me give you the twenty-five-cent tour," Stein said cheerfully as he guided me into the morgue itself. He first showed me a display of sad clown paintings by local serial killer John Wayne Gacy that would get Stein into trouble a year later for their inappropriateness. He was used to controversy, having been nearly fired for his decision to autopsy the body of Mayor Richard J. Daley against the wishes of his family. Stein led me down a corridor lined with large walk-in refrigerators. He threw open the doors one by one. Each refrigerator held several gurneys piled up with bodies, some stacked two or three thick. Men, women, children, and even babies. There were at least thirty to forty bodies in each refrigerator. I had assumed that the corpses would be in the neat little drawers you saw in the movies, but this was not the case.

David Gale as Dr. Hill (*above*) and Jeffrey Combs as Herbert West (*below*) pictured on French publicity stills for *Re-Animator*.

above (from left): Barbara Crampton, Jeffrey Combs, Bruce Abbott, me, and Brian Yuzna on the set of *Re-Animator*.
opposite top: Directing Barbara Crampton and Bruce Abbott.
opposite center: The simple costume design solution that brought the decapitated body of Dr. Carl Hill to life.
opposite bottom left: Another gallon of stage blood is spilled as a scene is filmed on the morgue set of *Re-Animator*.
opposite bottom right: A team of four crew members help David Gale perform the role of Dr. Carl Hill's disembodied head.
below: Filming the "University of Zurich Institute of Medicine" opening scene in *Re-Animator*.

OPEN THIS SIDE
30100
IVORY
02871

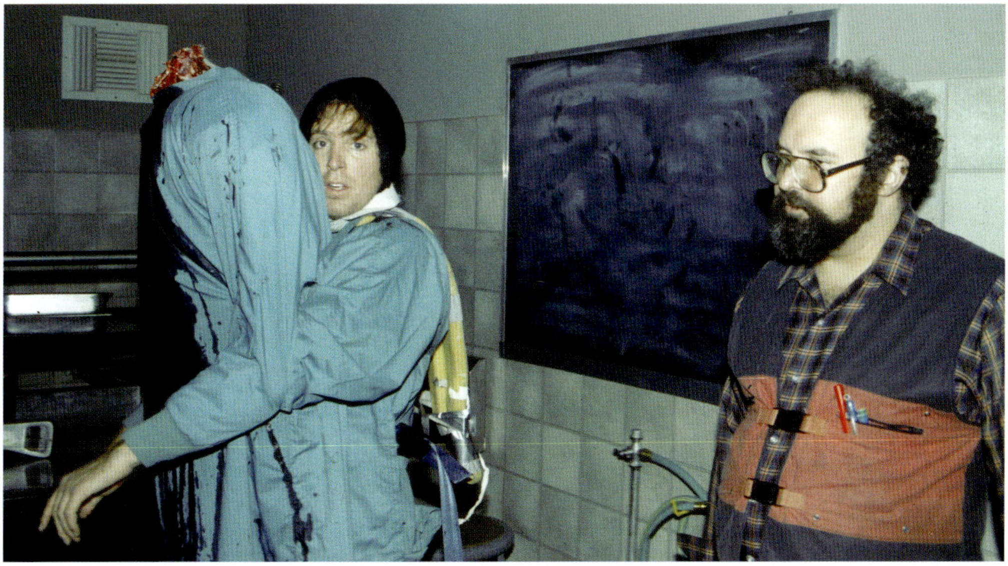

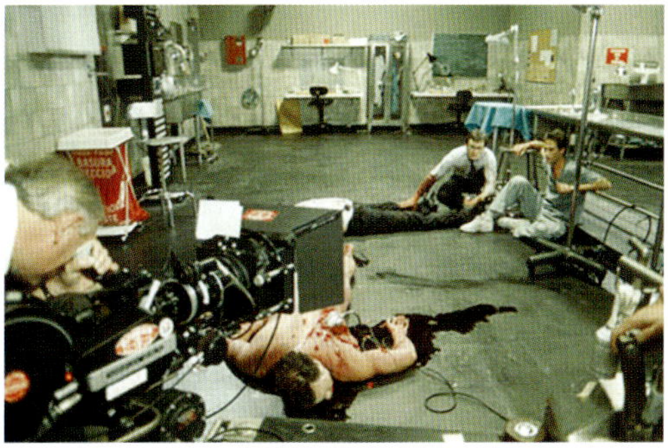

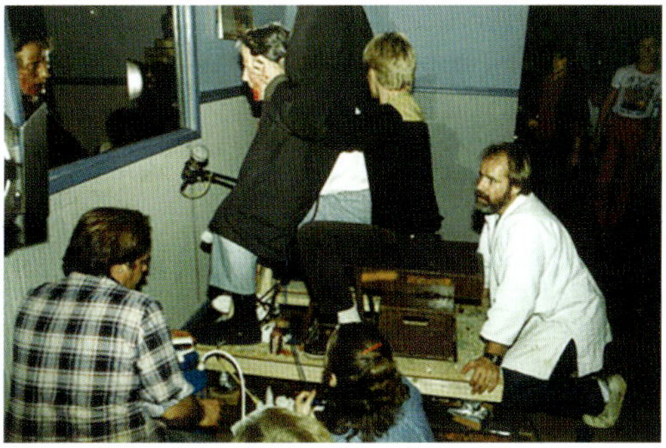

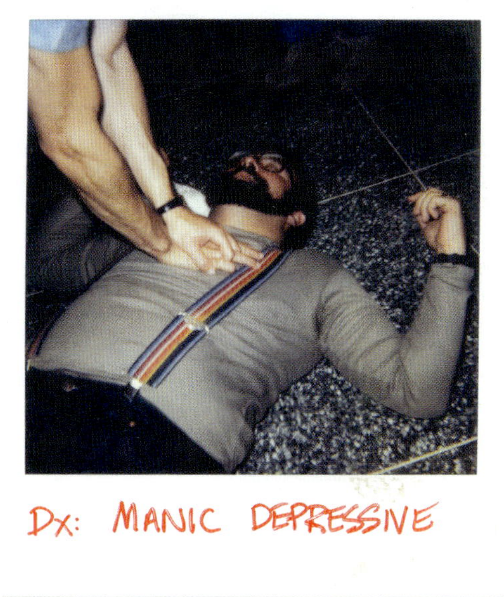

top left: A polaroid shot of me with Brian Yuzna during the filming of *Re-Animator*.

top right: Rehearsing a scene on the set of *Re-Animator*.

above: Sitting with Brian Yuzna (next to me on the sofa) and the crew to strategize *Re-Animator*'s tight shooting schedule.

right: Framing a shot with DP Mac Ahlberg (pointing).

opposite page: Directing Jeffrey Combs as Herbert West.

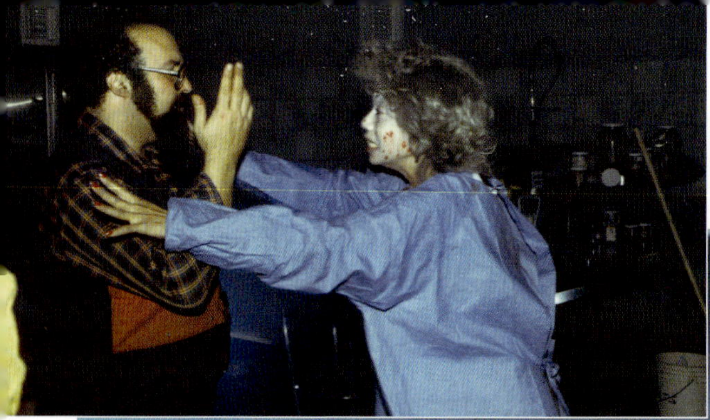

left and below:
Prepping and shooting *Re-Animator*'s final scenes of an experiment gone very wrong.

below: Working through a scene in *Re-Animator* with Bruce Abbott and Gerry Black.

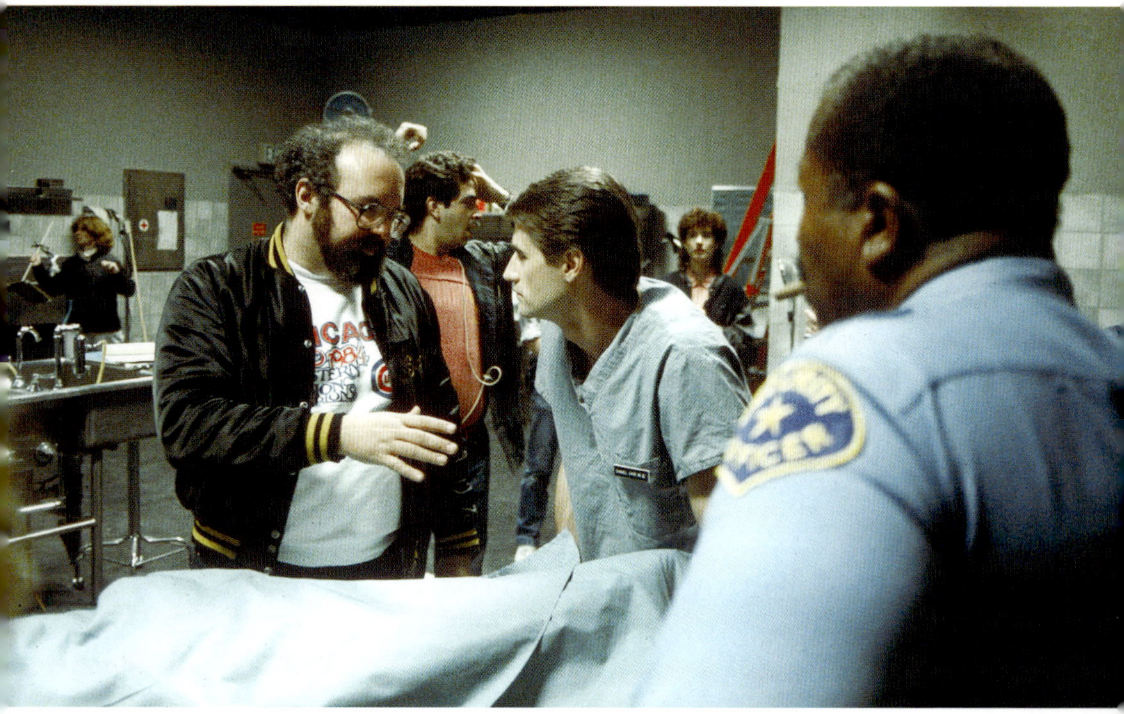

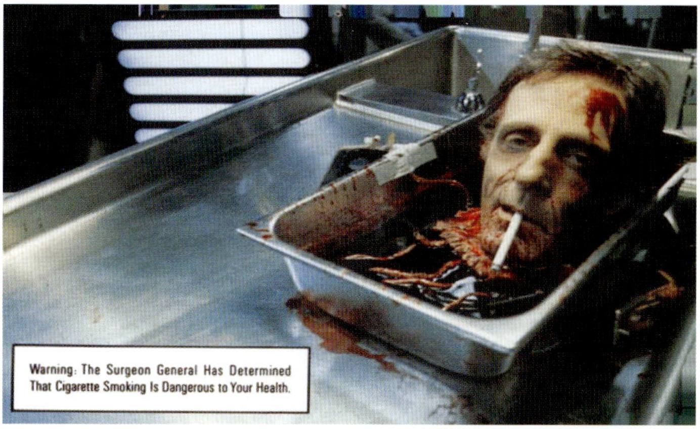

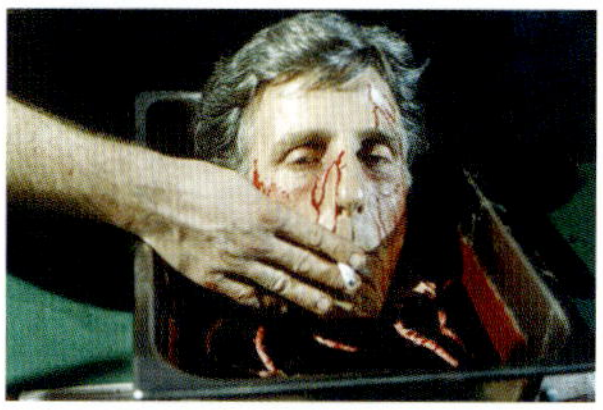

above and top right (both photos): Behind-the-scenes fun and hijinks with David Gale (and his head) on the set of *Re-Animator*.

right: With Brian Yuzna (center) and David Gale.

below: With "Rufus" on the set of *Re-Animator*.

bottom: Carolyn and me, September 1985.

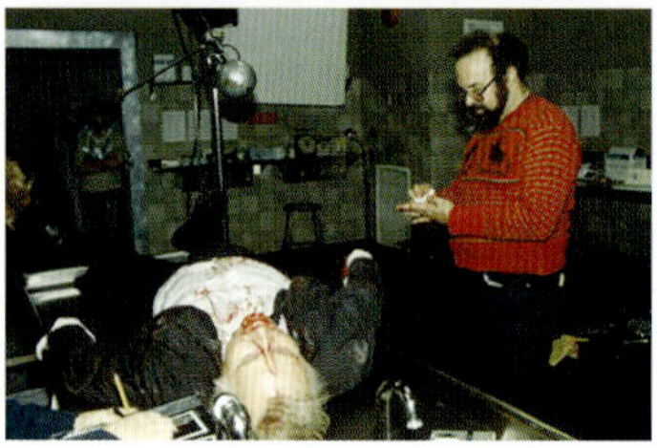

top: Filming a tracking sequence on the hospital set for *Re-Animator*.

above: Blood on my hands! Alongside Robert Sampson as Dean Halsey.

right: Lunch break with Barbara Crampton during the making of *Re-Animator*.

left: Directing *Re-Animator*'s socially awkward dinner scene with David Gale (lower left) and Robert Sampson (center).

below: Getting ready to saw a skull open with David Gale as Dr. Hill.

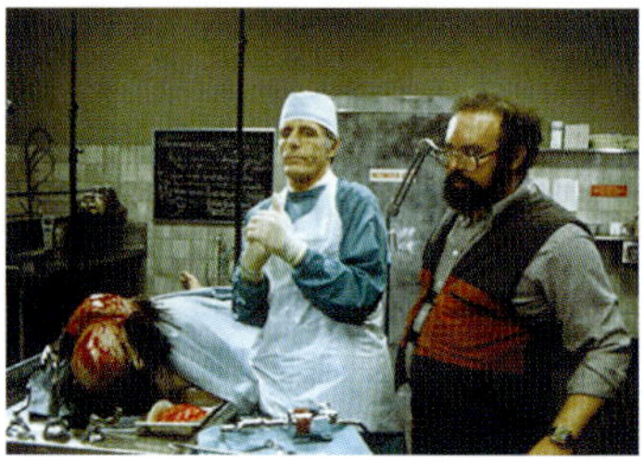

They weren't even in zippered body bags, but lay there cold and naked, some half covered by black plastic garbage bags. I saw patients who had died in surgery, the tubes from the operations still in place. Why bother to remove them? The bodies looked nothing like the corpses you see in movies. They were a variety of colors. Many had large purple markings on their backs where the blood settled after death. I learned that this is called lividity. Others were bright yellow (jaundice) or dark red or blue (pulmonary dysfunction) and a few were almost as white as ivory from loss of blood. Stein flung open door after door until we reached the end of the corridor. He looked at me to see if I was still standing. "You made it," he said laughing, and turned to his assistant, "I think he's ready to see the Rose Room." The assistant laughed and nodded.

"The Rose Room?" I asked.

"That's where we keep the ones who have been dead for weeks before their bodies are found." I was getting my first taste of the black humor that distinguishes pathologists, a necessary survival skill if you're going to work in a morgue.

My second trip to Los Angeles involved meeting Bob Burns, whom Bob Greenberg had asked to be our production designer. "You're lucky to have him," Bob told me. "He did *The Texas Chain Saw Massacre*, *The Hills Have Eyes*, and *The Howling*." Burns was a bearded little gnome with crooked teeth and was prone to cackling at his own jokes. He told me in his strong Texas accent that he liked the script and I told him about my visit to the Cook County Morgue. He asked me if I could go back and photograph it so he could use the pictures for reference.

* * *

When I went back to visit Dr. Stein, I discovered that the morgue had been completely remodeled. No longer dark and creepy with stained and cracked plaster walls, it was now spotlessly clean with shiny beige tiles covering the walls and a new air conditioning system that could replace the air every ten minutes (although it didn't seem to help much in removing the stench). I took pictures and sent them to Burns. When I got back to Los Angeles, I asked Bob Burns to show me his production concepts. He showed me the photos of the morgue I had sent him. I was confused. "What's the morgue going to look like?" I wanted to know.

"Like this," he said, holding up a photo.

"Don't you have any drawings?" I asked him.

"I don't draw," was his reply.

I was completely taken aback. A production designer that doesn't draw? "How did you do *Texas Chain Saw*?"

"I went to a slaughterhouse and found some cattle bones and the rest I just scrounged from here and there," he replied with his crooked-tooth grin. I went to Bob Greenberg and asked him what he thought.

"He's the best in the business," Bob told me. "Don't worry about it."

We needed to find a director of photography, and Brian decided to screen all the successful horror films of the last five years to help us in the selection process. I think he also wanted to make sure that I was aware of the state-of-the-art and what had worked in the past. Our goal was to find a way to top it – to separate our film from the hundreds of other horror films made each year. We sat in his red living room watching films on his enormous projection TV screen. We saw *The Evil Dead*, *The Driller Killer*, and dozens more that I have long since forgotten. We watched Polanski's masterpiece *Rosemary's Baby*, and I was taken with the extremely subjective way the film was shot, making the audience feel that they were Rosemary. I ended up watching it again and again, studying it to the point that I now tell people that *Rosemary's Baby* was my film school.

One of the other films we watched was *The Being*, shot by a DP named Robert Ebinger. We liked the look of the film and decided to meet with him. Bob Ebinger was an enthusiastic young man who loved our script and felt he could do a good job shooting it. But Bob Greenberg had some reservations, "He hasn't shot that many features and with a first-time director and a first-time producer, it would be helpful if we had someone with a little more experience," he told us. But we all liked Ebinger, and the last thing I wanted was for the cameraman to be telling me how to shoot the picture, so I was relieved when Brian decided to hire him despite Bob's objections.

I had brought along my newly-drawn storyboards and once again we went through the entire film, talking about how each of the effects would be done. Finally, Tony Doublin asked the question that all of us were afraid to ask. "Brian, when are we shooting this picture? I really need to know because I'm being approached about other projects."

There was a long pause. Finally, Brian answered, "Between Thanksgiving and Christmas." We all looked at each other. This was a momentous announcement. *Re-Animator* had just been green-lit! Then it struck us; here it was, mid-August, and we'd be shooting in less than three months. We had better get started pronto.

Brian had made a deal with Charles Band, whose new company, Empire Pictures, would distribute the film in exchange for providing postproduction facilities. Band offered us his casting director, Anthony Barnao, a large guy with shoulder length curls and a winning personality. Soon we were auditioning actors for the various roles. I was disappointed that I couldn't use my actors from Organic, as the production couldn't afford to fly them to California and put them up in hotels. But I was able to cast Carolyn as Dr. Harrod, the emergency room doctor. Harrod bookends the story, first appearing in a scene at the beginning of the film in which medical student Dan Cain ignores her instructions to stop CPR on a patient that she has already pronounced dead. “A good doctor knows when to stop,” she testily tells him. This scene had been added at the last minute, as we felt we needed to give the audience a reason for immediately liking our hero. Showing his idealism and willingness to go above and beyond the call of duty to save a patient’s life did the trick.

Many viewers think that Herbert West is the film’s hero, but we realized that the audience needed a protagonist that they could relate to; a normal guy who reacts the way they would react and asks questions about the things that they want to know. I had learned the importance of this from my kids when reading them their bedtime stories. I’d begin with, “Once upon a time, there was a princess…” And they would immediately ask, “Can I be her?”

I also had learned that it is essential for the protagonist to grow as a character and learn something. The events of the story must cause him to transform, and he needs to be a completely different person at the end of the story than he was at the beginning. In *Re-Animator*, and in Lovecraft’s original story, Herbert West really doesn’t change. For better and worse, he is always the same. Although his is the flashier role and the one that audiences remember most vividly, it is actually Dan Cain who is the film’s protagonist. If they don’t care about him, there is simply no movie.

At one of the first casting sessions, a young actor named Jeffrey Combs appeared. Slight and with large eyes, I asked him if he were familiar with H.P. Lovecraft, and Jeffrey nodded. Later, I was to discover that he thought Lovecraft was a boat. He was there to read for Herbert West and at first, I didn’t think he was right for the part as Lovecraft describes West as being a blond and Jeffrey has dark hair, but as soon as he began to read, I knew we had found our man. I felt an instant rapport with him and, as soon as he left the room, I turned to Brian and Anthony. “Cast him,” I said, and we did. Bruce Abbott looks like the ideal Lovecraft hero, bright, unassuming and appealing. We cast Robert Sampson to play Dean Halsey. Distinguished and good looking with silver hair, Bob really went to town in the scenes where Halsey has been turned into a re-animated corpse, drooling and out of control. It was as if he had waited all his life to find a role that would let him go nuts. David Gale became our villainous Dr. Carl Hill. Tall and angular with a protruding jaw and a deep imposing voice, David reminded me of a younger Boris Karloff, and his New England accent was perfect for the Arkham, Massachusetts setting. “I hope you don’t take this the wrong way,” I told him, “But you have a great face for horror movies.”

But what about our ingénue? Who would play Megan Halsey, the love of Dan Cain’s life who is hideously defiled by a living headless corpse?

When casting began, many actresses refused to even audition for this role as it not only required nudity, but also participating in a sex act that could only be politely described as necrophilia. But to our relief, a willing actress was finally found. Our joy was short-lived as a few days later she dropped out of the film, deciding that this was not a wise career move. For the life of me, I can't even remember her name.

We scrambled to recast the part as shooting was scheduled to begin in two weeks, and that is when Anthony Barnao, our casting director, introduced me to the astonishingly beautiful and supremely talented Barbara Crampton. I explained the demands of the role to her and told her that it would involve full frontal nudity. Barbara nodded and then asked me how I intended to shoot the nude scene. I stammered as I tried to explain, and then remembered my storyboards. She studied them carefully and finally nodded – but the deal was not to be closed before several intense days of negotiations with her agent.

How long would she be shown onscreen in full frontal nudity? Five seconds. It would also be a "closed set," meaning that only the most necessary crew members would be present and there would be no stills photographer allowed. Her contract was twice as long as anyone else's, as half of it involved the very particular rules for filming "the scene."

In our efforts to find something to separate our film from the thousands of other horror films made each year, we had realized that the "head giving head" scene was the central image of the film, the one that audiences would talk about and, we hoped, never forget. Brian hired artist William Stout to create a poster for the film featuring this scene, although the blonde heroine is shown wearing a see-through babydoll negligee as Dr. Hill holds his severed head in one hand and a syringe of glowing green reagent in the other.

After my tour of the Cook County Morgue, I was adamant that the re-animated corpses be naked. There was some concern about this, as Merchant-Ivory's otherwise demure film *A Room with a View* had just been denied an R rating because of one fleeting glimpse of Julian Sands' penis in a scene where he is discovered skinny dipping. Full frontal female nudity was allowed because, as the MPAA explained in frank anatomical terms, the female genitalia is internal and not visible, but with men it was clearly another story. It's hard to believe now, but at the time we were trying very hard to get *Re-Animator* an R rating. A plan was hatched in which we would cover the male genitalia with a little device known as a merkin. This is essentially a pubic wig and has existed since the Middle Ages, when women would shave themselves as an attempt to avoid lice and employed the merkins to cover that fact. Our DP would do his best to frame out the nude actors to avoid showing them below the waist but, if it was unavoidable, we'd employ the merkins. Boy, were we naive.

CHAPTER 24

Re-Animated

We put together our crew.

Many of them had just finished shooting another low-budget movie for a young director. They said that the movie had been a mess, and the director was a jerk who yelled all the time and didn't know what he was doing. A week or two into prepping *Re-Animator*, they had attended a cast and crew screening and returned singing a completely different tune, amazed at how well that film had turned out. The movie was *The Terminator*, and the director was James Cameron. Rob Roda had been a second assistant director on *The Terminator* but would be promoted to my First A.D. "He'll work his ass off to please you," Bob Greenberg had advised. And he did.

This was the first time since we had been married that Carolyn and I were apart for an extended time. She would join me for her hospital scenes during the first week of shooting, and I counted the days until I would be with her again. I discovered that pre-production is the most stressful part of moviemaking as you try to plan for everything that can possibly go wrong. Once you're on set shooting and dealing with the what-is (as opposed to the what-ifs), things are much, much easier.

I insisted that I rehearse with the actors for a week before we began shooting. We approached it like a play, going through the scenes in order. The actors were pleasantly surprised that we were doing this; I learned from them that in film and television, rehearsing in advance of shooting was very seldom done. Everyone usually just shows up on the first day as strangers and, as scenes are usually shot out of order, how does an actor know how to gauge their performance and how it fits into the whole? They also have no idea what the other actors will be bringing to their roles. Some feel that the spontaneity created by not knowing these things is helpful, but after the first take most of that spontaneity is gone. Coming from theater I knew the importance of rehearsal and how actors can use it to dig deeper into their roles and make amazing discoveries about their characters. I've found it so helpful that I always make it a part of my pre-production process.

Barbara Crampton graciously let us meet at her home to rehearse. I learned that she and Jeffrey Combs, Bruce Abbott, David Gale, and Bob Sampson all had strong theater backgrounds, and so we all spoke the same language and got along well. By rehearsing in advance, we were saving valuable time on the set. With a mere eighteen days to make our movie, you don't want to get into a long discussion with an actor about motivation while your entire crew stands around with their thumbs up their butts.

After our rehearsal, I pulled out a joint and offered it to the actors as we often did at Organic, and they looked at each other and politely refused. I then realized that the last thing an actor wants is to believe his director will be stoned on the set. As directing is about making decisions, and making them quickly, a clear head is essential. The one time I snuck off to have a few hits of a joint during shooting turned out to be a huge mistake. I found myself struggling to keep up with the pace and demands of production and I have never done it again.

The night before we started shooting, Bob Greenberg took me out for sushi, and I spent a restless night thinking about all the strange little creatures I had just ingested.

Our first day of production took place on location in the house that Dan Cain will share with his strange new roommate Herbert West. Things moved along at a pretty decent clip and we made our day, which means we completed shooting all the scenes scheduled. I always feel like a major league pitcher when directing, and making the day is like winning the game.

The next day I was surprised when Peter Bonerz, the director of the *E/R* sitcom, showed up on the set. I'm not sure how he even knew I was making a movie, let alone where we were shooting, but there he was. He wanted to know who was producing the film and I introduced him to Brian. I told him it was a very low-budget affair, but he asked if I would recommend him as a director for any future projects. This amazed me because he had clearly not helped me with my shot at directing an episode of *E/R*. I've since learned that the entertainment business is a very small world where everybody knows everybody, but the bigger lesson was that even a successful television director like Peter would much rather direct a feature film, even if it is just a little low-budget horror movie.

After the second day of shooting, we all headed over to a screening room on Highland Avenue to watch dailies. The room held about fifty seats but most of them were empty. Some of the crew, including my director of photography Bob Ebinger and my editor Lee Percy, were there. "Where are the actors?" I asked Greenberg.

"The producers usually don't want them to see dailies," he told me. "They're afraid that the leading lady won't like the way her hair looks and will want you to reshoot all of her scenes." They had waited for me before starting the projector but as soon as I took my seat between Greenberg and Lee Percy, an older man in his fifties sitting at the back of the room pushed a button on an intercom to tell the projectionist to start rolling. Bob nudged me, "That's Albert Band."

"He's distributing the film?" I asked.

"No, his son is," whispered Bob, "The one he's talking to."

I couldn't believe my eyes. Albert was talking to a baby-faced kid with shoulder-length hair who looked like he was a teenage pop star. Next to Charlie sat a beautiful blonde. Charlie fondled her knee as he conferred with his father. After the screening, Charlie, Albert, and the blonde headed for the elevators. Bob and I followed at a distance, hoping to get a sense of what they thought of the dailies. When we were close enough to hear them, I realized that they were not speaking English. I looked to Bob, confused.

"Italian," he muttered through barely moving lips. "Charlie grew up there." Then the elevator arrived. Charlie, Albert, and the blonde got in, the doors closed, and they were gone.

The next day Brian Yuzna informed me that Charlie wanted to replace Bob Ebinger, our director of photography. I couldn't believe it.

"He says everything is too dark."

"What should we do?" I asked Brian.

"Get rid of him, I guess. He wants us to use one of his guys." His guy was Mac Ahlberg, the urbane Swedish DP who shot all of Empire's films and who had directed tons of films himself, including the international hit *I, a Woman*, that my friends and I had seen while playing hooky from high school. Bob Ebinger finished out the week, shooting all of the emergency room sequences at a hospital in Altadena. The hospital had been damaged by an earthquake and was deemed too dangerous for medical staff and patients, so it now was used only as a location for films (clearly not too dangerous for us). I should point out that every scene that Ebinger shot ended up in the finished film.

Mac took over as Director of Photography. He also brought along his own camera crew, so it was like starting over. The first time I met him was on the set, a situation that was awkward at best. But Mac immediately put me at ease. "I'm here to do whatever you want," he told me. Mac was a handsome man in his fifties with snow white hair that reached his collar. His partner Julie always told me she thought he looked like Phil Collins, but I always thought he looked more like a slightly younger version of Pope John Paul II. Like the Pope, Mac always dressed in white: white shirt, white pants, and white shoes, although sometimes he wore a tan suede jacket. Very dapper, with a Swedish accent and, I would soon learn, a wonderful sense of humor.

The first scene Mac shot was the one in the basement where Dan discovers West being attacked by the re-animated cat. The hand-held camera, aided by a swinging overhead light, gave the scene a sense of chaos and urgency despite the fact that there really is no cat at all. The actors pointed and yelled, smashing at the imaginary beast with a baseball bat and a croquet mallet as the effects technicians yanked on monofilament to send props and set dressing flying as if the cat had knocked them over. It was a baptism of fire for Mac, who had to make sure that his own shadow would not be visible by the swinging light. The whole scene ended up being carefully choreographed for actors, effects crew, and camera. After we finished the shot, Mac immediately started the next set-up (or "up-set" as he liked to call them). He asked Dennis Bishop, his cowboy-hat-wearing gaffer, how long it would take to hang a light. "Five minutes," Dennis told him.

"Nothing takes five minutes!" Mac shouted in response, "Except my sex life."

It soon became clear to Mac that I knew very little of the basics of filmmaking. When I suggested a camera position, he told me that I was "crossing the line." I looked down at the floor to see what line he was referring to. "It won't cut with what we just shot," Mac quietly explained, but I still didn't get it.

"Of course it will," I told him, "You just glue the two pieces of film together." Mac rolled his eyes and his camera crew laughed. He was trying to explain screen direction to me and here I was arguing about it. Later he took me aside and showed me how important it was that if the actor is on the right side of the frame in one shot, he needs to remain on the right in subsequent shots. "It's like grammar," he patiently taught me. "Once you know it, you can sometimes break the rules, but you have to know the rules first." Mac was my first and best film teacher and I soon christened him "The Professor."

Mac loved to place lights in strange places: under tables, in closets and drawers. Once I asked him where the light was supposed to be coming from. "Where's the music coming from?" was his reply. Sometimes I would explain to him what I had in mind for a shot and he would let me know that what I was asking for was very complicated (and time consuming) and that, if I planned to intercut it with another shot, it might be simpler to break it down into two shots. Because of my theater background, I preferred long takes that could be used without cutting, believing, as I still do, that cuts can disrupt the power of the moment. I also used dolly shots so often that Mac soon christened me "Orson Rails."

Everyone seemed happy with the dailies. There is an old Hollywood maxim that nothing looks better than the dailies and nothing looks worse than the first cut. But I was intoxicated by the excitement of making a real movie. I broke the long-standing rule and allowed the actors to watch dailies with me, if they so chose, thinking that it could help with their performances. I remember sitting next to Jeffrey Combs in the little screening room, both of us unable to stop laughing, giddy with the images we were creating together. More and more members of the crew started showing up to see the dailies until all fifty seats were always filled and it was standing room only. Bob Greenberg told me it was a good sign that the crew was getting excited about the film they were making.

We soon moved from the basement set to the morgue set, and I was amazed to see that Bob Burns had duplicated the Cook County Morgue exactly. There have been rumors that we shot *Re-Animator* in a real morgue, and I think it's due to a combination of Burns' skill and Dr. Stein's invitation to film in his actual morgue. We used over thirty gallons of stage blood during the shoot. "More blood!" became my mantra and soon everyone's feet were sticking to the linoleum floors due to the corn syrup base of the fake plasma. "Haven't you ever heard that less is more?" Mac asked me one day.

"I've heard the expression, but never could understand it." I told him. "'More is more' makes more sense to me."

"More is more. I like that," Mac mused.

"I think your motto should be 'more is not enough,'" chimed in Barbara Crampton. She may have had something there.

When the day came to finally film the "head gives head" scene, the set was cleared of all unnecessary personnel, per our agreement with Barbara, and she finally appeared from make-up wearing a plaid woolen robe. She took it off and started to lie down on the metal autopsy table, "It's freezing!" she cried and quickly jumped off, throwing on her robe. The cold steel was heated with hair dryers for several minutes to warm it up for her. As we started filming the full-frontal scene, Barbara began to count out loud, "One one thousand, two one thousand...." to time the five seconds she had agreed to do. I had to remind her that the contract specified five seconds of *cut footage* and that we were not limited in how long we could shoot. She laughed and the rest of the scene went off without a hitch.

Our first inkling of how powerful the sequence would prove to be occurred during the screening of the dailies the next day. David Gale, who brilliantly played the villainous Dr. Hill, had brought his wife to the screening and apparently had never discussed the scene with her. As she watched her husband kissing Barbara's bare breasts on screen, Mrs. Gale suddenly stood up and turned to her husband, "David, how could you!" she exclaimed loudly before hurriedly leaving the screening room, her husband chasing after her trying to explain that we had "made him do it."

Finally, we reached the last day of our eighteen-day shoot. "We have to finish today," Dennis Murphy reminded me, "We have to return the rented gear tomorrow." So, this last day became the longest day I have ever worked on a film set. We were shooting all the climactic action of the film, the attack of the re-animated corpses, the death of Dean Halsey and Dr. Hill, and, finally (SPOILER ALERT) Meg strangled to death in the elevator. Tons of action, gallons of blood, and a crew that was moving like greased lightning. We shot more than eighty set-ups that day (twenty-five to thirty is normal). We started at 7:00 AM and when we reached the end of our twelve hours at 7:00 PM we just kept on going. We were shooting the scene in the hallway where Meg and Dan get attacked by a re-animated corpse. Brian Yuzna motioned for me to come over so we could talk. "Stuart, I can see his dick," he whispered to me.

I asked Mac if he was seeing it. “It’s hard not to,” Mac responded, making a gesture with his hands indicating that the actor was hung like a horse.

“Let’s put a merkin on him,” I responded. Problem solved, or so I thought until Robin Burton, our costume designer, was soon at my side, “I threw the merkins out,” she told me. “You never used them.” Both Ebinger and Mac had been able to frame out the exposed male genitalia that would have resulted in the dreaded X-rating. In fact, one of the re-animated corpses had once asked if Mac was seeing his dick.

“Don’t worry,” Mac responded, “It’s no big thing.”

Morning was now approaching, and we knew that when we hit 24 hours of shooting, the plug would have to be pulled. But it wasn’t, and we kept shooting until noon: 31 hours of non-stop filming. Carolyn had come back to Los Angeles with our kids to celebrate Christmas and, luckily for me, she was on the set. We said our goodbyes to Brian and the crew and got into my rented blue monstrosity from Ugly Duckling Car Rentals and headed back on the 101 Freeway to the Oakwood Apartments. But the bright afternoon sun was too much for me and I swear that my eyes just suddenly stopped working. “I’m blind,” I told Carolyn, “I can’t see a thing.” We pulled over to the side of the freeway and thank God she took the wheel.

CHAPTER 25

Goodbyes

Carolyn, the kids, and I returned home right after New Year 1985. The whole *Re-Animator* adventure now seemed like a wonderful dream, and it felt like I had never left Chicago. I immediately began work on re-mounting a new production of *Huckleberry Finn* for the Goodman Theatre. Artistic Director Greg Mosher had asked if we would allow him to present it as part of the Goodman's subscription season.

My original Huck Finn, Brian Hickey, was, unfortunately, now too old to play the role and I held auditions at the Goodman. I ended up casting a young Northwestern University student named John Cameron Mitchell. John was amazing as Huck, and the role would later become a springboard for him as he went on to create the role of Huck in *Big River*, which became a huge hit on Broadway. John later wrote, directed, and starred in *Hedwig and the Angry Inch*, which he directed as his first film. Bill Norris was unavailable, so I cast J. Pat Miller as the King. We began rehearsals and J. Pat seemed to be suffering from a bad cold. We urged him to see a doctor and he returned with the terrible news that he had AIDS. The AIDS plague had come to America in the early '80s, and so many talented actors, directors, writers, and designers were taken from us. At first, J. Pat had believed he could continue with our production, but there was worry that he was contagious, and the other actors would be in jeopardy. In those days, many believed that saliva and sweat carried the virus, and so even touching J. Pat could cause infection. Carolyn had repeatedly kissed him while playing his niece. Years later it would be discovered that the HIV virus can only be transmitted via bodily fluids, but in those days the mere mention of AIDS would cause a full-scale panic. Our actors loved J. Pat and were ready to take the chance and continue working with him no matter what, but his condition deteriorated so rapidly that he soon had to be hospitalized.

When I visited him at Illinois Masonic, his already slim body was skeletal, his yellowed, jaundiced skin was covered with black lesions, and his huge expressive eyes had sunk back into his deep eye sockets. J. Pat thanked me for coming, as many people – including some nurses and doctors – were afraid to even be in the same room with him. We talked about the Arnold Schwarzenegger film *Conan the Barbarian*, which had just opened. I told J. Pat about a scene in which Conan is being crucified and a vulture lands on the cross to pick at his flesh. Conan turns the table by biting off the head of the winged scavenger.

J. Pat smiled. "That's good," he whispered. On April 10th, 1985, he was dead at age thirty-nine.

* * *

One day I was taking a break between rehearsals for *Huck Finn*, grabbing a nap on the floor of the Goodman's rehearsal room. "Excuse me," a voice said, waking me, "Are you Stuart Gordon?" I looked up to see a skinny young guy who introduced himself as Dann Gire, film critic of the *Daily Herald*. He wanted to know about *Re-Animator*. Had I completed principal photography? This reminded me that yes, I actually had shot a film and, as I talked to him, the reality of it all came back to me. I soon received a rough cut of the film on VHS from editor Lee Percy. It was very crude, ran over two and a half hours, and had no music or sound effects, but there was a movie there, by God. I watched it several times and made notes and sent them along to Lee. This was before the internet or even faxes, so it was agonizingly slow. I didn't hear anything from him until a month later when another VHS tape of the final cut arrived, and my jaw dropped as I watched it. Entire subplots had been removed, the order of scenes re-arranged, and the running time was now under 90 minutes. When I asked Lee about this, he told me that Charlie Band and his dad Albert had supervised the editing.

Soon I was on the phone with Albert asking why he had cut some of my favorite scenes. "There was nothing going on in those scenes," he gruffly informed me, "They were just talking." In retrospect, I now realize that Albert was being kind. He could have used his more frequent assessments: "Stinks on ice," or "Twenty pounds of shit in a ten-pound saddlebag." Albert, a gifted director himself, having made dozens of films including the '50s classic *I Bury the Living*, had excised a subplot involving Dr. Hill's ability to hypnotize people. His rationale was that there should only be one fantastic element in a movie, and, in the case of *Re-Animator*, it was the glowing green serum that could restore life. This made sense to me, and I have adopted this theory in my subsequent work. It's why I've never been a big fan of the *Harry Potter* movies or *The Lord of the Rings*, because there are so many magical elements that they seem to cancel each other out. You can only push the audience's willingness to suspend disbelief so far.

Soon I received a call from Brian Yuzna telling me that, after seeing the new cut, he felt that we needed to shoot the original scripted opening scene that had previously been cut for budgetary reasons. The scene was set at a Swiss medical school, and began with screams emanating from the office of Dr. Gruber. The police have been called, and they discover the kindly old doctor writhing on the floor. Next to him is Herbert West, holding a hypo of the glowing green serum. Gruber stumbles to his feet clutching his head and, to the horror of all, his eyeballs pop out of his skull, showering everyone with blood.

"You killed him!" a woman doctor exclaims, confronting West.

"No," he insists, "I gave him life." Cut to opening credits.

With the new scene in the can and a "locked picture" (which means no more changes), the final post-production work could begin. Charlie Band's brother Richard had been hired to compose the musical score of the film, and I sat down with him and our editor Lee Percy to "spot" the music cues. We watched the film together, stopping and starting it, discussing what kind of music should be used at each moment. Today, movies seem to have wall-to-wall music that never stops, but we couldn't afford that and, frankly, I still believe that there should be sections of a film without any music at all. I remember telling Richard Band that I loved the music of Bernard Herrmann, who had composed the music for so many great Hitchcock films. Richard made a note, and we slowly made our way through the film. "I think a cue should start here," Richard told us, "And should go until…" He closed his eyes as if listening to imaginary music. Lee let the film roll as we waited for Richard to say, "And end here." But he never did. Lee and I looked at each other, puzzled. Then we realized that Richard had fallen asleep in mid-sentence. So much for our hope of an audience sitting spellbound on the edge of their seats.

When Richard finally delivered the score, I was astonished that the opening theme sounded exactly like the music in *Psycho* in which Janet Leigh is driving through the rain on her way to the Bates Motel. When I mentioned this to Richard, he told me it was "an homage." He told us he wanted an end title that stated, "With apologies to Bernard Herrmann." When the final titles were prepared weeks later, however, this was left out, and Richard has been getting shit about it ever since. He even received a letter from the estate of the composer stating that if Mr. Herrmann were still alive, they would have sued.

I went back to Chicago and was not present for the final mix of the film that was supervised by Brian, Albert, and Charlie Band. I didn't even get to see a videotape of the final film. Instead, I busied myself directing a new project at Organic that, unknown to me at the time, would prove to be my last: it was entitled *Dope*. Based on a book by Sax Rohmer, the man who unleashed Fu Manchu on the world, it also concerned the dangers of "the yellow peril." Totally racist, the book is filled with lines like "the filth of the Orient makes the white man's seem positively hygienic in comparison." We felt *Dope* could be played as a campy comedy that would ridicule the idiocy of racism as well as the war on drugs.

Despite the lack of elaborate sets and only the simplest of effects, the production was well received, winning excellent reviews. But Organic's board was adamant that someone else would have to pay for a larger production, and the show closed after a brief six-week run. The writing was on the wall. After killing ourselves to build the big new theater, we were now forbidden to use it.

I had almost forgotten about *Re-Animator* until one evening in May when the phone rang. Brian was calling from the Cannes Film Festival, where the film was having its debut. Although not in official competition, it was being screened in a small theater on the Croisette at midnight. Brian was clearly very excited and had to yell above the uproar of the noisy crowd that I could hear in the background. "They loved it!" he shouted. "They absolutely loved it!"

The next day our first review appeared. It was by my old friend Roger Ebert reporting from Cannes. He wrote, "One of the pleasures of the movies is to find a movie that chooses a disreputable genre and then tries with all its might to transcend the genre, to go over the top into some kind of artistic vision, however weird." He continued with a nod to our past friendship, "Gordon's direction and particularly his use of special effects will come as no surprise to anyone who saw his famous *Warp* trilogy onstage. He borrows from the traditions of comic-book art and B-grade thrillers, using his special effects not as set pieces for us to study, but as dazzling throwaways as the action hurtles ahead." Roger's rave encouraged other critics to weigh in and Pauline Kael, who my old Madison friend Larry Cohen had regarded as a goddess of film criticism, supposedly infuriated editor William Shawn when she wrote this in *The New Yorker*: "A silly ghouly classic – the bloodier it gets, the funnier it is. It's like pop Buñuel, the jokes hit you in a subterranean comic zone that the surrealists' pranks sometimes reached but without the surrealists' self-consciousness."

I learned an important lesson here. I, assuming the critics would *hate Re-Animator*, wrote them off, simply attempting to make a movie that the horror fans would enjoy. Because I hadn't cared about the reviews, I received the best of my career. In fact, the film went on to win the Critics' Prize at the Cannes Film Festival, an award given to the best film screened at the festival, whether in competition or not. It turned out to be an art film after all.

Brian and I were offered a three-picture deal by Charles Band. The films would be produced by Empire Pictures. I was offered a director's fee of $100,000 for the three movies. Carolyn and I both felt this was an offer we couldn't refuse. We sublet our new house on Melrose in Chicago, said our goodbyes to my mom, relatives, and friends, and loaded up our Toyota Corolla with our two kids and as much as we could carry and left Chicago.

I was no longer the artistic director of the Organic Theater and, for the first time in fifteen years, I felt as if a huge weight had been lifted from my shoulders. I was no longer responsible for the livelihood of a theater company and its actors and staff. But would I be able to make a living as a director in the movie business? *Re-Animator* had yet to open in America (or anywhere else), and its future was still a big question mark.

PART THREE

HOLLYWOOD

CHAPTER 26

Westward Ho

Off we drove to California in our little Toyota Corolla packed with suitcases and a few essentials (like our television). Jim Belushi, who had befriended me after the death of his brother John and now was living and working in Los Angeles, graciously set up a meeting for me with his management group, the Brillstein Company.

The next week, there was a cast and crew screening of *Re-Animator*. This was my first time seeing the finished film. I was dazzled by the opening credits that featured old fashioned drawings from *Gray's Anatomy* in Day-Glo colors. It had been created by Bob Dawson and was inspired by the psychedelic credit sequences from those old Roger Corman / Edgar Allan Poe movies. We also borrowed Corman's practice of putting Edgar Allan Poe's name above the title of the film, so our movie was now billed as H.P. Lovecraft's *Re-Animator*. Like Corman's Poe movies, we planned to do a series of Lovecraft inspired films.

It was also the first time I heard Richard Band's music, and I was amazed and appalled that he had lifted Bernard Herrmann's *Psycho* theme so shamelessly, although he made it his own by giving it an '80s-style disco beat that clearly worked with the film.

It was a happy reunion for the cast and crew, and as each name came up onscreen there was loud applause. I was thrilled when my own name came up last and got the biggest reaction of all. Very heady stuff. Afterward everyone was patting me on the back and telling me how much they loved the film and how proud they were to have had a part in making it.

Their reactions had been sensational – lots of applause and wild cheering during the bloodiest moments – but I wondered if a real paying crowd would react the same way. I would shortly find out, as the marketing department was planning a sneak preview in a couple of months to test both the film and its marketing campaign. The following Monday I made a trip to the Hollywood offices of Empire Pictures, where Brian Yuzna and I were to meet with Charles Band, the emperor himself. Empire had just moved into new quarters in a three-story building on La Brea Avenue near Sunset, and Brian and I waited in the outer office under the watchful eye of Charlie's secretary, the unflappable Bennah Burton-Burtt. Finally, we were ushered into Charlie's spacious office.

The walls were covered with garish posters filled with monsters, half naked women, and titles like *Zone Troopers*, *Terrorvision*, and *Crawlspace*. Charlie, looking even younger than the last time I had seen him, immediately leaped up from behind his gigantic toy-covered desk, "Ciao, raggazi!" And it wasn't long before Brian and I were under the spell of his intoxicating charisma.

Charlie's genuine love of making movies is irresistible, and you're quickly caught up in his very palpable and very contagious excitement. Then he dropped a pair of bombshells on us. He told us he had just bought Dino De Laurentiis's "Mega studios" in Rome (every other word was *mega* or *bitchin'*), and this fall we'd be shooting our three pictures there with an all-Italian crew. This was a homecoming for Charlie. He had grown up in Rome while Albert, his director father, was shooting spaghetti westerns and sword-and-sandal epics. Now Charlie was returning to the land of his childhood, a conquering hero, buying the largest studio in Italy.

Then came the second bombshell; he told us that our first film would be *The Doll*. "It's about killer dolls. It's awesome," he enthused as he handed me the script written by the oddly named Ed Naha. I looked at Brian. We were hard at work adapting *From Beyond*, another story by H.P. Lovecraft, in an effort to capitalize on what we hoped would be the success of *Re-Animator*. Now, suddenly, we were doing *The Doll*. What about *From Beyond*? When I brought this up Charlie laughed and with a wave of his hand explained, "Dude, *The Doll* is just a little movie that you can knock off in a couple of weeks while you're prepping *From Beyond*. In fact, you can even use the same set."

I came home that evening not sure how to break this to Carolyn. Here we had just moved our entire family across the country to Los Angeles only to be told that we would soon be moving overseas to Rome, and we'd be there long enough to shoot three pictures. Carolyn was silent for what seemed like an eternity. Finally, she said, "Better learn Italian."

I was given an office at Empire and an assistant, Liz Wartenberg. Tall, bright, and good-looking with short brunette hair, Liz kept everything on track. Every morning, Carolyn would drive me to work and pick me up in the evening (with the kids in the back seat as we only had the one car). I went to work adapting Lovecraft's *From Beyond* into a film.

The story about a scientist who invents a machine that allows him to see other parallel dimensions is one of Lovecraft's earliest, and is only seven pages long. The longer he wrote, the longer his stories became, with his last, *At the Mountains of Madness*, a novella. In fact, we borrowed one of Lovecraft's ideas from *Mountains* to expand *From Beyond* as we had completely used up his short story in our pre-title opening sequence.

In *From Beyond*, the scientist is devoured by an unnamed creature from another dimension. We decided to make that creature a "shoggoth," a protoplasmic shape-shifting Lovecraftian creation that in *At the Mountains of Madness* was originally a slave of "The Old Ones," the alien race that preceded man on Earth. Somehow, Lovecraft tells us, the shoggoths "accidentally gained intelligence" and rebelled, wiping out the Old Ones. We pondered this. "Accidentally gained intelligence?" What did that mean? We finally realized that this occurred when the shoggoths devoured the Old Ones and, in a bizarre extension of "you are what you eat," absorbed the intelligence of their masters.

Lovecraft did not believe in the supernatural. No ghosts or demons for him. Instead, all of his stories have a scientific basis, and in *From Beyond*, it's clear that he had done extensive research on the pineal gland. Not much was known about it then, and not much more is known now. Positing that perhaps stimulating the pineal would increase the sex drive, we started defining the character of the scientist as a man who wasn't satisfied with the five senses, and he became a hedonistic sensualist wanting to see more and feel more. This led us to basing his character on the Marquis de Sade. In Lovecraft's story he is named Crawford Tillinghast, but we felt the name seemed weak and gave it to his meek assistant. We borrowed the name *Pretorius* from James Whale's brilliant classic *Bride of Frankenstein* in which it was given to the evil rival scientist played to perfection by Ernest Thesiger. And being Lovecraft, who never created female characters, we once again asked ourselves, "Who's the skirt?" The answer became the woman psychiatrist who is examining Tillinghast at the asylum after he claims that a creature from beyond devoured Pretorius's head. We named her Katherine McMichaels, using a young Katharine Hepburn as our model. She would be working with a police detective who acts as her bodyguard to protect her from the suspect Tillinghast, whom he believes to be criminally insane. We decided to make the cop a black former football player, feeling the need for a character to stand in for the audience and ask the questions they would be asking. We named him Buford "Bubba" Brownlea.

What about the creatures "from beyond?" Lovecraft refers to them as protoplasmic "jellyfish monstrosities" swimming through the air. I asked legendary comic book artist and friend Neal Adams to help with the design of the creatures and the bizarre images poured out of him, many looking very much like the nightmarish works of Hieronymus Bosch. We also went to Salvador Dalí for inspiration and ended up adapting one of his drawings into our poster, in which skulls appear in the eye sockets and mouth of a screaming head. We studied pictures of existing sea creatures, glowing deep-sea denizens, and sharp-toothed eels as well as microscopic organisms. It had occurred to me that, since Lovecraft was germaphobic (among a laundry list of his phobias), the idea of invisible creatures floating in the air and being capable of harming you was probably inspired by contagious viruses, bacteria and microbes.

It also became clear that, to create this menagerie of other-worldly creatures, we would absolutely need more than one effects company to design and build them. We had hired Tony Doublin, John Naulin, and John Buechler, who had delivered the headless effects for *Re-Animator*, and we had also been hearing great things about a young effects genius named Mark Shostrom. Thin with shoulder-length hair so blond he could be an albino, Mark did a series of sketches that were jaw-droppingly bizarre. Inspired by cancerous tumors, the final form of Dr. Pretorius was so grotesque that I asked Mark how we could accomplish this, as I couldn't imagine how an actor could possibly twist himself into this pretzel-like shape. "It's not an actor," he told me proudly. "It shouldn't look like a man in a suit. We can create an animatronic figure that can do it all." I nodded, visions of sugar-plums dancing in my head, imagining the amazing work he would do.

We also began prepping *The Doll*, which I had renamed *Dolls*, as there were so many killer toys in the script that even screenwriter Ed Naha wasn't sure which one was the title character. I also suggested a few tweaks to the script. I had been reading Bruno Bettelheim's brilliant book *The Uses of Enchantment*, in which he analyzes the true meanings of fairy tales. Bettelheim tells us that these stories are always being toned down for children in an effort to avoid traumatizing them. It was his opinion that fairy tales should be scary. He believes that they prepare a child for the difficulties of life, portraying a threatening world filled with monsters and characters capable of great harm. But they also teach the child that if one is brave and good and doesn't give up, they can ultimately triumph over these adversaries.

Ed's story was about a house in the woods inhabited by a kindly old dollmaker and his wife who are, in reality, witches. If their visitors are good, they are spared, but if not, they are attacked by the murderous dolls and end up becoming dolls themselves. Its main character was a little girl, and her evil stepmother and weak-willed father reminded me of the parents in *Hansel and Gretel*. This presented an ideal opportunity to put Betelheim's ideas about fairy tales to the test. Ed was a little skeptical at first, as he had been working for Charlie for some time, and who was this guy from Chicago with all these suggestions?

Writing about thousands of murderous dolls was one thing, but bringing them to life was another. In those pre-CGI days, my first thought was to use puppets. I ultimately found John and Vivian Brunner, expert puppeteers who they believed they could create doll puppets capable of fulfilling all the needs of our script.

At the same time, casting began on *From Beyond*. I was pushing for bringing back *Re-Animator* stars Jeffrey Combs and Barbara Crampton. There was some resistance from Brian, Charlie, and Albert as Barbara seemed too young to play a woman psychiatrist, but Dennis made some changes to the script referring to her character as "the girl wonder" and that seemed to mollify them. We cast Ken Foree, who had starred in *Dawn of the Dead*, as Bubba Brownlee and he brought tremendous energy and good humor to the role.

When we began casting *Dolls*, finding the little eight-year-old heroine was the biggest problem. I saw scores of adorable blue-eyed, curly haired blondes, but none of them seemed to have the vulnerability I believed the character needed. One day our casting director brought in Carrie Machacek, whose stage name was Carrie Lorraine. She was tiny with large blue eyes, and she made you immediately want to hug her. When she read her scenes, she seemed genuinely afraid. I've always believed that if the characters aren't afraid in a horror film, why should the audience be?

We began preparing for our trip to Rome. Carolyn and I had been calling my mother in Chicago every Sunday to tell her all about our crazy adventures in Hollywood, and she was genuinely excited that I would be shooting movies in Italy. "Why don't you come with us?" I asked her. "You're retired now with no job keeping you in Chicago. They're renting a house for us in Rome, so the only extra cost would be the air fare."

There was a long pause. "I've always wanted to go to Rome," she said. When I told Carolyn about my idea, I mentioned that my mom could also baby sit the kids while we were at the studio, but Carolyn thought that would be too much for her as my mom was now in her mid-seventies. She had another idea: "Why don't we take my niece Lisa with us and hire her to be our au pair?" Lisa, her sister Marilyn's beautiful blonde daughter, had just dropped out of college in Colorado and wasn't sure what to do next.

"Instead of my mother?" I asked, trying to get a handle on this.

"No, in addition to your mother."

Our small entourage took shape. We'd take a flight that stopped in Chicago on the way to Rome and my mom would board there. Lisa would meet us in Rome. One big happy famiglia.

Roma

Re-Animator opened in mid-October, just before we left for Rome. The reaction was amazing; ecstatic reviews and lines around the block. The film had been released unrated as the MPAA found it so bloody that they refused to give it an R rating. So all our worrying about full frontal male nudity was for naught. As only studio films are required to have their films rated, Empire boldly decided to forego one, although they were warned that newspapers and television would refuse to advertise an unrated film. Luckily for us, this turned out not to be true.

Carolyn and I went to the theater on Hollywood Boulevard that was showing it, and the line was so long that we didn't get in until after the movie had started. We entered the theater behind a large guy carrying a huge tub of popcorn and he opened the door just in time to see Dr. Gruber's bloody eyeballs pop out of his head. The guy jumped a foot and showered us with his popcorn. It was a proper baptism for my new career as a filmmaker.

The movie was in 800 theaters (twice as many as originally planned), and ended up making around $4 million the first weekend, which is pretty good, especially for a non-studio film. But it dropped to half that the second weekend, which I've come to learn is typical for a horror movie. The distribution guys at Empire didn't have much of an advertising budget to keep it going, but they seemed pleased with the numbers and told me that the film would make a fortune in six months when it was released on VHS for home video.

On Halloween 1985, Carolyn, the kids, and I said goodbye to our dog, Sally, a large yellow Lab and Malamute mix that we had gotten for Suzanna after Lefty and Phoebe had left us. Sally would be cared for by Brian's assistant (and our house sitter) Mike Muscal while we were gone. Then we boarded a plane for Rome. The plane stopped in Chicago as planned and my mother joined us, and off we all flew to Italia.

We were staying in a guest house in a villa on the Via Cassia on the outskirts of Rome. We arrived on a Friday, and the production company had left us a bag of groceries which, of course, included pasta and espresso. Carolyn looked around for a coffee pot but could only find a small espresso maker. Not realizing how strong the Italian espresso was, she made and poured large cups of the thick syrupy coffee, and the adults were soon shaking, clicking their teeth together, and bouncing off the walls. We discovered that the last occupants of our guest house had been actress Susan Sarandon and her then significant other, Franco Amurri, with whom she had just had a daughter. I had rich fantasies thinking that I was now bathing in the same tub that the incredibly sexy Susan Sarandon had recently occupied. When we were moving our things into the bathroom, we found a large marijuana joint in the cabinet above the sink. Thinking it a good omen, and since we had not brought along any of our own stash, Carolyn and I quickly smoked it. A few days later, there was a knock on the door and a handsome Italian man stood there introducing himself as Franco Amurri. He told us he had left something in the bathroom, and could he take a look around? Carolyn and I looked at each other. Hmmm… "Of course," we told him "Come in," and he quickly disappeared into our bathroom. He was there for quite a while and finally emerged carrying a small nondescript bathmat. "I found it," he told us. "I'm very sentimental about this bathmat."

On Monday, they sent a car to take me to the enormous studio complex. It had been built on the outskirts of Rome by Dino De Laurentiis in the 1960s and christened Dinocittà after Cinecittà, which translates to "Movie City," the famous Roman studio built by Mussolini in 1937. Due to non-payment of taxes, Dino's studio had been seized by the Italian government and Charlie had been able to buy it at the bargain basement price of $20 million. We now called it Band-Land or Charliecittà. As we drove into it, I was amazed by the size of the place. It had seven large soundstages, an administration building, a restaurant and a coffee bar, and seemed almost as big as Universal Studios. Getting out of the car, I quickly realized that the place had seen better days. Knee-high weeds grew between cracks in the broken sidewalks, and the buildings all needed a paint job. But it was here that John Huston had filmed *The Bible: In the Beginning...* Roger Vadim had directed Jane Fonda's famous zero-gravity striptease in *Barbarella* and, more recently, my good buddy Arnold Schwarzenegger and Brigitte Nielsen had starred together in *Red Sonja*. Brigitte really was a barbarian, I was told… when she needed to pee, she would just push aside her loin cloth and squat, doing her business in front of the entire crew.

I was given a tour of the studio, where two films were in production: *Troll*, directed by effects maestro John Buechler, and *Crawlspace*, directed by David Schmoeller. An excellent director, David had achieved fame with the now-classic *Tourist Trap* and would go on to direct the original *Puppet Master* for Charlie, which would become his most successful franchise. David took me under his wing, filling me in on his experiences both good and bad working in Rome with an Italian crew. I was given a small blue Fiat for my personal use. We fell in love with Rome all over again, and I still never get over its unique mixture of the modern and the ancient, where a three-thousand-year-old edifice like the Forum is right next door to a shoe store. Unlike Florence or Venice, which seem like museums by comparison, Rome is a living city that has never stopped working.

* * *

My Italian crew called me "Maestro," which I quite liked, although there was some culture shock on both sides. In those days, Italian films seldom recorded production sound, preferring to dub it later in post. One day, a workman was hammering on another set while we were shooting a scene with dialogue. Irritated, I confronted him myself. "Senor Fellini always lets me hammer," he told me.

"I'm not Fellini," I replied angrily.

He shrugged. "That's for sure," was his response.

One day, Suzanna and Jill visited the set. We were in the midst of shooting the scene where Carolyn is attacked by a horde of murderous dolls, and three-year-old Jill was upset when she saw a fake screwdriver sticking in her mother's foot. I explained to Jill that it wasn't real and later took her to the special effects studio to show her how it was all done. Unfortunately the room, filled with latex monsters, upset her even more. Unlike Brian Yuzna's kids, whom he brought to the *Re-Animator* dailies, mine were as prone to nightmares as I was as a child. Some people love horror and others never will.

My parents did not allow me to see horror films. But they must have let their guard down and I somehow saw the innocuous-sounding *Abbott and Costello Meet Dr. Jekyll and Mr. Hyde*. The result was three years of non-stop nightmares. "You were traumatized as a child and now you're traumatizing others," Dr. Joanne Cantor told me a few years ago when I met her at the University of Wisconsin where I returned as a guest artist. "It's the cycle of abuse."

Every morning, I would be picked up and driven to the studio by Massimo, a distinguished looking fifty-year-old gentleman who seldom smiled and looked like he could have stepped out of *The Godfather*. When I would buckle my seat belt, he would roll his eyes. "Do you think I am a bad driver?" he asked me one day.

"Not at all," I told him, "But you should wear a seat belt too."

"If your time comes, it comes," was his response.

A few days later I stood waiting, but Massimo never showed up. I called the studio and discovered that he had been in an accident on his way to pick me up and they were sending another driver. "Is he alright?" I asked. A few days later he was back on the job wearing an eye-patch. He had almost lost his eye. I noticed that he now always buckled his seat belt.

As the weather got colder, we discovered that the soundstages were not heated. De Laurentiis's creditors had torn out the ductwork and sold the heating systems to cover delinquent taxes. It was so cold that there were shots where you could see the actors' breath fogging. When I pointed this out to our producer,

Roberto Bessi, he suggested that they suck on ice cubes. I insisted that he find a way to heat the stages, so he rented some noisy gas heaters that had to be shut off when we were shooting, but it proved to be a workable solution.

Two or three Empire films were shooting simultaneously on the seven massive stages. The studio's coffee bar became the hangout for the various casts, who recovered from their jetlag by knocking back espressos and comparing notes. "When do you die?" the actors would ask each other, "I get murdered next Tuesday."

One day, someone showed me an article about Charlie Band that appeared in *Newsweek* under the title "The Prince of Schlock." "Well, I guess that makes you the king," John Huston told Albert Band when he showed the article to his old mentor. The *Newsweek* story mentioned that *Re-Animator* had made over twenty million dollars and, as it had cost only $800,000, and contractually I had 2 percent of the net, I was sure I had struck it rich. "Drinks are on me!" I naively shouted to the denizens of the coffee bar before I became familiar with Hollywood-style accounting.

From time to time we got messages from Charlie and Albert Band in Hollywood. They were not happy. Although our dailies looked terrific thanks to the beautiful sets created by Giovanni Natalucci and shot to perfection by Mac Ahlberg, we were falling further and further behind schedule. The Italian crew worked at a slower pace than American crews, and it didn't help that we had so many special effects, which were extremely time consuming. Mac did wonders hiding the wires on the Brunners' marionettes by coating the strings with black Magic Marker, but the powers-that-be felt the doll effects were unconvincing.

Entire scenes were cut to bring *Dolls* back on schedule and budget. One scene that we lost took place in an abandoned English town in which the inhabitants have all been kidnapped and turned into dolls by our all-powerful witches. As we neared the end of our six-week shooting schedule (which had stretched to eight), Brian Yuzna started striking sets and sending back the rented furniture and props to save money. I returned from lunch one day to discover that the set I was using that morning had been completely struck before I had finished the scene. Furious, I insisted that it be returned immediately, and I was barely able to shoot the remainder of the scene in the short time that was left. The actors were wrapped, some before all their work was done. Carolyn stood in for Bunty Bailey in the scene in which her character is discovered in the attic partially turned into a doll. It is the scene in which her eyeballs fall out of her mask-like face and roll across the floor until she picks them up to hold next to the empty eye sockets. I had added this shot to mimic the poster that hung on the wall of Charlie's office, which featured this iconic image. Even my niece Lisa filled in as we shot close-ups of her hands pulling off Cassie Stuart's "Boy Toy" belt buckle to use as a weapon.

From Behind

I had been walking through the famous old studio with my second assistant director after a casting session.

"Wouldn't it be cool if we bumped into Fellini?" I had mused out loud. At that very moment we went around a corner and I literally *bumped into* the legendary director. Both my assistant and I were in shock and we stood there dumb-founded with our mouths hanging open.

"Scusi," Fellini muttered, and continued on his way.

That evening I told Carolyn. "You met Fellini?!" she excitedly exclaimed. "What did you say to him?"

"Nothing," I admitted.

"Nothing?!"

"What could I say?"

"You could tell him you like his films," she suggested, a bit exasperated that I had missed a once in a lifetime opportunity. "Don't you like it when people tell you they like yours?"

I nodded dumbly. A few weeks later, I was in the studio restaurant and there was Toshiro Mifune, the world-famous Japanese star of *Rashomon* and *Seven Samurai*. Summoning my courage, I approached him. "Mr. Mifune, I'm a huge fan of your films," I told him and introduced myself. He smiled graciously and bowed. Carolyn had been right.

The next day when Brian and I arrived at Empire Pictures' headquarters on La Brea, we discovered that the studio had recut *Re-Animator* so it could receive an R rating, allowing the video to be rented at Blockbuster. At the time, Blockbuster was run by a born-again owner who refused to stock anything stronger than R-rated films. Most of the bloodletting had been excised (as had the famous head-gives-head scene), resulting in a very-very short film. To achieve a ninety-minute running time, Charlie and Albert had reinserted all of the exposition that Lee Percy had originally trimmed. The movie now played like an episode of Masterpiece Theater.

Brian and I were both furious. To make matters worse, our original unrated version could no longer be screened in the USA. Brian ended up having to go to the MPAA ratings board and ask them to take back the R rating to allow the film to be screened (and sold) in its original unrated version. The MPAA was astonished, as this was the first time anyone had ever rejected the much-sought-after R-rating. This was not the only problem. My editor, Lee Percy, had completed a rough cut of *Dolls* under the supervision of Albert Band and, to my horror, the film was now less than an hour in length.

CHAPTER 28

When I asked why it was so short, Albert responded with his usual, "Nothing was going on. They were just talking." I told him that I thought he had gone too far, and that the movie would be scarier if it were given a chance to breathe. But I knew that I wouldn't really have a chance to work with Lee on the film until after I had finished shooting *From Beyond*.

The night before we were set to begin shooting *From Beyond*, it snowed. This is a rare occurrence in Rome and many tree branches, unused to being weighed down by snow, cracked and came crashing to the ground, blocking the streets and causing huge traffic jams. I've always believed that rain was lucky on an opening night of a play, but snow on the first day of a film shoot? The effect was magical (like a scene in another Fellini movie) and I've never again seen snow fall in the Eternal City.

Things moved along smoothly for the first few days until we had to put Jeffrey Combs into his bald-cap make-up. This was complicated by the fact that the specially-built latex head piece had to house mechanical effects to control his protruding, writhing pineal gland. This necessitated an enlarged forehead, and when he showed up on set wearing the make-up, it just didn't work. The seams were clearly visible, and we ended up having to hide them by adding blood-soaked gauze bandages.

We began shooting the scenes where Jeffrey Combs' character escapes from his hospital room and is discovered by Carolyn as Dr. Roberta Bloch (named after Lovecraft's apostle and *Psycho* author Robert Bloch) munching on human brains. The brain, created by John Naulin, was made out of rigid latex and resembled the brains that are used as classroom anatomical models. I was fit to be tied. "How is he supposed to eat this?" I asked John. "We built one with a bite taken out of it," he replied proudly, apparently not realizing that real brains are soft squishy affairs, nothing like the hard rubber ones he had created. Could we find some real brains to use instead? The Italians are fond of cervelli (fried calves' brains that are often served with artichokes). I was told they could get them but it would cost valuable time.

"Alright, we'll use these," I grudgingly conceded, and Jeffrey pretended to take a bite out of the prop brain. "Isn't there anything that he can really chew on?" I asked Naulin. He ran off to find something and returned a few minutes later with tube of dental adhesive. I looked at him as if he were crazy. "It's all I could find," he sheepishly admitted. "But it's pink like the brain…" Frustrated but realizing we were running out of time to shoot the scene, I nodded, and the hole in the rubber brain was filled with the gooey stuff. The cameras rolled and Jeffrey gamely took a big bite. But when he tried to speak his lines, he couldn't seem to open his mouth. His lips were stuck together by the bright pink glue. "Cut!" I screamed, turning on Jeffrey, thinking that he was playing a sardonic joke at my expense. Jeffrey's response – as he was still unable to speak – was to pass me the brain with a "Go ahead and try it" gesture. I took a bite and, like the poor characters in Dr. Seuss' *Bartholomew and the Oobleck*, my mouth was instantly glued shut. Jeffrey later ended up miming the sequence as he had originally suggested.

Ted Sorel, who had been cast to play the demented Dr. Pretorius, had to wear an elaborate prosthetic that made him look as though grotesque tumors were covering half of his face and body. It took over six hours to apply the elaborate make-up, and Ted asked if it would be possible to shoot all of his lines in that make-up so he wouldn't have to again go through the agony of putting it on. I agreed and, unlike the normal procedure of starting with the widest shots and then going to close-ups, I began with the closest shots, knowing that the make-up would begin to disintegrate the longer we filmed it.

The shooting went on for several hours. After a while it became clear that Ted was having trouble remembering his lines. This was unusual, as Ted was an excellent actor who always was prepared and knew his scenes backwards and forwards. But his line readings got worse and worse, and his words sounded slurred. It suddenly hit me that the make-up was somehow having an effect on his mind. I called to the crew to get Ted out of the prosthetic make-up that covered half of his body, and they immediately began tearing it off of him. When he was freed from the confining latex that held him in place like a strait jacket, it was apparent to us all that his left arm, trapped under the makeup, had swollen to twice its normal size. All living beings need to be able to move so the blood can circulate throughout their bodies. If we remain motionless too long, like the guards at Buckingham Palace, we pass out because our blood is unable to reach our brains. This is what killed the victims of crucifixion – the inability to move – and this was what was happening to poor Ted Sorel. He was being crucified by the prosthetic make-up. Thankfully, after a few painful minutes, he was able to move his arm again and his mind seemed to be returning to its usual sharpness. I was learning a sobering lesson that movie sets are dangerous places. This is why it's not uncommon to see a film dedicated to a crew member who didn't make it through the shoot.

We all survived *From Beyond* despite more make-up catastrophes. It seems as if effects geniuses always want to play God. They want to emulate Dr. Frankenstein so they too can shout, "He's alive!! HE'S ALIVE!!!" Mark Shostrom was no exception. He had promised me that his animatronic version of the fully mutated Dr. Pretorius would be able to take the place of the actor playing him. When his creation arrived on set from Los Angeles, however, it could barely move its arms. I suddenly felt that I had been an idiot to expect more.

"We clearly need to put this make-up on an actor," I told Shostrom on the first of many long-distance calls. He was already hard at work on his next project and wouldn't be joining us during the shoot, having sent some young assistants to tend to his creations instead. Like mad Dr. Frankenstein, Shostrom was so convinced that his elaborate puppet would work that his response was to instruct his young crew not to aid us in duplicating his make-up on the actor. We were forced to hire another company to do the prosthetic work and the finished film is a combination of Shostrom's mechanical creature and actor Ted Sorel in matching make-up. Our ingenious cinematographer Mac Ahlberg saved the day by creating brilliant on-set practical effects that could convince an audience they were actually entering another dimension. Lovecraft refers to his characters' ability to see light waves beyond the ultra-violet spectrum, and Mac came up with the idea of using undulating purplish light. Lovecraft writes about jellyfish-like creatures swimming in the air, so Mac gave the purple and turquoise light a shimmering quality like the reflection of light on the bottom of a swimming pool. He did this by using sheets of bendable mirror-like Mylar to warp the light and give it an other-worldly effect. This was further enhanced by wind machines to create additional movement of the actors' hair and clothing as if they were under water or in zero gravity.

We had been instructed that *From Beyond*, unlike *Re-Animator*, would have to get an R rating from the MPAA so that it could play to a wider audience. We decided to use less blood. We had gone through over thirty gallons of the red stuff on our last Lovecraft opus, and it had made an R-rating impossible. So we decided to try a different substance in *From Beyond*. Somehow, we came upon the idea of using slime instead. Maybe it was inspired by *Ghostbusters* ("He slimed me!"), and after a little checking we discovered that the gooey stuff they had used on Bill Murray was methylcellulose, created from vegetable and plant material (also used as a thickener in fast food milk shakes). Not only did we cover our creatures with the gooey stuff, but our actors as well. Barbara Crampton's complaints about how cold it was necessitated us warming up the goop before applying it to actors. It reminded me that we had also warmed up the autopsy table before her famous scene in *Re-Animator*, so I had no problem making her and the other actors as comfortable as possible. We went through hundreds of gallons of the slimy gunk during the shoot.

Albert Band had joined us in Rome for the shoot, probably due to our running over budget on *Dolls*. It was a happy homecoming for him, and he generously took us to many of his favorite restaurants and introduced us to the Italian movie folk he had met when shooting spaghetti westerns and sword-and-sandal epics in the 1960s. Brian and I, however, knew that he was really there to keep us on schedule and within our budget. One day I was running behind schedule and Albert took me aside. "How many more shots do you have?" he asked me. I pulled out my shot list and counted them, "About six more shots," I nervously told him, "But maybe I can cut some." He looked over the list and then turned to me. "These are good shots and you need them all," he said. "Keep going." I was stunned. After Brian's constant worrying on *Re-Animator*, it was hard to believe that a producer would be so accommodating. But Albert, being a fine director himself, totally understood the filmmaking process and was encouraging me in a way that really meant something. He was allowing me more time, the most valuable commodity on any film, or as I have learned, in life itself. Albert wanted me to make the best movie possible. In fact, a few days later, he went well above and beyond the usual role of an executive producer. We were about to film the scene in which an ambulance crew is unloading a homeless man suffering from delirium tremens. The poor fellow is raving about seeing a man with a snake coming out of his head, and the paramedic thinks he is hallucinating, not realizing that the drunk is accurately describing Crawford Tillinghast and his writhing serpent-like pineal gland. That afternoon the first assistant director came to me looking a bit panicked, "The actor who is playing the drunk is not here," he told me. They had been calling him all morning and couldn't reach him and even his agent had no idea where he was. As Roberto Bessi would say, "What to do?"

Albert Band had the answer: "I'll play the part," he told me. In a few minutes he was in a tattered overcoat and covered with greasy make-up. I even had them mess up his teeth with black and brown enamel paint. Albert gave a wonderful performance as the terrified bum, and from that moment we became friends for life.

CHAPTER 29

Crash and Burn

We returned to Los Angeles right after Easter. It was good to be back in the little house in Van Nuys, and Suzanna returned to school at Los Encinos. One of her classmates was taking horseback riding lessons at a ranch in Sunland, and we accompanied her there one weekend. The ranch, which was essentially a large back yard, belonged to the trainer, Millie Chalk, and her family. Millie is a larger-than-life character who always reminds me of Calamity Jane. Boisterous and loud, with a great whooping laugh, she introduced us to her children: Brenda, who was Suzanna's age, and her son Tony, who was about Jill's age. Despite her cowgirl persona, Millie taught English-style riding. Her daughter was already an accomplished jumper.

It had been decided that *From Beyond* should be released before *Dolls* as Dave Allen would need more time to complete his stop-motion animation work on *Dolls*. Dave was small and blond and seldom smiled, but he could talk for hours about his painstaking technique. As the saying goes, he was the sort of person who, if you asked him what time it was, would tell you how to build a clock. But he was a genius of the craft and his work could give the famous stop-motion animator Ray Harryhausen a run for his money. So I focused on editing *From Beyond* with Lee Percy. The movie came together quickly. As I had previously agreed that the film would receive an "R" rating, the completed cut was dutifully submitted to the MPAA. Their reaction was pure horror, but not in the way I intended. The movie could never be given an R, we were told. They found the slime even more disgusting than blood and, in their opinion, the film was far too upsetting to be shown to anyone under 18. "Isn't that the goal of horror movies?" I asked, "To be upsetting?" To make matters worse they didn't suggest any cuts.

During this time, David Edelstein, who was then a writer for *Rolling Stone* magazine (but would later go on to write for *New York* magazine and coin the term "torture porn"), was doing a story about me and my new film. He called the *Rolling Stone* article "Shock Treatment" and had me pose for a photographer wearing a surgical gown, grinning like a madman as I leaned over a rubber dummy of a bald Jeffrey Combs lying on a gurney, grasping his erect pineal gland with forceps. Very tasteful. And there was another shot of me, Carolyn, and our family, with our daughters wearing grotesque monster masks. I had even shown the writer a screening of the original rough cut of *From Beyond* and he had loved it. "You can't let them cut this," he had told me. "It's genius!" But it finally became clear that the scene the MPAA was intent on removing was, of course, the most disturbing one in the film: the one in which

Dr. Bloch (played by Carolyn) has her brain sucked through her eye socket by a possessed Crawford Tillinghast (Jeffrey Combs). After making several trims and having the film returned again and again without the sought-after R rating, I requested a meeting with the MPAA.

This is seldom done, as the identity of the review board's members is top secret, but eventually I was allowed to meet with the woman who was judge, jury, and executioner of my film. She turned out to be a matronly woman who, I later learned, worked as a librarian when not serving as a censor. "I'm not a censor," she told me emphatically. "My job is to let parents know which movies their children can see without being traumatized. If you want to make changes to get a less restrictive rating, that's up to you." She clearly knew she had me (and every other filmmaker) by the balls. The studios are always insisting on a rating no more restrictive than an R, and I would have to make the cuts she demanded in order to get it.

Together, she and I watched a VHS tape of the offending sequence. "Look at that!" she shouted as Jeffrey Combs' mouth covered Carolyn's eye socket, "You keep pushing in! Closer and closer!" I felt like I was 10 years old being scolded in the principal's office. I wanted to start crying, "I'm sorry! I'm sorry! Please give me an R rating! I'll do whatever you want!" Of course, it turned out what she wanted was for the sequence to be truncated to the point of being barely in the movie. My film was being cut to ribbons for the safety of the American public. No arguments seemed to work. Comparing it to another film that had received an R rating for similarly disturbing scenes resulted in her saying that if it had been up to her that other film wouldn't have gotten off so easily. Was this payback for our sidestepping their authority and releasing *Re-Animator* unrated? Maybe, but the truth is that the MPAA has no hard and fast rules, so their decisions are entirely subjective and up to the whims of whoever is viewing your film.

Moreover, if the scene is in any way sexual, you haven't got a prayer. Years later, when I submitted my film *King of the Ants* – an incredibly violent movie that features scenes in which the protagonist is beaten to a bloody pulp – the only scene that they wanted to trim was a sex scene between the protagonist and the leading lady. "Too much thrusting," I was told. America remains a very puritanical country. So *From Beyond* was released with its most shocking moments lying on the cutting room floor, and I found watching the castrated version a pretty depressing affair. The movie received good reviews but did not create the excitement (or box office) that *Re-Animator* had.

Jump ahead twenty years later when DVDs appear on the scene, presenting director's cuts of popular titles. I was repeatedly asked if I had an uncut version of *From Beyond*. Unfortunately, I told them, I did not. But one day I got a call from the people at MGM, who now had obtained the rights to

From Beyond and were finally about to release it on DVD. They had found a small film can containing little scraps of celluloid and could I come to their laboratory to identify them? Feeling like a parent being called to the County Morgue to identify his child's body, I was handed the small film can and immediately recognized Lee Percy's handwriting on the metal container. "For video version" it read. Inside were all the trims that the MPAA had excised in 1986: little pieces of 35mm film that contained all the material that they had found so offensive. Over a period of several months the pieces were digitally cleaned and recut into the film. The process was like piecing together a jigsaw puzzle as there was no time code to guide us as to which piece went where. The results were amazing, and in the final version, it's impossible to determine which was newly-added footage.

The scene that had been the most brutalized by the MPAA was Dr. Bloch's brain sucking episode. Carolyn came back to record groans and gasps to bring the re-cut sequence to screaming life. It made me feel so good to undo the damage that the film had endured for over two decades. Unfortunately, there were never any 35mm prints struck of the new version, so it is still rarely screened at film festivals.

I also learned a bitter lesson about self-censorship on *From Beyond*. There was a scene near the beginning of the film in which Crawford Tillinghast, realizing that Pretorius' Resonator actually works, walks in on his boss to find him torturing a naked woman. The girl is trussed up, bondage style, and wears a leather gag. We see that her tongue protrudes from a slit in the gag and a large nail has been pounded through it. Crawford frees her and, terrified, she quickly throws on a coat and runs off. When I watched this scene in the editing room back in 1986, it became instantly clear that the MPAA would never allow this to remain in the finished film. "Maybe we should leave it so we can trade it for another scene," suggested Lee Percy. I stupidly told him to cut it. Today it seems that every other young girl has a pierced tongue, and what was so outré in 1986 is commonplace today. Unfortunately, Lee did not save that scene with the other trims so it has been lost forever. The lesson learned is to never censor yourself. And I have tried to follow that rule ever since.

Things were not going well in the partnership between Brian and Charlie. Brian had not received a dime from *Re-Animator* and, to make things worse, Charlie had bought himself a 14th century castle in nearby Giove, a picturesque little town between Rome and Florence. Brian had raised the money to make *Re-Animator* from private investors, many of whom were his personal friends, and Charlie's buying sprees did not go down well with them, particularly since they had yet to be repaid, let alone receive any profits. To make things worse, Vestron Video, which bought the rights from Charlie to release *Re-Animator* on home video, had also neglected to pay Brian his share in their profits, which were substantial. Brian realized that if he did not immediately distance himself from Charlie, it would appear that he was Band's accomplice. He left Empire and hired a lawyer to take legal action.

This put me in an extremely uncomfortable position. I understood and supported Brian in his struggle with Charlie to be paid what was due him and his investors (in fact I was one myself, having received points of profit participation in my contract). On the other hand, I was still under contract with Empire Pictures and owed them a third film. I decided to do my best to remain friends with both Brian and Charlie.

Since the early eighties, I had been a fan of the Japanese Transformer toys, and the anime based on them such as the *Macross* television series. Many of the toys featured cockpits for the pilots to control these gigantic robot weapon systems, and I kept waiting for someone to take advantage of this fully realized fantasy and do a live action film based on this imaginative concept. No one did, so I decided to pitch the idea of a giant robot movie to Charlie. I called it *Robojox*, the *jox* coming from *fighterjox*, an expression popularized in *Top Gun*. The story would be about the men and women who pilot these mechanical behemoths in futuristic single combats that have taken the place of wars. The plot came from Homer's *Iliad* (which, strangely enough, no reviewer or fan ever commented on) and would retell the story of the great warrior Achilles who refuses to fight but is forced to take the field when his lover steals his armor and is killed fighting in his place. Charlie loved the idea but realized that to pull it off we would need a much larger budget than any of Empire's previous films. The concept seemed perfect for stop-motion, so David Allen, the genius puppet master currently hard at work on completing *Dolls*, was given the job of creating an opening sequence that could be used to sell the concept. It took him and his talented crew almost six months, but the results were amazing. The scene began with a frozen landscape in which we dolly across the broken pieces of these fallen fighting machines lying half-covered in snow until the eerie silence is shattered by an explosion. A robot arm crashes into the foreground, and we join a fierce ongoing battle.

Meanwhile, I was developing the script with Joe Haldeman. Joe wrote several drafts of the script and came up with the phrase "Crash & Burn" which I believe is a bikers' saying that he discovered. Joe had the Jox use it as a "Break a leg" expression of good luck as they bumped knuckles. But Albert Band felt that Joe's script lacked heart, so I brought on Dennis Paoli to do a rewrite. His work attempting to humanize the characters still did not achieve the much-sought-after green light.

Charlie wheeled and dealed and in February of 1987, we were back in Rome prepping *Robojox*. We again stayed in the guest house on the Barzini's estate, and Suzanna was back at the Overseas American School. She had been nervous about returning and asked me to stay with her until she felt comfortable. I assured her I would, and we made a plan that she would let me know when she felt comfortable enough for me to leave by touching her finger to the side of her nose as a secret sign between us, (I had borrowed the gesture from the con men in *The Sting*).

I escorted her to her classroom and as soon as we walked in the door her classmates instantly recognized her. "Suzanna!" they cried, rushing to her happily and surrounding her. It was as if she had never left, and she quickly glanced back at me, her finger already on her nose. I smiled, thinking how wonderfully adaptable children can be. She was having such a good time with her Roman friends that I don't think she even noticed when I left.

The cast of *Robojox* featured the terrific Gary Graham (later the star of *Alien Nation*) as Achilles and the wonderful Anne-Marie Johnson (*In Living Color* and the television series *In the Heat of the Night*) as Athena. (Early on we had decided to change the legend and make the couple hetero.) Since Athena has to steal Achilles' armor, they needed to be the same height. According to their resumes, Gary and Anne-Marie were exactly the same height: 5'11". When we got them together, however, Anne-Marie towered over Gary. It turned out that they had both fibbed about their heights.

During the casting process in Los Angeles, I had a difficult time finding an actress to play Athena. We had decided early on that, as she was a Gen-Jock, a genetically engineered super soldier, she should appear to be a racial hybrid. We narrowed the search to an athletic black actress. Vanessa Williams, the first African American Miss America (who had to give up her crown after nude photos of her surfaced in *Penthouse*), had auditioned for me and was brilliant as well as stunningly beautiful, with hypnotic green eyes. I was ready to cast her, but her then-husband and manager, Ramon Hervey II, called to tell me that he had a big future in mind for his talented wife and had no intention of allowing her to appear in "some cheesy space movie." I asked him why she had auditioned twice for the part if he felt that way and he lamely mumbled something about if he had known she was auditioning he would have discouraged her from doing so. Oh well, back to the drawing board.

Around this time *Pumping Iron II: The Women* was released. It featured the gorgeous champion body builder, Gladys Portugues. I quickly had Anthony Barnao, my casting director, contact her agent and set up an audition. It turned out that Gladys had a high-pitched voice with a thick Brooklyn accent, and she struggled with the audition. I thanked her but had to ask her to flex for me before she left. She graciously obliged and I was blown away when she seemed to double in size in the blink of an eye. She had arrived with her husband, a scrawny European who proudly told me that he was a champion kickboxer about to star in his first film and that he was destined to become an even bigger star than Arnold Schwarzenegger. "Just what the world needs," I thought to myself, "kick boxing movies," and I didn't even have him read for a role. His name was Jean-Claude Van Damme.

Giant sets with full-size robot legs and cockpits were built by our talented production designer, Giovanni Natalucci. He took advantage of those enormous Dinocittà sound stages to work wonders. One scene features the actual 20-foot-tall studio door opening majestically as Achilles enters the gigantic robot hanger and steps into the gantry elevator to reach the cockpit of the 120-foot-tall fighting machine.

God bless Mac Ahlberg, our Swedish cinematographer, who managed to make our budget look five times as large. I remember him telling the set dresser that the interior of his Subaru looked more futuristic than the cockpit of Achilles' robot; the next day the dresser had completely redone it way beyond Subaru. (If you watch the movie closely, you can see a few shots where the cockpit is still pre-Subaru.) When we wrapped principal photography, we believed we had the makings of a movie that could take its place alongside *Star Wars*. The only thing missing was the robots.

Now it was time for Dave Allen and his legion of effects guys to do their magic. Dave Allen had done the opening scene of the Robot Burial Ground in conventional miniature fashion on a tabletop in a studio – the most easily controlled situation. But when I returned to Los Angeles after wrapping principal photography in Italy, he informed me that he had an even better way to shoot the rest of the robot battles: outdoors under real sunshine, in a dry lake bed in the Mojave Desert. Dave's reasoning was that sunlight provides enough natural light to allow the camera an enormous depth of field so that objects like the miniatures can be close to the camera looking big while other elements can be very far away looking tiny, and everything will be in focus.

Then we received the letter from Orion Pictures, the producers of *Robocop*. It was from their legal department. They threatened to sue us if we used the title *Robojox*. It was too similar to their title they told us, and it interfered with their ability to do business. We argued that we had started shooting our film before they had. The problem was that they had already released *Robocop* and we were still shooting effects. Our lawyers told us we had to change the title. So, our movie became *Robot Jox*. In my mind, though, it will always be *Robojox*. I always tell people that the *T* is silent.

One day, I showed up to work at Empire and was stopped at the door by hulking security guards. I had to identify myself and show them my driver's license. "What's going on?' I asked, but was met by a wall of silence. I quickly discovered that a very hostile take-over was in progress. Suits were walking around carrying clipboards. The bank, Crédit Lyonnais, had demanded that its loan of over twenty million dollars be repaid immediately. I got into the tiny elevator and headed for the third floor. I found Charlie's assistant, Bennah, cleaning out her desk, but she buzzed Charlie to let him know I was there. I discovered him sitting in the dark, holding his head in his hands. The blinds were closed, and his walls were completely stripped of the outrageous posters for insane new Empire movies. When he looked up at me, he seemed like an old man.

"It's over, dude." he told me. I tried to tell him that he would find a way to turn things around. Maybe we could show the bank some of the footage from *Robot Jox*. But he just shook his head. "It's over," he said again.

When I tried to leave the building, security guards were searching everyone's brief cases at the door and patting us down. I even saw them confiscate a can of prunes that Albert was carrying out. The reasons for Empire's sudden demise were vague: overexpansion, too many productions, the decline of the Italian lire. But the story that has emerged over the years is that it was *Robot Jox* that killed Empire. With its budget rumored to be ten million dollars (but actually less than six), it supposedly stretched Empire's resources to the breaking point. The truth is that Empire had eleven other pictures in production at the time. In fact, I always believed that *Robot Jox* was the film that could have saved the studio. But Charlie was denied time to even find new funding. The bank had seized all of Empire's assets, one of which happened to be the movie that we had been working on for over two years.

Everything ground to a halt while the new company Epic Productions reviewed the *Robot Jox* footage. Six months dragged by. Finally, I was called in to meet with Moshe Diamant, the new CEO, who told me he had decided to complete the film. There was only a small problem: during the delay the world had changed. In 1989 the Berlin Wall came down and soon the Soviet Union became a distant memory. Our film, begun three years earlier, had mirrored the politics of the Cold War: two superpowers rebuilding after a nuclear war, The Market (us) and The Confederation (them), were now using robot battles to settle territorial conflicts. The bad guys had Russian accents and were knocking back vodka and the film suddenly seemed hopelessly dated. When it finally opened in 1990, four years after we had begun, even the Transformer craze that had originally inspired our film was dead. As a result, as we say in the movie business, our film didn't open.

But God bless the fans. Many were ten years old when they first saw my movie on HBO or on VHS and they never forgot it. When I meet them at film festivals or conventions, they always want to bump knuckles with me and say the *Robojox* greeting that now seems more appropriate than ever: "Crash & Burn."

1987

Brian Yuzna wanted to make a movie his children could see. A Disney film had been screened at his kids' school. *The Journey of Natty Gann* had been directed by a classmate's father. Brian knew there was absolutely no chance of them screening one of ours.

"Why don't we make a movie for kids?" I asked him.

He brightened. "What should it be about?"

Suzanna and Jill loved Lily Tomlin's *The Incredible Shrinking Woman*, the story of a housewife who begins shrinking after being exposed to an array of toxic household products that her advertising biz husband promotes. My daughters found it hilarious and watched it over and over.

What if we did a movie in which the *kids* were able to shrink? I knew my kids would love it. Brian was also charmed by the idea and together we created a treatment. The story was about a scientist who develops a ray that can shrink matter, but accidentally reduces his own children to the size of ants. As a matter of fact, they become even smaller than ants, as we had a scene in which they ride on the backs of the tiny insects. We named the film *Teeny Weenies*, a title inspired by the old Sunday newspaper comic strip.

My new agent, Jeremy Zimmer, set up a meeting for us to pitch the idea at Disney. It was a very exciting day when we were passed through the studio gates. I remembered that my family had been invited to tour Disney Studios long ago when I had first visited Los Angeles as a ten-year-old child. That trip never happened when my mother's father, Isidore, had a stroke and we rushed home; he died two weeks later. Now, here I was walking toward the Animation Building where so many of the favorite films of my childhood were created.

The studio had fallen on hard times. Walt Disney's nephew, Roy Jr., had just saved it from a corporate takeover. He quickly replaced studio head Ron Miller (Walt's son-in-law) with Michael Eisner and Frank Wells. Michael, who had been the head of production at Paramount, was the creative idea man and Frank would have control of the financial decisions, a situation that mirrored the original partnership of Walt the dreamer and his businessman-brother, Roy Sr.

Brian and I met with David Hoberman, a creative executive (a term that some believe to be an oxymoron) on the fourth floor of the Animation Building. Hoberman, a good-looking young guy with dark, curly hair, pushed a button on his desk that automatically closed his office door behind us. He motioned for us to sit in leather armchairs around a coffee table and, as we talked, he leaned back in his chair and put his Italian loafer-covered feet onto the table. I was shocked when every other word out of his mouth was *fuck* or *bullshit*. This was Disney, after all. We pitched our story and he quietly listened, chewing on his almost non-existent fingernails. After we finished, there was a long pause.

"We could turn this into a ride," he finally said.

"A ride?"

"At Disneyland," he patiently explained. Brian and I looked at each other. Had we just made a sale? "How much would this cost?" Now it was Brian's turn to spring into action.

"We've been making our movies for less than five million," he told Hoberman. "We could do this for less than ten." This seemed to please the young executive.

"I'll have to talk to Jeffrey," he told us. "We've been told to stay away from family films." This, of course, surprised us. No family films at Disney?

"We'll get back to you," he told us.

I immediately called Jeremy to report on the meeting, but before I could say anything, he told me that Hoberman had already called him and said that Disney wanted to put our film into development immediately. A deal was quickly negotiated for us to write *Teeny Weenies*, for me to direct, and for Brian to produce. My payday was over half a million dollars plus profit participation.

In our minds, there was only one person to write it with us: Ed Naha. Ed had written *Dolls* and seemed particularly good at creating believable children's characters. He loved the idea of the film, and soon he was approved by Disney. Brian, Ed and I hammered out a detailed outline of the story. We named the mad scientist Wayne Szalinski, the last name coming from my high school home room teacher. We named Wayne's daughter Amy after then-President Jimmy Carter's popular young daughter.

Ed's method is to first write what is essentially a prose version of the story, which I'm sure comes from his background as a novelist. Soon there was a very detailed seventy-page treatment which we handed in to the studio. In what seemed like ten minutes, we received their notes: over a hundred pages. What made things even more confusing was that many of the notes were contradictory. "We like this scene" they would say and then in the next paragraph, "This scene should be cut." The notes had clearly been written by several different people. I called Jeremy and asked him what to do. "You have to figure out which notes are Katzenberg's," he told me. "Those are the only ones you need to pay attention to." It soon became clear that the most copious notes were from Katzenberg and his notes were always the most blunt: "This scene is a do-over." No sugar-coating from him.

We discussed the suggested changes and once again I was on the phone with Jeremy. "What if we don't agree with his notes?" I asked him. "How many do we have to follow?" Jeremy's answer was exactly what I hoped it would be, "Just do the ones that you think will make the script better."

The process of writing our first draft began. It took about three months for Ed to turn it in. Once again, the next round of notes immediately appeared and, again, they far outnumbered the actual page count of our script. This process continued for over a year, during which time we handed in more than a dozen drafts of the script. We were frustrated and knew we needed to do something to move the process toward production. Bob Greenberg suggested we find a graphic artist to render some of the key scenes. "Most executives can't make heads or tails out of a script," he told us. "You need to show them some pictures to excite them."

This is exactly what George Lucas had done after every studio in town had passed on *Star Wars*. They couldn't make sense of Jedi knights and characters with names like: "Chewbacca" or "Obi Wan Kenobi," so Lucas hired artist Ralph McQuarrie to show them what the movie would look like and the iconic paintings he created were able to get Twentieth Century-Fox enthused enough to finally produce the film. Bob recommended we hire the great Mentor Huebner, the artist who had done production illustrations and story boards for *Blade Runner*, *Fiddler on the Roof*, *The Time Machine*, *North By Northwest*, *Forbidden Planet*, and *Ben-Hur*. Mentor did some brilliant charcoal drawings, and Disney's enthusiasm for our project seemed to suddenly grow, just as Bob had predicted. When I called Bob to thank him, his wife Brenda answered the phone. She was beside herself with worry and told me that Bob had been in a terrible car accident. A drunk driver had veered across the double yellow line and had smashed into Bob's car. "Thank God he didn't have the baby with him," Brenda sobbed. They had been trying for children for years and she had just given birth to a son, Justin, their pride and joy. Bob had been taken to the hospital with a severe head injury and was in intensive care. It soon became apparent that the damage to his brain was so extensive that he would never recover.

After several weeks, with no signs of improvement, a decision was made to take him off the respirator. Miraculously, he continued to breathe on his own. Weeks later, when he was finally taken out of the ICU, I was able to see him and I was shocked by Bob's condition. His eyes moved around constantly, never focusing on anything, and his tongue lolled out of his mouth like an infant's. I tried to show him the Mentor Huebner drawings, but he couldn't even focus on them, let alone speak. He wasn't even aware that I was there. After several more weeks, it appeared that this condition was permanent. When I called Ron Berman to ask his opinion, he offered little hope, "This is what we all dread," he said, "to be so compromised that we've become a vegetable." Was there nothing that we could do? His assessment was bleak. "The only thing that can be done is to pull the plug." But this clearly was not an option. "As doctors, we're not allowed to put people out of their misery," Ron told me. "That's something that needs to change, but until it does, there isn't much that can be done besides withholding nourishment."

I was shocked. "You mean starve him to death?"

"That's about it." He answered grimly.

After weeks of visiting Bob and hoping for a sign that he was responsive in any way, but receiving none, Brenda had come to the same inevitable conclusion. I asked if I could see Bob again before the hospital began withholding food and water. When I entered his hospital room, it was clear that his condition remained unchanged. I told Bob what was happening, that unless he could show them that he understood, he would be starved to death. I pleaded with him to show me a sign.

"Blink your eyes," I begged him. "Tap a finger! Please, Bob! Please! Show me you can understand!" But there was nothing, no discernible change in his behavior. The hideous plan went forward. It took him several weeks to die, and by the end the once chubby man with his cherubic smiling face had withered away to a skeleton. He died September 9th, 1987, at the age of forty-one. The man who destroyed Bob while driving drunk – depriving his wife, Brenda, of a husband, his infant son, Justin, of a father and me of a dear friend and mentor – served just one year in prison.

Bob had generously given up his chance to direct his first feature film and allowed me to take his place. I had come to Los Angeles at his urging and after the success of *Re-Animator*, he had told me that now I would be able to direct feature films for the next twenty years. And I have. He had been my most trusted advisor, always looking out for me. And I had been forced to stand by and watch him slowly die and now he was gone. I felt terribly guilty. I also felt abandoned. Alone.

A production meeting was called for *Teeny Weenies*. Instead of taking place in Hoberman's office as they had in the past, this one was held in a large conference room on the fourth floor of the Animation Building, at a table that seated over twenty people. Joining us were production accountants and special effects experts. At the head of the table was Jeffrey Katzenberg himself. A small, thin man in his mid-thirties with oversize glasses, Jeffrey dominated the meeting.

"Welcome to the first production meeting for *Teeny Weenies*," he began. Were we actually in production? "Clearly we have to find a new title," Jeffrey continued. Then he turned to me. "*Teeny Weenies*. Is the title autobiographical?" and the room burst into laughter. "You've told us that this movie can be made for ten million dollars," Katzenberg went on. "Is that really possible?" Brian was about to answer, but before he could, Jeffrey turned to another person at the table, an older bearded fellow. "Tom?" This, we would learn, was Tom Smith, former general manager of the best special effects company in Hollywood (or anywhere else), George Lucas's Industrial Light and Magic. Tom now headed up special effects for Disney.

"The original *Star Wars* was made for eleven," he answered, "But that was ten years ago."

"We did a ballpark budget based on the last draft of the script," a woman in a suit chimed in, "And we don't think the movie can be made for less than twenty million." This set the table buzzing. I turned to Tom Smith, "But isn't it true that until the film is storyboarded, it's really impossible to determine how much the effects will cost?" Tom agreed with me, and the result was that Jeffrey told me to hire a storyboard artist and begin the process.

Tom Smith recommended Marty Kline, who had worked with Steven Spielberg on *Who Framed Roger Rabbit*. Soon we began storyboarding, but the number of effects scenes was so numerous that we ended up hiring a second artist, David Russell. Soon, my days were taken up working with these two excellent artists as they sketched each shot based on my suggestions. Both were witty and imaginative, and we soon became friends. When a sequence was fully boarded, I'd discuss with Tom Smith the various processes for realizing each shot, and a fairly accurate effects budget was created. Unfortunately, it seemed that the lady bean-counter's original estimate of twenty million dollars seemed to be correct. We discussed this at another meeting around the giant conference table.

"The characters shrink to a quarter inch in height, is that correct?" someone asked. "Would we save any money if they only shrank to half an inch?" Tom Smith had the answer, "Not really," he said, and then added, "But we'd save a fortune if they only shrunk half an inch." Again, the room erupted with laughter.

Don't think that working for Disney was all fun and games. Jeffrey Katzenberg was a harsh taskmaster, expecting everyone to work just as hard as he did. The workday often went on long into the night. "If you don't like coming to work on Saturday," Jeffrey would say, "Don't bother showing up on Sunday."

We wrestled with the budget, looking for ways to save money and receive the long-sought-after green light. The head of production at Disney at the time was always coming up with innovative schemes to save money and he decided that *Teeny Weenies* would not officially be a Disney film, but would instead become what is termed a "negative pick-up." This means that the production company making the film would be independent of the studio and could work for lower rates, ultimately selling the finished film to Disney. This would enable us to hire crews at far less than the full studio rates and, although we would not be able to use the enormous Disney soundstages, we could also avoid the high rentals that we would be charged. It was also decided that it would be a great idea to shoot the movie at Churubusco Studios in Mexico City, the largest studio in Latin America. *Romancing the Stone* and *Rambo: First Blood Part II* had both been shot there, the crews were excellent, and they would work for a fraction of the cost of an American crew. They also had incredible set builders, carpenters and plasterers, who could build the oversize sets, cutting down on the need for expensive blue screen shots.

We were told to shoot the scenes that took place in the neighboring houses of our protagonists in San Diego, which would be far cheaper (Los Angeles, being the center of production since the beginning of cinema, is notorious for high location fees). We quickly hired a location scout who eventually found two houses next door to each other in a suburb of San Diego that seemed ideal: one neat and homey like the family's house on *Leave It to Beaver*, the other a more ramshackle place that looked like it could be the home of our mad scientist and his quirky brood.

Altogether these cost-saving ideas cut our budget down to fifteen million dollars and the project (still named *Teeny Weenies*) was finally greenlit. Now we could begin serious pre-production and hire our crew. Mac Ahlberg had worked with Gregg Fonseca, a talented production designer and, based on Mac's enthusiasm, Gregg was quickly hired to work on our film. Gregg, tall, thin, and very intense, and his crack team of designers and draftsmen photographed every square inch of the two houses so he could match the interiors on sound stages in Mexico. It later was discovered that it would be cheaper to build the complete exteriors of the two houses from scratch on a back lot at Churubusco. The Mexican studio was ready to absorb the construction costs of the American-style houses for use in future films. The duplication of the houses was so exact that when the owners of the houses in San Diego eventually saw our finished film, they thought that we had somehow secretly filmed our movie in their homes while they were away at work without compensating them. In fact, they originally threatened to sue Disney until the truth was explained to them.

Fonseca had been sent to Mexico to begin building the sets, and the producers and I set up a trip to visit Churubusco Studios. The only problem was that I had yet to be paid a penny for my services and, when I mentioned this to my agent, he told me not to get on the plane to Mexico without a check in my hand. When I pointed this out to David Hoberman at Disney, he got rather huffy. Didn't I realize that I was no longer working for these fly-by-night companies? This is Disney Studios, for chrissake! I should be kissing their asses to be working there! I responded that the fly-by-night companies always paid me before they expected me to go on location. So here I was at the boarding gate, and no check had arrived. I was just about to turn and go home when an accountant arrived, out of breath, check in hand.

I returned to Los Angeles, where the studio was still struggling to bring down the budget. Jeffrey was still throwing concepts at us. Once, he suggested that the minuscule kids should encounter an enormous pile of dog shit, "As big as the Beverly Center!" he enthused. Now thanks to Jeffrey, whenever I see the Beverly Center, I think of it as an enormous turd. He also started talking about a scene where the kids end up in a shopping cart at a grocery store and ginormous boxes of food products are bombarding them. I couldn't imagine where this idea was coming from until someone explained that Jeffrey was looking for ways to amp up "product placement," a system that allows corporations to have their products on display in major motion pictures in exchange for paying the studio sizeable fees that could help offset production costs. One day, Hoberman asked me what the ant that befriended our tiny kids would look like. "Like an ant," I answered, puzzled by the question.

"Don't you think that might scare little kids?" he wanted to know. "Maybe it could look like E.T. and have blue eyes." It turned out that he had been approached by someone who envisioned blue-eyed ant plushy dolls.

"Everyone knows what an ant looks like," I told him, "And if we make it cartoony, the reality of the whole movie will go down the tubes."

"But ants are so fucking ugly," he whined, used to getting his own way.

"I'm sick of movies where the good characters are always beautiful and the bad characters are always ugly," I argued. "Sometimes ugly creatures can be good."

I finally had to bring Hoberman to the effects studio where John Naulin was building an anatomically accurate giant ant puppet for the film. I asked John to have the puppet ant snuggle with me, lovingly wrapping its antenna around my shoulder to hug me. This seemed to convince Hoberman, and I never heard about the blue-eyed ants again. But years later I saw DreamWork's animated film *Antz*, produced by Jeffrey Katzenberg, and guess what? All the cartoon ants had blue eyes.

I started doubting if my concept of creating a film that my kids could enjoy would ever be possible with a company that seemed so obsessed with the bottom line. My subconscious must have been stressing as well, for that night, I had a dream in which Walt Disney himself appeared to me.

"These people aren't storytellers, they're salesmen," he said, looking just like he did when I used to watch him on the old *Disneyland* TV show. This immediately comforted me. He went on, "We were artists. We were back-alley Picassos. If you want to see what we were about, go to the studio library. It's all there."

I awoke grinning, feeling as if a huge weight had been lifted from my shoulders. I must have laughed out loud because I awakened Carolyn and she asked me what was so funny at three in the morning? "I just went over Katzenberg's head," I told her.

She was confused, "You talked to Eisner?"

"I went over his head too," I told her, grinning from ear to ear. "I just had a meeting with Walt."

The next day I asked someone at the studio where the library was. This seemed to confuse him. "There is none, as far as I know," I was told. And then there was a pause, "Unless you mean the archives."

The archives were in a little room on the first floor of the Roy Disney building across the street from the Animation Building.

I spent the whole day there reading and could see how Walt, the most expert storyteller of all time, got his ideas and developed them. I felt like Salieri looking over Mozart's original compositions. I was in the presence of true genius.

Now I wasn't so threatened by Katzenberg and the other suits. As Walt had told me in my dream, they were salesmen, not artists. I was making a Disney film. And it was up to me to lead the way and create a movie that could join the best of Disney's classics.

I had an idea that I knew would please Jeffrey; a way to use product placement to make our movie even better. It involved one of the kids falling into his father's bowl of Cheerios. Using the O-shaped cereal as a life preserver, he is lifted up in a spoonful of milk and almost devoured by his inventor dad. Luckily, his father spots him just before swallowing his son and the kids are rescued. This idea replaced an involved effects sequence, saving hundreds of thousands of dollars. Even better, it had a Freudian perversity ("Please, Dad, don't eat me!!") that I loved and knew would be one of the most memorable scenes in the entire movie.

Crash!

In August of 1987, I celebrated my 40th birthday. I walked into the backyard after parking my car in the garage and was greeted with a huge "Surprise!" All of my Organic friends, now living in Los Angeles, were there: Joe Mantegna and his wife Arlene, Dennis Franz, Meshach Taylor, Mike Saad, Patrick Williams and Josephine Williams, now husband and wife. We reminisced and told stories about our adventures on tour in Europe, and it was a wonderful evening – a nice break from the building tension of working at Disney studios.

I was now in the process of casting *Teeny Weenies* (as it was still called), and I remember that the first person to audition was John Goodman. He was perfect for the role of Big Russ Thompson, the next-door neighbor to our mad scientist. But in those days, he was a fresh-faced newcomer, and Hoberman told me to see a few more people before signing him. The result was that John quickly was snapped up by another production.

Coincidentally, I also had the idea of auditioning Roseanne Barr for the role of Big Russ' wife. Keep in mind that this was several years before her television series in which she and John Goodman would famously star together. In those days, she was a stand-up comic whose material could politely be termed "blue." (One of her jokes involved her husband accidentally getting a garage door opener as a penile implant and all she had to do was hit the button on the remote control.) Hoberman was horrified by the notion of this raunchy comedienne appearing in a Disney film and made me swear that I would never ever suggest the idea of hiring her to Katzenberg.

I am a big fan of *SCTV* (*Second City Television*), which was a syndicated late-night competitor to *Saturday Night Live*. Most of the Organic Theater Company members were hooked on the hilarious series, and I remember us all rushing home after our double shows on Saturday night, ordering a pizza, and watching the brilliant John Candy, Rick Moranis, Eugene Levy, Catherine O'Hara, Andrea Martin, and Joe Flaherty. I thought Flaherty would be great as Wayne Szalinski, but the studio wanted a bigger name. They ended up casting Rick Moranis.

Casting the kids was a more difficult problem. A teenage Jennifer Connelly had auditioned and was quite wonderful. She had already starred in several big studio films including *Once Upon a Time in America*. She turned down our offer. So did the parents of Heather Graham, who was sixteen at the time. She could have been Barbara Crampton's younger sister with her blonde curls and big blue eyes, but her parents were worried about her going to Mexico. It didn't surprise me that, when she turned eighteen and could choose her own projects, her breakthrough movie was *Drugstore Cowboy*, in which she played a teenaged hooker/heroin addict.

It was at this time that Mac Ahlberg told me that he had accepted another job and wouldn't be our director of photography. This was a big blow, as Mac and I had done four films together and it was hard to imagine working with anyone else.

I chose several young actors to play the kids who are accidentally shrunk to the size of fleas. They included John Cameron Mitchell, who had been so wonderful as Huckleberry Finn in our production at the Goodman Theatre. I also chose Alexandra Auder, who was the teenaged daughter of Viva, Andy Warhol's favorite actress, and the Timony twins from New York city. They had never acted before but were wonderfully funny and engaging. The studio had insisted on screen tests, which I supervised and later sat with the Disney executives to watch the results. "You've been making too many horror films," said Rich Frank, the head of Disney television who, for some reason, Katzenberg had brought in as a producer on our film. "These kids are monsters!" It was true that our child actors were not your typical blonde, blue-eyed movie-kids, but they all had a natural, non-show-biz presence that made them believable as real kids. And they were all excellent actors.

The next day I was told that none of them were acceptable to the studio and that I would have to keep looking. This struck me like a knife blow to the heart. When I met with Hoberman to protest this and plead for the studio to change its mind, he held firm. As I argued with him, my nose started to bleed. It was not your typical nosebleed in which the blood runs down your upper lip. The blood literally shot out of my nose and showered the papers on Hoberman's desk. Shocked, he jumped up and grabbed for a box of Kleenex. I pulled out a handful to stop the deluge, and holding them to my bleeding nose, quickly retreated. It took over an hour for the nosebleed to completely stop and when I called Carolyn, she insisted I see my doctor right away. He took my blood pressure and discovered that it was 350/200 (normal is 120/90). "You're lucky it was your nose that blew," Dr. Saliba told me. "If it had been higher up (he pointed to his head), it would have been all over for you." He told me that until my blood pressure was under control I should not continue working on the film. The stress was simply too much for me. When I discussed this with Carolyn, she asked me, "Is this movie good enough to be your last?"

I was devastated, but in some ways relieved to be removed from the daily battles that seemed to be an integral part of working for Disney. I called my agent, Jeremy Zimmer, and of course it turned out he had already spoken to Hoberman. I asked for his advice. If I had to quit the film, would I ever work again? His answer was unforgettable. "I don't know," he began, "But I do know one thing: dead directors never work again."

I called Brian Yuzna and we discussed what to do. We both knew that if I quit, Brian's chances of staying on the project without me were minimal at best. To his great credit, he was supportive, so the next morning I phoned Hoberman and told him that I had to drop out. A few hours later the phone rang. Carolyn answered it. It was Jeffrey Katzenberg himself. He spoke to her first (something she has never forgotten) and seemed genuinely concerned. He then told me that he hoped I'd make a speedy recovery. I thanked him. He was the only executive from Disney who ever called.

My doctor put me on a new regime of blood pressure medication and bed rest and, amazingly, in a few days I was back to normal. A week later I went back to the production offices. It was a very strange return. Everyone gave me odd "What's he doing here?" looks. When I entered my office, I found my personal things had been put into cardboard boxes. Special effects expert Tom Smith now sat at my desk, and he appeared to be running the show.

I called my agent. Jeremy explained that the studio had indeed replaced me and were now looking for a new director. Brian's services were also no longer needed. I felt terrible that my illness had cost him his job too. I realized that I had made a major mistake by resigning. I had lost my chance to direct my first studio film, and I still find myself wondering how my life would have changed if I had been able to hang in there and direct the film that would become the blockbuster *Honey, I Shrunk the Kids*.

Here I was, having just moved into a new house and wondering where my next paycheck would come from. Was I now damaged goods? Would I ever work again?

And Carolyn had some big news for me: She was pregnant. Would we be able to afford another mouth to feed? I hugged her and told her that of course we would. "Babies are lucky," I told her, and something would turn up to keep us in the game. It did.

Jim Belushi (John's younger brother) showed up one day telling me that he was there to whip me into shape. He had heard about my leaving Disney from our manager Sandy Wernick, and talked me through an exercise regime of push-ups, sit-ups and squat thrusts that had me ready to pass out. When I complained, his reply was, "Hey, you ain't pukin' yet!" After a few of these sessions, he tape-recorded the routine so I could exercise on a daily basis without him. We called it the "You Ain't Pukin' Workout." It seemed to help; whatever doesn't kill you makes you stronger. I still call Jim "Coach."

As the weeks went by, I learned that Tom Smith got the studio to hire his protégé, Joe Johnston, as the new director.

above: The *From Beyond* crew posing with the Resonator.

below: With Brian Yuzna and festival director Freddy Bozo (crouching) while visiting Brussels International Festival of Fantasy Film (BIFFF) in 1986 for a screening of *From Beyond.*

bottom: With Brian Yuzna (left) and Carolyn (right) at the same Brussels International Festival of Fantasy screening of *From Beyond.*

above: Making a few adjustments to the Resonator on the set of *From Beyond.*

above: Ted Sorel and the effects team on the set of *From Beyond.*

opposite: Transforming Dr. Edward Pretorius (Ted Sorel) during the filming of *From Beyond.*

left: Ted Sorel in full make-up during the filming of *From Beyond.*

below: The effects team working on a cast for the transformation of Dr. Edward Pretorius in *From Beyond.*

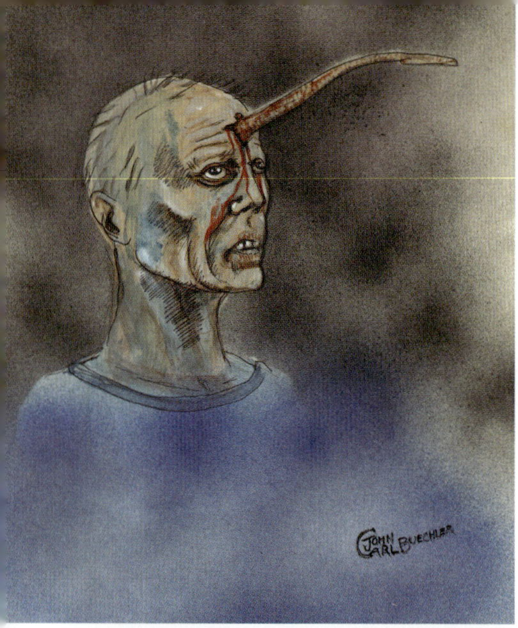

above: Ted Sorel in make-up during the filming of *From Beyond.*

left and opposite: Original special make-up effects concept art sketches for *From Beyond* by John Carl Buechler.

below: An extensive effects and make-up crew was engaged to realise the unspeakable, trans-dimensional horrors described in H.P. Lovecraft's *From Beyond.*

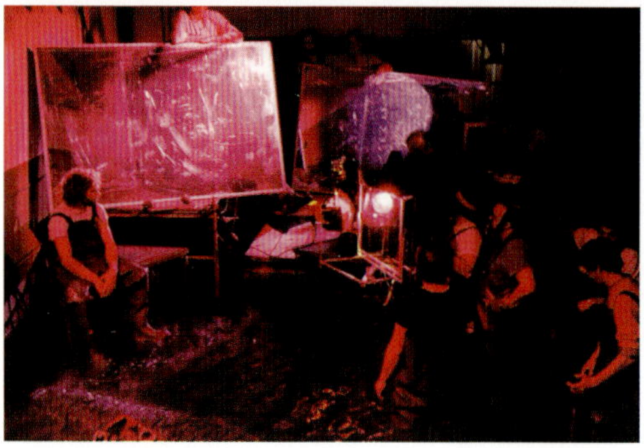

JOHN CARL BUECHLER

above: Shooting with a large cable-puppeteered Achilles at El Mirage Dry Lake bed during the making of *Robot Jox*, 1987.

opposite top: A publicity still for *Dolls*.

opposite bottom and below: Concept art for *Robot Jox* by Ron Cobb.

right: Costume design concept sketch for Achilles by Kathie Clark.

above:
Behind the scenes during the filming of *Daughter of Darkness.*

left and below:
Daughter of Darkness set design concept art by Tamás Hornyánszky.

I'm frequently asked how my version of *Honey, I Shrunk the Kids* would have differed from Joe Johnston's film. The main difference would have been that I wanted the miniature world to be stunningly beautiful. I had been studying micro-photography of insects and blades of grass and was astounded by how surreal and exotic it all seemed when highly magnified. Even the simplest things like wood grain became amazingly complex textures when enlarged, and I made sure that production designer Gregg Fonseca duplicated these photographs in his oversize landscapes and objects. The moment that the children emerge into the jungle that is their own backyard, I saw as being comparable to Dorothy's first look at the wonders of the Land of Oz and had planned for the scene to be accompanied by Ravel's sumptuous tone poem *Daphnis et Chloé*. Instead, we ended up with James Horner's score that was so derivative of Nino Rota's music for Fellini's *Amarcord* (and a swiped jazz piece called *Powerhouse* by Raymond Scott) that Disney was sued and forced to settle. As a result more than two decades passed before a soundtrack album was belatedly released.

Honey was released in the summer of 1989 on the same day as Tim Burton's first *Batman* film. Everyone (including myself) thought that our film was doomed, reduced to cannon fodder. Miraculously, it ended up in second place. "Counter-programming!" crowed Katzenberg. As the weeks went by, it remained in the top five, eventually leading the list at #1 after all the other films had faded away. It became the most successful live-action movie in Disney history, a title it held for seven years.

After the success of *Honey*, my agent was able to negotiate a bonus of $100,000 and a first-look deal at Disney with an office and assistant. This lasted for a number of years. Amazingly, although my profit participation was cut to only one percent, I ended up making well over a million dollars and the money is still trickling in.

I also executive produced the first sequel, *Honey, I Blew Up the Kid*, but had nothing to do with the second sequel, *Honey, We Shrunk Ourselves*, which was released direct to video. I did get a chance to direct an episode of the syndicated television series based on the films, which ran from 1997-2000 (produced, incidentally, by John Landis). I got the job because Ed Naha had been tapped as showrunner for the second and third seasons of the series.

If I had directed *Honey*, I would have become a studio director with big budgets and a far bigger salary than I have ever received. But would I have made the strange and disturbing films that I am known for if I had continued working within the studio system? Do I regret it? Sometimes. I often wish I had access to the powerful distribution machines available to the major studios, spending as much on marketing as they do on making their films. But at least I can look at myself in a mirror and still call myself an artist.

For whatever that's worth.

Margaret

1988 was the year Charlie Band started a new production company that he christened Full Moon. I pitched him a new version of Edgar Allan Poe's *The Pit and the Pendulum*, the idea inspired by a tour of the Tower of London with Brian Yuzna. We were both horrified by the treatment of the unfortunate prisoners who must have felt that their ultimate beheadings were merciful compared to the daily tortures they were forced to endure. It made me think about Poe's great story (my favorite). Dennis Paoli and I soon wrote a treatment and showed it to Charlie. He loved the idea and saw it as a way to put his new company on the map. It was planned to be a grand epic. Vestron, the largest video company of the day, agreed to put substantial money into it. I believe our budget was seven million dollars, the most substantial Charlie had ever had.

Anthony Barnao was again my casting director, and we went after name actors. We had signed *The Empire Strikes Back*'s Billy Dee Williams to play a Moorish prince and the red-hot Sherilyn Fenn of *Twin Peaks* fame to play the lovely baker's wife lusted after by the Grand Inquisitor, Torquemada. I was once again working with Charlie's dad, Albert, who served as Charlie's consigliore. It was decided that he would be my producer. We had become good friends, and I was often invited to his home for lunch followed by a game of gin rummy for half a penny a point. I would usually get blitzed, but hearing his wondrous tales of old Hollywood and never-ending off-color jokes made it worth it. His lovely wife Jackie was a former model whose picture Albert had seen on a billboard on Sunset Boulevard and fallen madly in love with her at first sight. Born in Oklahoma, she cooked us the best baked beans I've ever had. Albert gave me a picture of him and Jackie sitting in a booth with Marilyn Monroe and Joe DiMaggio, which I still have. Albert only has eyes for Jackie, who is even more beautiful than Marilyn.

One day, Albert excitedly told me that an agent friend at William Morris had called to say that the legendary Peter O'Toole was interested in the role of Torquemada. I couldn't believe my ears. I had been a fan of O'Toole from the moment I saw him in *Lawrence of Arabia*, and the idea of working with him was a dream come true. We made what we believed to be a generous offer, but the agent called telling us that Peter was passing on the project. Without skipping a beat, Albert offered O'Toole a million dollars and the next thing we knew he was on board. The only hitch was that we would have to accommodate Peter's schedule, which meant shooting the film in England instead of Italy as planned. The reason? Peter shared custody of his son Lorcan and couldn't leave Great Britain during the six months he was looking after the boy. The next thing I knew, Albert and I were in London casting the supporting roles while our sets were being built at Elstree Studios where Hitchcock had shot his early films. It was April and it rained every day. I was reminded of the prologue of Chaucer's *The Canterbury Tales*, which begins with a verse about April showers, but since Chaucer had written his stories in Middle English, I could not for the life of me remember how it went. As a result, I ended up asking every actor who auditioned if he or she knew the opening lines of *The Canterbury Tales*. No one did, and as the auditions went on, it became a joke between Albert and me. We decided that we would cast whoever knew those lines, whether they were suitable or not. But every single one of these excellent English actors failed our test. We had pretty much completed casting when Albert walked in one day and announced that we were going to Nice to have lunch with our star Peter O'Toole. "I'll have to stop at my hotel to pack a bag," I told him. "Bullshit," he replied in his usual no nonsense style. "We're just going for the day. We'll be back in time for dinner."

We bought our tickets at Heathrow, where we were informed that we needed visas to enter France. "But we're just going for the day," Albert explained. It didn't matter. The visas would take a couple of days to process, but Albert was not to be dissuaded. "Can we talk to the immigration people when we get there?" he asked. We could, but most likely they would send us back on the very next flight. Unfazed, Albert bought the tickets and told me to keep my mouth shut when we talked to the immigration officers. He would handle it. My heart was pounding on the entire hour-long flight.

As we deplaned, we were ushered to the immigration authorities. Suddenly Albert began to sob as he pleaded with the officers in perfect French. I had known that Albert had been born in Paris, but this was the first time I had ever heard him speak his native tongue. He gestured to me a few times and I nodded, taking my cue from him and looking as sad as I could. After a few moments the officials waved us through the checkpoint.

"I told them that my mother had died," Albert explained. "And I told them you're my nephew and that we're going to her funeral." Before I could reply, he added, "I've gotta take a piss." And he ducked into a men's room. As he stood at the urinal relieving himself, he started laughing, "I can't believe those idiots fell for it!" I started to laugh with him until I looked up and saw the same immigration officials entering the bathroom behind him. I tried to signal Albert, but he went on, "Those dumb French pricks, what a bunch of assholes…" Then he saw them and his face went white. They looked us up and down as we zipped up our flies, somber once again as we left the bathroom. Luckily, they didn't stop us.

We had a lovely lunch with Peter O'Toole, who was utterly charming. He told me that he had always wanted to do horror, ever since he was an acting student at the Royal Academy and would sneak into the balcony to watch Laurence Olivier in *Titus Andronicus*, Shakespeare's bloodiest play. As our time together was coming to an end, I turned to Mr. O'Toole and asked him if he, by any chance, knew the opening lines of Chaucer's *Canterbury Tales*. He seemed a little startled by this odd question. "No," he said shaking his head, "I don't think so." I was about to explain when he said, "Wait a minute, is it…

> Whan that Aprille with his shoures sote
> The droghte of Marche hath perced to the rote,
> And bathed every veyne in swich licour
> Of which vertu engendred is the flour;"

I looked to Albert grinning. He too was smiling from ear to ear. I turned to Peter O'Toole and shook his hand. "You've got the part," I told him. A few days later I headed back to Los Angeles to scoop up Carolyn and the kids and take them back to England to make the film. When I got off the plane there was a message waiting for me from Albert, who had stayed in London, telling me that Vestron was no longer financing our film. The project was dead. I was crushed. If I had just stayed in London, the movie would have somehow gotten made I thought, but I know this is completely irrational. There I was, out of work with no project and absolutely nothing on the horizon to take its place.

Our new baby was born on June 8th, 1988 – a little girl with blue eyes and blonde hair, just like my mother. We named her Margaret after Carolyn's freewheeling aunt. Although I had only met Aunt Margaret once or twice, I had instantly liked her. She reminded me of a cross between my father's larger-than-life sister, Eleanor, and Rosalind Russell's Auntie Mame.

The new baby's middle name is Berni, named after my father, a name that Margaret still hates ("Dad, it's a boy's name!"). I've discovered that children always dislike the names they're given no matter what. I remember Suzanna asking us why we couldn't have named her something pretty like Jennifer or Jessica (the *noms du jour* in the '80s). We had been thinking of giving Margaret the middle name of Elisabeth, but both of her older sisters thought that it would be completely unfair to give her such a pretty name when we had stuck them with such awful ones. Margaret is our only native Angelino, born at Cedars-Sinai Hospital where I was allowed to cut her umbilical cord (photo-op).

In November of 1988, George H.W. Bush was elected the 41st president of the United States. He had been Reagan's Vice President and, in a move seen by many as a gambit to prevent his own assassination, had chosen dim-witted Dan Quayle to be his running mate. We girded ourselves for more "trickle down" economics, which only seemed to trickle into the pockets of the super-rich. Our two older daughters were still going to school at Los Encinos where they often complained about the hot lunch that was being provided (at an extra charge). It always seemed to be some form of fast food: McDonald's, KFC, or hot dogs, usually cold by the time they arrived, and the kids were forced to eat them in the ten or fifteen minutes left of their lunch break.

"I could do better than this," Carolyn remarked one evening as the kids complained.

"Why don't you?" I asked. "After all, you served hot lunch to the theater company when we first started Organic."

Carolyn met with Mr. Holabird, the founder and principal of Los Encinos School and he seemed overjoyed with her idea of serving nutritious meals to the children at the same prices that they were paying for fast food. Carolyn ended up doing this job for almost fourteen years, long after our kids had moved on to high school.

* * *

One day I got a call from Anthony Barnao, my casting director from the days at Empire, and now Full Moon. He had been hired to cast a made-for-television movie of the week for CBS. It was a story about a young woman who discovers that her father is a vampire, and they were looking for a director. Was I interested? Anthony couriered the script to my home that afternoon and I quickly read it. Entitled *Daughter of Darkness* and written by Andrew Laskos, the script is set in Romania during the reign of the feared dictator Ceaușescu. I liked the concept of the heroine discovering that she herself is half vampire. Her ability to walk in the daylight makes her much sought-after as a mate for the full-blooded undead.

I met with the film's producers: blond and good-looking Harry Chandler and seasoned television producer Gerald W. Abrams (father of J.J. Abrams.) They seemed impressed that I had made three movies in Italy. Also present was producer Andras Hamori. Short and squat with a thick Bela Lugosi accent, he told me that the film would be shot in his hometown of Budapest, Hungary, as Romania was far too dangerous and unstable. How soon would I be ready to begin pre-production?

Budapest was a bustling city (actually two cities: Buda and Pest, one on either side of the Danube) with the gorgeous royal palace on a hill above the cities looking like something straight out of a Disney fairy tale. On closer inspection, one can still see the bullet holes in the cities' walls from the ill-fated uprising of 1956 as the Hungarians tried to free themselves from their Soviet masters.

The production was a chaotic mess, but no one seemed at all worried except me. Anthony Perkins had agreed to play our vampire-father. "You better be careful with him," Line Producer Ken Gord warned me, "I hear he's a handful. He's directed movies himself and doesn't suffer fools gladly." Nevertheless, the idea of working with one of my favorite actors overcame any fear. "I can be a handful too," I told Ken, not realizing that this statement would turn out to be prophetic.

I had been talking to several locals who all told me that Budapest looked nothing like Romania. "Budapest is a paradise compared to Bucharest," they said, "Romania is a complete shit-hole." This concerned me as the locations I had chosen for *Daughter* were very picturesque.

"Can I visit Bucharest before we start shooting?" I asked Andras Hamori.

"The US won't allow you to set foot in Romania," he told me. I was crestfallen. Then he added, "But since you'd be coming from Hungary it may be possible."

"It would be incredibly helpful," I responded.

"I'll see what I can do," Andras replied. "But it's very dangerous. I can get you in, but it may be more difficult for you to get out. I'd hate to start looking for another director."

CHAPTER 33

Psycho Killer

It was on my forty-second birthday, August 11th, 1989, that I got off the plane at Bucharest's airport. The short flight from Hungary had been made in a beat-up Soviet Aeroflot plane. There were no overhead compartments, only a crude netting that barely held our carry-on luggage, and if memory serves, a few cages containing live chickens. After we deplaned, we were herded into the main terminal and waited in long lines to be interviewed by the immigration personnel.

When it was finally my turn, they looked at my American passport in disbelief. "Why do you want to come to Romania?" they asked.

I told them that I was a tourist and had always wanted to visit their country. They looked at each other. Was I kidding? How long would I be staying? "Just the weekend," I answered. More strange looks.

They examined my carry-on bag and quickly found my camera. "What is this for?" they wanted to know. "To take pictures," I replied. More looks back and forth. Finally, they stamped my passport, and I was told that every tourist has to buy thirty dollars worth of leu, their local currency. The exchange rate was six leu per dollar, so I ended up with 180 leu.

I left the airport and climbed into a dilapidated cab. It was a Trabant, one of those Soviet cars made out of cardboard. "Do you want madam?" the cabdriver immediately wanted to know. I shook my head and told him to take me to one of the two hotels in Bucharest that accepted foreign visitors. As we left the airport, he asked me if I wanted to buy leu. "I already have some," I told him.

"I give you better rate," he replied, "Ten thousand leu for one hundred dollars." This was more than ten times the exchange rate. I thought about it for a few seconds and agreed.

He quickly took my money and handed me a large shopping bag full of Romanian currency. "This is real money?" I asked, not believing this could be true.

"Is real," he assured me, and I jammed the money into my carry-on bag. I had chosen not to stay at the more modern Inter-Continental Hotel because I wanted to see a more typical Bucharest hotel. I had also been warned that the Inter-Continental was a hangout for Romanian hookers. The first thing I noticed when I entered the lobby of my chosen hotel was a portrait of Vlad Tepes, aka Vlad the Impaler, and even better known by his nick-name – Dracula.

Mustached, with large piercing eyes, Vlad is considered a great hero in Romania. He saved the country from the invading Turks in the fifteenth century by impaling thousands of his own subjects and placing them like telephone poles along the road to his castle. The Turks took one look at this carnage and thought if he does this to his own people what will he do to us? And so, they quickly turned around and fled Romania.

My hotel room was very old-fashioned but seemed clean, and I grabbed a handful of leu out of my bag full of money and decided to go shopping. As I left the hotel lobby, I was aware that I was being followed by a pair of burly guys in badly fitting suits. I would soon learn that they were the secret police.

As I walked down the main drag I immediately saw, as I had been told, that this city looked nothing like Budapest. Most of the older buildings were crumbling and the newer ones had been built with the cheapest materials possible. Everything seemed sad and dreary. I looked into the shop windows and saw that most of them were empty, with almost nothing for sale. The only things you could buy were poor quality clothes made of synthetic fabrics. No cotton or wool in sight.

The proprietors seemed very nervous when I would enter their stores. Shouldn't they be happy to see an American tourist whose pockets were bulging with money? But they couldn't wait for me to leave. I later discovered that they would be taken to the headquarters of the secret police and interrogated for hours. "What did the foreigner want? What did he say to you?"

The shelves of the grocery stores were also empty. Only a few cans of food were available for sale, and they looked like they had been sitting on the shelf for decades. There was absolutely no fresh produce or meat in sight. Again, more terrified stares.

At five o'clock that afternoon, everyone was herded to the main street in Bucharest. Crowds lined both sides of the wide tree-lined boulevard leading from a large white office building. This was called The White House and it was where the dictator Ceaușescu conducted his business. Eventually an old-fashioned long black limousine drove out of the White House and the people all half-heartedly cheered. I learned that they were forced to do this every day when their fearless leader arrived for work and when he left. I found a restaurant and had dinner. The food was sparse and poorly prepared. I had heard that the people of Romania were starving because Ceaușescu was exporting all their crops to other countries, and it seemed to be true.

At 9:00 PM the curfew began. No one was allowed on the streets on penalty of arrest and even the electric power was shut off. So much for late night television, which was fine with me as the only programming consisted of old propaganda films continuously praising Ceaușescu.

The next morning, I went for another walk, and again the secret police followed me wherever I went. It was Saturday and all the stores were closed, so it looked like I'd have a very hard time spending my 10,000 leu. The day was sunny and hot, and I looked for a place to sit down and have a cold drink;

eventually, I came across a beer garden. It was packed with people and I couldn't find an empty table. A pair of young men beckoned for me to join them and to my amazement they spoke English.

They were students and saw this as an opportunity to try out the language. When I told them I was there prepping a new film, they became very excited. They wanted to know what it was about, and when I told them it was about vampires, they stared at me blankly. "You know, like Dracula," I explained.

They looked at each other. "You mean Vlad Tepes?"

I discovered that Bram Stoker's famous book had been banned in Romania and the idea that their national hero was portrayed as a blood-sucking ghoul seemed absurd and more than a little insulting. It would be like telling an American that Abraham Lincoln was a werewolf.

The students' names were Tibbi and Stefan, and Tibbi was studying geography but as he was not allowed to leave Romania, he might as well have been studying the craters of the moon. "Don't worry," I told them, "Ceauşescu won't be in power forever."

This made them nervous and they looked over their shoulders and I realized that my secret policemen were now sitting at the next table taking notes feverishly. "He was in power when I was born," Tibbi whispered, "And he will be in power when I die."

I decided that we should probably talk someplace more private and invited them back to my hotel. "Your hotel is not safe," they informed me. I was shocked. "You mean my room is bugged?" I asked.

They nodded. "They think you are a spy."

That night I barely slept. I kept waiting for the door of my hotel room to be broken down and I could envision myself being dragged off for an interrogation, but thank God, it never happened.

There was more questioning at the airport the next day, and finally I was allowed to board the plane. All the other passengers seemed nervous too, especially when our take-off was delayed for more than an hour. Finally, we pulled away from the gate and taxied down the runway. As the plane lifted off, the entire cabin broke into loud cheers.

I was still carrying the shopping bag full of Romanian currency and after I arrived in Hungary, I went to cash it in at a currency exchange in the Budapest airport. I was handed the equivalent of about two dollars. "But it's six leu to a dollar!" I complained to the teller.

"Maybe in Bucharest," she smirked.

When I returned to the production office, I was told that Tony Perkins had arrived. He had requested a daily copy of the Los Angeles Times. "What does he want with that rag?" I asked our producer Harry Chandler. This clearly disturbed him.

"Stuart," he slowly began, "My family owns that newspaper." Oops. He was one of those Chandlers. I was also told that Mr. Perkins wanted to meet with me. Could we have dinner together that evening? I called the best restaurant in town, but when I arrived, I was told that they had no record of my reservation. Worse yet, the restaurant was completely booked.

At this point, Tony Perkins showed up. Tall and thin and extremely well-dressed, he looked every inch the movie icon that he was. Embarrassed, I told him that we had no table. Not a great way to begin our relationship. "Don't worry," Tony replied. "I'll just throw 'em a profile." (He pronounced it "profeel.") With that, he turned to the side and lifted his chin. The maître d' looked up and immediately recognized him. "Oh, Mr. Perkins! So sorry! Right this way!" and he quickly led us to the best table in the house.

Tony and I instantly hit it off, especially when he told me that he had seen *Re-Animator* and had liked it so much he had agreed to do *Daughter of Darkness* just to work with me. He was full of wonderful stories about working with Hitchcock on *Psycho* and told me that Norman Bates' habit of eating candy corn throughout the film had been his own idea. I asked him if he had been upset that *Psycho* had so drastically changed his image – that he would no longer be able to play the boy-next-door types. "Are you kidding?" Tony replied. "I was relieved. Those were the most boring roles in the world."

At the end of the meal the maître d' showed up with a large autograph book for Tony to sign. "Orson Welles told me to never write anything but your name," he said as he autographed a page. "But I started thumbing through the book and discovered that Orson had been there before and had previously signed 'Delicious meal!' When I showed it to him, Orson grabbed the book and ripped out the page!"

We had such a good time that Tony and I frequently dined together during the shoot and he regaled me with wonderful stories. He even told me how he had undergone therapy in the fifties to reverse his gay tendencies. His therapist had showed him a copy of *Vogue* magazine and asked him to pick out the woman that he was most attracted to and could possibly see himself marrying. He pointed to a picture of the beautiful photographer Berry Berenson. Several years later he actually did marry her. He also told me that actress Victoria Principal had pursued him so relentlessly on the set of John Huston's *The Life and Times of Judge Roy Bean* that he ended up going to bed with her. It was his first time with a woman, and he was so nervous that he couldn't perform. "Don't worry," Victoria had told him, "We'll just try again tomorrow night." They did, and everything had gone splendidly. "Isn't that a wonderful thing for a woman to say?" he asked me. I could only smile and nod.

Tony was always helpful. One day he arrived on the set and saw that the camera was sitting on its tripod. "Didn't you want a dolly shot?" he asked me.

I told him that I was behind schedule and we didn't have time to set up the dolly tracks. "Don't worry," he told me, "I'll give you your dolly shot." As the shot rolled, he gracefully slid toward the camera barely moving his feet. The effect on film looked exactly like the dolly shot I had originally wanted. One day, I played the Talking Heads song "Psycho Killer" for Tony. He had never heard it before and loved it, especially when I told him that it had probably been written about him. A few days later I again found myself behind schedule and line producer Ken Gord told me that there would absolutely be no overtime. When we hit midnight, he was pulling the plug and all work would have to stop. It was our last day at that location, and I complained that this was a crucial scene and we had to complete it for the film to make any sense. Ken just shrugged, "Too bad." Tony sensed my frustration when he arrived on the set and I told him the situation. "Here's what you do," he advised me, "Just keep singing 'Psycho Killer' and keep working. When midnight arrives, keep singing and don't stop working no matter what." Faced with no other choice, I decided to take his advice and so I began singing, "Fa Fa Fa Fa! – Fa Fa Fa Fa Fa Fa!" The crew looked at me like I was crazy, but we continued shooting. When midnight arrived Ken Gord announced that it was a wrap. Tony turned to me. "What's the next shot?" he asked. I told the crew and they began setting it up as I started singing again.

"It's a wrap!" Ken screamed at the crew but, amazingly, they continued working. "We're not paying overtime!" Ken shrieked, his voice becoming very high and screechy, but the crew, God bless 'em, continued working. Finally, Ken stomped off the set, probably looking for producer, Andras Hamori. He never returned, and we didn't wrap until three in the morning.

The final days of shooting involved grabbing some insert shots. These included POVs out the window of a moving cab to show "Romanian" life during the Ceauşescu regime. I had sent a second unit cameraman to film the red stars displayed on many of the Hungarian buildings. He returned and told me that there were no red stars. Thinking he had gone to the wrong street, I jumped into his car and asked him to show me where he had gone. It turned out that he hadn't made a mistake; amazingly, all the red stars had disappeared from the buildings. Even a red star flower arrangement in the center of a square in a public park had been dug up and replanted. Huge bronze statues of Lenin and Marx had suddenly vanished. What was going on? It turned out that the Berlin Wall had come down, and the Russians would soon be leaving Budapest. I couldn't believe it, and neither did the Hungarians, who were sure it had to be some sort of a Russian trick. As the days went by, it became clear that Hungary was now a free country. But the people still didn't celebrate, their skepticism outweighing their joy.

I returned to Los Angeles, where my editor Andy Horvitch quickly turned in two cuts: a direct-to-video version that featured all the bloodletting and nudity, as well as a tamer television version that could be easily accepted by Standards and Practices. I brought in Tony Perkins to redo a couple of lines that had been ruined when an airplane flew overhead, interfering with the sound recording, and he quickly re-dubbed the lines. It took him about ten minutes. "Is that all you wanted me to do?" he asked, and I nodded.

"That should do it," I told him, "The rest of your performance is fine."

"Fine?!" Tony shouted. "That's the best thing you can say about my performance? THAT IT'S FINE?!" I knew he was kidding, but Tony wanted to look at some more of his scenes. "I can do better than that," he said after watching them. So, he went through almost every one of his scenes and he redid his dialogue, improving his work in every instance. I marveled at his ability to redub himself, not an easy job for most actors. "I have a theory that when you die, not only does your whole life pass before your eyes, but you have to redub it all. Every word you ever said in life," he explained.

Before I knew it, CBS aired *Daughter of Darkness* as a movie of the week, and it proved to be the most anemic vampire movie ever made. They had cut out every drop of blood.

Tony Perkins and I remained good friends. He and his wife Berry and his two teenaged sons Osgood and Elvis even came to lunch at our home in Van Nuys. It was a wonderful afternoon and Carolyn, who had never met Tony until that day, instantly fell in love with him and his wonderful family. It was with great sadness a couple of years later that we read the horrible news that Tony had been diagnosed with AIDS. I called him immediately, and he told me that the *National Enquirer* had originally run the story. He knew it wasn't true and called his lawyer to sue the tabloid for defamation of character. But his lawyer encouraged him to be tested, as he needed a clean bill of health to be able to sue them for libel. The test confirmed that Tony did indeed have AIDS. He later discovered that a lab technician at his doctor's office had discovered that Tony had the disease from a routine blood test but, instead of alerting him and his doctor, he had sold the story to the *Enquirer*. Tony was devastated, as were his family and many friends, myself and Carolyn included.

Tony Perkins was gone in a few months. He died on September 12th, 1992, shortly after his 60th birthday. "I chose not to go public about this because, to misquote *Casablanca*, I'm not much at being noble," he wrote, "But it doesn't take too much to see that the problems of an old actor don't amount to a hill of beans in this crazy old world."

I had a made a wonderful friend and lost him in just three short years, but I will never forget his great wit, grace and good humor. He was a true movie star, and even better, a great human being. His intelligence, honesty and personal generosity made him a natural-born aristocrat. Although I hate arguing with him, even posthumously, I never knew anyone more noble. We will not see his like again. I just hope the angels didn't make him redub his whole life.

A few years after Tony left us, I happened to be paging through a copy of *Variety*, and I saw that a film called *Daughter of Darkness* had been given an R rating by the MPAA. I called the company that was listed as its distributor. "This couldn't by any chance be my movie?" I asked them. "I doubt it," replied the executive, "It's an old movie that stars Anthony Perkins." It *was* our film, of course and, amazingly, it had been restored to the original cut, every drop of blood and ounce of bare flesh intact. I couldn't believe it. Who was responsible for this amazing new lease on life for this forgotten little film? None other than Count Dracula himself, Andras Hamori.

Rainbow

Charlie Band, never one to throw in the towel, had somehow found the money to produce *The Pit and the Pendulum*. It would now be shot in Italy at Charlie's castle in Giove, with less than half of the original budget, and it would have to be a significantly smaller production than the one we had originally planned. Sadly, this meant we could no longer afford the great Peter O'Toole, Sherilyn Fenn, or Billy Dee Williams. I went back to Lance Henriksen, who had originally agreed to be Mendoza, the torturer, and asked him if he was still interested in playing the role. "I really want to do this movie," he told me, "but only if I can play Torquemada."

In the original script, Dennis Paoli and I had written a scene in which the Pope sends a Cardinal from the Vatican to shut down the bloody Spanish Inquisition. We had hoped to get Vincent Price to play the Pope in a nod to his wonderful work in the original Roger Corman version of the same story. I had met Price several years earlier when he was performing onstage in Chicago as Oscar Wilde in his terrific one man show. I'd even been able to spend time with him backstage in his dressing room after the performance. He was a delightful man, full of wonderful stories. Now I met with him filled with optimism that he would take the part. Instead, he seemed a bit amazed that we were remaking his classic film. "You'll certainly have your work cut out for you," he told me, his eyebrow arching in pure Vincent Price style, the subtext being "How can you possibly even hope to come close to equaling my work?" When I pressed him to play the role of the Pope he demurred, telling me that his health would not permit him to travel to Italy.

Dennis and I went back to the drawing board and decided to cut the scene with the Pope, but we would still have his cardinal showing up with an order from Rome to stop torturing heretics. I had been watching Ken Russell's controversial film *The Devils* while preparing *Pit*. It, too, deals with the Inquisition, and the protagonist is a debauched priest played by Oliver Reed. Reed had been one of my heroes ever since I first saw him in the Hammer Film Productions classic *The Curse of the Werewolf*. Since then, he had done great work as Bill Sykes in the film adaptation of the musical *Oliver!* and created a sensation wrestling nude with Alan Bates in *Women in Love*. I looked forward to working with him.

In the summer of 1990, our family once again flew off to Italy, but this time we stayed as guests in Charlie's magnificent castle. It had been beautifully restored since we had last seen it and now had large antique tapestries and vanitas paintings hanging on the high-ceilinged walls. The paintings were of skulls reminding the viewer that "All is vanity as only death awaits us." The bathrooms had modern plumbing fixtures that were gold plated. It was nice to finally be able to share, even indirectly, in some of the profits from *Re-Animator.*

* * *

In September, Suzanna and Jill had to return to school in Los Angeles. We couldn't bring ourselves to uproot them again. Meg, however, was now a toddler, so Carolyn kept her with us. Margaret would run around in only her diapers, her hair so blonde it almost looked pure white. Michaela, the costume designer, would bring her bejeweled plastic necklaces, which the child loved to wear. She looked like a merry little sprite, a magical fairy princess, and captured everyone's hearts.

Mac Ahlberg, sadly, was unavailable to be our director of photography and so, after some searching, we hired Adolfo Bartoli. Short with curly hair and a mustache, Adolfo spoke with a pronounced lisp but was an excellent DP. He often used real candlelight to give the shots a sense of period authenticity. We got along fairly well until the day came that a thunderstorm materialized while we were shooting a big scene involving hundreds of extras. Large black clouds had quickly rolled in, and the dramatic sky now looked like a painting by El Greco. Adolfo said that we could no longer shoot, but I insisted that we keep going. Fofo, as Adolfo was called by his friends, refused, saying it wouldn't match the previous shots, which were filled with bright sunlight. But I saw it as a "happy accident" and remembered Mac telling me about how he was on the set when legendary cinematographer Sven Nyquist was shooting Bergman's *The Virgin Spring.* The sky had been overcast all day but, as the villain lay dying, a shaft of sunlight miraculously penetrated the clouds and hit his dead body like a spotlight. The shot had been lavishly praised by the critics, but it had been completely unplanned – a happy accident. Adolfo filmed the scene for me under protest and, at a key moment a bolt of lightning cut through the sky as if cued by the special effects team. I was ecstatic, but my producer and friend Albert Band took me aside and told me that I had to listen to my cinematographer. To ignore his insistence that we stop shooting could create a rift between us that could hamper the entire film. He also told me not to use the lightning shot no matter how well it turned out as it would be perceived as a slap in the face to Fofo. So, although the shot turned out to be every bit as dramatic as I had hoped, it remained on the cutting room floor.

We had been shooting about a week when Lance Henriksen arrived. He had been making another film and had been unable to join us for the week of rehearsal that I always conduct before filming begins. None of us was prepared for the intensity that he brought to the role of Torquemada the Grand Inquisitor. The first scene he shot involved him stopping the torture of Maria as she is stretched on the rack, lifting her unconscious body and carrying her off. He began the scene by grabbing the large book that Jeffrey Combs' character used to record confessions and slamming it against the torture device. BLAMMM!!! As this piece of business was unscripted and totally unexpected, everyone jumped a foot. Lance had begun Torquemada's reign of terror from his first moment on the set. He had also done his homework and knew that Torquemada was an ascetic who dined only on bread and water. Because Lance was a true disciple of The Method, he too followed this Spartan diet. The fact that he was in Italy, depriving himself of the best cuisine and finest wines on the planet, made no difference to him. Torquemada never wore shoes, so Lance, too, always went barefoot. Thank God he didn't incorporate the Inquisitors' other habit of always wearing a hairshirt under his robe to mortify his flesh. With the strange bald cap that make-up artist Greg Cannom devised to recreate the bizarre hairstyle of the Dominican friars, Lance looked like Death incarnate. His presence was so fearsome that, on one occasion, our focus-puller literally fell to his knees begging for Torquemada's forgiveness for blowing (buzzing) a take.

Lance always argued about every direction I gave him, which made working with him a constant battle. The results were so amazing, though, that it was well worth the aggravation. Once, toward the end of the shoot, he began questioning another of my directions and, exhausted, I replied, "Do whatever you want. I don't care anymore."

He looked stricken. "Come on man!" he pleaded, "Don't give up on me!" I finally realized that this was his process, arguments and all, and he needed to argue with me to do his best work.

We had been searching for a place to screen our dailies. Somehow, we managed to obtain permission to use the Vatican screening room in Rome. I found this incredibly ironic as many of the scenes showed the Grand Inquisitor and Dominican monk, Torquemada, torturing heretics and finally attempting to have sex with the baker's lovely wife, Maria. We usually watched our dailies on the weekends and would use our excursions into Rome as an opportunity to have a wonderful dinner afterwards at one of the city's many fabulous restaurants. The footage was gorgeous, the acting was brilliant, and so we always returned happy and inspired, our stomachs full of delicious Italian food.

On one of these excursions, we had just finished dinner when Albert got a call from the castle. Oliver Reed had arrived and had told poor Tonni, the castle cook, that he wanted every bottle of wine in the place lined up before him on the enormous banquet table. Reed then proceeded to drink bottle after bottle, becoming so inebriated that he began chasing Tonni's wife around the table, causing Tonni to lock his wife in their apartment to protect her from being ravaged by this madman (who was a famously formidable presence). When we got to the castle, the hulking Oliver Reed was indeed sitting alone at the great bottle-covered table. He loudly invited us to join him for a drink with his young wife, Josephine, whom he had married five years earlier when she was 21. How could we refuse? By this time Oliver was so drunk that he could no longer even get up to pee, so he simply grabbed an empty wine bottle and pissed into it while still sitting at the table. Before he put it back in his pants, he showed us the tattoos on the tip of his penis. "Eagle claws," he told us proudly.

"I always thought they were lightning bolts," said Josephine, who was almost as drunk as he was.

The arrival of the wild Oliver Reed even caused Lance to join the party and drink for the first time in weeks. At one point, Reed showed Lance a drawing he had made on the cover of his script of a prone victim under the swinging pendulum of the title. Lance admired it and so Oliver Reed grandly presented it to him as a gift. Lance hugged it to his chest as he profusely thanked Reed, telling him he would have it framed. Later, when Lance left to relieve himself, Oliver noticed that Henriksen had left the drawing on the table. Reed picked it up. "Look at how he treats my gift!" he exclaimed, taking the drawing back. When Lance returned, Oliver innocently asked him if he was missing anything. Puzzled, Lance patted his pockets. "No, I don't think so," he finally replied. At this point Reed held up the drawing. As Lance reached for it, Oliver pulled it away and dramatically tore it in half. Lance screamed as if he himself had been ripped apart and fell to his knees sobbing. It looked like Torquemada had finally met his match.

Later, Oliver told Lance that he was going to take him to the best whorehouse in Rome that evening, but soon Lance was unconscious on the floor. "Can't hold his liquor," Reed said dismissively and again whipped out his dick. I was afraid he was about to piss on his co-star, but his wife handed him another bottle and he quickly filled it. The drinking went on all night until we finally crept off to get some sleep. When we awoke on Sunday morning, we discovered that Oliver and his wife were across the street at a coffee bar knocking back beers. That evening, I sat with Mr. Reed in front of the castle's enormous fireplace, where he recited the poetry of Lord Byron. It was the most beautiful recitation I have ever heard. I asked him if he had ever performed Shakespeare. "Never been onstage," he told me. "Got my first job from my uncle, Carol Reed (the great director of *Oliver!* and *The Third Man*)."

Monday morning arrived, and I nervously asked the first AD if Mr. Reed had shown up yet. "He's all ready to go," I was told, and when I went into his dressing room, I found him in costume and make-up, and totally sober. Lance later stumbled onto the set with a massive hangover. Their scene involved drinking Amontillado wine in a nod to another great story by Poe, and we had a cask of real Italian white wine standing by for Mr. Reed. After a couple of takes, he asked for colored water instead. "If I have another glass of this, I won't be able to remember my lines," he explained to me. Thus, I discovered that Oliver Reed was a consummate professional, doing what he wanted (raising hell) on his own time but ready to get the job done, and done magnificently, when on yours.

The next day, after he had left, we discovered the hard way that he had left his urine-filled bottles in the refrigerator. No one at the castle drank white wine again.

Reed died less than ten years later, having a heart attack while arm-wrestling sailors in a bar in Malta during a break from the shooting of *Gladiator*. Director Ridley Scott completed Oliver's work in the film with a combination of outtakes and CGI but, as always, Reed's performance is amazing. In fact, he was posthumously nominated for a BAFTA Award (the British equivalent of an Oscar).

So, let's drink a toast to the great Oliver Reed… just make sure it's red wine.

* * *

Dennis and I had decided to include a scene from Poe's famous story that, as far as I know, is seldom, if ever, shown in adaptations. It involves our hero being freed from the ever-lowering blade of the pendulum by hundreds of hungry rats who chew through the leather straps holding him down. I hired Maurizio Garrone, an animal wrangler who had often worked with Dario Argento, providing trained cats, dogs, ravens and even insects for his films. He was a small man with curly dark hair and, as I discussed our scene with the ravenous rats, he nodded, indicating that it would be "non c'è problema."

He suggested that we use white laboratory rats, as they were clean and disease-free, so we wouldn't have to worry about anyone getting rabies from interacting with them – a thought that I must admit never crossed my mind. We could easily dye their fur black, he told me, the only thing that might give away our ruse was that the albino rats' eyes would remain red. But the idea of a horde of hungry black rodents with blood-red eyes did appeal to me. Soon he had set up a series of cages filled with the little buggers in an upstairs room in the castle. Jonathan Fuller, who would be their unfortunate victim, decided that it would be in his best interest to get to know them and let them become acquainted with him so they would feel comfortable around him (and preferably not bite him).

When the day came for the rats' big scene, our trainer brought them to the set. Most of the crew decided to stand on chairs or ladders to avoid interacting with the rodents, but in a few minutes, it became clear that the rats were far more afraid of us than we were of them. The animals huddled together in a tight group, shivering and looking for somewhere to hide. We ended up smearing peanut butter, which the rats adored, all over Jonathan – but still the rats kept their distance. We ultimately discovered that the only way to make the rats advance was to drive them forward, much as cowboys make a herd of steers go into their pens. I found myself whooping and hollering like I was at a miniature rodeo. No wonder Maurizio was called an animal wrangler. Soon, the whole crew was stamping their feet and shouting, and eventually the tight cluster of rats began to move forward. Clearly, we would have to cut the shouting voices from our soundtrack in post-production. It also was clear why no one had ever attempted to film this scene as Poe had written it. As the old maxim goes, "Never work with animals or small children."

Getting the rodents to climb around on Jonathan was even more problematic. I had initially been terrified of the creatures, but as the day progressed, I found myself casually picking up the small animals and placing them where I felt they needed to be. Everyone seemed to be getting more comfortable on the set – rats and humans alike – and eventually we were able to get them to do what they needed to do, and poor Jonathan only ended up being bitten a few times.

We were in the final days of shooting when our leading lady, Rona De Ricci, came running down the stairs to the dining room where I was finishing lunch. "Stuart!" she cried, "You must come right away! Marion has died!" Marion Mertes was our script supervisor, a tough old lady with a German accent. She had been doing her job since the 1950s and had worked on countless movies including *Cast a Giant Shadow* with Kirk Douglas. My first altercation with her occurred when I looked at the clapboard (which is called a *ciak* in Italy) and saw that it had been given a new shot number. I reminded her that we were still doing another take of the same shot, and this was Take #21 not Take #1. She replied that we certainly didn't want our producers in Hollywood to know that we had exceeded twenty takes. She clearly had been around the block a few times and had my best interests at heart. I told her not to worry about the producers and that this was Take #21. "Let's not confuse our editor," I explained.

She was a character. Once when someone was looking for me, she told them that I was "around somewhere fucking around." I liked her very much, and she was an excellent extra set of eyes and ears. I quickly followed Rona to the castle's veranda where I found the poor old woman lying motionless on her back with our line producer trying to shoot a breath inhaler spray into her open mouth. Instantly, all of the training in CPR that my friend Ron Berman had taught us in the days of *E/R* at Organic Theater came back to me. I pushed the line producer aside and felt for Marion's pulse.

There was none. And worse, her skin was cold as ice and her lips had turned blue. Rona was right. She was dead. I felt for the base of her breastbone as my old friend Dr. Ronald Berman had instructed, and lacing my fingers together, began compressions on her chest. I pushed hard, forcing her ribcage down four inches as CPR requires. After ten of these, I leaned over and placed my lips over hers. They were deathly cold, but I blew air into her lungs. Then I went back to the compressions as I shouted to the crew to call an ambulance.

I leaned in to give her a second breath, and suddenly she gasped and miraculously began to breathe. I instantly stopped CPR as the color slowly began to return to her face. I stayed with her until the ambulance arrived. She was loaded onto a stretcher and taken to the nearest hospital. Everyone circled me, patting me on the back, and I felt that I had witnessed a miracle. What an amazing feeling – to save a life!

It was a Saturday, and we were only working a half day. The car was ready to take me and Albert Band to Rome to view the dailies. As we drove away from the castle, the driver pointed to the sky. There we saw a brilliant double rainbow – glorious, arching across the bright blue heavens like a sign from God. I gasped at its beauty. It was a blessing.

A few days later, I visited Marion in the hospital. She complained that I had broken her ribs when I had performed CPR, which Ron Berman had told me often happens if you do it correctly. She was clearly not happy with me. "Maybe I should have just let you stay dead," I kidded her, and she smiled. Her son was there, and he took me aside, thanked me for saving his mother's life, and apologized for her behavior. I told him that I understood. She was an old soldier, and now she wouldn't be able to complete the film. I wished her a speedy recovery and kissed her on her forehead. It was nice and warm.

CHAPTER 35

High-Tech Prison

The Pit and the Pendulum went directly to video without a theatrical release. This was a new concept, conceived in the late 1980s by Charlie Band, and eventually adopted by the major studios who were soon creating direct-to-video divisions of their own. Amazingly, it led to Paramount hiring Full Moon to produce direct-to-video films for them. This "too good to be true" deal involved them providing Charlie with two million dollars per film and releasing one every month. Soon, Full Moon was churning out picture after picture for Paramount, supervised by Jim Gianopulos (who later became Chairman of Twentieth Century Fox). Charlie, with the help of his father Albert and new wife, Debra Dion, was even able to expand and create several new Full Moon lines: Moonbeam, to produce family films, and Torchlight, for softcore fantasy sex films.

I was disappointed that after all our hard work, *Pit* was never to be shown on the big screen. I was learning that, as a filmmaker, I could have almost total control of the making of my films but had absolutely nothing to say about how they would be released. I came to believe that my only hope was to work again with a major studio that had a solid distribution network that could give me a real release.

In 1990, I became entranced with the idea of making a movie based upon the Marvel comic book *Iron Man*. What set Iron Man apart from the other superheroes was that his powers didn't come from the planet Krypton or a radioactive spider bite, but came from his ingenious inventions. After working on the stage version of *The Forever War*, with its high-powered exoskeleton fighting suits, I knew that real scientists were in fact attempting to create a strength-enhancing suit not that dissimilar from Iron Man's. In other words, the comic book story seemed possible, and the film could be set in the real present-day world. I was also fascinated with the character of the suit's inventor, Tony Stark. A charismatic genius industrialist inspired by Howard Hughes, Stark, like most Marvel characters, had a fatal flaw, and one that I could easily relate to: he had a damaged heart. A piece of shrapnel had lodged in his heart while he was fighting in the Vietnam war, and he used electromagnetism to prevent it from killing him. That technology had become the basis for the development of the flying exoskeleton that would turn him into Iron Man.

But he also had another flaw that made him even more interesting to me: Tony Stark was an alcoholic. I met with Stan Lee at Marvel about adapting the comic books into a film. Stan and I had first met during my adventures with legendary comic book artist Neal Adams when we prepared for the Broadway production of *Warp* in late 1972. Now, almost twenty years later, I found Stan to be a little grayer, but with his unbridled boyish enthusiasm and great good humor intact and undiminished.

Stan desperately wanted a movie based on a Marvel superhero. It particularly galled him that DC Comics, his archrival, was having great success with the *Superman* and *Batman* franchises. It seems unbelievable now, with the enormous success after success of Marvel's movie projects, but back in 1990, the company had not yet made a single movie.

Not that there weren't plans to make one. Stan invited Carolyn and me to a party at his home where I was introduced to James Cameron, who was developing a *Spider-Man* movie, and Wes Craven, who was hard at work turning *Doctor Strange* into a film.

"Spider-Man, this is Iron Man. Iron Man, this is Doctor Strange." Sadly, none of these projects became realities until decades later, and every one would end up with a different director. Even Stan Lee had to leave Marvel before the films would happen. Working with Stan was amazing. "You can do anything you want," he once told me, "As long as the villain wants to destroy the world." I immediately thought of Lord Cumulus's rejoinder upon hearing a similar line in *Warp*, "Destroy the world? Where's he gonna live?" Stan also stressed that I should never forget that Iron Man is also a businessman, and that the plot needed to feature a business deal at its center.

I got two old friends from Empire Pictures to help me develop the story: Danny Bilson and Paul De Meo. We came up with an excellent scenario which we were able to sell to Universal Studios. Then another of Danny and Paul's projects, *The Rocketeer*, got picked up by Disney (and directed by Joe Johnston) and the writers had to leave *Iron Man*. Their replacement, Michael Miner, who was one of the creators of *Robocop*, immediately threw out Danny and Paul's scenario, calling it unfilmable, and replaced it (over my objections) with one that really *was* unfilmable. The project was shelved. I watched with bitter amusement as *Iron Man* became Marvel's first blockbuster eighteen years later, in 2008.

One day, I got a call from my agent that an independent producer was planning to make a film of Kurt Vonnegut's great book *The Sirens of Titan*. This producer had discovered that I had adapted the book into a play during my Organic Theater days and wanted to meet. Who was this producer? None other than Jerry Garcia of the Grateful Dead. Jerry flew me to San Francisco to meet with him and Tom Davis, his writing partner on the screenplay they were developing. I was familiar with Tom; he was then a regular on *Saturday Night Live*, often appearing with Al Franken. Upon arrival, I was taken to Garcia's downtown office, where I met Tom and was shown into a nondescript conference room. We chatted for a few minutes, and then Jerry Garcia walked in. I couldn't believe my eyes. He was wearing a three-piece suit, a tie, and button-down shirt, and had his hair tied back into a neat ponytail.

We talked about his ideas for the film. He had purchased the movie rights from Kurt Vonnegut, and wanted Bill Murray to play Malachi Constant, the richest man in the world, who is abducted and taken on outrageous adventures across our solar system. I was shown conceptual designs and budgets and schedules, all paid for by Mr. Garcia. There were many questions about our stage adaptation at Organic, which Vonnegut himself had supervised, and they laughed when I told them that the author had felt that we were too faithful to his novel. After meeting for several hours, Jerry told me he was performing a concert that evening, and would I like to go with him? Before I knew it, we were speeding to the venue in his limo. Jerry had changed his clothes and now wore his emblematic tie-dye T-shirt, blue jeans and head band. If memory serves, he carried his own acoustic guitar into the hall.

The concert was Jerry playing a solo gig to a packed audience. The adoring fans (myself included) gave him a standing ovation. Strangely, he did not return to the stage to perform an encore. I asked him about this, and he sighed, "The whole show's an encore, man." Jerry died of a heart attack in 1995 at age 53, and the movie project never materialized, but I will never forget that one day I spent with this gentle, good-natured icon.

In November of 1990, we were making plans to visit Carolyn's brother Roger for Thanksgiving when I got a call from my Uncle Donald, my mother's older brother. I knew immediately from the tone of his voice that this was very serious. My eighty-year-old mother had been found wandering, disoriented, in the basement of her apartment building. Upon hospital examination, it was determined that she was the victim of a series of small strokes called TIAs (Transient Ischemic Attacks). When she returned home, we felt that she should not be left alone. Although the strokes had not impaired her physically, she was extremely confused. I made plans to fly to Chicago immediately and told Carolyn that she and the children should join me after their visit with her family in Minneapolis. When I arrived at my mother's apartment, it was clear that things were not as they should be. There were boxes of paperwork scattered around her usually pristine quarters. I quickly realized that she was not herself; she would ask me the same questions over and over. Her memory was severely impaired, and she was extremely concerned about her financial situation. She had collected her checkbooks and bank statements and continually paged through them. I tried to calm her, to no avail.

I stayed the night on the pull-out couch in her living room but was awakened several times in the middle of the night when she came into the darkened room, turned on the lights, and began going through the drawers of her desk. This became a nightly occurrence no matter how many times I reassured her that everything was alright. Soon, lack of sleep began taking a toll on me.

I talked things over with my uncle, and we agreed that she needed full time help. Would she get better? I asked him. My uncle seemed to believe that it was possible for her condition to improve. I called Carolyn, and we discussed the idea of bringing my mother to Los Angeles to live with us until she recovered. "But how long will that take?" Carolyn wanted to know, her hands already more than filled with raising our three children.

Carolyn and the kids arrived in Chicago after Thanksgiving and helped me gather a suitcase full of my mom's clothing. Then we brought her to California to live with us. We celebrated Christmas together and, at first, I was reminded of growing up with my grandfather in our little house on Keystone Avenue. But it soon became clear that taking care of my mother was a full-time job, and 99 percent of the work fell on Carolyn's shoulders while I looked for my next project.

My agent Jeremy Zimmer set up a meeting with the producers of a new sequel to *Invasion of the Body Snatchers* at Warner Bros. Bob Solo had produced the successful 1978 remake directed by Philip Kaufman. A new script had been written by filmmaker Larry Cohen (not our friend from Madison, who now went by the name Lawrence D. Cohen). This Larry Cohen had achieved fame as a writer and director and was well known for *It's Alive*, *God Told Me To*, and *The Stuff*. Dennis Paoli and I felt that the most successful section of Cohen's script focused on the happenings at an army base that is being taken over by the pod people. At my pitch meeting with Solo and the executives from Warner Bros, I presented our idea of focusing on a family who arrive at the army base only to be replaced one by one by the body snatcher duplicates. Solo, a small balding man with a sharp mind and wonderful sense of humor, loved the idea, and Dennis and I were quickly hired to rewrite the film, which I would also direct. Two months later, we turned in our first draft, which closely followed the outline that the studio had approved. But like my experience working on *Honey, I Shrunk the Kids*, we soon found ourselves stuck in the quicksand of development hell. After a dozen drafts, the studio executives wanted me to bring on another writer, which essentially meant firing Dennis and myself as screenwriters. When they asked me to suggest our replacement, I facetiously suggested that they hire Stephen King. Before I knew it, he had been sent a copy of our script.

A few days later I was shown the letter King had sent to the development executives at the studio. "I'm going to decline to work on this project," he wrote, "because the screenplay falls under the old Navy maxim that goes, 'If it ain't broke, don't fix it.' My feeling about Body Snatchers II is that it ain't broke – that it is, in fact, a very tidy and very effective piece of work… and is, in one aspect, brilliant." True to form, the studio still insisted on hiring another writer and soon I was working with him on yet another draft. As this was going on, I received a script from my agent entitled *Fortress*. It was a science fiction action movie set in a high-tech prison in which the hero (a futuristic garbage man) is imprisoned for destroying a robot. I thought the script was a derivative mess and told Jeremy I was passing.

"They really want to meet you," he told me, "You should take the meeting."

"But the script is terrible," I told him.

Nonetheless, he insisted that I meet with them. "Just don't tell them that you hate the script," he cautioned me. That February I met with John Davis, the producer of *Predator*.

"What did you think of the script?" was Davis' first question. I hemmed and hawed and finally told him I thought it needed work.

"We know," he replied. "What would you do to make it better?"

Suddenly, the meeting got interesting. "I think he has to be imprisoned for something stronger than destroying a robot," I began, not sure where I was going.

Davis nodded. "Like what?" he asked.

"Maybe overpopulation is the big issue in the future," I began, "And it's like China, where you can only have one child and his wife is pregnant with their second baby."

Davis clapped his hands, "I love it!" He turned to his partners Greg Coote and John Flock, who both nodded enthusiastically. Before I knew it, I was hired to direct the film and supervise a rewrite. The budget was $14 million. We all shook hands and, as I was leaving, Greg Coote mentioned that his company, Village Roadshow, was financing *Fortress* and that we would be shooting it in their native Australia and what did I think of that?

"I've always wanted to visit Australia," I answered truthfully.

My deal was quickly drawn up. I was to get paid nearly half a million dollars and they wanted me to start immediately. I then had to tell Bob Solo that I was dropping out of *Body Snatchers*. He was not pleased. Warner Brothers' inability to green-light the project was wearing him down too, and my departure would further delay its start.

I was given an office in Davis's complex in the Die Hard Building and soon met with the writers, Troy Neighbors and Steve Feinberg. Both were in their mid-twenties and were very excited, as this was the first script they had ever sold. I learned that the project had originally been intended as a vehicle for Arnold Schwarzenegger, but he had dropped out to do another film. In keeping with typical Hollywood economics, this meant that, without this very bankable star, the budget had been cut in half.

"I tried to guilt Arnold into staying with the film," John Davis later explained to me. "I told him that there was no way we could make the movie with such a small budget, and he just grinned and said, 'Get Stuart Gordon. He made

Re-Animator for nothing. If anyone can figure out how to do it, he can.'" Arnold had become a fan after seeing my film, which presented his buddy and stunt double, Peter Kent, as a featured zombie. This finally explained my agent's insistence that I meet with Davis. I also learned that the film had to start shooting by the beginning of September. The reason? It was to be the first movie filmed at Warner Movie World, an amusement park recently taken over by Village Roadshow that surrounded their studio in Queensland, Australia. Using Universal as their model, Village Roadshow planned a tram ride that would allow visitors a studio tour. They needed a film to be in production as an attraction at the theme park and we were it. So, our date was firm – whether the movie was ready or not.

At the same time, there was a good side to all of this: as far as *Fortress* was concerned, I could do anything I wanted as long as it came in on budget and shooting commenced by September. It was a tight pre-production schedule, but it gave me tremendous freedom if we could get everything ready in time. Like a trapeze artist, we had to pray that the other trapeze would be there for us to grab onto as we went flying through the air with the greatest of ease. The first question was who would replace Arnold?

I was going over a list of possible candidates with our casting director when John Davis burst in. "I just got off the phone with Christophe Lambert and he wants to meet you for lunch," he excitedly told me. "Are you free tomorrow?" I nodded and the meeting was quickly set for Le Dome, the trendy industry restaurant du jour. I busied myself going over Lambert's career. I had seen him in *Greystoke*, in which he played Tarzan. It was his first feature film, and he had gone on to become an international sensation in the *Highlander* films. I believed he was French and wondered about his accent. I later learned that he had been born in New York and moved to Switzerland when his diplomat father was posted there.

I walked into the Sunset Boulevard restaurant at the designated time and told the hostess at the front desk that I was meeting Mr. Lambert. "Is he here yet?" I asked her. Before she could answer a voice behind me said, "Yes, it's a pleasure to meet you." I turned around, and there stood a small man wearing very thick glasses. His shoulders were stooped, he wore a grey pullover sweater, and I later noticed that it was inside-out with the tag apparent on his back. He held out his hand. "I'm Christopher, but you can call me Chris," he said with a gravelly, slightly accented voice that always reminded me of Peter Lorre.

My first reaction was to insist, "You're not Lambert!" as he looked nothing like the handsome statuesque figure I had seen on screen. With his slouched posture, unshaven face and messed-up hair, he looked more like Woody Allen than an international movie star. As we took our seats at the banquette he continued: "I've seen all your films and they're all great. I'm really looking forward to working together." I remained silent, not sure what to say. As the lunch went on, however, I found Chris to be a bright, charming, very funny, and self-deprecating character. He told me that he had originally been an investment banker but soon traded in his suit and briefcase for a leopard-skin loincloth, swinging from vine to vine in his first film.

"You've done a lot of theater," he went on, "And I hear that you always rehearse your films before you start shooting." I was amazed. It was clear that Mr. Lambert had done his homework.

"How do you feel about that?" I asked him.

"Great!" he enthused, "I've never had the luxury of rehearsing before." Sensing that I didn't know how to respond to this, he continued. "But I promise you will never find anyone more willing to learn." I smiled and we shook hands. I liked him, and I felt that he liked me. "Welcome aboard," I said.

I also liked the idea that Chris was not a heavily muscled action hero like Schwarzenegger. You never worry about Arnold when you see him onscreen. You just sit back and wait for him to tear apart all the bad guys. Chris could be more of an everyman, someone that the audience could relate to and imagine themselves in his place. When I told John Davis that I liked Lambert and we should cast him he was ecstatic. "Great," he cried, "We should be able to get him for a couple of million!"

"A couple of million?" I thought, "I've done entire movies for less than half that."

One day, I was rushing into the lobby of the *Die Hard* building (probably late for a meeting) and, as I rounded a corner, in my hurry, I bumped into an elderly gentleman. He was accompanied by two young men whose hands immediately went into their jackets. I gasped, and it was at that moment that I realized that the man I had bumped into was former President Ronald Reagan, who also had an office in the *Die Hard* building. Luckily, Reagan waved to them that he was okay. I quickly apologized and went on my way. It was the closest I've ever been to a U.S. President.

As is my M.O., I set up some visits to nearby prisons as research for *Fortress*. I was able to get permission to visit Pelican Bay, a newly built super-maximum-security penitentiary in Northern California. It boasted high-tech features such as video surveillance and an electronic system of locking the cells that no longer needed keys.

I was concerned that I might be denied access to Pelican Bay because of my arrest record. The obscenity charges from *Peter Pan* were never officially dropped but instead "withdrawn," which implied that they could be reinstated at any time. Nevertheless, permission was granted for our visit, and it seemed the powers-that–be were very proud of their new high-tech prison. Ironically, the facility is located in the midst of a glorious state park. As we approached the prison, we passed through forests of towering sequoias and even saw bald eagles flying overhead. In harsh contrast to its magnificent surroundings, the prison is a stark series of poured concrete buildings standing in the midst of barren grounds, stripped of all vegetation. Gravel covers pressure-sensitive pads that will alert the guards if anyone sets foot on it, and we had to go through three armed checkpoints before entering the facility. A gatekeeper slid a pole with a mirror attached back and forth under our car, and our trunk was thoroughly searched to make sure that we were not hiding contraband or helping someone escape. Then we were carefully patted down.

We were met by a guard (who we learned must be referred to as "Officer") who handed us stab-proof vests, which we were instructed to put on for our own protection. "These probably won't help you," the officer casually informed us, "They always go for the eyes." "How do they get weapons?" we wanted to know. "They can make a shiv out of anything" he replied. "An officer was stabbed with a paper knife last week."

As they buckled us into the thick vests, a public relations assistant arrived to give us the tour. He told us that Pelican Bay was for convicts who continued to commit crimes while already incarcerated, and that they had been sent here to be broken of these bad habits. We were told the prison housed serial killers, gang leaders, and white supremacists: the baddest of the bad. The prisoners were kept in solitary confinement for twenty-two-and-a-half hours daily with ninety minutes in the yard. We later discovered that they remained alone even in the yards; a small space surrounded by twenty-foot-tall cinderblock walls topped with broken glass, razor wire and chain link fencing as a roof. Video cameras looked down from above.

As we entered the prison, I was struck by how quiet it was. Most prisons are noisy places, but at Pelican Bay, you could hear a pin drop. The cells were enclosed by solid white walls instead of bars, so we couldn't see the prisoners, and they couldn't see us. There had been much criticism of the prison for creating a world of sensory deprivation that could cause the inmates to go mad. This, as we learned, was the philosophy of the Reagan Administration, during which the purpose of incarceration had changed from rehabilitation to punishment.

While walking through the silent hallways, my fears quickly evaporated, and I realized that I was in the safest place I had ever been in my entire life. Finally, we were taken to meet the warden, and he asked us about our film. When we told him about the script's "Intestinators" – explosive devices implanted in the prisoners' stomachs that can be detonated if they get out of line – his eyes lit up. "We could sure use those!" he said, chuckling, and we all laughed with him as we looked nervously at each other.

Chris Lambert wanted to be locked in a cell to see what it felt like to be imprisoned, so I nodded to the officer who immediately granted his wish.

As the door clanged shut, I turned to the guard. "Let's go," I said, and we walked away, leaving the star of our film in that claustrophobic cell until we returned a half hour later to free him.

"Very helpful," was Lambert's reaction. But I knew he would find a way to get even.

The research helped us with the script rewrites, but I felt that we needed more help, so I brought on my old friend, Terry Curtis Fox. The success of the play *Cops* had enabled Terry to become a television writer for *Hill Street Blues*.

We wrestled with the budget. I had to kill my darlings, which included eliminating a great chase sequence in which our heroes are pursued by the Strike-clones, half-human cyborgs that have been reprogrammed as members of a souped-up tactical squad. The clones are able to move at great speed by the use of hanging tracks that pre-dated zip-line rides. I also had to agree that half of my fee wouldn't be paid until the movie had gone into profit. Usually this means you will never receive it, due to what is politely termed "Studio Accounting," but a few years ago I was pleasantly surprised to receive a large check making up the balance. The film had made so much money that they couldn't hide the profits.

A few days before I was scheduled to leave for Australia, I received word that Greg Coote, our executive producer and the head of Village Roadshow's movie division, wanted to talk with me. I waited nervously until I was ushered into his office. Greg sat me down. "So how do you think it's going?" he asked.

"Pretty well," I replied.

"Do you think you're ready?"

I nodded. "Yes, I do."

He got up and began to pace. "I've been thinking a great deal about this movie, and there's something that I feel I need to tell you."

I braced myself for the worst. Was I being replaced? "What is it?" I asked him.

"Alright, here it is," and he sat down facing me. He looked me right in the eye.

He cleared his throat.

There was a pregnant pause.

"Good guys and bad guys fight," he began. I nodded, wondering where this was going. "Good guys win."

There was another long pause.

"That's it." Greg said.

"Okay," I told him, greatly relieved. "I can make that work."

He stood up. "Have a great time in Queensland," he said shaking my hand. "And make us a great movie."

"I will," I told him, and as I headed for the door, he stopped me.

"Remember, Stuart – good guys win."

Australia

Terry Curtis Fox and I boarded a Qantas 747 to Australia. We were still working on the shooting script, but I knew that changes would come fast and furious on a daily basis, so it was simpler to have him with me than to work long distance, and I frankly welcomed his company as Carolyn and the kids couldn't join me until Christmas vacation.

When we were about to land in Sydney, the flight attendants appeared wearing surgical masks and sprayed insecticide throughout the cabin. We were told the chemicals were harmless and would kill any foreign bugs or life-forms that we might be bringing inadvertently into the pristine biosphere of Australia.

Australia is a wonderful place where the skies are big and the people are larger-than-life. Crocodile Dundee's line, "*That's* a knife!" as he faces down a gangbanger's switchblade with his enormous Bowie is very true to the Australian character. I felt like I was back in the frontier days of the old American West, and I absolutely believe that some day, when they are able to irrigate the outback, Australia will take our place as the breadbasket to the world. I found the positive "can-do" attitude of the Australian people exciting. Anything is possible. Americans are made to feel at home, but there is still great animosity toward the "pommie bastards" (their derogatory term for the "whinging" – complaining – Brits who so cruelly ruled them in colonial days).

In Sydney, we assembled our crew, and I ended up hiring many of the same folks who had made the terrific *Mad Max* films: director of photography David Eggby, editor Tim Wellburn, costume designer Terry Ryan, and stunt coordinator Glenn Boswell. I was even able to hire actor Vernon Wells, who had made movie history by playing the Mohawk-wearing Wez, who climbs up the grill of Mel Gibson's truck as it rockets along in *The Road Warrior*. Then it was off to the studio in Queensland. When I first saw the place, I couldn't believe my eyes. It was an exact duplicate of Dinocittà in Rome where I had shot three films. This was because both studios had been built by Dino De Laurentiis, and he had clearly used the same blueprints. I amazed the Australians by immediately knowing my way to the commissary. The only difference between the two studios was that the one in Queensland was surrounded by a swamp filled with enormous crocodiles, so it turned out to be a very good thing that I knew where I was going.

I was still jet-lagging when filming began and once had to be awakened during a take by my script supervisor tactfully nudging me so I could call "cut." Chris Lambert had a picture taken of us with me fast asleep on a recliner that he signed and dedicated, "Just another day at the beach."

CHAPTER 36

The Australians were always full of surprises. When one of our scenes called for a semi-truck to flip upside down, fly through the air, crash into a barn and blow up, I had assumed that this would be accomplished with miniatures. "Why miniatures?" Glenn Boswell, the stunt coordinator, asked me. "We have trucks, we have barns…" It was decided to do the scene in full size. The truck would hit a hidden ramp that would flip it and then the barn, filled to the brim with explosives, would be detonated as the truck crashed down onto its roof. We would have to turn on the five cameras and run for our lives before the stunt could be performed. I watched from about a mile away, and the blast still knocked the wind out of me. It was so spectacular that I was afraid the continent of Australia would look like a doughnut.

Vernon Wells played Maddox, a murderous prisoner who fights it out with our hero, Chris Lambert. At one point, Maddox is thrown into the laser bars of the futuristic prison cells, igniting a spark effect. Unfortunately, the sparks hit Vernon in the eye, and he crumpled to the ground rolling in pain. He was quickly sent to an emergency room where it turned out that his eyelid had been singed. Luckily, his eye was fine, and he returned to the set a few hours later. I told him he should take the rest of the day off to recover, but Vernon, being an Australian, insisted on continuing. As soon as we began the first take, though, he suddenly collapsed again, grabbing his eye and howling in pain. I yelled cut and ran to him. As he removed his hand from his eye for me to see, his eyeball fell out onto the floor. I gasped in shock until I saw it bounce and I realized it was a glass eye. Vernon and the entire crew roared with laughter. I'd been had.

Christopher Lambert did most of his own stunts, and the only time we ever argued was when I wouldn't let him stand in front of an oncoming truck and blast it with a flamethrower to make it to veer off and narrowly miss him. "If it was your last day of shooting, I'd have no problem," I kidded him, "but I need you to finish the film." We devised a compromise: a stunt double would do the first take and Chris would do the second. As the truck barreled toward the stuntman, he fired the flamethrower and when the flames struck the truck they bounced back, hitting him full in the face. Both of his eyebrows were completely burned off. I turned to Chris, "You still want to do this?" He just grinned and nodded. His take came off perfectly. Either he was the bravest actor I had ever worked with, or he had just been in Australia too long.

We also had a scene that featured poisonous snakes. One day, a snake wrangler showed up at our production offices. I asked to see his snakes and, before I could stop him, he dumped several pillowcases full of the reptiles onto the office floor. In an instant, the snakes were slithering around at great speed. Everyone was standing on their desks screaming for help. "Don't worry!" cried the wrangler as he quickly scooped them up with his bare hands, "they won't kill you. You'll just need to be hospitalized for a few days and then you'll be immune to the venom!" Now, *that's* a snake wrangler!

Jeffrey Combs had brought along a cassette of the Dire Straits album *On Every Street* and, during filming, their song "Heavy Fuel" became our theme song. Lines like, "My life makes perfect sense: Lust and food and violence" really spoke to us in those days, and when we discovered that Dire Straits was on tour in nearby Brisbane that weekend, Jeffrey and I immediately got ourselves a couple of tickets. We drove to the concert in my rented car (steering wheel on the right), playing the cassette at full volume as we smoked half a bag of weed. We arrived at the venue, jumping out of the car in a cloud of smoke, and we rushed into the arena. It was the best concert ever. Mark Knopfler's solos were mind-bending, and when they went into "Heavy Fuel," Jeffrey and I went apeshit.

After the concert, we stumbled out of the arena, found our car and discovered that the motor was still running!

"Oh shit!" Jeffrey screamed grabbing his head, "We've locked the keys in the car!" I reached for the door handle, and to my shock and surprise, it swung right open. I had left the car unlocked with the motor running during the entire concert. Even more amazing, no one had stolen it.

Now you may be wondering where we got the weed. Since the film took place in a high-tech futuristic prison, we had found the most badass-looking extras to play the prisoners, and the meanest and toughest were an Aussie motorcycle gang. Each looked like he had stepped right out of *The Road Warrior* – three hundred pounds of solid muscle, tattooed and pierced with shoulder-length hair and braided beards. We soon discovered that they were really some of the gentlest creatures the planet. Their frightening appearance, like much of nature's protective coloration, scared away any potential threats. We made friends with one of them, a bloke named Shorty (he was the smallest of the group), and he provided us with dynamite grass. We decided that we should repay his kindness by featuring him in the film.

There was a scene toward the end of the movie where Zed 10, the computer that runs the prison (later voiced by Carolyn) is infected with a virus by Jeffrey Combs' character D-Day and goes berserk. The laser bars that kept the prisoners locked in their cells begin to blink on and off, and one of the inmates tries to make a break for it, only to be sliced up like sushi when the laser suddenly comes back to life. I decided that this unfortunate soul would be played by our pal Shorty.

As the scene involved seeing his sliced-off arms, legs, and head, our special effects team photographed every inch of Shorty's heavily tattooed body and matched it perfectly with prosthetic limbs. The day arrived when we were to shoot the scene but, to our surprise and dismay, Shorty did not show up.

After a series of frantic phone calls, it was discovered that he had been busted for selling weed and was in the slammer for real. We finally ended up having to make-up one of the effects guys to look like Shorty in order to match the prosthetics, and shot the scene.

* * *

And of course, there were kangaroos. Thousands of them. I was told that the Australians regarded them as pests: "The fur's no good. You can't eat 'em." (But I have sampled their meat since, and it was delicious.) Most of the Australian cars and trucks had what they called bull-bars attached to their front bumpers to protect them from destruction if they happened to hit anything from the smaller wallabies to the massive red kangaroos.

One early morning when I arrived at our farmhouse set ahead of the rest of the crew, I stepped inside the barn and encountered a big red. It seemed to tower over me, and as we looked at each other, I slowly backed away having heard stories of how aggressive they could be. The kangaroo suddenly bolted and, in an instant, disappeared through an opening in the dilapidated wall.

Carolyn and the girls joined me for the last week of shooting. When I picked them up at the airport, Meg, who was now three years old, was sucking on a pacifier. Without thinking I grabbed it out of her mouth and threw it out of the car's window. Meg broke into tears. "She's jet-lagging!" Carolyn shouted at me, and I felt like a complete shit.

The production wrapped principal photography right before Christmas and, as December down-under is early summer, the temperatures were now over a hundred humid degrees Farenheit. The closest we could find to a Christmas tree was a large fern that bent as we hung our ornaments that Carolyn, as usual, had brought with her from Los Angeles. It reminded us of Charlie Brown's scrawny tree. Among their presents, the older girls were given boogie boards, small Styrofoam surf boards. The next day Suzanna, Jill, and I went to the beach so they could try them out. I was lolling in the sun when Suzanna ran up to me. She was very upset. "Dad!" she cried, "Jill's being pulled out to sea!" She pointed to the ocean and I could barely see a little speck on the horizon: nine-year-old Jill clutching her shocking-pink boogie board. I jumped up and ran toward the water.

"Here, take this," Suzanna yelled holding out her board. But I waved her away thinking it would slow me down, and I jumped into the water. The tide quickly carried me out to Jill, at least a half mile from the beach. She had already been rescued by some surfers who put her on a surfboard and were paddling back to shore. Did I want a lift? I waved them off, and in a moment they were gone. I turned around and headed back toward shore. But after several minutes of swimming, I realized that the tide was against me, and I was farther out to sea than when I began. I kept at it to no avail and soon was completely exhausted. I was alone in the water, and it suddenly hit me that I no longer had the strength to make it back and could easily drown. I fought to keep my head above water, but the current was carrying me further and further out to sea.

The surfers were nowhere in sight as I started yelling for help. Could anyone hear me? My arms and legs had turned to wet noodles and I started sinking. They say that your whole life flashes before your eyes as you go down for the third time, but all I remember seeing were the newspaper accounts of my death. "American Director Drowns at Sea" Who would finish the film? The next thing I remember is being pulled onto a surfboard and an Aussie voice telling me to hang on. He soon got us back to shore and dropped me on the beach. "Was I okay?" he wanted to know, and I wearily nodded, too exhausted to speak. And then he was gone.

Suzanna and Jill came running to me and we hugged as I fought to catch my breath. I looked around for the surfer, but he had disappeared. When I recovered, we hurried home, and I told Carolyn what had happened. "Thank God!" she exclaimed as she hugged us all.

"He saved my life!" I told her.

"And mine too!" Jill added.

"How much money do you have? We need to give them a reward!"

We scraped together what we had – a couple hundred Australian dollars – and Carolyn quickly drove us back to the beach, but by the time we got there, all the surfers were gone.

"Maybe they were angels," I stammered trying to make sense of it all. According to the Bible, angels are messengers from God, and as soon as they complete their assigned tasks, they disappear.

"Surf Angels?" Carolyn asked, never one to believe in divine providence. But we all hugged each other again, feeling very lucky to be alive.

CHAPTER 37

Documentaries Don't Count

When we returned to our house on Crewe Street, it was time for my mother to come back from Seattle to stay with us in Los Angeles. Her condition had deteriorated. After three months with my brother, he had to put her in the Ida Culver House, an assisted-care residence for retired teachers. She was asked to leave, however, when, in her confusion, she started wandering into other residents' rooms. It was clear that she now needed to be supervised on a full-time basis. We needed to find a facility for her in Los Angeles.

We found a senior residence for my mother on Ventura Blvd in Encino and every Monday, Wednesday, and Friday we would bring her to our home for dinner. She especially enjoyed the Friday night Shabbat with the whole family. She had, by then, suffered more small strokes, and it was clear that her condition was worsening, but she had good days and bad days, and she often reminded me of a broken radio whose constant static could become clear as a bell for brief occasions. We discovered that her long-term memory was in far better shape than her short-term, and she could remember events that had taken place when she was a child as if they had happened yesterday. She had dictated a lovely remembrance to my brother about a car trip she and her family had taken to visit relatives in the countryside when she was a small girl. It seemed so unfair that a woman with such a brilliant mind, who had graduated Phi Beta Kappa from the University of Chicago, could no longer read a book, as she was unable to remember what she had just read.

I began editing *Fortress* with Tim Wellburn, our Australian editor whom we had brought to Los Angeles. We were about to lock picture on *Fortress*, but the producers wanted to test it first. This involved conducting a screening with questionnaires and a focus group. I have always done this informally, but this was my first professional research screening. The results were mixed, with the film scoring in the high sixties (not particularly good). This surprised me, as I had been in the audience for the focus group (a small portion of the audience asked to stay and discuss the film), and they seemed to like it very much. Why was our score so low? When the focus group was asked this question the response was, "Well, it's not *Citizen Kane*." My usual response to a comment like this would be, "You're right. If it had been *Citizen Kane*, we wouldn't have called it *Fortress*." The audience seemed to have the most trouble with the ending of our film in which the evil computer Zed 10 takes control of the semi-tractor that our heroes have used to make their escape. The scene ends with Chris Lambert firing his flame thrower at the truck as it races toward the barn in which his wife is giving birth to their child. The scene climaxes with our spectacular explosion. But audiences couldn't believe that the wife and child could possibly live through such a conflagration. This surprised me, as I had just watched the film version of *The Fugitive*, in which Harrison Ford somehow survives a leap from a dam.

In Hollywood, they say you have to kill your darlings, so I cut the entire battle with the truck, massive explosion and all, and the film scored slightly higher (mid-seventies). This is the version of the film that was released in Europe, where it ended up breaking attendance records in its first week. "We've got lightning in a bottle!" Village Roadshow's Greg Coote crowed. Then the distributors in Great Britain contacted me. They told me that the film would get the equivalent of a PG-13 rating which, in their mind, would not help its release. Did I have any other more violent footage that would help it get an 18 and older rating? This was the first time anyone had complained that my movies weren't violent enough. It's not as if *Fortress* is devoid of blood and guts. After all, a character's entire midsection is vaporized by a laser cannon. I sent them the excised truck explosion, and they loved it. Many of the Asian territories followed Britain's lead, and now there are two versions of *Fortress*, both of which are approved by the director.

The film was released in just about every country except America and was a huge international hit. This must have galled Twentieth Century-Fox who initially had the U.S. rights, but passed on distributing the film. It was eventually released a year later by Miramax under their new Dimension label, which was supervised by Harvey Weinstein's younger brother Bob. I was worried that Bob would follow in "Harvey Scissorhands" tradition and completely re-cut the film, but, except for a couple of minor trims, he left it alone. Then Gerry Rich, the Weinsteins' marketing guru, decided that no one wanted to see a prison movie. He had reached his own odd conclusion based on the fact that Sylvester Stallone's last film, *Lock-Up*, had bombed. In his mind, the reason for its failure was that it was a prison movie. So, despite the fact that *Fortress* had become a huge international hit and all the advertising had focused on the high-tech prison concept, Rich decided he knew better.

Marketing guys like to make sweeping generalizations. "No one wants to see a movie set in the past" was their mantra for decades until Jim Cameron made *Titanic*. Before that it was "No one wants to see science-fiction" until *Star Wars* opened. Thanks to the genius of Mr. Rich, no mention could be made of the fact that *Fortress* was a prison movie. His advertising concept aped the campaign for *Total Recall* with a close-up of Chris Lambert's face and a glowing ruin of a city. This meant that no one had the slightest idea what the hell the movie was about. Worse yet, they decided not to have the movie reviewed even though its international reviews were quite good. I called Bob Weinstein and begged him to reconsider. Not allowing critics to review a film sends the signal that the distributors think it's a piece of shit. Then if it somehow manages to score positive reviews, with a Friday opening the reviews won't run until Saturday at the earliest, a day when almost no one buys newspapers. They also chose to release the film on Labor Day weekend, a dumping ground for the worst films of the year. Bob Weinstein told me not to worry, he knew what was best, and that was that.

Miraculously, the film ended up getting excellent reviews in *The New York Times* and *Los Angeles Times,* among others, but no one read them – except for Bob Weinstein, who called me on Monday, believe it or not, to apologize. Despite this, *Fortress* quickly disappeared from the multiplex screens without a ripple. Gerry Rich, on the other hand, continued to fail upward, ultimately becoming the head of worldwide marketing at Paramount.

In October of 1992, I was invited to serve on the jury of the Sitges Film Festival in Spain. Sitges is the oldest festival devoted entirely to fantasy, science fiction, and horror. *Re-Animator* won the award for best picture in 1985. Carolyn and I were flown business class to Barcelona, and the plane was overrun by a raucous crowd who whooped and hollered the whole twelve hours of the flight. I later found out that the offenders were Quentin Tarantino and the cast of *Reservoir Dogs*.

Sitges is a beautiful seaside town an hour south of Barcelona. We stayed in a large 4-star hotel that was also the home of the festival, and I was introduced to my fellow jury members. The president was Ellen Burstyn, star of *The Exorcist.* The line-up of films that we judged included *Reservoir Dogs, Braindead* (an amazingly bloody horror comedy directed by a New Zealander named Peter Jackson) and *Man Bites Dog*, a Belgian mockumentary in which a film crew follow around a serial killer while he commits numerous murders. I got to meet the filmmakers and, after watching *Braindead* and its climactic scene in which a power lawn mower is used against a horde of marauding zombies, I had to ask Peter Jackson how many gallons of stage blood he had used in his film. We had gone through almost thirty gallons in *Re-Animator,* which I assumed was the all-time record. Jackson thought a minute, doing the math to convert from liters to gallons. "We used three thousand gallons," he finally told me. So much for my record.

I also met Quentin Tarantino. He told me that his film education had taken place working in a video store in Manhattan Beach where he had watched just about every movie they had in stock. It became a game to try to stump Tarantino by naming a film he had not seen, but the only one turned out to be *Harlan County, USA*, which Quentin said didn't count because it was a documentary.

We also became friends with Ellen Burstyn, who was very down to earth and funny as hell. She told us she had started out as a chorus girl on

The Jackie Gleason Show. Poor Ellen, the president of our jury, was reprimanded by Thomas Spieker, the representative of the festival, because she often put her hands over her eyes during the most disturbing moments in the many horror films we watched. "How can she judge our movies, if she covers her eyes?" the filmmakers wanted to know. I kidded her about this. After all, I told her, she had starred in *The Exorcist*, one of the scariest movies ever made. "I was in it, but I never saw it," she responded, then quickly amended her statement. "Well, I did see it once," she admitted. It was in a little town in Arizona where she was shooting *Alice Doesn't Live Here Anymore* with Martin Scorsese. She and the crew had gone to the tiny local theater to see *The Exorcist* and a woman sitting in the row in front of them fainted and fell into the aisle. Ellen went to help her. When the woman came to, opened her eyes, and saw Ellen she screamed her head off. "She thought she had gone into the movie!" Ellen told us, laughing.

When *Reservoir Dogs* was screened, the film broke during the scene in which Michael Madsen cuts off the policeman's ear. While they were repairing the film and rethreading the projector, I went to the men's room and discovered Wes Craven at the next urinal. "I'm not going back in there," he told me.

"But it's only a movie," I replied, not being able to resist throwing back his famous line from the ads for *The Last House on the Left*.

"It's too real," Wes insisted. True to his word, by the time the film continued, he had left. I've since discovered that many horror movie makers are, like me, the biggest cowards on Earth. We know what scares us and have no problem scaring others, but whenever I see a movie and realize that the director knows what he's doing and isn't going to hold back, I immediately panic. I've walked out of many movies over the years. I have to say that I found serving on a jury to be a stressful experience, as many of my fellow jurists had their own agendas and favorites. After much arguing, we ended up giving the Best Picture prize to *Man Bites Dog*. Quentin won for best screenplay and Peter Jackson received the award for best special effects. As soon as the decisions were made, I felt as if an enormous weight had been lifted from my shoulders. We all went out together and got very drunk.

CHAPTER 38

Beauty and Truth

On September 8th, 1993, my mother died.

I was having lunch with Christopher Lambert at a Beverly Hills restaurant a few days after the American release of *Fortress* when Carolyn called with the awful news. I quickly excused myself and drove to my mother's nursing home, where I found her body lying peacefully in her hospital bed. She looked incredibly young; all the wrinkles she had accumulated over her eighty-three years of life had miraculously vanished. She looked at peace and so beautiful. I kissed her forehead, and it was as cold as marble.

I had tried to prepare myself for losing her as her condition had continued to worsen during the final months. She could no longer eat as her swallowing reflexes had ceased working and a stomach tube had been surgically implanted to feed her. I had visited as often as I could, and she always seemed to know who I was. Her blue-grey eyes lit up when I entered her room. Sometimes I would read to her. I was reading her Keats's *Ode on a Grecian Urn*, and to my amazement, she began reciting the beautiful poem with me.

> 'When old age shall this generation waste,
> Thou shalt remain, in the midst of other woe
> Than ours, a friend to man, to whom thou say'st,
> "Beauty is truth, truth beauty," – that is all
> Ye know on earth, and all ye need to know."'

My mother's long-term memories were stronger than her short term, but this poem seemed to be coming from the very core of her being. And this core was filled with sweetness and sunshine.

Over the years, I have noticed myself becoming bitter and cynical with life's defeats. I wish I had her tremendous inner strength and genuine goodness to help me resist these weak responses to adversity and remain gentle and kind like her. My mother is like Keats's Grecian Urn; she can never fade. Her stroke-ravaged mind held onto that poem and kept it alive within her. I pray that there is a poem that will always live in me.

* * *

Like my father, my mother's body was cremated. We buried her ashes beside her beloved husband in Chicago. She has been gone for many years now, but the pain of losing her is still as strong as if she had left us yesterday.

Saving King Kong

My mother's death plunged me into the depths of depression. It didn't help that I had no work. Strangely, the international success of *Fortress* had not encouraged any studio to hire me, and the original projects that I developed cratered one after the other. I hadn't made a movie in almost three years. There had been talk of a sequel to *Fortress*. I had suggested the idea that the new prison could be in high Earth orbit, above the stratosphere. I did some work on a treatment with Troy Neighbors and Steve Feinberg, but soon was booted off the project. I initially found this hard to understand as I believed that my involvement had turned *Fortress* into the enormous international hit it had become, but no one seemed to know or care. All that matters to Hollywood is how much the film grosses domestically and, thanks to Bob Weinstein and Gerry Rich, it had been perceived as a flop.

Abel Ferrara had been chosen to replace me as director of *Body Snatchers*. He had made a name for himself grinding out shocking low-budget affairs in New York such as *Ms.45* and *The Driller Killer*, films I had watched with Brian Yuzna prior to shooting *Re-Animator*. These projects had led to his bigger successes with *King of New York* and *Bad Lieutenant*. Now, he was being given a chance to direct his first studio film at Warner Brothers. I met Ferrara and found him to be a weird, chain-smoking hipster who constantly referred to the shape-shifting aliens in *Body Snatchers* as "Martians." Producer Bob Solo often found himself at odds with Ferrara and repeatedly called me to bitch about him screwing up the film. The initial research screenings had been abysmal, and the project was soon turned over to legendary editor Dede Allen (*Bonnie and Clyde*, *Little Big Man*, *Dog Day Afternoon*, *The Breakfast Club*) who, at seventy years old, was now the head of post-production at Warner Bros. Disappointingly, Dede's solution to "fixing" *Body Snatchers* was to add a voice-over to explain the story to the audience (a sure sign of desperation). I found myself tangling with her, as I believed that the voice-over telegraphed to the audience who would survive, robbing the movie of a great deal of its tension. After all, Lovecraft himself said, "Never explain anything." As I was no longer involved except as a writer, my concerns were ignored. I also suggested to Bob Solo that he should reinstate effects sequences from our original script that Ferrara had cut. These involved the idea of using Agent Orange, a chemical defoliant from the Vietnam war, to kill the plant-based pod people. Comic book artist Bernie Wrightson had worked with me to create amazing conceptual artwork showing the dissolving pod people.

CHAPTER 39

Plans began moving forward for a reshoot when I received a frantic phone call from Abel Ferrara. He was livid. "What are you doing, man?!" he shouted at me. "You left this project two years ago! This is my movie!" I tried to explain that Bob Solo had sought my help and that the melting effects could help save his film, but he was having none of it. "The pod people aren't fucking vegetables!" he screamed. "It says in the book that they are exact cellular duplicates of the people they have replaced."

He was right about this. Jack Finney, the author of the classic novel, had been very clear about this concept; Dennis Paoli and I had taken creative liberties and changed this basic idea. But what cut through me like a knife was that Ferrara viewed me as a traitor, a fellow director interfering with his artistic freedom. "How would you like it if somebody else did this to you?" he pleaded. I instantly knew that he was absolutely right. I felt like a total shit. I apologized to Ferrara and walked away from *Body Snatchers* and had nothing more to do with it.

Warner Brothers planned to shelve the film but in the summer of '93 Ferrara, who is considered a god in France, was somehow able to get it screened in competition at the Cannes Film Festival where it received excellent reviews. Warner Brothers gave it a half-hearted American release and it died a quick death. Nevertheless, I was quite impressed with Ferrara's work on the film; the performances he pulled from Meg Tilly, Terry Kinney, Gabrielle Anwar, and Forest Whitaker were spectacular, deep, and terrifying.

* * *

I'm not sure what brought me to Full Moon's new headquarters in Los Feliz, but in February of 1994, I found myself sitting in Charlie Band's office staring at a poster that showed a grotesque Quasimodo-like monstrosity whipping a nearly naked young woman who was chained to a stone wall. The title read *Castle Freak*. Intrigued, I asked Charlie what the movie was about. "There's a castle and there's a freak," he told me, and I realized that, like most Charles Band concepts, there was no script yet. Then his eyes lit up. "Do you want to do it?" he asked.

The plan was to shoot it at his castle in the little town of Giove that May. To make it even more enticing, Charlie told me that, unlike the movies he was cranking out for Paramount, this one could be unrated. And I could have my name above the title. Like most directors, I had been offered the "A Joe Blow film" credit that one sees on nearly every picture, but I ultimately learned to turn down this possessory ego stroking. As a member of the Writers Guild, I couldn't fathom why a director would be given this credit, especially if he hadn't even written the script. I began to notice that people I respected, like

Woody Allen (who always wrote his own scripts) never ever took this credit. After all, filmmaking is a team sport. But, as Frank Capra pointed out in his wonderful autobiography, *The Name Above the Title*, using the director's name to sell the film was the highest honor one could aspire to. For that reason, my new project would be called *Stuart Gordon's Castle Freak*. For the first time, I would contractually receive final cut.

Accepting this assignment, however, meant that I would have to drop out of the B'nai Mitzvot class at Temple Beth Hillel. We had joined the temple shortly after moving to Los Angeles, and Suzanna had attended religious school there. She originally chose not to be Bat Mitzvahed, but now, at sixteen, she had changed her mind. Knowing that I had never had a Bar Mitzvah, she asked me if I would join her in learning Hebrew, so we could be B'nai Mitzvahed together. I had agreed. Directing *Castle Freak* would mean that once again I would be a dropout. I agonized about letting my daughter down, but work is work and you have to take it when you can, so I accepted the assignment knowing that I would be in Italy when she would be reading from the Torah before the entire congregation. It killed me to not be there for her, not even as a proud parent. I wrote her a letter on the day of her B'nai Mitzvah – June 24th, 1994 – and faxed it to my assistant Tom Bradford at Disney (where I still had an office) to deliver to Suzanna:

> It's been such a pleasure watching you grow from baby to child to a young woman. Each phase had special pleasures and I will cherish these wonderful memories all of my life. Like the time I took you to see *King Kong* when you were 6 years old. At first you were scared of this gigantic gorilla, but I assured you that Kong was "a good monkey." This seemed to do the trick until we got to the final scene on top of the Empire State Building. You watched horrified as the biplanes machine-gunned this magnificent creature. And with tears running down your cheeks you whispered "Daddy, who's going to save King Kong?"
>
> I sometimes think that there are two kinds of people in this world: life-givers and death-dealers. It's always been clear to me that you are a member in good standing of the first group. Your appreciation and love of animals, your abilities to understand and care for children, and your skill at relating to all people, young and old, is such a great gift. I wish I could take credit for it. But it has always been a key part of who you are.
>
> This is the source of your strength and now that you are taking your place as an adult, I feel I can talk to you as an equal and answer that question you tearfully posed those many years ago: No one could save King Kong. But Kong rose to the occasion and heroically sacrificed himself to save the love of his life.

> Life is wonderful. It is God's greatest gift, but it can also be tough. Life isn't always fair. Bad things can happen to good people. And when those biplanes start circling, you have to look within yourself for strength. You have to save yourself. This is not to say you are alone. Belief in God means you are never alone. But as some unknown philosopher once said, "The Lord helps those who help themselves." Your sisters, your mother and I, your family and friends create a bond of love which will always be there for you. Love, like God, is forever.

Looking back now at those words I wrote more than twenty years ago, I marvel that they still seem true. Sometimes you do get a glimpse of the big picture. Suzanna became a high school English teacher, just like her grandmother.

A Castle and a Freak

Dennis Paoli and I immediately went to work on *Castle Freak* and developed a story about a family that inherits an Italian castle unaware that there is a hideous creature trapped in the bowels of the darkest dungeon. Because we needed the script yesterday, we ended up shooting the first draft of the screenplay – something I have never done before or since. Perhaps because of this, the script has an inherent purity like none of my other films. Sometimes fast is good.

During the rehearsal period, I screened Robert Wise's spooky masterpiece *The Haunting* for the cast. We had heard rumors that Charlie's castle was haunted by the spirit of a little girl who still can be heard crying at night. Although we never actually heard her, we ended up incorporating this legend into the script, and even used a Ouija board in an attempt to contact her spirit. This initially failed – but one night we did manage to contact a Latin-speaking ghost (an ancient Roman?).

On the evening that Carolyn and my daughters arrived from Los Angeles, I was shooting an outdoor scene in the castle's stone courtyard. Meg, who was now six years old, had been repeatedly told that she had to remain completely silent during the filming. But as the Assistant Director called "Roll sound!" and then "Roll camera!" she couldn't control herself, and at the top of her lungs shouted "ACTION!" The entire crew (myself included) burst into laughter.

Jonathan Fuller had lost almost fifty pounds to play this starving monstrosity. Seeking inspiration from the great Lon Chaney, he found ways to establish pathos for this abused child who knew only pain and suffering. John Vulich – who, as a beginner in creature effects had created many of the grotesque little monsters hidden inside the innocent-looking porcelain dolls in the movie of the same name – was now designing and building the disturbing full body suit that Jonathan would wear as the freak. He created a horrible looking teeth-baring split lip that was truly the stuff of nightmares. Jonathan's extensive full body make-up required six hours to apply each day, so during the morning, we would shoot scenes without the freak. Then all hell would break loose when he appeared on set after lunch. The Castle Freak's make-up was so grotesque that I worried it would give my youngest daughter nightmares, so I asked Jonathan if he wouldn't mind eating his lunch alone in the make-up room so as not to frighten Meg. He graciously agreed until one day at lunch when Meg, who had often talked with Jonathan when he was out of make-up, asked me where he was. I explained that he was eating alone because he didn't want to scare her, and her face fell. "That's so sad that he has to eat alone," she told me. And then she got up to leave the dining room.

CHAPTER 40

"Where are you going?" I asked her.

"To have lunch with Jonathan," she called over her shoulder as she quickly took off down the stairs to the make-up room. Jonathan's grotesque appearance didn't seem to faze her, and she continued having lunch with him every day. Eventually she asked to try on the prosthetic mask herself, so make-up artist Mike Measmer turned her into The Littlest Castle Freak.

As shooting continued, I was constantly clashing with our producer. Maurizio Maggi seemed to be spending as little money as possible. While this is standard operating procedure for most producers, in Maggi's case it went far beyond what the crew and I had ever experienced. Tonni, who once again cooked for the entire cast and crew, complained that he wasn't given enough to feed everyone properly, and I noticed that even the wine had been watered down. I finally discovered that Maggi's deal with Charlie Band allowed him to pocket whatever money he didn't spend on our film. I tried to explain to Maggi that, despite its tiny budget, *Castle Freak* had the potential to be a classic horror film. But he assumed it was just another Full Moon quickie and my words fell on deaf ears. The situation came to a head when I was told that we couldn't afford to hire a taxicab for the scene in which Barbara Crampton's character and her daughter leave the castle. "You can use my car," Maggi told me, pointing to a beautiful white Mercedes. I protested that the scene wouldn't make sense with such an upscale car, but my Italian producer was adamant. Finally, I turned to one of the grips. "Drill some holes in the roof and put a taxi sign on the car," I told him. Within seconds Maggi relented and soon enough a real taxi appeared.

One of the most disturbing scenes in the film is when the freak bites off a nipple of the prostitute he has captured and imprisoned in his cell. When writing the script, Dennis and I had joked that the character of Castle Freak confused food and fucking. His development had been permanently stunted by his abusive mother, and so he was stuck in the early oral phase of childhood. A prosthetic device concealing a blood pack had been attached to Raffaella's breast, but Jonathan Fuller must have been slightly carried away in the playing of the scene and accidentally bit through the prosthetic and into the actress's breast. She screamed bloody murder and we thought she was just playing the scene, but after I called cut, she began pulling off the latex to reveal real teeth marks around her nipple. Oops!

When we got back to Los Angeles, I began working with my new editor, Bert Glatstein. Because we had left without finishing the last few scenes, a reconstruction of the freak's bleak cell had to be built, and the scenes shot on a stage in Full Moon's large Los Feliz studio. It added almost another hundred thousand to our small budget, and I still can't believe that Charlie threw us out of his castle without first finishing the film. He clearly believed his amazing deal with Paramount was of the utmost importance. So, I was flabbergasted with what happened next. One day as I was sitting with Bert editing *Castle Freak*, a guy in a suit with a clipboard entered the editing suite. He told us he was from Paramount, and could we please tell him the name of the film we were working on? We gave him the title and watched as he leafed through several pages on his clipboard. "*Castle Freak*? That's the title?" We nodded. "I can't find it," he finally said, and then quickly left. Bert and I looked at each other. Weird. The next day the other shoe dropped. It was announced that Full Moon's fabulous deal with Paramount was cancelled. It turned out that several of the films Charlie had promised to deliver had never even been started, Paramount's money had been pocketed or spent on projects like *Castle Freak* that had never been approved for production in the first place. I felt a strong sense of déjà vu. This seemed like a replay of the end of Empire Pictures seven years earlier.

Completing the film proved almost as difficult as finishing *Robot Jox*. Maurizio Maggi refused to send Charlie the negative until he had been paid in full. The Italian wolf had been tricked by the quick American fox. Somehow Charlie managed to use the work print to generate a print which was never properly color corrected. Everything ended up looking various shades of green, and this poor print is the only 35mm copy in existence. The technicians were somehow able to adjust the color on the transfer to video, so the film was completed. There were two versions: one rated R and the other, a director's cut, that was unrated. Unfortunately, Charlie didn't have the money to release the film theatrically, so I asked him if I could show it to Bob Weinstein at Miramax. He agreed.

A few days later, I got a call from Bob's assistant telling me that the film had scared the crap out of Bob. "He wouldn't let me leave him alone in the screening room," he told me. I was delighted. A sale to Miramax would guarantee a real theatrical release. Then the phone rang again, and it was Bob himself. "Your movie is pretty damn scary," he told me. "But then you fucked it up." This was typical no-bullshit Bob. The film was too bloody for him. He could never release it. I was reminded of a conversation in which Bob had once told me that he believed *The Omen* was the scariest movie ever made. "That scene where they dig up the kid's mother and find the skeleton of a dog. It doesn't get any better than that," he had told me.

And so *Castle Freak* became another orphan, receiving a very limited release direct to video. It was my last film shot in Italy, my last film for Charlie Band, and my last film with both Barbara and Jeffrey. I believe it is the best of the films they starred in together, and that I had the good fortune to direct.

The film is as incredibly shocking today as it was twenty years ago, but it's not shocking in a fun way like *Re-Animator. Castle Freak* is a very disturbing, dark tale about the responsibilities of being a parent. The script came from a very dark place inside of both me and my old friend Dennis Paoli. I was still reeling from the recent loss of my mother, and Dennis was still hurting from the death of his beloved wife Heidi. For me the film harkens back to the line from *Dolls*, "Being a parent is a privilege – not a right." In *Castle Freak*, the terrible actions of the parents permanently damage their children. I was lucky to grow up in a household filled with love. My mother was always understanding and supportive – never anything close to the monstrous mother in this film. So where did this horrendous character come from? Was I angry at her for leaving me? Was I angry at God for taking away everything that she loved – her quick mind, her ability to think and dream and all of her beautiful memories?

I was in a dark place, darker than I had ever been, exploring the evil possibilities of a life that had become a curse, one that had destroyed the beauties of childhood and the possibilities of any future happiness. For me, the worst possible thing imaginable – the thing I feared the most – would be the loss of my sweet family, of my dear wife and children and, now, my loving grandchildren. Many have remarked on the fact that, unlike my other movies, there is very little humor in this film. Nevertheless, *Castle Freak* ends with a little ray of hope: a shot of the prostitute's now-motherless child, whom the carabiniere has never acknowledged as his own. Barbara Crampton's character watches as the man goes to the small child and takes his hand. The child looks up at him.

And Barbara smiles.

Untitled Irish Space Movie

Back in my college days when I was driving the endless highway between Chicago and Madison, I became fascinated with the semi rigs that owned the road. In the late '80s, *National Lampoon* writer Ted Mann and I joined forces to set that memory in outer space. The film that would ultimately become known as *Space Truckers* was about working-class guys pulling long trains of cargo to colonies throughout the solar system.

We assembled an amazing array of talented artists to refine the look of the film: Ron Cobb, who had designed our giant robots in *Robot Jox*, created the beat-up space truck. Bruce McCall, famous for his fanciful car and airplane designs as well as classic covers of *The New Yorker*, envisioned the rotating space diner as a shout out to *2001: A Space Odyssey*. I began casting our untitled space movie as production designer Simon Murton left for Dublin to begin prepping the picture. I had a meeting in New York with Harvey Keitel, who was having a manicure while we met in his office. Clearly embarrassed, he made me agree never to tell anyone about the manicure, but he ultimately passed on the project, so I feel no compunction about spilling the beans. A week later casting director Heidi Levitt called to let me know that Dennis Hopper was interested in playing the role. I've always been a big fan of his work, but Hopper's career had been derailed after *Easy Rider* by his out-of-control substance abuse, although Heidi insisted he had been clean for five years. Dennis wanted to meet me, and I was invited to his home in Venice Beach.

When I got to his house, I had to check the address twice to see if I had made a mistake. The strange house was made entirely of plywood sheets and had no windows. It was surrounded by gravel and a high cyclone fence topped with razor-wire. Very off-putting, to say the least. I rang the doorbell and was asked to identify myself. Then I was buzzed in, and the cyclone fence automatically slid open. Dennis Hopper greeted me at the door, and as I walked in, my jaw dropped. The stark windowless building, which I later learned had been designed by Frank Gehry, was filled with light streaming down from enormous skylights that covered the 20-foot-tall ceilings. The gleaming hard-wood floor was carpeted with gorgeous oriental rugs. But what immediately captured my attention were the walls covered with the most amazing paintings I had ever seen: Warhol, Haring, Rauschenberg, de Kooning, Lichtenstein, a veritable Who's Who of the greatest artists of the 20th century. Not prints, but all originals and, unlike the works displayed in museums, which are usually more sedate, middle-of-the-road samples of the artists' works, these were some of the most outrageous and brilliant paintings they had ever done. In the center of the room stood a statue of four life-size figures in business suits (but no pants) each holding onto the others' erect penises. Mind blowing.

"This is my fifth collection," Dennis told me as I admired his artwork.

"What happened to the other four?" I asked him.

"My ex-wives got 'em," he answered with his cawing laugh. "I started collecting when I first came out here. No one had ever heard of these artists, and I got them for next to nothing. My agent told me I was wasting my money... so I got a new agent."

* * *

Charlie Band asked me to join him at the Cannes Film Festival on my way to Dublin so I could meet with prospective buyers and help him sell *Castle Freak*. Even though *Re-Animator* had been shown there (and won a Critic's Prize) in 1985, this was my first time on the Croissette. Charlie, as always, did things in grand style, and I was picked up at the airport by a stretch limo and taken to the Carlton, the most chic and expensive hotel in Cannes, where all the biggest stars were staying. As we approached the hotel, I saw a huge crowd standing in front. We turned into the driveway and the crowd surged forward quickly surrounding the limo. Holding autograph books and snapping flash pictures, the people pushed their faces against the tinted glass of the limo's passenger windows trying to see inside.

"Who are you?" they yelled, "Who are you?"

"Who do you think I am," was my reply.

There was a long pause and then someone yelled, "It's Coppola!" And the crowd went nuts. "Coppola! Coppola!" Security men had to push the admiring fans back, clearing my path into the hotel. Later that day I told my friend Steve Blum, the former Full Moon gofer who was learning foreign sales, about what had happened. He thought it was hilarious. We decided to grab some dinner and ended up at a toney French restaurant on the beach. "Do you have a reservation?" the snooty maître d' asked. We shook our heads. "Zen I am very sorry but zere is nossing I can do."

I started to say something, but Steve held up his hand, "Come on Francis, let's go." I laughed and we began to walk away, but the maître d' was now frantically chasing after us. "Monsieur Coppola! Monsieur Coppola! I am so sorry! Please, right zis way!" Now he was leading us to his very best table. Steve and I looked at each other. It's good to be the king. We ordered some wine, but the maître d' insisted on only the best champagne for us. Mais oui! So, we enjoyed a fabulous meal. When we asked for the check, the maître d' waved his hand. He was comping our dinner. Then he opened a box of Havana cigars. As we started to leave, the maître d' was back holding a large book. "Monsieur Coppola, Did you enjoy your meal? Would you please write somesing." I looked at Steve nervously. I took the book and opened it looking for a blank page, flipping past pages signed by Cary Grant, Marilyn Monroe, Orson Welles, Frank Sinatra.

"What was it like working with Sinatra?" the maître d' asked. Sinatra? I wracked my brains. Did Coppola ever work with Sinatra? The only connection I could think of was *The Godfather*, where there's a character who's supposed to be Sinatra (Johnny Fontane, the guy who gets cast after they cut off the head of the producer's prize racehorse).

"That was Al Martino," I told him as I signed the book. The maître d' nodded, taking back the leather-bound volume "Delicious," I had written and then I signed "Stuart Gordon." The maître d' wrinkled his brow as he tried to read it as Steve and I walked away.

A few years later I was at a film festival in San Francisco and guess who was there? That's right, Francis Ford Coppola. I couldn't resist telling him the story about being mistaken for him at Cannes. Coppola didn't laugh. He slowly looked me up and down.

"You're much too fat to be me," he finally said.

* * *

Simon Murton persuaded his father Peter to help him with his maiden voyage as a production designer. Peter was the art director on *Dr. Strangelove* and brought along several of his favorite crew members to help us. It was his first time working in Ireland, and I remember an embarrassing meeting in which he loudly proclaimed that the Irish technicians and craftsmen were incapable of doing professional-level work. Unfortunately, he said this while sitting at a table full of Irishmen.

The animosity between the English and Irish was (and is) alive and well. I was shocked by the stories of the cruelty of the British rule, destroying Irish castles and churches and even forbidding the Irish to speak Gaelic.

Our casting directors quickly set up a meeting with English actor Charles Dance at the Groucho Club in London. A very exclusive members-only club in Soho, Peter Newman, Greg Johnson, and I were initially refused entrance. "Don't you know who this is?" Greg had asked the bouncer, pointing to me, "He's a very famous director."

The bouncer had just shrugged. "This place is full of 'em," he replied.

Luckily, Charles Dance came to our rescue, and we were finally allowed in. Utterly charming and very funny, Charles told us that his daughter had encouraged him to do the part. "She wants to see me do something less stodgy," he explained. Charles and I immediately hit it off, especially when I discovered that he could do a dead-on impersonation of Dennis Hopper's cackling laugh.

* * *

Interestingly, the celebrity who caused the biggest stir in Ireland was George Wendt. He couldn't walk down the street without everyone wanting to have a beer with Norm, the character he famously played on *Cheers*. He had to be dropped off in the alley behind his hotel to avoid causing a riot.

We began rehearsals, and for the first (and only) time, I encountered an actor who didn't want to rehearse. It didn't help that the actor was none other than Dennis Hopper. Stephen Dorff, who now saw Hopper as his role-model and mentor, also blew off the rehearsals. Although Hopper had studied with Lee Strasberg, he had never appeared on stage in his entire life, and he believed that rehearsals would somehow spoil his spontaneity. Later, when we started shooting, I asked Dennis for a second take and he asked me why. I told him I needed to see more of this or that. "I did it, man," he told me. When I explained that I hadn't seen it, he became irritated. "That's because you're sitting way over there and the camera is right here!" he informed me, pointing to his face. I was later to discover that Dennis Hopper's first take was always his best. The more takes we shot, the worse his performance became. This put the other actors at a severe disadvantage. They had to be able to deliver their best work right from the jump on the first take.

By the way, Hopper was correct. When I watched the dailies the next day, I saw he had given me the little nuance I was looking for but couldn't see from where I was sitting. Hopper could be a pain in the ass, but he was also an amazing teacher. "The movies are only a hundred years old," he once told me, "and I've worked in them for half that time."

Hair in the Gate

It had been decided that, despite the cartoony nature of *Space Truckers*, we should follow as many of the rules of physics as possible. This meant that, unlike *Star Trek* or *Star Wars*, there would be no gravity in the ships traveling through the starry reaches of deep space. I soon learned why this is so seldom done in films or television, and I also learned that our $27 million budget was much too small to do it all properly. Taking our cue from *2001: A Space Odyssey*, we designed the larger space craft and space stations to have artificial gravity created by centrifugal force caused by rotation and decided that the space trucks would have magnetic floors. But this still meant that objects needed to float and so did our characters if they weren't wearing their iron-soled boots. We used a ton of wire work, some of which could be hidden if we put the camera on its side so the wires would not appear above the "floating" objects. We also used a few computer-generated opticals to achieve some of the effects, such as squirting a line of mustard that remains floating in the air until the hot dog and bun are brought into contact with it. Our wonderful DP, old friend Mac Ahlberg, enhanced the zero-gravity effect by using a crane that made the camera seem to float, and the actors helped things along by creating the illusion of weightlessness with their underwater-like movements.

It was the first time I used computer generated effects and the Regalia, the space pirates' mother ship, was created entirely this way. Simon Maddocks, the British effects genius at Electric Image who beautifully brought the pirate ship to life, told me how he was constantly getting into trouble in elementary school when he'd be caught doodling pictures of spaceships during his lessons. "You're never going to be able to earn a living drawing spaceships," his teacher had scolded him. Hah!

We had the longest shooting schedule I've ever had: twelve weeks. We needed every minute. We had a crazy British pyro guy who used such massive charges in the bullet squibs during the opening scene that flying chunks of plaster hit the actors, sometimes drawing blood. We had a scene where a hand grenade is tossed into an elevator and the doors buckle with the explosion. The pyro guy wanted to show us a test of this effect during our lunch break, so Mac and I went to have a look. We stood over thirty feet from the elevator doors. Nonetheless, the explosion was so massive that it blew the metal doors completely off their tracks, and they came pin-wheeling through the air straight at us. I jumped out of the way, but poor Mac was hit in the thigh. Luckily, he wasn't seriously hurt, but I was furious. I later learned that this crazy pyromaniac blew himself up on his very next picture.

CHAPTER 42

Back in those ancient days of shooting movies on 35mm film, the last thing that happened before moving to set up the next shot was for the assistant director to call out "Check the gate!" This meant that the first assistant cameraman would open up the front of the camera, remove the lens, rotate the shutter, and make sure that there is no obstruction on the plate that holds the film in place. If there is a problem, it's called a "hair in the gate" and it can be anything – a shred of torn film, a piece of dirt or lint, or an actual hair. If this occurs, it means that you can't use what was just shot and need to reload the camera and reshoot the scene as the film is probably so damaged as to be unusable. This rarely happens. It had only occurred once or twice on all the films I had made up to this point. Usually, the first assistant calls out that the gate is clean, and you continue. But on *Space Truckers*, we heard "hair on the gate" not just once or twice, but literally dozens of times. This would mean losing a minimum of a half hour to an hour of your shooting day each time it happened. Why was it occurring so often?

It turned out our Irish first camera assistant had a bushy black beard that today would make the Taliban envious. When I pointed out to him that this might be the problem, he denied that it was possible. He insisted that the hairs he was finding in the gate were blonde. I urged him to shave off his beard, but he refused, and I was told that the union would not allow us to replace him, so this problem plagued us during the entire twelve-week shoot. We must have lost more than an entire day's shooting as a result. The capper was when I happened to run into him a few months later, and he was working on his next movie. I almost didn't recognize him, as he was now completely clean shaven.

Universal Studios had approached us during our shoot after seeing some early edited footage and wanted to buy our film and distribute it worldwide. This would give us a real release with the massive advertising and promotion that a blockbuster demands. What made this offer even better was that they were willing to put a significant amount of money into post-production to improve and add to our special effects. Peter Newman and his partner Greg Johnson were as excited about the prospect as I was. Universal needed a quick answer, and we were about to agree when our new partner, John Quested, vetoed the entire deal. He argued that if we were getting such an amazing offer now, we would get an even better one once the film was completed. We all tried to talk him out of this – a bird in the hand and so forth – but he held firm and Universal's offer was ultimately withdrawn. Heartbreaking.

Peter Newman and Ted Mann then met with Bob Weinstein at Miramax in New York to screen our thirty minutes of cut footage, but he told them he'd need to see the finished film before making an offer. "Then you'll have to buy a ticket," Ted had cheekily replied, and that was that.

As we reached the end of our shoot and the actors were departing, I asked Stephen Dorff if he had any thoughts on a new title for our film (as he had contractual approval of it). He looked a bit perplexed, and it was obvious that he hadn't really given this a second's thought. There was a long pause, then Stephen said, "How about *Space Trucker*?" I reminded him that everyone would think the title was referring to Dennis Hopper's character. "Oh…" Dorff replied. Another long pause. "Okay, how about *Space Truckers*?"

"Good idea," I replied, and so we were no longer "Untitled Irish Space Movie."

* * *

One evening I got a call from Tom Bradford, my assistant at Disney, where I still had an office. Carolyn and Margaret had been in an auto accident. Margaret was unharmed but Carolyn had badly broken her right hand. She had been taken to hospital and was awaiting surgery. Tom gave me the hospital's number and when I spoke to Carolyn, she sounded groggy. I later learned that she had suffered a compound fracture; the bones of her hand had broken through the skin causing her to go into shock. The operation, which took place that evening, involved putting titanium plates and seventeen screws into her hand, and thank God it was accomplished without a hitch.

I was able to talk to her the next day as she recovered, and she told me how she had been taking Meg to school when a car had shot out of a side street and struck her vehicle near the passenger door where Margaret had been sitting. It hit them with such force that her car ended up on the front lawn of a house across the street. Carolyn had been sounding her horn when she first saw the car, but the impact had set off the air bag in her steering wheel, and that was most likely how her hand had been broken. But those air bags also saved the lives of my wife and daughter. We had just gotten the new Toyota Camry with the money I had made from *Space Truckers*, and the car had been nearly totaled.

We talked about whether I should come home to help her with the kids while she recovered, but we decided that she should come to London and recuperate with me, away from the many duties of taking care of our house and home. She stayed with me for a couple of weeks and I have to say that, despite the severe pain from her injuries (hands have a great many nerves), it was wonderful to be together. I was again reminded that without her, I was only half alive. Suddenly London, which had seemed so cold and unfriendly, became a magical place and its usually reserved inhabitants opened up their hearts to us. Our editor, John Victor Smith, invited us to dinner at his home and his lovely wife Jane cooked a delicious Indian meal of chicken curry.

* * *

When *Space Truckers* was finished, we showed it to the other studios, but no one was interested in acquiring it, making it clear that we should have taken Universal's original offer. One of the things I've learned is that (with a few exceptions) there's nothing more promising than a work in progress and nothing less tantalizing than a finished film. Peter Newman was able to get *Space Truckers* shown out of competition at the Sundance Film Festival. Unfortunately, we still had no takers except for an offer from HBO to premiere it on their pay channel. So our $27 million opus became a TV movie-of-the-week and then went direct-to-video. Peter Newman and Greg Johnson ended up suing John Quested for not allowing them to accept Universal's offer. Peter also asked Ted Mann and me to tear up our WGA writers' contract. This meant that not only would we receive no future royalties or residuals, but we would also be reprimanded by our own union for breaking the rules. Ted Mann agreed to accommodate Peter, and I had no choice but to go along with the same shitty deal. But I never agreed to waive the balance of my director's fee (over two hundred thousand dollars) which I have yet to receive.

Over the years, *Space Truckers* has established itself as a guilty pleasure, often ending up on lists of the best movies no one has ever seen.

Get Your Work Done

In June of 1996, Suzanna was graduating from high school. Besides applying to California-based universities, we had suggested she think about attending the University of Wisconsin in Madison. We visited the campus that spring, and Carolyn and I enjoyed showing her around our old stomping ground. I even returned to the theater department for old times' sake and found myself knocking on the office door of Professor Ed Amor, who had been prepared to testify in my defense during the *Peter Pan* trial back in 1968. He turned as white as a sheet when he saw me, and I felt like an apparition. When I told him that my daughter was thinking of applying to UW, he looked ready to pass out. Carolyn quickly reassured him that Suzanna had no interest in studying theater, and Ed finally regained his composure.

Suzanna was very taken with Madison and, after being accepted, chose to attend. That August, we bought her a new set of luggage which we loaded with all of the newly-purchased warm clothing we knew she'd need. I would accompany her on the plane trip to Chicago where I'd rent a car to take her to Madison and help her move in. I parked the rental car at the curb of the baggage claim at O'Hare, where Suzanna and I gathered up her many suitcases. "The Midwest always makes me feel more grounded," I told my daughter.

"What do you mean?" she asked.

"Everything is more real here," I explained. "In Los Angeles, I always feel as if I'm floating."

We walked out to the car, and on its windshield was a parking ticket for seventy-five dollars. My jaw dropped in disbelief.

"Does this feel real enough?" Suzanna asked with a grin.

We loaded up the car, and off we went. As I drove the familiar route I had taken so many times during my student days, driving to Madison or to Janesville to visit Carolyn before we were married, the reality finally began to sink in: I was taking my daughter off to college. Except for holidays and summer vacations, she would no longer be living with us. She was leaving home. I suddenly found my vision blurred by tears.

"What's wrong?" my daughter asked. "Do you want me to drive?"

"I'm okay," I told her, and it suddenly hit me that you teach your child how to drive and then they drive away. We spent the day unloading her things and meeting her new roommate and the girls on her floor. The next day I returned to Los Angeles feeling very alone.

I probably should have spent some more time in Chicago. The Organic Theater Company was in a state of upheaval. Tom Riccio, whom I had originally appointed to replace me, had resigned as artistic director and in 1988 my old friend, actor/playwright Richard Fire, had taken over. He transformed the small storefront theater where we had done *Dope* in 1985 into the Organic Greenhouse. There, new works could be produced far less expensively than using the large 350-seat theater. Instead, Richard and Organic's board chose to hire out the larger space, using the rental income to finance these smaller productions. I have to admit that this irritated me; we had almost killed ourselves to create that large flexible space in the shell of the former Buckingham Theater.

In 1996, the Organic board ultimately chose to merge with the Touchstone Theater Company under the direction of Touchstone's Ina Marlowe. The name was changed to the Organic/Touchstone Theater. Ina reached out to me in 1997 about directing a production that would utilize many of the old company members such as Joe Mantegna, Dennis Franz, and Meshach Taylor, all of whom, in the intervening years, had become well-known in films and television. I was planning a new adaptation of Shakespeare's *Julius Caesar* when I received the news that Ina had sold the Buckingham Theater for over a million dollars. Our magnificent theater with its uninterrupted sightlines and perfect acoustics was broken up and turned into condominiums.

Feeling stabbed in the back like Caesar myself, I broke off any further contact with Ina Marlowe and the Organic Theater. Over the ensuing years, I watched as Ina moved Organic (she had dropped the Touchstone moniker) from theater to theater until in 2005 she sold the Organic name to Northern Illinois University. Although it no longer produces original work, the good news is that Organic still exists, as does the Broom Street Theater in Madison, Wisconsin.

One day in Westwood I heard someone call my name, and I turned to see Ray Bradbury waving to me. He wore white Bermuda shorts held up by brightly colored suspenders and a blue and white long-sleeved striped shirt with a pristine white collar. The outfit, which made him look a bit like Tweedle-Dee from *Alice in Wonderland*, happened to be, I was soon to learn, one of his favorite ensembles. As always, Ray was exuberant. When I told him I was making movies now and had an office at Disney Studios thanks to the success of *Honey, I Shrunk the Kids*, he slapped me on the back. "We should make a movie of *Ice Cream Suit*! he exclaimed, as if it would be the easiest thing in the world. Still, I set up a meeting with the head of live-action production at Disney who, for the sake of discretion, I will call Derek. Ray arrived for the meeting wearing a pure white ice-cream suit. How could anyone say no to him? Ray Bradbury, a living legend and American treasure, wearing a snow-white suit. "The last time I was here, I had lunch with Walt," Ray announced ebulliently as he entered Derek's office.

"Walt's dead." was Derek's dour reply. I was shocked and so was Ray, but he attempted to carry on, congratulating the prematurely balding Derek on the success of the studio's animated films (which, by the way, Derek had nothing to do with).

"You don't have to lie to me," Derek sourly responded. "The only person you have to lie to is your mother."

Without skipping a beat Ray replied, "Well sometimes you just feel like you're in a room full of mothers."

Derek's jaw dropped and so did mine. And with that the meeting was over.

A few days later I got a call from Derek that he was passing on *Ice Cream Suit*. "Too small a story," he told me.

"*Pee-wee's Big Adventure* is a pretty small story," I replied, "It's about a kid losing his bike."

"We would never have produced that," Derek told me to my amazement. After all, it only had made tens of millions of dollars and launched Tim Burton's career.

When I called Ray to relay the bad news, he seemed shocked. "I can't understand it," he told me, "Roy Disney has always been a fan of the play."

"Roy Disney?" I asked, *The* Roy Disney? The guy who hired Michael Eisner?

"He saw the play half a dozen times," Ray explained as if he were talking to a sweet but slow-witted child. "He thinks it would make a great movie."

The next thing I knew we were in Roy Disney's office. "I think we should do it," Roy (who by the way looked exactly like Walt) told Michael Lynton, the head of Disney's other division, Hollywood Pictures. "Don't you?" What else could Lynton do but cheerfully nod? The easiest thing in the world.

Turning *The Wonderful Ice Cream Suit* into a feature film was far from easy. Roy Disney ran the Animation Department; having already created the studio's biggest hits with *The Little Mermaid, Beauty and the Beast*, and *Aladdin*, his first thought was that *Ice Cream Suit* should be an animated film. His artists soon produced wonderful concept illustrations of the characters and the barrio locations, but eventually the decision was made that the story seemed too slight and the project was put on hold. It looked like the dream was over until one day in early 1997 I received a call from a junior executive at Disney. *Ice Cream Suit* would be given a green light if I would agree to the following terms: 1. The budget would not exceed five million dollars, 2. The film would go directly to video and, 3. The film would be supervised by the head of live-action production, Derek – the very man who had originally passed on the project.

I immediately agreed to the terms, sensing the powerful hand of Roy Disney behind the scenes. Ray Bradbury was quickly hired to adapt his own play into a film script. A few weeks later, Ray's script was delivered and I had never seen anything quite like it. Most scripts are broken down into scenes (Interior – Pool Hall – Day) but Ray's script was more like poetry, describing everything so beautifully that you felt you were watching the finished film. I did have a few suggestions, and Ray patiently listened and finally said, "Stuart, I'm the tailor who made this suit, and I think I know where every button should go. Leave it to me."

"Ray," I replied, "That's the nicest way anyone has ever told me to go fuck myself."

I hired the exceptional Laura Medina to be my line producer. We got along so well that I had to ask her to pretend to be more adversarial so the studio would believe she was holding my feet to the fire and would trust her to bring the project in on budget. Line producers and directors aren't supposed to be buddies and Laura, being extremely good at her job, managed to bring the film in under budget, pleasing everyone.

We hired Ricardo Matta as my First Assistant Director. Extremely well organized and extremely funny, the Puerto Rican kept the set friendly and humming along at a brisk pace. It didn't hurt that he was fluent in Spanish as I made sure that the majority of the crew were also Hispanic. I wasn't at all surprised that Ricardo later moved up the ranks to become an excellent director himself.

Casting soon began, and every Latino actor in Hollywood wanted to be part of the production, including the great Edward James Olmos of *Stand and Deliver*, *Blade Runner*, and later *Battlestar Galactica* fame. I wanted to cast him as Villanazul, the intellectual poet of the group, but Eddie had different ideas. "I'll be happy to play whatever role you'd like," he politely told me, "But what I really want is to play the dirtball." The dirtball was Vamenos, a filthy homeless guy who lives in a dumpster and is only allowed to share the pristine white suit after his first bath in a dozen years, a haircut, and a long list of rules to protect the suit (don't walk under trees with birds in them, etc.). The role calls for a terrific physical comedian, a brilliant clown in the tradition of Charlie Chaplin mixed with Cantinflas. I hesitated.

"What's wrong?" Olmos asked.

"Well, Eddie…" I began, not knowing how to say this, "I've never seen you… be funny. You're always so serious." And with that Eddie did a series of pratfalls and comic business that had me rolling on the floor with laughter. Like everyone else in Hollywood, he had been typecast, and this was his chance to break out of the mold. I knew he was the man to play the part when he first tried on the raggedy clothes, scraggly wig, and filthy make-up and was so convincing that the studio security guards tried to throw him off the lot.

For the role of the old haberdasher who sells the suit to the five amigos, I first tried to interest Mel Brooks. I had become friendly with him over the years after discovering that besides being one of the funniest men on Earth he was also a big fan and producer of horror movies. His company Brooksfilms had made David Lynch's *The Elephant Man* and David Cronenberg's *The Fly*. But when I described the role to him, he told me that he "didn't play Jews." He suggested that I call Sid Caesar, the great comedian who had given Mel his first job on *Your Show of Shows*, the '50s live television sensation that paved the way for *Saturday Night Live*.

"Do you think we can get him?" I asked Mel.

"Only if you ask him," he replied.

On the day that we were to shoot Sid's scene in Zellman's clothing store (the actual Boyle Heights location that had inspired Bradbury's original story), Ray showed up with his friend Stan Freberg, the genius satirist whose hilarious song parodies I had so enjoyed as a boy. I felt like I had died and gone to heaven. Here I was surrounded by men I had worshipped my whole life: Ray Bradbury, Sid Caesar, Eddie Olmos, and Stan Freberg. Pinch me! We had begun shooting on August 11th, 1997, my fiftieth birthday, with a mariachi band serenading me with Happy Birthday. But this magical day, on a set filled with my idols and friends, was the best present a kid could ask for. Sid, being the king of improvisation, never did the same scene twice. Every take was completely different and funnier than the last. From time to time he would turn to Bradbury and ask, "I changed a couple of lines. Is it okay?" Ray, who was laughing so hard he couldn't talk, just made the okay sign with his fingers.

"That suit's been in the window so long it used to be brown," is one of Sid's many original lines that I'll never forget.

I had more fun shooting *Ice Cream Suit* than any of my other films. Like Eddie Olmos, I too had been typecast. I was a horror director whose movies usually took place in mad scientist laboratories, graveyards, and haunted houses. Here I was making a colorful comedy with beautiful dancing girls and my old friend Joe Mantegna playing the same role he had performed onstage twenty years earlier. Little did I realize that my joy would be short-lived, that this happy little movie would be the inciting incident in a war that would end up tearing Disney Studios apart.

I should have realized that my happy little comedy was in trouble after I had my meeting with the guys at Disney's Product Placement Department. These are the people who can provide additional money for your budget, and at the very least free products, if you have your star drinking a Coke or using a particular brand of cell phone on camera. They told me that, unfortunately, they could provide no products for my film, that in fact none of the corporations they were dealing with would have anything to do with *Ice Cream Suit*.

"But the Latino market is huge," I argued. "They are avid consumers just like everyone else."

"But the characters in your movie are losers," one of the suits explained, looking to his associates like he was stating the obvious. "They have no money and live in the ghetto. No one wants their products associated with these types of people."

"But they're losers who become winners!" I argued, getting angrier by the minute. "This is a movie about friendship and sharing, about turning your life around." I was preaching to deaf ears. Deaf racist ears. The meeting was over.

When I reported this to Roy Disney, who had joined me as a producer on the film he had championed from the beginning, he too couldn't believe it. He would talk to studio head Michael Eisner, the man he had put in charge of Disney back in 1984. Roy had fought off a hostile takeover of the creatively bankrupt studio by bringing in Eisner and Rich Frank to save it, and they had miraculously turned things around. Roy believed that Eisner would appreciate the chance to reach a whole new market with *Ice Cream Suit* and release it theatrically, although we both knew that one of the conditions for the studio's agreeing to make the film was releasing it direct-to-video.

Both Roy and Ray Bradbury loved the film. Ray felt it was the best movie that had ever been made of his work because, for the first time in his career, he had been allowed to adapt his own story without some "hot young screenwriter screwing it up." Roy Disney, who usually stayed in the background, started flexing some muscle and I became his messenger boy. Amazingly, many of the suits didn't even know who Roy Disney was, since he didn't attend their day-to-day department meetings. Didn't the name Disney tip them off? Those who stupidly ignored or underestimated him usually found themselves up to their necks in deep shit. I started to feel like Robert Duvall in *The Godfather* saying things like, "I don't think Mr. Disney is going to like this."

Meanwhile, Roy found other ways to expand our budget, allowing us to hire Aleksandra Korejwo, an amazing Polish animator, to do a miraculous title sequence out of colored salt that she moved into place frame by frame with a condor feather. Why a condor feather? "I get from Warsaw Zoo," she told me. "Very strong."

When the film was completed, I found myself sitting next to Derek, the man Bradbury had called "a mother," in the executive screening room. It was just the two of us, and Derek never cracked a smile. The movie seemed to take weeks to finally end. After it was over, he turned to me as the lights came up. "Do you think you could introduce me to Roy Disney?" he asked.

I set up a lunch and sat there as Derek proceeded to tell Roy that family films were dead. "Who did he think he was talking to?" Roy asked me as the two of us walked back to the Animation building. "What a horse's ass." Eisner refused to distribute *Ice Cream Suit* theatrically. After a quick release on VHS the film seemed to disappear, never to even play on the Disney Channel.

It was the beginning of a rift between Roy and Michael Eisner that escalated with Eisner firing Roy from Disney's board. Like the other fools who had underestimated Roy, however, Eisner found himself tossed out of the studio a year or two later, the victim of a stockholder's revolt orchestrated by... guess who?

Thanks to Roy, I was able to keep my office at Disney three times longer than my original three-year deal. When I had first told him that I was being evicted he replied, "We can't let the usurpers win," and I was able to remain at Disney until the end of the nineties.

Sadly, Roy passed away from stomach cancer in December of 2009, but I treasure the time I spent with him. I fondly remember setting up a screening of *Ice Cream Suit* in his fourth-floor projection room at Disney for Carolyn's family when they visited us at Thanksgiving, and we were all amazed when Mr. Disney himself appeared and asked if he could join us. Afterward, he gave my in-laws an unforgettable tour of his office, which had originally belonged to Walt.

Ray Bradbury continued to sing the praises of our little movie. He was made a Commander of Arts and Letters by the French government and wore the star-shaped gold medal around his neck at a free screening of *Ice Cream Suit* held at the Los Angeles Public Library in honor of his 90th birthday in 2010. "I'm a Commander now," he told me, his face beaming with pride, "and I command you to make another one of my stories into a film." But on June 5th, 2012, the great Ray Bradbury left us. I always considered him one of my mentors, and I found myself wondering what he'd tell me about dealing with his loss. Then I remembered a telephone conversation I had with him shortly after his beloved wife Maggie had died in 2003. They had been married for 56 years, so I knew when I called that he must be hurting terribly. But the Ray I talked to that day answered my lame, "How are you doing?" by telling me his two rules – rules that I immediately wrote down and pinned to a bulletin board in my office where they remain to this day:

1. To hell with it.
2. Get your work done.

Although often described as sweet and gentle, Mr. Bradbury had a will of iron, a fact he proved over and over throughout his life. When a stroke in 1999 confined him to a wheelchair and prevented him from typing his stories (he wrote one every day), he began dictating them to his daughter Alexandra who input them into her word processor, a device Ray himself never would use ("too many machines!"). Like Matisse, who was prevented from painting by medical complications but continued creating stunning canvases by cutting out patterns of colored paper, or Frank Frazetta, who learned to paint left-handed after suffering a stroke similar to Ray's, Bradbury never stopped creating his amazing stories, and I have no doubt that he probably completed one the day he died.

Much has been written about Ray Bradbury as the ultimate Angelino. Yes, he loved our city. He arrived as a teenager and lived in Boyle Heights, where many of his friends were equally poor Mexican-Americans. He told me he got the idea for *The Wonderful Ice Cream Suit* when he saw how the large Mexican families would share clothes, passing them down from older brother to younger. Yet Ray had been born in Waukegan, Illinois, and his days growing up there stayed with him always. His version of Waukegan – Green Town, Illinois – was the setting of *Dandelion Wine*, *Something Wicked This Way Comes*, and countless short stories. It was a touchstone that he returned to again and again in his mind.

One of his favorite stories was about the day that he was supposed to attend his grand aunt's funeral when he was 9 or 10 years old but, instead, took off to a little carnival that had been set up on the outskirts of Waukegan. "I chose life over death," he told me. There he saw Mr. Electrico, a performer who sat strapped into a "working electric chair" while thousands of volts supposedly passed through him causing sparks to fly and Electrico's hair to stand on end. At one point, he held out a sword over the audience and brought it down close to the head of young Ray Bradbury. A spark arched from the sword to the boy's head as Mr. Electrico exclaimed, "Live forever!"

"You will live forever!" I gushed as Ray smiled his Cheshire Cat grin. But now that he has left us, and although his treasured stories remain, it's hard to live in a world without Ray Bradbury. But I know what he'd tell me:

To hell with it.
Get your work done.

Fish Story

In 1999, I was invited by Professor Tino Balio to spend a week at the University of Wisconsin as a Brittingham Visiting Scholar. I would have a chance to meet with students in both the theater and film departments to talk to them about working professionally in their respective industries. The irony of this was not lost on me, as I had left Madison without ever receiving a diploma, and at that time was still being pursued by the local police department who couldn't wait to arrest me for producing obscene theatrical productions. Even after all these years, the felony obscenity charges against me from *Peter Pan* had still never been dropped, but only "withdrawn," so I was worried that I would be arrested upon setting foot in Madison. Luckily, this didn't occur, and I spent a wonderful week at the university enjoying the unbridled enthusiasm of the bright graduate students. Being around excited young artists always reminds me how consumed I was with theater and film when I was their age. But one thing nagged at me: the university's film and theater departments had absolutely nothing to do with each other. Wouldn't the acting students benefit by making short films with the film department directing students? And wouldn't the young film directors learn a great deal by working with the highly trained actors of the theater department instead of being forced to cast their roommates in their films?

I mentioned this notion to Tino, and it intrigued him. A year later, he invited me to return and set up the first inter-disciplinary classes in the history of the university between the film and theater departments. I should have realized how radical my idea was when J.J. Murphy, the head of the film department, got lost taking me to the first meeting with the theater department, even though both departments were located on the same floor of the same building. I was further astonished when I discovered that the graduate acting students of the theater department had never been taught the Method. This meant that Madison was turning out actors who were absolutely clueless about the most common approach to acting practiced in film and television, as well as most American (and Russian) theater. The theater department was still teaching the old English-style basics: voice, movement, mime and so on.

I ended up teaching the Method to both the actors and film directors, and they took to it like ducks to water. I'd watch enthralled as the actors did beautifully sensitive scene work in my classes, only to want to kill myself when I'd see them in the awkward shows ineptly directed by their professors. I urged all my students, actors and filmmakers alike, to think about moving to Los Angeles. "Who'd hire us?" they would ask me. "We're just a bunch of hicks from Wisconsin."

above: Directing Frances Bay as Esmeralda on the set of *The Pit and the Pendulum.*

right: With Charlie Band (left) and Albert Band (seated) on the set of *The Pit and the Pendulum.*

below: Lance Henriksen and Jonathan Fuller in *The Pit and the Pendulum.*

top: On a lunch break while filming *Fortress* with Christopher Lambert.

above: With Loryn Locklin on the set of *Fortress*.

right (from left): Kurtwood Smith, Jeffrey Combs, me, Clifton Collins Jr., and Christopher Lambert on the set of *Fortress*.

above: Jonathan Fuller in effects artist John Vulich's make-up, as the Castle Freak.

left: Jonathan Fuller (center) with crew members on the set of *Castle Freak*.

below: Directing Jonathan Fuller on the set of *Castle Freak*.

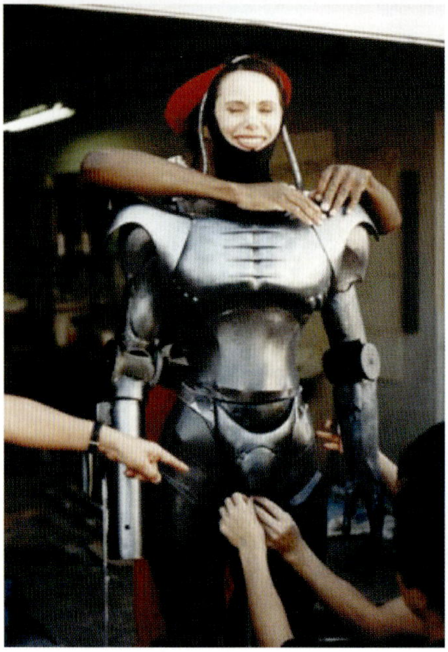

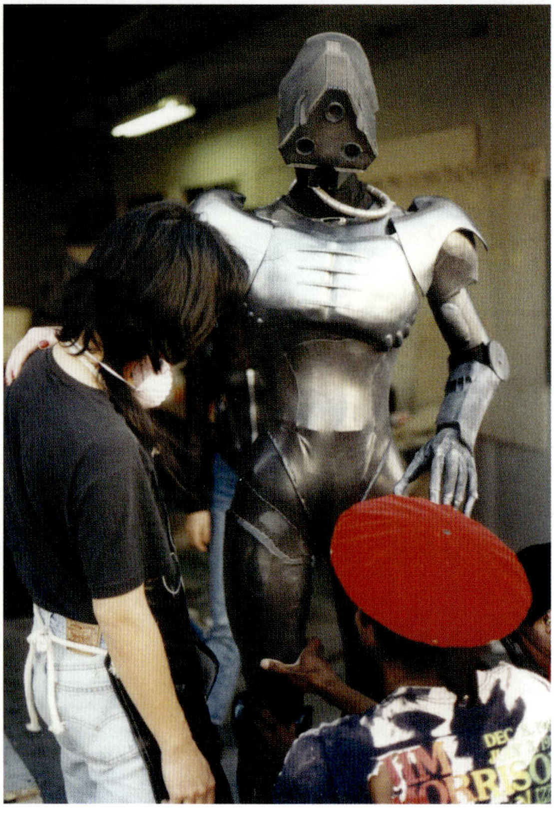

top: On the set of *Space Truckers.*

above and right: Bio-Mechanical-Warrior costume fitting on the set of *Space Truckers.*

opposite main image: A Bio-Mechanical-Warrior with members of the *Space Truckers* crew.

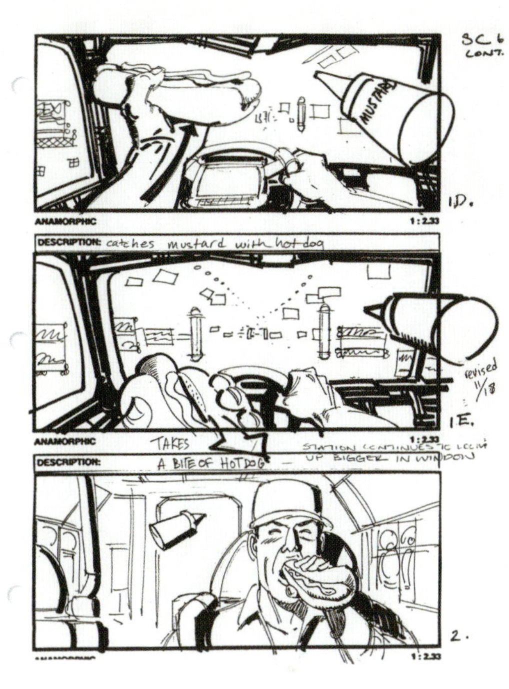

top left: (from left): Stephen Dorff, Barbara Crampton and Debi Mazar suit up for *Space Truckers*.
above (from left): Dennis Hopper, Barbara Crampton, Debi Mazar, and Stephen Dorff on the set of *Space Truckers*.
top right: A storyboard page from the production of *Space Truckers*.

The HUB DINER

above (from left):
Ray Bradbury, Mercedes Ortega, Clifton Collins Jr. and me on the set of *The Wonderful Ice Cream Suit.*

left:
On location in Boyle Heights for *The Wonderful Ice Cream Suit.*

below:
On the set of *The Wonderful Ice Cream Suit* in Boyle Heights with Bradbury.

opposite top:
Directing George Wendt and film extras on the set of *Space Truckers.*

opposite center left:
With George Wendt on the set of *Space Truckers.*

opposite bottom left:
Charles Dance as Macanudo in *Space Truckers.*

opposite bottom right:
Creating the Macanudo make-up design for *Space Truckers.*

above: Setting up a shot for *The Wonderful Ice Cream Suit* with cinematographer Mac Ahlberg (in white) and Edward James Olmos (center).

right: Legends Sid Caesar and Howard Morris filming a scene for *The Wonderful Ice Cream Suit*.

below: Signing a poster for *The Wonderful Ice Cream Suit* alongside legendary author Ray Bradbury.

CHAPTER 44

"Everyone in LA is from somewhere else," I'd tell them. "And they're going to hire someone. Why not you?"

Sometime later, I got a phone call from Brian Yuzna. He was in Spain where he had made a deal with Filmax, a Barcelona-based company, to develop a series of horror and fantasy films for them under the label Fantastic Factory. Was I interested in finally getting *Dagon* made?

Dagon was to be the follow-up to *Re-Animator* way back in 1986, but Charles Band, the young head of Empire Pictures, had thought the story of a town in which the inhabitants are transforming into fish too ridiculous even for him. We did *From Beyond* instead. During the intervening years, Brian and I had tried many times to convince other studios to make the film, but their reactions were always similar to Charlie's. "If you make them werewolves," one of the studio heads had told us, "We'd make it in a minute. But fish people? No way!"

Years had gone by, and the project had languished. Now Brian Yuzna had finally found a way to get *Dagon* made. The catch was that it would have to be shot in Spain. The original story is set in the isolated fishing town of Innsmouth in Lovecraft's gothic Massachusetts, but Brian had visited Galicia on Spain's western coast and was convinced the film could be set there.

In August of 2000, I brought our family to Barcelona as I began to prepare *Dagon*. We stayed in a second story apartment on Mallorca Street rented by the production company but, being August, the month when everyone in Europe goes on vacation, the city seemed deserted. So Carolyn and the kids and I had fun exploring Barcelona.

Dagon was being partially financed by subsidies from the various regions of Spain, so we had to submit the script to the province of Galicia where the film was set. I wasn't sure how they would react to our portrayal of Galicians as monstrous inhabitants capturing tourists and skinning them alive. A few days later, I received a call from the Galician film fund. The woman on the phone spoke excellent English. "We have a problem with your script," she told me.

"Here it comes," I thought to myself.

"The script refers to Gallego as a dialect," she began.

"Yes?" I muttered, waiting for the other shoe to drop.

"Gallego isn't a dialect," she curtly told me, "It's an actual language."

"Alright," I said, "We'll make that change. Anything else?"

"No," she said. Amazingly, that was that.

Our line producer, Miguel Torrente, suggested that I meet director of photography Carlos Suárez, as Mac Ahlberg was again not available to shoot our film.

The biggest problem we faced was how to create a town full of mutated inhabitants all in various stages of transforming into sea creatures. I was introduced to David Martí and his female partner Montse Ribé, who ran a make-up effects company called DDT. The prospect of creating literally hundreds of monsters on our small budget did not seem to discourage them in the least. Both were in their late twenties (although Montse looked even younger), and David had a wonderful sense of humor. Soon, we were discussing how many creatures we would need for each scene and in what stages of mutation. They hit it off with Richard Raaphorst, one of our conceptual artists, who once insisted that they throw an actual (dead) octopus on their Xerox machine so they could capture its unique texture. The work they created for us was sensational, and I was not surprised when they both won Academy Awards® a few years later for Guillermo del Toro's *Pan's Labyrinth*.

I had always thought that we would need dancers and mimes to play the half-human inhabitants of the cursed town, which we had renamed Imboca (a Spanish version of Lovecraft's pun Innsmouth). For *Dagon*, I hired a Spanish mime company under the leadership of Joan Minguell to create the strange movements of the half-human sea creatures. Incredibly thin and supple, Joan (the Catalan equivalent to John) ended up playing many of the featured monsters in the film and appears on the cover of the American DVD as the shark-like monster with two sets of pointy teeth.

I began casting in September and soon discovered that Julio Fernández did not see any value in hiring name American actors. I have never believed that you need recognizable stars in horror films, as the genre itself is the big draw, but distributors often insist that there needs to be at least one recognizable name for them to sell the movie. This made no difference to Julio as he was distributing the film himself in Spain. But one day, he burst into our office so excited he could barely speak. Legendary Spanish actor Francisco "Paco" Rabal wanted to meet about playing a role in *Dagon*. Paco is considered a national treasure in Spain and has been in hundreds of movies internationally, including several of Luis Buñuel's most famous films. Upon meeting him, I discovered why he was interested in our project: it turned out Rabal was a big fan of H.P. Lovecraft. Paco was in his early seventies at the time and his nose was scarred, almost split down the middle, from a recent automobile accident. His unique growling voice and expressive features made him ideal to play the role of Ezequiel, the last living human being in the cursed town.

I had offered the role of Uxia, the young high priestess of the sect, to the beautiful Mercedes Ortega, a Spanish actress from the Canary Islands. I had met her at Sitges a few years earlier and had cast her in *The Wonderful Ice Cream Suit* as Celia Obregon. She speaks Spanish with the Castiliano lisp and kept calling her on-screen lover "Jose Martineth." But she had turned in an adorable performance, and I was looking forward to working with her again. She gave me a beautiful letter opener of Toledo steel as a thank you gift, which

I still use to this day. I was not prepared, however, when a young eighteen-year-old actress showed up at auditions and asked to read for the role. Her name was Macarena Gómez, and she had never appeared in a film, but she proceeded to "hit it out of the park." Her incredible audition and her large luminous eyes made a lasting impression on me. She seemed both vulnerable and dangerous, and I knew she was born to play the part. I was forced to call Mercedes and let her know that I was casting Macarena in the role I had previously promised her. She began to cry, and I felt like two cents. I wouldn't blame her if she wanted to stab me in the heart with her lovely letter opener.

Dagon started principal photography in November of 2000 on the Costa Brava (sometimes referred to as the Spanish Riviera). There was a lovely beach which featured a large reef of enormous rocks about twenty feet from the shore. This proved to be ideal, for it allowed us to put our sailboat close to our base camp, and if we shot toward the water, it looked like we were in the middle of the ocean. Turning around, we could make our boat appear to be stuck on the rocks. The weather cooperated, and it was sunny for the first few days and overcast for the next few, allowing us to create a sense of the gathering storm that traps our protagonists and ultimately runs them aground.

Next, we flew to Galicia where our wonderful art department had already transformed the town of Combarro into the decrepit Imboca. Again, the weather helped us by consistently providing overcast days but little actual rain. It was an odd state of affairs as we couldn't shoot our film on sunny days and had to use a cover set – the exact opposite of the usual procedure. We created our own rain with twenty-foot-tall rain towers because actual rain doesn't photograph well. Both cast and crew were constantly cold and wet. But it was young Macarena Gómez who put us all to shame when it came time to shoot the underwater sequences. A nearby high school swimming pool had been found for these, but it needed to be filled with water. When we arrived, we discovered that the water was cloudy and, worse yet, freezing cold as it hadn't been heated. Even the underwater camera crew, who wore wetsuits, were hesitant to dive into the icy pool and the stunt people flatly refused. When I told this to Macarena, who had to swim topless as a mermaid, she said she would give it a try. Without a moment's hesitation she bravely dove into the water. "This isn't so bad!" she shouted upon surfacing, and the crew had no choice but to join her and the scenes were filmed. The cloudy water seemed to add an eerie mystery to the footage.

There were other heroes among our cast. Our lead actors, Ezra Godden and Raquel Meroño, both gamely paddled an inflatable Zodiac life raft in the cold Atlantic waters as the crew filmed from nearby boats. The little raft, which was supposedly leaking air, had to be deflated for each shot, and by the end of the sequence, it was half-filled with seawater. But the two actors bravely soldiered on, with Raquel happily singing a pop song between takes. During the shooting of this scene, the two camera boats somehow collided and luckily were not severely damaged. We had dodged a bullet, but the possibility of a real disaster was not lost on me. "Do we have life jackets on board?" I asked my first assistant director, Manolo (called Lolo by the crew) who faced the cold damp by imbibing large quantities of alcohol to the point that his speech was slurred. He told me he'd check and later informed me that there were no life jackets on board. I'm not sure which horrified me more: no life jackets, or a drunken assistant director. If the boats had sunk, what would have happened? We were shooting these scenes quite some distance from the shore. Manolo's reaction was to laugh and insist that nothing of the kind had happened or could ever happen. But I was unconvinced.

The next night, we were shooting a dialogue scene with Ezra and Paco Rabal underneath one of the many corn cribs on the shore. These picturesque ancient structures, called *hórreos*, are built of stone and stand on three-foot-high legs to protect them from the rising tide. Most have crucifixes on their roofs, which we replaced with tridents for our film. We were more than halfway through the scene when Manolo told me that we had run out of time and had to wrap. I replied that we could complete the scene in a half hour if we continued shooting, but he refused.

"That's a wrap!" he called out to the crew, and in an instant, they were striking our lights. I was furious. Returning to complete the scene would cost us hours the next evening, and our schedule was tight enough without adding this to our workload. I didn't sleep that night, and finally came to the conclusion that Manolo would have to go. He had put the crew in jeopardy in the unsafe boats, and now he was costing us valuable time by refusing to let me complete the scene. I met with Brian Yuzna and told him that I couldn't continue working with Manolo. Brian tried to encourage me to relent; I was in Spain, and people here are never fired as it is considered a great personal disgrace. But I was adamant. "It's him or me," I told Brian.

The next day was our last one in Combarro and I was assured that Manolo would no longer be working on *Dagon*.

We continued working the next day and things seemed to be going much more smoothly, but as I was walking through the twisting streets of Combarro, I turned a corner and literally bumped into Manolo. He was clearly still there working on the film. We looked at each other, neither of us knowing what to say. Then I continued on my way. When we returned to Barcelona a meeting was held in the office of Carlos Fernández. Carlos is Julio's younger brother, but one would never know by sight that they were even related. Unlike Julio, who is gregarious, boisterous and loves a good joke, almost as much as his ever-present cigar, Carlos is quiet and unassuming. Julio is short and round and Carlos is tall and thin. As Brian had warned me, I had clearly put Carlos in an embarrassing position. "You cannot force us to fire Manolo," he told me. There was a long pause.

"No, I can't," I replied. "I have no control over what you do. But I do have control over what I do. And I will not continue working on this film unless Manolo is replaced." Eventually a compromise was agreed and Manolo was put to work elsewhere at the studio

We wrapped principal photography just before Christmas, and I headed back to Los Angeles to spend the holidays with my family. Before I left, Julio Fernández asked me to complete the post-production on *Dagon* in Barcelona rather than LA as my contract had allowed. He offered me a generous increase of my fee to do so, and I agreed. After a few short weeks with my wife and kids celebrating Christmas and ringing in the New Year 2001, I came back to Spain.

* * *

One of the things I did in Spain was to go to the bullfights. I didn't tell Carolyn or the kids as I knew they would be horrified that I was endorsing animal cruelty, but I had met many Spaniards who talked of the bullfight as if it were a religious experience, and I knew that the sport was the last vestige of the spectacles of ancient Rome's Circus Maximus and the even earlier bull dancing of Crete. I couldn't get any of my Spanish friends to go with me. "Only the tourists go," they told me. So, undaunted, I went alone. My seat was close to the ring, and there were times I wished I couldn't see so well. The picadors rode padded blindfolded horses. They stab the bull repeatedly with their lances until the great loss of blood slows the creature down, making him ready for the kill. The matador, using a smaller cape, attempts to thrust his sword between the creature's shoulder blades directly into its heart. It's a small, fast-moving target and an inch to the right or left will cause him to hit solid bone. The moment I'll never forget was when a matador expertly drove his sword home, instantly bringing the bull to its knees. Then, to the surprise of everyone, the impaled animal rose again to its feet and slowly and majestically walked around the entire ring, the hilt of the sword visible, sticking out of its back. The crowd rose to its feet applauding and cheering this brave bull. Finally, still holding its head high, it slowly lay down. A man approached the dying animal with a small knife to administer the coup de gras and, as he neared the bull, the animal seemed to welcome him. The bull had been pampered its entire life and couldn't understand why the humans were now hurting him. The poor creature seemed surprised when the man slit his throat, and I was relieved that his suffering was over at last.

Dagon was completed in June, and before I left Spain I was notified that we had been accepted into the Sitges International Film Festival where the film was set to premiere in early October. Would I be able to come back? I had such a good time in Sitges in the past that I immediately agreed. My lovely assistant, Inés, drove me to the airport, and her driving was as wild as it had been when we had met five months ago. I had told her that the first rule as an assistant was not to kill the director. "Don't you remember the first rule?" I admonished her.

"I'm not your assistant anymore," she replied. And we both laughed.

The summer gave me a chance to relax and catch my breath after having spent an entire year in Spain. But at the end of August, I was notified that the great Paco Rabal had died. He was on a plane returning from the Montreal Film Festival where he had received a lifetime achievement award. The actor had suffered an attack of compensatory dilating emphysema. I dedicated the film to Paco: "a wonderful actor and even better human being." *Dagon* had been his last film.

* * *

Like so many others, I was not prepared for the morning of September 11th, 2001. Carolyn called me into the living room. We were babysitting Gabriela, our niece Lisa's three-year-old daughter, when *Sesame Street* was interrupted by the news that a plane had crashed into the World Trade Center. I assumed it was an accident and thought they meant a small private plane. I was trying to make sense of it all when a second plane crashed into the other tower. Now it was clearly deliberate, and the planes were 767s filled with passengers and aviation fuel.

We watched in shock as the towers collapsed, and I have never before witnessed anything as horrific. Thousands had been killed before our eyes. It was hard to imagine the scope of the tragedy, but I couldn't shake the feeling that I was watching some Hollywood disaster movie. I had to keep telling myself it was real. The entire world changed in that moment. We had enjoyed a few years of peace since the Berlin wall had come down in 1989, but those days were clearly over. Another plane crashed into the Pentagon, and there was word that another United Airlines plane had crashed in Pennsylvania. How many more would die?

As the media scrambled to cover the world-shattering events, we got word that all flights had been grounded. We saw images of our president reading a children's story to a kindergarten class as he received the terrible news and then, amazingly, completed the story before being quickly whisked away.

There were no commercial flights for three days. No one had any desire to fly, especially overseas. Filmax wanted to know if I would still be willing to come to Spain for the opening of *Dagon* four weeks after 9/11. I talked it over with Carolyn, and we decided that we should go. The company needed us there to promote the film. We reasoned that airport security would be tighter than ever, and it was. The plane was half empty, but the journey was uneventful, and we arrived safely.

I was totally unprepared for what happened next. I realized that I was in trouble after the early morning journalists' screening of *Dagon*. The first question at the press conference was, "Is this movie supposed to be funny or scary?" Being the eternal wisenheimer, I had answered, "Yes." The early reviews were abysmal. It seemed as if I had insulted the entire country by suggesting that a town full of monsters could exist in Spain. They thought the film was absurd, and I was reminded of all those people at the studios who had thought the concept of Lovecraft's story ludicrous. I was devastated. I even considered not attending the opening night screening, but Carolyn rightly let me know that I had to tough it out. After all that hard work, after risking my wife's and my own life by making the flight in these dangerous days, this was the result. I felt sick to my stomach. How could I go on? Then I remembered the brave bull who had walked around the entire arena with a sword through its heart. And keeping that image in mind, I walked into the enormous auditorium.

I wish I could say that it was a triumphant evening, but it wasn't. Eventually, I did learn that the movie played extremely well in every country but Spain. The rest of the world had no problem believing that there could be half-human fish creatures in Galicia. Today the film is regarded as my most Lovecraftian.

Ia! Ia! Cthulhu fhtagn!

Short Ends

A few weeks after 9/11, Suzanna began a new job as a high school English teacher at Sherman Oaks Center for Enriched Studies, her alma mater. In 1999, she had left the University of Wisconsin after two and a half years. She told us the brutal winters had been too much for her, but we suspected it was being away from Harold Avila, her boyfriend. She had met Harold when they were both high-school students at SOCES. I soon learned to appreciate this bright, personable young man who could coax conversation from a rock.

Suzanna's decision to drop out of the University of Wisconsin upset me. I even tried to bribe her to stay with the promise of a new car. Carolyn had to remind me that I was also a college drop-out, and now I could understand how my mother must have felt. My mom had never complained about my decision to quit school, but I must admit that I still regret not receiving my degree.

After graduating from the University of California Riverside in June of 2001, Suzanna was offered a job teaching English to 9th graders. The fact that this was the same subject and grade that my mother had once taught was not lost on me (or Suzanna, who adored her grandmother). I couldn't help feeling that this might be some form of divine intervention. Suzanna blossomed in this career and today is Chairman of the English Department at SOCES.

I had left Disney Studios in 1999 and rented an office on the first floor in a charming courtyard building on Magnolia and Hollywood Way in Burbank. Although the rent was only five hundred dollars a month plus utilities, I found that the additional cost was putting a strain on our finances. I began looking for someone to share the office. I soon struck a deal with producer Duffy Hecht. Duffy's father, Harold, had been Burt Lancaster's producing partner and their company, Hecht-Lancaster, had created many notable films including Academy Award® winners *Marty* and *Birdman of Alcatraz*, as well as *Sweet Smell of Success*. Duffy, who possesses a keen intellect and enormous enthusiasm, was looking for an inexpensive office that he could use on a part-time basis, and we quickly struck a deal. I greatly enjoyed Duffy's company. We had many lively lunches at the nearby Chinese restaurant, Century Dragon, which we nicknamed "The Commissary." I loved Duffy's wonderful stories about growing up as a movie brat with his famous producer father.

We started looking for a project to produce together. I soon discovered that Duffy was not a fan of horror films, which caused him to turn down most of my suggestions, but there was one script which piqued his interest. It was entitled *King of the Ants*. Although the title makes it sound like a '50s science fiction film with giant bugs, it's actually a crime story about a young slacker who becomes a professional hit man. Based on a brutal British novel by Charles Higson, the book was brought to me by my old friend George Wendt, who had met Higson on an interview show in the UK. Charlie Higson is well known there, as one of the creators of *The Fast Show*, a popular sketch comedy TV series. Also a novelist, Higson had given George a copy of his book and Wendt had read it and decided that it would make an excellent film. "If you like it, I'll option it," he told me. I couldn't put the book down and found myself shocked and surprised by the fact that the young hero really does go through with the murder of an innocent accountant. Even more shocking: somehow, we still care about him. It would be a nifty trick if we could pull this off on screen. George and I partnered with Higson, and he adapted his book, resetting it from London to Los Angeles. I found the soft-spoken author to be an excellent screenwriter, not afraid to make major changes in his novel for the good of the film. We ended up with a powerful script and I began meeting with the studios looking for someone to finance our film.

Unfortunately, the darkness of the material, the very thing that had attracted me in the first place, made it impossible for potential producers to embrace it. "If you change it so he's revenging his brother, we might be interested," one executive told me, unaware that he was removing the very element that made this story so original and disturbing. His suggestion would turn it into every other film we had ever seen. After five years of disappointing meetings, the script had ended up sitting on my office shelf.

I gave Duffy a rundown of our travails, showing him the long list of every studio and production company that had turned us down, but he was undeterred. "There's a whole new world of tiny new production companies that we can try," he suggested. "It will mean doing the film for a minuscule budget, but maybe we can partner with one of them as producers and make our money on the back end." One of the companies we met with was The Asylum, run by David Rimawi and David Michael Latt. They had just started producing small genre films (many directed by Latt), and Duffy and I believed that with the proper encouragement, they could produce excellent edgy projects for a price. The two Davids had met in film school. In their early thirties, Rimawi, handsome with dark hair, and red-headed Latt were both bright and witty, and they introduced us to Sherri Strain, their CFO. The three seemed to immediately appreciate the potential of *King of the Ants*. We met at their offices at the well-known Crossroads of the World on Sunset Boulevard and soon hammered out a deal. We would split all proceeds 50/50 after recouping the production costs. Normally, a deal like this wouldn't make sense, as the common Hollywood wisdom is that "There is no net (profits)." Initially, the budget was only $100,000, the same as most of Asylum's other films. We struggled with the production costs, as our script had almost thirty locations, making it a far more expensive proposition.

Unwilling to shoot digitally, which in 2002 was still not considered professional quality, Asylum insisted that we shoot on 35mm, but suggested we use left-over stock from other movies. These scraps of film (called short ends) meant that you would constantly run out of film and had to continually reload. I thought the extra time this took erased any potential savings, but Asylum was adamant.

The Davids ultimately found an investor who was willing to substantially increase our budget to $325,000. It would still mean that none of us would receive much (if anything) as a fee. My directing fee was only $5,000, an all-time low, but we had faith in the project and believed that the film would gross far more than its budget, so we would share in the substantial profits. I was able to hire Mac Ahlberg in what would end up being the last film we worked on together. Mac was paid a pittance, a fraction of his usual fee, but never complained. Mr. Wendt, already a producer, joined the cast as Duke Wayne, an electrician who seems like a genial good ole boy, but is revealed to be a brutal monster. It was a mind-blowing turn for "Norm," so beloved on the long-running sitcom *Cheers*. His wife Bernadette had attended an early reading and was absolutely horrified. "I don't know who you are anymore," she told her husband afterward.

I cast my old Aussie friend Vernon Wells and Chicago actor Lonnie Smith as two construction working henchmen, and we were able to get a couple of other name actors onboard: Kari Wuhrer to play the beautiful wife of the murdered accountant, and Daniel Baldwin as the cold-blooded owner of the construction company who, in a drunken rant, hires our hero to murder the accountant who is investigating him.

But who would play Sean Crawley, the murderous hero? We clearly needed someone that the audience would instantly like and continue to care about even after he has killed an innocent man. Ron Livingston, who was George Wendt's assistant at the time, had played the role brilliantly in the earlier reading but had since become a young actor on the rise, and his manager did not want him playing a murderer. We offered Ron the role of the poor victim, and his reps allowed this only on the condition that his name would not appear in the credits. Weird.

Many name actors did audition for the role of the well-named Crawley, among them Ethan Embry, who got so carried away during his audition that he slammed his fist into the wall, breaking his hand and thereby disqualifying himself. I was very taken with a young actor named Chris L. McKenna, who had worked as a child actor on the soap opera *One Life to Live*. Tall, good looking, with a likeable grin and a terrific sense of humor, I knew Chris had the talent to star in our film and eventually was able to convince the folks at Asylum to allow me to cast him. It was a decision that I have never regretted.

I also hired Carolyn to be our caterer. Her new company, christened Café Carolyn, successfully served independent film productions for the next dozen years until her retirement.

We began shooting in a movie ranch near the picturesque Vasquez Rocks. It was August, and the temperatures were well over a hundred degrees Farenheit every day. It was so hot that our perspiration instantly evaporated. Daniel Baldwin arrived and immediately began flexing his muscles by loudly disagreeing with every direction I gave him. He had recently directed his first film and felt he knew far more than I did. Having gone through the travails of Dennis Hopper, I had no trouble holding my ground and not letting him get to me. One of the first scenes we shot was the climactic fight between him and Chris McKenna during which Baldwin was shoved and smacked his head against the camera's matte-box. We stopped shooting and examined him. There was no bleeding or even any mark, and Baldwin insisted he was fine, so we continued shooting. But the next day, he didn't show up. After many calls to his home and his agent, we finally located him, and he was complaining about a headache. I suggested that he go to an emergency room to be X-rayed. They found nothing wrong with him. We had to scramble to find other scenes to shoot so as not to waste the entire day.

The next day, Daniel showed up, and I met with him in his honey wagon. He still complained about headaches, and I suggested that he take the day off to fully recover. This seemed to astonish him, but I didn't want to be held responsible if there was a concussion of any sort. Daniel went home, and we rearranged the schedule so he could have two weeks off. When he finally did return, he was as sweet as pie. We shot his longest monologues and, as we were using short ends, the camera would run out of film every two minutes, breaking any rhythm or flow that Baldwin tried to establish. He never lost his cool and delivered the speech brilliantly, and we parted on good terms. He later was so happy with the finished film that he accompanied us to the Seattle Film Festival, where it had its American premiere.

With twenty-eight locations, we could never have afforded to film them all on our meager budget without the help of a program called California First, which allowed us to use any facility owned by the state free of charge. Through this, we were able to shoot on Los Angeles' new subway system and were even given a train for our own use. It ran back and forth on a short track beginning at its North Hollywood station. The folks at the Midnight Mission in LA's skid row were kind enough to allow us to shoot in their facility, and we were able to hire the homeless to serve as extras in our film. Carolyn ended up donating the leftovers of her catered meals, and they were greatly appreciated.

Things were moving along, and we somehow stayed on budget, but this wasn't enough for The Asylum. Duffy and I were repeatedly called in to meet with them on weekends, where we would be berated by the Davids and Sherri Strain, who supposedly was keeping track of our expenses. "You're using too much film," I was told. "We can see by the dailies that you got the shot on Take 2 but you went on and shot three more takes." Mac Ahlberg had always told me that film is the cheapest item in the budget, and, in those days, you only printed the chosen takes. But they could not be reassured. These meetings went on every weekend, and one day, I walked into David Rimawi's office to see a red, white and green flag hanging on the wall behind his desk. "What's that?" I asked him.

"It's a Palestinian flag," he tersely answered. I wondered what the Jewish buyers from other companies would make of this (let alone his partner David Latt, who I knew was also Jewish), and in a few days the flag disappeared, never to be seen again. But the haranguing continued.

"We only shoot one or two takes on our movies," I was told. And that was the straw that finally broke my back.

"You don't make movies," I angrily told them. "They may look like movies, but they aren't movies. This is the first real movie you have ever made, and despite all your bullshit, it's coming out well. When it's done, it will be something we can all be proud of."

The kicker was when Sherri Strain finally admitted that we weren't over budget after all. She had not been keeping up with her bookkeeping and, as a result, she and the Davids were operating in a constant state of blind panic. The result was dispiriting and totally unnecessary. The constant browbeating about money was responsible for some unbelievably stupid occurrences. The most outrageous was the evening we could no longer film a key scene because our line producer had allowed the generator that powered the lighting to run out of gas, completely shutting us down. In order to save a few bucks on gasoline, we lost several precious hours of shooting while a PA ran to a nearby gas station.

There were, of course, some good things about working with Asylum: David Latt proved to be an excellent editor using Final Cut Pro on the office's computer. Karl Hirsch, a bright young assistant, managed to do all the sound work on the computer as well. It was the first time I didn't use a professional sound company to complete a film. The music was composed and played by a talented newcomer recommended to me by my old Full Moon friend Daniel Schweiger. Dan was now working for Modern Music, finding and cutting temp music for many of Hollywood's biggest blockbusters. When I told him that I thought all movie music sounded alike, he suggested that I check out Bobby Johnston, a one-man band who uses only acoustic instruments and by multi tracking can create the sound of a full ensemble. His score for *Ants* worked extremely well, and I have used him on all my subsequent features.

The finished film was quickly purchased by DEJ, the production arm of Blockbuster Video. The deal was for significantly less money than I felt the film was worth, but the Davids were nervous about repaying their investor and made the sale before the film had played a single festival. Foreign sales were brisk, but just as we approached the $450,000 in sales that would allow us to begin sharing profits with Asylum, all financial reports abruptly ceased.

Duffy and I met with a litigator. It turned out that there was no way to determine how much *King of the Ants* had made. As Asylum often sold the film in bundles with their other films, we were only entitled to a small percentage of each sale, even though it may have been our film that made the sale happen in the first place. The attorney, who would only take the case for a percentage of the money he could recoup, turned us down. As the saying goes, we were shit out of luck.

Asylum began making knockoffs of successful studio films like *Snakes on a Train* (instead of a *Plane*) and producing their own versions of films with public domain titles like *War of the Worlds* that they hoped the public would confuse with the Spielberg film of the same name. They finally hit pay-dirt with *Sharknado*, a film so bad that it became the butt of jokes on *The Tonight Show*. But to the Davids, there is no such thing as bad publicity as long as there is a hefty check to cash.

Every Fear Hides a Wish

"You know what you should do next?" Lonnie Smith asked me one blistering hot day as we worked together on *King of the Ants*.

"What?"

"*Edmond*." Lonnie was referring to David Mamet's controversial play. I had seen its original production at the Goodman Theater way back in 1982 and had never forgotten it. The story begins as Edmond Burke, a middle-aged, middle-class bureaucrat, visits a fortune teller. She tells him that he is not where he belongs. He immediately leaves his wife, telling her he no longer loves her and, in his one-night quest to get laid, ends up abused, beaten, and incarcerated for murder. The play packs an enormous wallop; it features several insanely racist rants that Edmond delivers throughout his misadventures. Mamet wrote the play after the breakup of his first marriage, and the work is filled with extreme anger and bitterness. It also was written like a movie, with a series of short scenes and characters that are reductively named Wife, Cop, Pimp, Whore, and so on. It follows Edmond's descent into the hellish underworld of an unnamed city that is clearly New York.

"When I first saw it, I wanted to kill David Mamet," Lonnie, a gifted black actor, told me. "And I actually went looking for him, finding my way backstage. But by the end of the play, I realized that this was the most truthful thing I had ever seen on stage, and when I finally found David I hugged him. It wasn't long before I joined the cast myself."

Because Mamet and I had parted company on not the best of terms, Lonnie spoke to him about the idea of doing his play as a film. Mamet seemed intrigued by the idea and suggested we ask William H. Macy to play the title role. He also suggested we contact Julia Stiles about playing the doomed actress that Edmond murders.

With Mamet's blessings and a screenplay version of the play that he had written, Lonnie, Duffy Hecht, and I started making the rounds of the studios and production companies looking for backing. When the executives heard that we had a script by Pulitzer Prize-winning Mamet with William H. Macy and Julia Stiles attached as stars, they were extremely interested. "We'll read it this weekend," they had told us.

Then we never heard from any of them again.

So, we proceeded down the food chain, meeting with smaller and smaller independent production companies. Eventually, we ended up at Muse Productions, the company founded by Chris and Roberta Hanley and located in Venice Beach. Soon they were talking about making a deal with us.

CHAPTER 46

We met with them several times to discuss terms, and it was not unusual for us to show up at the appointed time (usually two in the afternoon) and then be kept waiting, often for more than an hour. Chris and his associate Molly Hassell would finally come breezing in, all smiles, saying that they had stopped to get coffees at Starbucks or something. I later learned that Molly was a trust-fund baby and Chris was married to a billionaire's daughter, so they both possessed a sense of entitlement that apparently didn't require them to ever apologize for keeping us waiting.

One of the first meetings was with Gary Rubin at his First Independent Pictures. Gary, a high-strung fellow, turned out to be a huge Mamet fan. His main concern seemed to be the scene in which Edmond is sodomized by his cellmate. "How would this be portrayed?" he wanted to know.

The scene is not shown on screen as scripted, but Gary seemed to be so nervous about it that I began to suspect that he really did want to see it. As Mamet says (in my favorite line in the piece), "Every fear hides a wish." When I kidded Gary about this, he got so offended that the deal almost fell through on the spot, and I had to profusely apologize to him to get things back on track. First Independent would be the American distributor of the film, and the final contract stipulated that I would have to call Gary Rubin before shooting the sodomy scene to quell any and all of his fears/wishes.

Hanley ended up piecing together the financing from twenty-nine little production companies. "Instead of asking one company to give us a million dollars, we got a million companies to each give us a dollar," Bill Macy later said. There were so many production companies that when all their names came up during the opening credits, it would often get a laugh. But I've since noticed that this is pretty typical for the way independent movies get financed these days.

Molly Hassell was friends with Bai Ling, the beautiful Chinese actress. I thought she would be perfect to play the peep-show girl that repeatedly encourages Edmond to "Take your dick out!" Bai wanted to meet to discuss the film, and we got together in an udon noodle restaurant near La Cienega Boulevard. She showed up wearing a tiny mini dress unbuttoned to her navel, and the entire place went completely silent as she walked in. The girl really knows how to make an entrance.

"I've read the script," she told me, "and I'd like to do it."

"Great!" I replied.

"I want to play Edmond." I was stunned and stammered something about the fact that we had already cast Bill Macy in the role. She quietly took this in and then replied, "Then I'd like to play the Prisoner."

I wasn't sure if she was kidding, but she seemed deadly serious.

"I don't think they allow men and women in the same cell," I replied.

"But I think you'd be terrific as the peep show girl."

There was a long pause and Bai finally nodded. "Okay. What does a peep show girl do?"

I tried to explain what a peep show was, but finally realized that it might be best for Bai Ling to visit one and see for herself. She and I headed to a peep show in North Hollywood and together we entered one of the tiny cubicles where a surprised dancer did her routine for the two of us.

When we filmed her scene, she was absolutely fantastic – funny and sexy and a bit threatening. I was just about to release her when she took me aside. "Stuart," she whispered, "You didn't shoot my butterfly."

I was confused, "What butterfly?" I asked her.

And with that, she pulled down her G-string to show me a glittering fake tattoo of a colorful butterfly right above her shaved… I instantly called back the crew to grab a shot of her butterfly.

Directing a David Mamet script definitely had its perks. Every agent in town was calling to sell us on using one of their clients. As the script was essentially a series of short scenes with characters who didn't reappear, it meant that most of the actors would work only one day. This made it extremely easy to fit our shoot into their schedules. One agent called to recommend his client Mena Suvari of *American Beauty*. When I told him we'd want her to play the Whore, he seemed happy. "Do you have anything for Denise Richards?" he wanted to know. So we were able to get them both. I had a stellar cast that included Dulé Hill of *The West Wing* and *Psych*, Dylan Walsh of *Nip/Tuck*, and Bokeem Woodbine of the television series *Fargo*. It was also the first time I worked with Russell Hornsby, who went on to star in my next film *Stuck* and later the television series *Grimm*. I was also able to cast old friends like Joe Mantegna, Debi Mazar, Frances Bay, George Wendt, Jeffrey Combs, and former Organics Mike Saad, Bruce Young, and Vinnie Guastaferro. I cast Rebecca Pidgeon (Mrs. David Mamet) to play Edmond's wife, and even offered to make David a producer, but he turned me down. "That's like asking someone at the Nuremburg trial if they want to be a Nazi," he told me. He visited the set on our first day of shooting and seemed pleased with what he saw. I told him he had an open invitation to join us during the shoot, but he demurred. "This is your honeymoon," he replied, and indeed it was. Working with Mamet again reminded me of our days together on *Sexual Perversity* thirty years earlier. It made me feel young and alive.

We began shooting before we had raised the complete budget, never a good idea. Normally, this would not be allowed by the completion bond company, but in an effort to save money (and avoid the medical physical), I had convinced the producers not to have a bond. Duffy and I offered to cover any overruns ourselves, confident in our ability to keep within our meager budget.

This ended up biting us in the ass when one of our cinematographer's assistants pulled the rug out from under us by turning our non-union shoot into a union one. The teamsters showed up, shutting down our production until we signed our entire crew to union contracts. Duffy and I lost most of our fees paying for the additional costs of pension and welfare. This was bad enough, but the situation got worse when our producer, Chris Hanley, disappeared. There had apparently been a falling out between him and Molly Hassell. We were initially told she had been let go, but the next day, there she was, and Hanley was nowhere to be found. We later discovered that Hanley and his wife had left for their vacation home in Africa, and the inexperienced (and appropriately named) Ms. Hassell was now running the show. This added a whole new level of chaos, but working with Bill Macy more than made up for it. He was an absolute delight. Although the character of Edmond had more dialogue than *Hamlet*, Macy never seemed stressed but was always completely at ease. I called him the Fred Astaire of actors as he made it all look so effortless. The other performers had no choice but to follow his good-natured lead, and as a result, the set was always happy and productive.

A very nervous Julia Stiles arrived to do her most demanding scene, which climaxes with her murder. It's a fifteen-page scene and builds from comedy to horror, perhaps the most difficult scene in the film, so Julia's nerves were well justified. After a few awkward takes, she nailed her first sequence and announced that she was "Out of the gate," and from that moment, the then-twenty-two-year-old actress was confident and absolutely brilliant. My job as a director was incredibly easy on *Edmond*. All I had to do was point the camera at the actors and let them and Mamet's exceptional dialogue do all the work.

We shot with downtown Los Angeles doubling for New York. The problem was that we needed the hustle and bustle of crowded nighttime streets, and LA's downtown emptied quickly after 5:00 PM quitting time. Because we couldn't afford to hire extras, we only had a couple of hours to shoot before downtown turned into a ghost town. We spent nearly every evening from five to seven shooting our street scenes. Several of these involved Edmond interacting with a pair of black guys playing Three Card Monte, a gambling game in which you try to pick the red queen. Dulé Hill played the sharper, and he became quite good at it. Real passers-by would stop to play the game, plunking down five- and ten-dollar bills, unaware that they were being filmed. Dulé would artfully fool them every time. I kidded him that if he ever decided to give up acting, he could easily make his living at Three Card Monte. Of course, after each take we'd get the unwitting participants to sign releases and we'd return their money.

Russell Hornsby played Dulé's shill, and he would keep up a steady stream of conversation, riffing with the passers-by. I found his patter hilarious but worried that Mamet wouldn't be amused, as he is notorious for insisting that his lines be read exactly as written, however when David saw the finished sequence, he was as charmed as I was.

When we wrapped principal photography, I discovered that Molly Hassell had neglected to pay the crew for their final two weeks of work. Instead, she headed off with a friend to a vacation in the Bahamas. I was livid, as it put the rest of us producers in an extremely awkward position, and Molly was not responding to any calls or emails. I had no choice but to refuse to work on post-production until my cast and crew were paid. They finally received their salaries – months later.

Andy Horvitch again was my editor, and David Mamet showed up one day with his wife Rebecca to watch a rough cut. When the peep show scene with Bai Ling came up, Mamet was transfixed. "I'd like to fuck her," he said.

"So would I," added Rebecca.

Gary Rubin (whose email address earned him the nickname Grubin) showed us the American poster, which looked exactly like the poster for Mamet's last film, *Heist*. It featured a large close-up of William H. Macy, Julia Stiles, Denise Richards, and Mena Suvari, and called the film "A heart-pounding thriller!" Bai Ling broke down in tears when she saw that she had been left off of the poster. It was very dispiriting to think that Rubin had so little faith in our film that he wanted to present it as something other than what it was. When the film was released on DVD, a forty-five automatic was prominently featured on the box cover artwork, even though no gun appears in the entire movie.

Edmond was invited to screen out of competition at the Venice Film Festival. The screening was scheduled for midnight on, I believe, a Tuesday evening. I expected the theater to be half empty but was amazed to find a full house. It was hard to read the reactions of the audience, because there were none. The film was subtitled, but I wondered if they were getting Mamet's unique and, in many cases, darkly funny dialogue. But when the film ended, the entire audience leapt to their feet and gave us a standing ovation that went on for at least twenty minutes. Bill Macy and I stood and bowed again and again.

William H. Macy won several acting awards for his exceptional work in our film, including the Astor Award at the Mar del Plata Festival in Argentina. We were invited to screen our film at the prestigious Telluride Festival, high in the Rockies. I exchanged my first-class ticket for several coach seats so I could invite Duffy Hecht and Lonnie Smith to accompany me. This was the first time that the film had been screened for an American audience, and some outraged audience members loudly shouted insults as they walked out, while others stuck around for spirited discussions.

It reminded me of the first time I had seen the play.

CHAPTER 47

A Dream Within a Dream

In 2002, I took part in a documentary entitled *Masters of Horror*. It was the brainchild of Mike Mendez and Dave Parker, who both have gone on to successful careers as directors. They interviewed just about everyone involved in the making of scary movies, a virtual Who's Who of horror. The list included (among many others) Dario Argento, John Carpenter, Joe Dante, Tobe Hooper, George Romero and myself. A few weeks later I received a call from writer/filmmaker Mick Garris. He lamented that, although we all had taken part in this documentary, we had been interviewed separately and never had a chance to meet each other. Would I be interested in having dinner with the other participants? Of course I would, and so we all met at Café Bizou on Ventura Boulevard in the San Fernando Valley. We sat at a long table in the middle of the dining room. The conversation was lively, and the evening a great success.

At one point, another table was celebrating a birthday and Guillermo del Toro encouraged us all to rise and sing "Happy Birthday" to the celebrants. "The Masters of Horror wish you a happy birthday!" Guillermo loudly exclaimed as we finished the song. And so, the group was officially born and christened at that moment. We continued meeting every so often, and the membership continues to grow. Wes Craven and Quentin Tarantino joined us, and even the great British director Ken Russell showed up one memorable evening. We found that all of us had a great deal in common (besides often being up for the same jobs). We had all been branded as directors of the most popular but also the most maligned genre, considered by snooty cineastes just a half step above pornography. We were all fellow prisoners in the ghetto of horror.

We discussed how wonderful it would be if we were given the chance to work together, and it wasn't long before Mick Garris devised the concept of an anthology television series in which we would each make an hour-long episode of our choice, uninhibited by censorship and limited only by the boundaries of our imaginations and the size of our budgets. The title of the show? *Masters of Horror*. With the help of Mick's manager, Keith Addis of Industry Entertainment, a deal was struck with Showtime to air the programs that were financed by IDT Entertainment, a company run, I was told, by orthodox Jews. In 2005, I was invited to join the party and chose to do an adaptation of the first Lovecraft tale I had ever read, *Dreams in the Witch House*. Dennis Paoli and I had often talked about adapting it, but since the titular witch sacrifices and feeds on human babies, the chances of getting past the politically correct studios and the MPAA censors seemed insurmountable. But now there was a forum without any such impediments, so the story was quickly approved, and we went to work. The tale concerns a young physics student at Miskatonic University who moves into a house that was once inhabited by a seventeenth century witch. The odd "non-Euclidean" angles of his garret apartment allow the old hag and her familiar, a human-faced rat, to travel through space and time. Soon, the poor student is under her power and serving as her accomplice in procuring an infant for her evil machinations.

The show was scheduled to premiere in the fall of 2005. In late August, there is a yearly television ritual called the Press Tour in which each network trots out its new series for the critics. This usually takes place at the Beverly Hills Hotel, and the stars and creators of the new series are there to generate a buzz and answer reporters' questions. Bob Greenblatt, the head of Showtime (and later the head of NBC), met with us in his hotel suite before we went downstairs to make our presentation for the critics. "They'll try to bait you," he warned us. "But you have to keep your cool and keep everything positive." We nodded, and soon we all went onstage to meet the press. The first question was, "Do you think that horror needs to be gory to be scary?" It seemed like a reasonable question to me, and I was about to answer when John Landis jumped in. "How dare you?!" he angrily began. "An idiotic and offensive question like that indicates that you have absolutely no idea how horror works!"

I was relieved when Mick Garris, usually the voice of reason, tried to intercede. To my amazement, he began talking about the effect horror can have on children. Out of the frying pan, into the fire. I looked over to Bob Greenblatt, who was standing at the back of the auditorium with one of his lieutenants. He put his finger to his head, miming a gun, and pulled the trigger. The next thing I knew, the press conference was over and we were leaving the stage. It had only lasted ten minutes.

In spite of this bizarre baptism, the series was a big success and Richard Band, who composed the music for my episode, was even nominated for an Emmy Award (the only one that the show ever received), and I was invited back the following year to direct another episode.

I had been visiting my daughter Suzanna's high school English class every Halloween to talk with her students about Edgar Allan Poe. I found that the kids loved the gothic writer with his scary tales and romantic poetry. One year, I read them Poe's great story "The Black Cat," and it scared the crap out of them. I realized that although the story had been dramatized a million times, no one had ever presented it as Poe had intended. The story, which is told in the first person, involves a man who is normally a gentle soul, but when he has had a few too many drinks he becomes sadistic and violent, taking out his frustrations on the family pet. In one traumatic scene, he cuts the poor cat's eye out with a pen knife.

I mentioned the story to Jeffrey Combs, and he told me that he had always wanted to play Poe; in fact, he had been researching the poet's life. Poe's own story is as grim and horrifying as many of his tales. His mother, a stage actress, had died when he was only two years old, and he and his brother and sister were separated, parceled out to various families in Richmond, Virginia. He was raised and educated by the wealthy John Allan (the source of his middle name), but was disowned as a young man for running up enormous gambling debts. Later, his child bride and first cousin, Virginia (whom he had married when she was not yet thirteen years old), contracted consumption (tuberculosis). There is a famous story of her entertaining Poe's friends with her beautiful singing voice, only to begin vomiting blood from a burst artery.

Suddenly it hit me that by making Poe the protagonist of his story, we could combine the tale with elements of Poe's own life. Like the protagonist of "The Black Cat," Poe also had an acute drinking problem. Dennis Paoli and I put together a script, and soon the folks at Reunion Pictures, the Vancouver production company, were budgeting it. "We can bring it in on budget if you make two changes," producer Lisa Richardson told me. "Set it in the present day," she began, "And cut the cat." Of course, neither was possible.

Lisa was right about the cat. It was the most expensive single line-item on the budget. We ended up using seven cats: five with two eyes and two with only one eye. Each cat was capable of doing a single task on cue. For example, if we needed the cat to hop on the piano, walk across the keys, and then hop down to the floor, we would use one cat to jump on the piano, a second cat to walk across the keys, and a third cat to hop down. Frankly, I was amazed that anyone could train a cat to do anything.

* * *

Jeffrey Combs' portrayal of Edgar Allan Poe was nothing short of extraordinary. Jeffrey affected a deeper voice and a Virginia accent and, with the prosthetic nose and wig, looked exactly like the famous author. The fact that he was the same height as Poe and had the same large grey eyes made the transformation complete. I felt that I was in the presence of this great, but deeply troubled, genius. The episode became one of the most highly regarded in the series.

A couple of years later, in 2009, Poe's bicentennial celebration took place. I was so excited by Jeffrey's portrayal that it occurred to me how wonderful it would be for a live audience to feel that they were witnessing a public appearance of America's greatest writer. Jeffrey and I talked about the idea of recreating one of Poe's recitals in which he would tell one of his famous tales and recite his poetry. We began choosing poems and stories for the performance and immediately contacted Dennis Paoli about writing the scenario, the connective tissue that would hold the piece together.

While the production, which we named *Nevermore*, was taking shape, Amit Itelman of the Steve Allen Theater and I worked out a plan to present it on weekends at the theater beginning in August. We initially scheduled a four-week run. Jeffrey had kept his costume from *The Black Cat*, a black frock coat and a flowing white shirt whose tattered sleeves were spattered with copious ink stains. Per Amit's suggestion, we advertised only in the *LA Weekly*, taking out a small ad each week. Would an audience show up to hear someone recite poetry? The answer turned out to be an enthusiastic YES, and the little 99-seat theater was filled to overflowing every night. My hope that the audience would believe they were in the actual presence of this long dead genius became a reality thanks to Dennis' brilliant script, Jeffrey's incredible channeling of Mr. Poe himself, and, of course, the power of those unforgettable words. We had re-animated Poe.

* * *

The show played to packed houses through the Christmas holidays. Jeffrey and I called it our little lemonade stand. As the running costs were so low, we even managed to make a little money. Our original plan had been to take the show to each of the five cities where Poe had resided: Boston, Richmond, Baltimore, New York, and Philadelphia. We were invited to bring the show to Baltimore for Poe's 201st birthday celebration in January of 2010. We played in the large chapel of the cemetery in which Poe and Virginia are buried, literally a few feet from their graves. Jeffrey passed their final resting places on his way to the stage, and one night, he touched Poe's headstone. Later, he told me he heard a voice saying, "Do it for her."

Sadly IDT, the company that had originally produced *Masters of Horror*, was sold to Starz, and the cable company decided to cancel the show even though it was one of Showtime's most popular series. Keith Addis at Industry Entertainment was able to sell the concept of a horror anthology directed by well-known auteurs to NBC. Although Mick Garris christened the new incarnation *Fear Itself*, after Roosevelt's famous quote, he ended up leaving the series due to what is often called "creative differences," but is almost always about money.

It didn't help that a major strike by the Writer's Guild was about to begin. The WGA's main issue was royalties for DVDs and what was then called "new media." The strike began on November 5th, 2007 and I joined the picket lines, as I had back in 1989 when that strike had lasted almost a year. A group of us horror writers got together and created shirts that read "Horror Writers Eat Scabs" in a reference to those who continued to accept jobs while the rest of us struck. The Screen Actors Guild's contract was also up for renegotiation that year, and they too joined the strike. Little headway was being made until the two guilds boycotted the Golden Globe Awards, forcing the telecast to be cancelled for the first time in its history. With the Academy Awards just around the corner, it looked like the strikers finally had the leverage to gain approval of their demands. At this point, the Directors Guild began negotiating with the producers, even though their contract would not lapse for six months. Those of us who were members of both guilds wrote a letter to DGA President Michael Apted begging him to please back off until the Writers Guild had finished negotiating their new contract. Apted's response was to announce that he'd only wait two weeks before beginning negotiations. What was the big hurry? Clearly, it was the Academy Awards and the knowledge that the writers and actors had the power to shut it down. This would be an enormous economic blow to the producers and could force them to accept the writers' terms.

The situation was further complicated by the fact that Gil Cates, the DGA's treasurer and "negotiating chairman," was also producing that year's Academy Awards. This was clearly a conflict of interest, and Cates should have recused himself, but did not. He encouraged the DGA to accept a terrible deal that shared insignificant revenues from streaming and nothing for DVDs in order to save the 2008 Academy Awards telecast (and his own job). The actors and writers, worn down by months of picketing, had no choice but to also accept the same rotten deal.

The only good news was that with the strike finally over, *Fear Itself* could at last begin production. The show would no longer be shot in Vancouver, but in Edmonton, and I was asked to direct the first episode in February of 2008. The story was about a shape-shifting cannibalistic serial killer able to take the form of anyone he has eaten. It all takes place in the police station of a small upstate New York town on a snowy evening while the local cops wait for the Feds to pick up their high-profile prisoner.

The network had suggested that the protagonist be changed from a policeman to a policewoman. They sent me a list of possible actresses to play the role. Most were beautiful blonde television stars who didn't look like they'd last ten minutes on the force. It seemed to be a given that the star had to be recognizable to a mainstream audience and, as Canadian mini-major, Lionsgate, was now producing the show, they were pushing me to hire someone from one of their television series.

I suggested Elisabeth Moss of *Mad Men*. She had turned Peggy Olson, her character on that series, from a plain-Jane secretary to a formidable force to be reckoned with. Like the character she played in "Eater" (our episode), it turned out that Moss was also a big fan of horror movies. She immediately agreed to do the role, and I had a wonderful time working with her.

February in Edmonton is like being at the North Pole. Twenty below zero was a warm day. The car that picked me up at the airport had a big crack in its windshield, which I soon discovered was typical. It was so cold in Edmonton that simply warming the interior of the car could cause the glass to break. You had to keep an electric blanket on your engine overnight even if you parked inside a garage or the engine block would freeze solid.

The evening that the actors arrived, I invited them to join me for dinner at a nearby Chinese restaurant. About an hour before the appointed time, I got a phone call from Stephen Lee (who had been the hero in my film *Dolls*), whom I had cast in *Fear Itself*.

"Hey man, do you have any pants?"

"Pants?"

"Yeah, the toilet on the plane exploded after I had taken a massive dump and my pants are covered with shit."

This was classic Stephen Lee. "Didn't you bring another pair?" I asked him. He hadn't. I told him he could wear a pair of my pajama bottoms, and so he did. I don't think he ever bought himself another pair of pants during the entire shoot.

Sadly, Stephen left us in 2014 after a massive heart attack. I was told that he had friends smuggle drinks and cigarettes into his hospital room. Stephen lived life on the edge, never allowing any issues, including the state of his own health, to interfere with having a good time. No one ever made me laugh as hard as he did.

Post-production on *Fear Itself* was hardly a good time. Unlike *Masters of Horror*, in which we had complete freedom from censorship, Lionsgate and NBC were now running the show, and each gave us a ton of notes in an effort to soften the fright factor. As "Eater" was the first episode of the series to be filmed, I felt that I needed to hold the line for my fellow directors. After all, this was a horror series, and it needed to be horrifying. The most disturbing scene was one in which our serial killer cuts out the tongue of one of his female victims. He then proceeds to fry it, slice it up, and then feed it to her. I fought long and hard to keep this scene from being cut, and my tenacity began to irritate my own producers. "Stop being such an asshole," Andrew Deane, a fellow manager at Industry Entertainment, cautioned me. "You're pissing them off."

Finally, a compromise was reached. We could show the killer cutting out and frying the tongue, and even taking a bite or two, but we couldn't show him feeding it to his victim. Ahh, the strange ways we earn our living. As things turned out, the complete uncut sequence was reinstated for the

DVD release. (As a footnote, I should point out that "Eater" scored the highest ratings of any of the *Fear Itself* episodes that aired on NBC.) Sadly, the summer Olympics interrupted showing all thirteen episodes, and after the games ended, so did the series.

Presenting horror on network television is a difficult process. You have to keep an audience on the edge of their seats while commercials constantly interrupt the story, becoming more numerous and intrusive as the show goes on. In my opinion, most of the horror-based TV shows on the air these days aren't scary at all. And I am nostalgic for those old episodes of *The Twilight Zone, The Outer Limits*, and *Alfred Hitchcock Presents* that burned themselves into my young and impressionable brain.

And the Ship Sails On

The longer I've been making horror movies, the more I've realized that the scariest stories are the ones that actually happened. Our daily newspapers are filled with hair raising events, many so bizarre that if a fiction writer suggested them, no one would believe they could ever have occurred. So it was with the story of Chante Mallard, a twenty-five-year-old woman in Fort Worth, Texas who, on October 26th, 2001, drove her car into Gregory Biggs, a thirty-seven-year-old homeless man. The impact was so powerful that he went flying through her windshield and was lodged with his head and upper body inside the vehicle and his legs and lower body on the hood of her car. Chante had been partying and was under the influence of booze and drugs. She knew she'd be charged with a DUI. So instead of taking Biggs to an emergency room, she panicked and drove home, leaving his broken body in her garage, still half impaled on her car. The fact that Mallard was herself a caregiver at a local senior citizen facility makes her actions even more difficult to comprehend.

Maybe her fear was based on the fact that the man she had struck was white and she was a black woman who realized that her chances of receiving a fair trial in Texas were slim at best. Biggs was still alive when Mallard checked on him the next morning, and he pleaded with her to take him to a hospital. She assured him that she would, but instead waited two days for him to bleed out, frequently returning to see if he was still alive and apologizing to him as he begged for help. After he died, she enlisted her boyfriend to help dispose of Biggs' body and the bloody car. Mallard was arrested four months later after bragging about the incident at a party, and her trial made front page news. She was eventually convicted and sentenced to fifty years without parole.

Writer John Strysik and I discussed the idea of making a film based on Chante Mallard's bizarre story. We did several drafts that stayed fairly close to the actual events but one day Strysik, in an effort to make the victim more active, suggested that maybe the Biggs character should try to free himself. If this had ever happened, the poor man clearly wasn't successful, but good screenwriting is fueled by the tantalizing question, "What if…" We pursued this idea, creating a suspenseful screenplay that became a cat and mouse game between Chante (named Brandi in our script) and Biggs (renamed Bardo by Strysik after the Buddhist term for a lost soul). We developed the script for a super-low-budget, taking advantage of the new digital technology.

One day, I got a call from producer Bob Katz who told me he had acquired the library of Amicus Productions, an English rival of Hammer

Film Productions back in the '60s and early '70s, famous for horror films such as *Dr. Terror's House of Horrors* and *Tales from the Crypt*. Was there any Amicus film that I was interested in remaking?

I had met Bob many years earlier when he was partnered with Moctesuma Esparza. Together, they had made *Selena* and other Latino themed films as well as historical epics such as *Gettysburg*. I had approached them with the idea of making a film based on Terry Curtis Fox's play *Cops* starring Jim Belushi, but it had come to naught. Now Esparza and Katz had ended their partnership, and Bob wanted to make horror films. I happened to mention our script based on the Chante Mallard case, which was now entitled *Stuck*, and he seemed interested. I sent him the script, and the next thing I knew, he called to tell me that he loved it. Could it be made for under three million dollars?

"How far under?" I jokingly asked.

"Two million nine hundred ninety-nine thousand, nine hundred ninety-nine dollars and ninety-nine cents," he replied.

We had a deal.

The next thing I knew, I was meeting with Bob and his assistant Julie at his office on Beverly Boulevard. Bob was in his early sixties, but was clearly trying to look younger. His hair was dyed an unearthly orange/brown, which he wore in a weird comb-over, but he was a charming guy who had seen it all and had a million colorful stories. He told me he used to go on motorcycle runs with Steve McQueen. He also told me he absolutely loved the script but had only one concern: the fact that our leading lady was black. Would I be willing to change that? I explained that in my opinion the race of the character contributed heavily toward her motive for not turning herself in.

"A black actress can't open a movie," Katz bluntly stated.

"What about Halle Berry?"

"She'll never do it," Julie chimed in, "She has been charged with a hit and run herself."

"Does she have to be black?" Katz wanted to know.

The question was answered for me when I received a call from Mena Suvari's agent Chuck James at the Gersh Agency. "Mena loves the script," he told me. "She wants to do it." This surprised me. I know Mena loves edgy roles, but what amazed me was that she had read our script. Where had she gotten it? It turned out that Katz had "slipped it" to a few agents. He knew I had worked with Mena on *Edmond*, and that I liked her.

I tried to think of a way to make it work.

I called Mena and asked her if she would be open to the idea of playing Brandi with corn rows? "No problem," she told me. We were able to cast the great Irish actor Stephen Rea as Thomas Bardo, the homeless man who is struck by Brandi's car. But could he do an American accent? "I'll work on it," he told me, and we hired a dialogue coach to help him. When I met him, he tried it out for me, and I was astonished how much he sounded like Humphrey Bogart. When I mentioned this to Stephen, he smiled and admitted he was a big Bogart fan.

I had assumed we'd shoot the film in a location that could pass for Texas, such as New Mexico, a popular right-to-work state (Republican code for no unions) but Jay Firestone, a Toronto-based producer, had come on board and he insisted we consider the Canadian Maritime region where the government subsidy was close to 90 percent. This meant that for every dollar you spent, the government would match it as an incentive to get you to work there. In September of 2006, I arrived in Toronto.

Like all of my films, we rehearsed for a week before shooting began. This pleased the actors, and I learned that Stephen Rea had been doing experimental theater in Europe at the same time Organic was performing at the Mickery Theater in Amsterdam. In fact, he had even been a member of the political theater company 7:84. Stephen told me that he used to give its leader, John McGrath, a hard time about driving a Rolls Royce. "But it's used!" McGrath would cry in an effort to defend himself.

Mena Suvari was thrilled to be working with Rea, but he seemed to think she was a self-absorbed narcissist, much like the character she was playing. During an early conversation, I suggested that Mena not play Brandi as a psychopath. "She's afraid," I told her, "and people do terrible things when they're afraid."

"She's a monster!" Rea piped in. "She has absolutely no conscience. All she cares about is herself!" There was a long silence. One of the things I had learned during my days studying Method acting at the University of Wisconsin was that an actor can't think of his character as a villain because no one in real life ever believes they are doing evil. Even Hitler thought he was saving the world. In order to play a role, you have to sympathize with your character and see the onstage world through their eyes. Rea's comment may have been helpful to him, but it wasn't helping Mena.

During the course of the shoot, Stephen would realize that he had misjudged Ms. Suvari and ultimately appreciate that she was a tremendously bright woman and a totally fearless actress. The two of them delivered fantastic performances, working brilliantly together to take the film beyond its tabloid roots. During their final confrontation, Brandi is set on fire, and Mena allowed flammable gel covering her arm to be ignited. Now *that's* commitment. When it came time to do a nude sex scene, however, she refused. "I've done topless scenes," she told me, "but that's as far as I can go." I explained that this movie was attempting to show the world as it really was, and that she needed to be completely naked for it to be believable. Without another word, she angrily stalked off to her dressing room. I wasn't sure what to do. Mena and I had never argued about anything before. When it came time to shoot the scene, she showed up wearing a robe. "Alright," she told me. "I'm naked." Indeed, she was. Thank you, Mena.

But we weren't out of the woods yet. Russell Hornsby also had problems with the nudity and refused to remove his boxers. By positioning Mena on top of Russell so her legs covered his underwear, we were able to make it look as if both characters were completely nude. The result was one of the steamiest scenes I have ever shot.

Stephen Rea had his own challenges, the main one being that he had to be made up every morning with the nasty gashes across his face that his character suffers from going through the windshield. This usually took at least a couple of hours in the make-up chair. Then he would be inserted through the shattered windshield with his legs on the bloody hood and his upper body hanging in the car. He asked that we wait until we were completely ready to shoot before he took his place, as it was extremely uncomfortable to hold this position. He often joked that he knew all his lines: "Help! Help! Help me!" The physical demands took a toll on the actor, who turned sixty during the shoot. (His birthday is on Halloween.) The day that his character manages to pull himself out of the car's windshield was the happiest that I've ever seen him. He even threw a party for the entire cast and crew.

Filming in Saint John was a delight. The city closed down its major intersection and allowed us to shoot the accident scene three nights in a row. In fact, the whole town became our backlot, and the locals were always friendly and helpful.

In a nod to Hitchcock, I ended up playing a small cameo in the film myself. Brandi discovers that her boyfriend Rashid is cheating on her and literally drags the other woman (gorgeous actress/stuntwoman, Sharlene Royer) out of his bed, beats her up, and throws her out of Rashid's apartment into the hallway completely naked. I come walking out of an elevator carrying shopping bags and am shocked to discover her. As my actors often say, "It gets a laugh."

The film had its debut at the Cannes Film Festival in June of 2007. Like *Re-Animator*, it was shown out of competition at the market. The reaction was so strong that extra screenings were quickly added. It was invited to be shown at the Toronto Film Festival's Midnight Madness in September. At a pre-screening dinner, Jay Firestone and John Lange, who headed our foreign sales company, got into an argument about who would end up sitting next to movie star Mena (Firestone won). Stephen Rea was unable to attend the screening in Toronto, but he did make it to a screening at the USA Festival in Dallas. There, he met the real-life son of Gregory Biggs, the homeless man that was hit and killed by Chante Mallard. Stephen told me the son was upset that his character didn't die like his father in our film. He thought we trivialized his death by giving the film a Hollywood ending. Maybe we did. "This is the way it should have ended," is what I would have told him.

I won a Silver Raven at the Brussels International Fantastic Film Festival, my first award there since *Re-Animator*. The film was well received by critics and audiences alike, so I was not prepared when I learned a few years later that *Stuck* had been remade by an Indian company as *Accident on Hill Road*. At first, producer Bob Katz denied knowing anything about it, which seemed odd as the Indian film mentioned *Stuck* in its publicity. Eventually, Katz admitted that he had sold them the rights to remake the film. "It wasn't a lot of money," he insisted. As writers of the original script, the Writers Guild insists that we should receive at least a third of our original fee, but Katz refused to pay us. We eventually had to send the WGA lawyers after him. He ended up declaring bankruptcy rather than pay us, which was a shame, as I had enjoyed his friendship.

Despite its success, *Stuck* would turn out to be my last feature film.

When I was in Saint John making *Stuck*, I shared a Boston-style brownstone with our director of photography, Denis Maloney, and Craig Lathrop, our production designer. My apartment on the second floor had a wonderful view of the harbor, and I could see the ships coming and going. One day, the Queen Elizabeth II arrived, and the night it left, I watched from my window as this glittering giant, lights ablaze, looking like a floating city, slowly left the dock on its way to its next port of call. The sight reminded me of the famous scene in Fellini's *Amarcord* (which means "I Remember") in which the Italian townsfolk take their tiny boats out to sea to watch the huge luxury liner go by. Like them, I watched as the enormous glowing ship got smaller and smaller until it was as small as a star in the sky on the distant horizon, and then it was gone. I wished that I could be on it. I wished that I was going with it. Maybe this was a sign that my adventures in the glittering world of movie making were finally coming to an end.

CHAPTER 49

Ob-La-Di, Ob-La-Da

In 2004, Jill graduated from Berkeley. We went to the graduation and, as Jill's name was called to receive her diploma, we saw that she had written "Thanks Mom & Dad" on the top of her mortarboard in big Day-Glo letters. The people sitting next to us held a large handwritten sign that read "The World is Yours!" That sentiment expressed the way we all felt about the graduates. After the ceremony, a tattered homeless street person stood on the corner crying out, "Happy, happy, happy!" and indeed we were.

Margaret's dream was to go to UCLA but she, like so many excellent local students, had been turned down, so she went to UC Irvine instead. She doggedly kept applying for transfer to UCLA and, after her third or fourth letter of rejection, I finally took her aside and told her that this was one dream she would probably have to forgo. Killing anyone's dream is the last thing I ever want to do, but UCLA seemed like an impossible one. Margaret wouldn't give up and, to my amazement and delight, she was finally able to transfer to UCLA in her junior year. I let her know how impressed with her I was and told her that if she pursued all her goals as relentlessly as she had UCLA, nothing would stop her from becoming a huge success. She graduated in 2010 and, after a series of other jobs, entered the demanding world of movie public relations. The fact that one of my daughters has joined me in the movie business really delights me. (Although I must admit that Margaret operates in a much higher sphere than I do.)

In 2006, Carolyn and I were invited to a film festival in Tucson Arizona. We had just arrived and checked into our hotel when the phone rang. It was Suzanna's boyfriend, Harold. I was surprised, and I asked if everything was alright. He assured me it was, and then told me that he was calling to ask me for my daughter's hand in marriage. He was calling from the top of a cliff in Malibu overlooking the Pacific and was about to pop the question, but before he did so, he wanted my blessing. I was completely taken aback, not because I hadn't seen this coming, and not because I was against the idea, but because it was so formal and traditional. It also reminded me of that day almost forty years earlier when I had asked Dr. Purdy the very same question about his lovely daughter. Shakespeare said that throughout life we play many parts. I was no longer playing the lovesick suitor; I was now cast as the fearsome father-in-law. I thanked Harold for calling and told him that the only person who could answer that question was my daughter. He sounded very relieved. When I told Carolyn about the call, we hugged each other.

They were married a year later in Guatemala, where Harold's family comes from. The enormity of the occasion didn't really sink in for me until I accompanied my wife, daughter, and her future husband to the florist who was providing the flower arrangements for the wedding. Suddenly, it became real for me, and that night in our hotel room I couldn't stop crying. I was losing my beloved firstborn daughter. Carolyn, who hates it when I cry, finally was able to calm me down. "Suzanna's not dying," she reminded me. "You'll still see her. Nothing has really changed. She hasn't lived at home for years." Which I had to admit was true.

The next day at the wedding, I was about to walk Suzanna down the aisle when she turned to me. She had never looked so beautiful. "I love you, Dad," she whispered. My heart soared, and before I knew it, she and Harold were husband and wife. Three years later, Carolyn and I became grandparents when Suzanna gave birth to Isabel Rosalie Avila. Carolyn and I would baby sit with her while her mother and father taught school (Harold is also a teacher). When Isabel learned to talk, she called me Papa, and I was playing another role. Next, Suzanna had a little boy. She and Harold named him Benjamin Isaac Avila (a nod to my father Bernie and grandfather Isidor). Ben reminds me of myself when I was a toddler, and I still have a picture of me as a two-year-old sitting in my grandfather Isidor's lap with my arm around his neck hugging him. Now, I am the grandfather.

"We always remain all the people we've been," Joe Haldeman wrote in his script for *Robot Jox*, "The oldest man has a child inside him." The truth in this simple statement makes it my favorite line in any play or film I've ever done.

In 2009 I was made president of the short films jury at the Venice Film Festival. Although watching the films was easy, there was a great deal of arguing amongst the jury about who should receive the prize, with the Russian juror pushing hard for her country's film, and so on. I was exhausted from all of the debating and was looking forward to visiting Mac Ahlberg at his apartment overlooking the Adriatic Sea in the Italian town of Cupra Marittima.

Mac had retired there in 2006, and I missed him terribly. He had extended an open invitation for Carolyn and me to visit him there since our early days working together. Carolyn and I took a train from Venice to Cupra, our enormous wheeled suitcases in tow. We walked along the boardwalk overlooking the beautiful white sand beach until we found Mac's apartment building. It was September, and the beach town seemed practically deserted. Although the day was sunny and the ocean bright blue, a cold wind blew. The tourist season was over, and there was a sadness about the town. We boarded the tiny elevator to his apartment. His wife Mary greeted us at the door. When we saw Mac, we were shocked. He suffered from congestive heart failure, and his legs were so full of fluid he could barely walk, but his spirits were high, and he seemed genuinely happy to see us.

It was a lovely visit, but my heart broke seeing Mac, always a pillar of strength, so compromised by his illness. We could only stay a couple of days and, when it was time to leave, I hugged my beloved "Professor." We both knew it was the last time we would see each other. Mac died on October 26th, 2012, at the age of 81.

Mille baci, Sr. Ahlberg.

background: Atmospheric water-drenched imagery from the Filmax pressbook for *Dagon*.

above: Make-up concept art for *Dagon*.

right: On location in Spain directing *Dagon*.

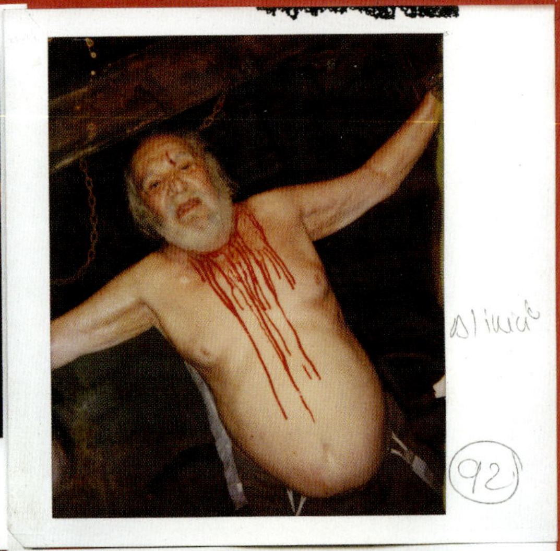

Lok d is my Paulin

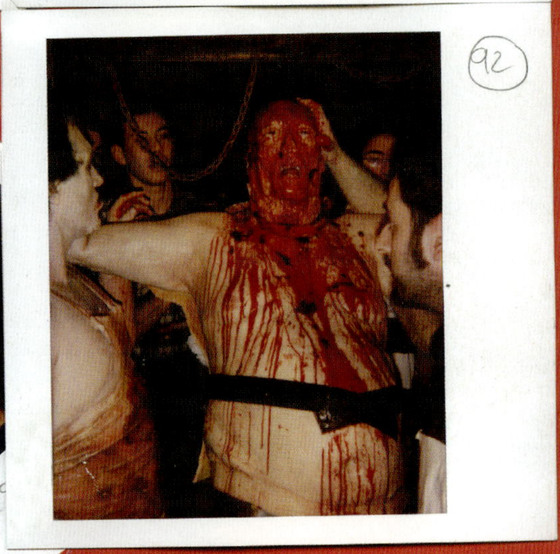

I no want. He make me lie down

Saaaahhhooo!!!

The end of Ezequiel.

Ia, Ia,
Cthulhu fhtagn!
Ia, Ia Dagon fhtagn!
Ia, Ia, Ia.

¡¡ Te voy a matar hija de puta !!!

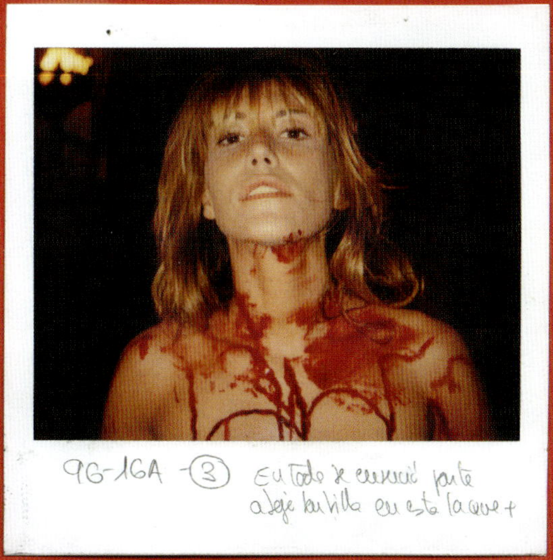

this page and opposite:
Reference snapshots from the filming of *Dagon*, including Uxía Cambarro (Macarena Gómez), Bárbara (Raquel Meroño) and Ezequiel (Paco [Francisco] Rabal).

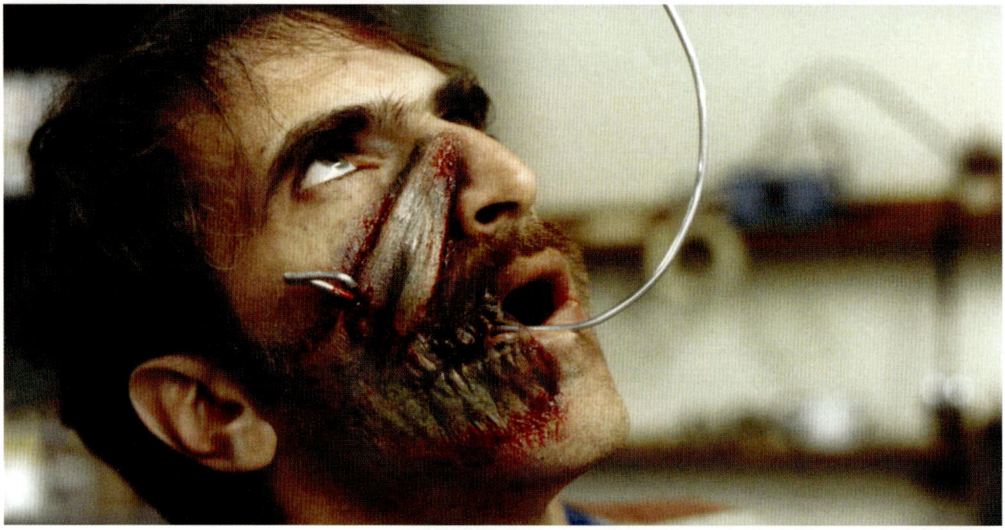

top:
Directing on location in Galicia, Spain during the filming of *Dagon*.

above:
Special effects make-up for *Dagon* by artists David Martí and Montse Ribé.

right (from left):
Mac Ahlberg (cinematographer), Danny Draven (director), me (producer), and John Strysik (writer), collaborating on *Deathbed*, a loose 2002 reimagining of the 1977 cult favourite *Death Bed: The Bed That Eats*.

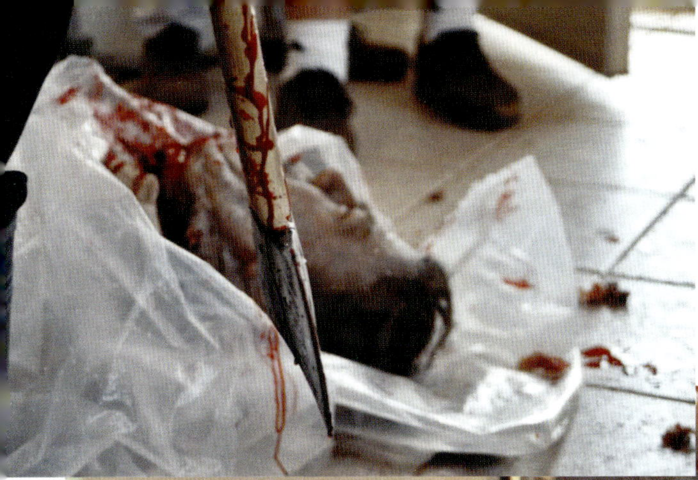

left:
Chris McKenna in *King of the Ants.*

below:
Signing an autograph during the promotion of *King of the Ants.*

bottom left:
Ron Livingston in *King of the Ants.*

bottom right:
George Wendt's frozen demise in *King of the Ants.*

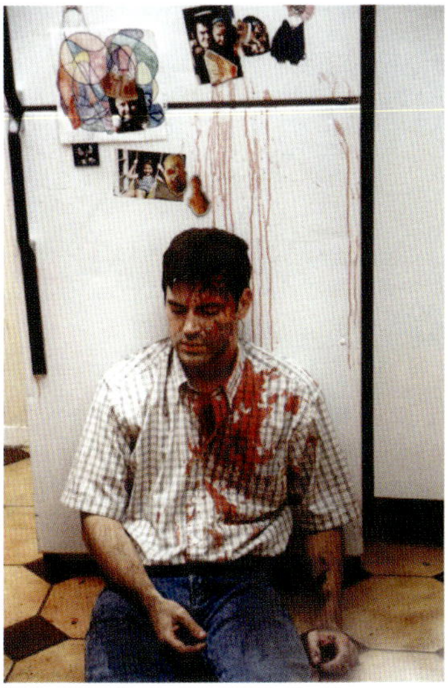

above:
Jesse Merlin (front) as Dr. Hill with George Wendt as Dean Halsey in *Re-Animator: The Musical.*

opposite both images:
With William H. Macy on the set of *Edmond*.

right:
With leads Mena Suvari and Stephen Rea during the making of *Stuck*.

below:
With Julia Stiles on the set of *Edmond*.

bottom right:
With my daughters in 1989, Jillian (back center), Margaret (left), Suzanna (right).

Celebrating Carolyn and my 50th wedding anniversary in 2018 with our daughters. From left: Margaret, Jillian, Carolyn, and Suzanna.

I was discovering that once you turn sixty, the offers for directing jobs are few and far between. Never one to wait for the phone to ring, I had gone back to creating theater after the success of *Nevermore* and began working on a new project – a musical version of *Re-Animator*. People had been suggesting the idea to me for years, and my response had been to laugh, thinking it absurd. But I also realized that since we had used practical special effects while making the movie, these same effects could work live on stage. I sat down and made a list of possible song titles and figured out where they would be sung. But who would compose them?

This question was answered when actor Ezra Godden invited Carolyn and me to join him at a performance of *The Bicycle Men*, a witty musical playing in Santa Monica, written by Mark Nutter. Mark, a fellow Chicagoan, had worked for the Organic as a musician when we performed *Warp* at the Apollo Theater in the early eighties. We had lost touch, and it was good to see him performing this hilarious show with three other talented actor/singers. When I later approached him about the idea of a *Re-Animator* musical, he immediately agreed to collaborate with me. We worked on it for over two years and, to my amazement and delight, Mark turned the show into something approximating an operetta, non-stop music with literally dozens of songs. Entire scenes were now sung. The music was captivating and the lyrics hilarious. The score reminded me of a cross between Gilbert & Sullivan and Tom Lehrer, the brilliant composer of twisted songs like "Poisoning Pigeons in the Park."

In 2010, we did our first staged reading. George Wendt was an early cast member. He encouraged us by championing our new production. He also agreed to take the role of Dean Halsey, the unlucky head of Miskatonic Medical School who is murdered only to be re-animated as a mindless zombie. Chris McKenna, who had done such an amazing job starring in *King of the Ants*, became our new Dan Cain, the young medical student who assists Herbert West in his grotesque experiments. Who knew he could sing? George introduced me to Graham Skipper, a talented young actor he had met while performing in New York. Graham came to Los Angeles to audition, and I was so impressed with him that he became the new Herbert West. Dean Schramm, who had been my agent for the last ten years, attended that first reading and liked it so much that he asked if he could join me as a producer. He invested his own money, breaking the first two rules of producing: never use your own money and NEVER USE YOUR OWN MONEY!

I was able to get the original FX team from the film – Tony Doublin, John Naulin, and John Buechler – to recreate the special effects for the musical. We designated the first three rows of the audience as a "Splash Zone," so named as gallons of blood soaked the spectators during each performance. During our two weekends of previews, I would talk to the audiences after each performance, as I had during my days at Organic, and would ask for suggestions to improve the show. "More blood!" they would always cry, so we ended up showering them with the red dyed baby shampoo (soap-based so it could wash out of their clothes). No matter how much we used, it was never enough, and I realized the only thing that would ultimately satisfy them would be to fill the entire theater with blood and let the audience swim out.

We opened the show in March of 2011, and *Re-Animator: The Musical* was an immediate hit. We took the show to the New York Musical Theater Festival the following summer and were also invited to bring the show to the Edinburgh Festival in Scotland. We had always wanted to bring the Organic Theater to the famous international festival, but never had the opportunity. Now, I wished that I was thirty years younger. There were over six thousand shows running at the festival, and we shared our stage with three other productions. We had to strike and reset the stage for every performance. Exhausting, but great fun.

In October of 2013, I moved out of my office in Burbank. I had been there for ten years. Clearing a decade's debris was a major undertaking. I had produced three movies and three television shows while in that little office. Duffy Hecht had left a few years earlier, and I now paid the full rent myself. The economics no longer made sense, and so I enlisted Zane Grant and Jackson Stewart, two of my former interns, and my son-in-law Harold and his father Carlos to help me. I moved into what had been Margaret's bedroom in our house on Crewe Street (where I now sit writing this).

In September of 2015, we celebrated my father-in-law Dr. Marshall Purdy's 100th birthday in Janesville, Wisconsin. It was touch and go for a while, as two weeks before the party, he took a fall and broke several vertebrae in his neck. But Carolyn, who planned the entire event with help from our niece, Lisa, managed to make it possible for her father to attend (in a neck brace) and be fêted by his entire family (all thirty-five of us) and his closest friends. When Doc saw the slideshow, that Lisa and her teenage son Matt had prepared, of pictures that began with him as a boy and covered his two marriages, children, grandchildren and great grandchildren, he seemed astonished. "This could start some crying," he remarked as he watched his life flashing before his eyes. A kilted bagpipe player entered playing "Scotland the Brave" and provided a rousing "Happy Birthday." We all joined in as Dr. Purdy blew out the candles on his cake with a little help from his great grandchildren.

Jillian married Brandon Alinger in January of 2016. He runs the American branch of Prop Store, a UK-based company which collects and sells movie memorabilia. He had started his own collection of *Star Wars* artifacts when a teenager and, like me, has found a way to make a living by doing the things he loves best. In November of 2016, Jill gave birth to Flynn Stuart Alinger. Her second son, Colin Henry, joined us in December of 2019. We are truly blessed.

These happy events were a joyful respite from the deaths of several old friends and members of the Organic Theater Company: Meshach Taylor, Tom Towles, Roberta Custer, Richard Fire, Rick Obadiah and John Heard. They left us much too soon. Sometimes they visit me in my dreams.

On March 22nd, 2016, Carolyn's dad passed away. She was at his bedside, and he wished her goodnight, closed his eyes, and went to sleep, dying the sweet and painless death we all wish for.

Adjusting to retirement has not been easy. I know I drive my poor wife crazy by being constantly underfoot. But we are slowly getting used to the new arrangement. I spend some of my days writing. These memoirs have taken several years to put on paper and have given me a chance to examine my life in great detail.

As the farm hands ask Dorothy at the end of *The Wizard of Oz*, "What did you learn?"

I learned I should have been more patient. Many of my greatest mistakes came about because I was in such a damn hurry. As the saying goes, "All things come to he who waits."

Unfortunately for me, my listening skills have never been the best. I need to keep quiet and pay more attention to what is going on around me. I now take great pleasure listening to the chirping of the birds at dawn. Why did it take me so long to hear them?

I've tried not to be so quick to anger. When I lose my sense of humor, I know I'm in trouble.

My old friend Albert Band, who passed away in 2002, once asked me why I had become so bitter. Coming from Albert, one of the most cynical people I have ever met, his question really took me aback. I always think of myself as optimistic and positive, but life has a tendency to beat you down.

Most biographies chart the rise and fall of an individual. During the first half of your life, everything seems possible, and as you reach the end, nothing seems to work anymore – including you. But as Billy Wilder said, "You have to have a dream so you can get up in the morning."

I receive great joy from the triumphs of my children and their loved ones. Margaret and her film editor husband Blake Carlile married in 2018. And nothing can beat grandchildren. I call them "the people from the future," and the ones who will someday take our places on this orbiting ball we call Earth. I pray that we can leave our campsites for them as we found them.

I'm very proud of my assistants and interns, many of whom have gone on to have successful careers as moviemakers in the treacherous minefields of Hollywood: Tom (now Ty) Bradford, Scott Forte, Jorge Falcone, Stuart Ortiz, Joe Begos, Zane Grant and Jackson Stewart.

Many thanks to Patrick McGilligan, Nat Segaloff, and Tim Lucas who helped me edit this unwieldy tome. (Although it comes as a shock to be told that your life is way too long.)

Most of all, I'm blessed with the love of my wonderful wife, who makes life an adventure and every day a joy. When we first met over fifty years ago, she told me that she couldn't imagine growing old with me. And somehow, we haven't. When I'm with her, I always feel young as we continue our delightful ongoing conversation that began as a wrong number.

Carolyn doesn't believe in a God who watches over you, but I wonder if our very meeting wasn't meant to be. You can call it fate or kismet, but I believe at the bottom of my living soul that she had to have been heaven-sent.

Speaking of Heaven, I visited it once, thanks to the wonders of nitrous oxide (often called laughing gas). I kept asking our dentist, Paul Landman, to crank it up more and more, and soon was reaching astounding heights, flying among twinkling stars and glowing planets. Eventually, I must have entered the Pearly Gates, and there sat God himself. Instead of a long flowing white beard, he had a well-trimmed mustache and wore glasses. His robes were replaced by a white lab coat. He looked exactly like my childhood pediatrician Dr. Aronow. He smiled at me.

Then He turned to one of his angels, "I like this one," He said. "He makes me laugh."

"That is not dead which can eternal lie,
And with strange aeons even death may die."
~ Abdul Alhazred ~

A Tribute to Stuart Gordon by Jeffrey Combs

I almost got Stu into a lot of trouble once.

In 1991 we were shooting *Fortress* near Brisbane, Australia. We were filming on a soundstage situated on the grounds of a movie-themed amusement park, kind of a small-scale Universal Studios. *Fortress* is a futuristic prison movie so most of the actors, including me, were costumed in grimy orange jumpsuits. One day, some of us were outside taking a break between shots when one of the many tourist trams slowly approached. Vernon Wells, an imposing, mischievous, big-hearted Australian actor, said to me, "Let's have some fun." Next thing I know we're jumping onto the tram and declaring that this was a prison break and that we're hijacking the tram to make our escape. Vernon removed the driver, hit the gas and began weaving the tram back and forth until finally he crashed it into a curb. We jumped off and ran away to raucous applause. Great fun. But about an hour later. Stu is approached by a rep from the amusement park informing him that the 'suits' in administration needed to speak with him immediately. Uh oh. Stu had already heard about our little escapade and so he left with a very serious look on his face. So clearly, because of us, Stuart was in trouble. About half an hour later, Stu returned looking very stoic. "So what happened?" we cautiously asked. Stu said, "Well, I started to profusely apologize for your reckless behavior, but they stopped me and said 'No, you don't understand. We LOVED what they did and we were wondering if they could keep doing it!'"

We all had a good laugh at that, but Vernon and I were greatly relieved and vowed to never hijack another tram ever again.

Back in the '80s and '90s, Stu and I had the joy of shooting a number of films together in Italy. Early on, we decided to give each other Italian names. I called him "Stuarto." Adding an "o" to the end of his name is pretty lame, I know, but there really isn't an Italian equivalent for Stuart.

He called me "Giofreddo", which is about as close as you can get to Jeffrey in Italian. Since then, whenever we would see each other or talk on the phone the conversation always began the same way:

"Stuarto!" "Giofreddo!"
"Come stai?"
"Molto bene, grazie!"
How I miss that.

Stu was my North Star. He plucked me from relative obscurity and gave me the kind of juicy role that every actor dreams of. He's the one who got me on the dance floor, who jump-started my film career and my gratitude to him is and always will be profound.

In one of our last conversations, Stu asked me how many projects we had done together over the 35-plus years that we'd known each other. We came up with about a dozen. If there was ever a role, big or small, in one of his projects, Stu always thought of me. That kind of consistent loyalty in our line of work is a profoundly rare thing.

I wish I could say that it was always harmonious on set between Stu and I, but that's not the case. Nor should it be. Film is a collaborative art form. A little friction is a natural part of the process. Something more interesting always came from our debates. We both understood this because, in a heartbeat, we were laughing again either at a new joke or an old one – usually an old one. We had quite a few of them in our repertoire, and we relished retelling them. Even though we already knew the punchlines, we'd end up laughing until we cried. Sometimes one of us would blurt out just the punchline of an old joke, and that's all it took for us to be in stitches.

That's what I will cherish and miss most about Stu: our laughter together.

My favorite experience working with Stu, which may surprise, was our last. For years, ever since we'd filmed *The Black Cat*, Stu had urged me time and again to consider doing a one-man show of Edgar Allan Poe. Typical of me, I resisted the idea. It seemed like a hell of a lot of work and, deep down, the notion of a one-man show scared the holy crap out of me. But Stu, true to form, was persistent and so after literally a couple of years of his urging, I finally relented.

We both had cut our teeth in the theatre and yet, throughout all the years, we had never done a play together. So for months it was just the two of us getting together at my place or his and honing the piece, finding the colors, discovering the arc of the evening. But there was something different about Stu's directorial approach throughout the process that I had never experienced from him before. A movie set is a pressure-cooker, and the director is at the center of that storm, but now, without the constant barrage of problems to solve, Stu was gentle, sparse, serene, Zen-like. It was a revelation and one of the most generous and spiritual experiences I've ever had.

To our delight the show was a huge success and the initial four-week run turned into years and performances across the country. To this day, whenever I have a chance to perform the show, I reflect on Stu's unshakable faith in me, his gentle approach and his unwavering vision. The show simply would not have happened without him. I see it as Stu's last and most powerful gift to me.

Many directors are wary of actors. They see their importance, but they don't quite understand them or their process, but Stu loved actors. I saw it many times. He loved their company. He loved their spirit. He loved their willingness to take a leap of faith into the unknown.

Stu was a masterful storyteller. It was perhaps his greatest talent. He knew how to construct a tale to get the most out of it. And he definitely delighted in compelling an audience to step out of their comfort zone.

The tragedy of losing his father too soon was a heartbreaking trauma for Stu. No child should have to endure that. The loss taught Stu early on a hard truth about life: that it is fleeting and unpredictable. No wonder 'defeating death' was a recurring theme in his work.

But the early loss also taught him the deep importance of family. Family was central to Stu. He was devoted to Carolyn, and he cherished his three daughters and later his grandchildren with all his heart. In a business that can take a heavy toll on families, Stu was steadfast in striking a balance between work and home and, no doubt about it, he succeeded.

I'm confident the appreciation for Stu's films will only grow with time. He left behind some truly indelible, iconic films that will continue to entertain and titillate audiences for generations to come.

I was beyond blessed to have him in my life and to call him my friend. I miss him.

Ci vediamo dopo, Maestro.

~ Jeffrey Combs (aka Giofreddo)

Acknowledgments

On behalf of the author, the Gordon Family would like to thank the following people for their loving support on this project:

To Mary Huelsbeck and the University of Wisconsin Center for Film and Theater Research archive team (Jeff Smith, Matt St. John, Amanda Smith), thank you for sourcing and expertly scanning the majority of the film artwork, photographs and behind-the-scenes material included in this memoir. Stuart was deeply honored to have these items in your care, and we are forever indebted to you for your service on this project. You helped bring these pages to life.

To Brian Yuzna, thank you for scouting near and far for behind-the-scenes photos and never-before-seen snapshots. We are so grateful for your help, and most importantly, your friendship.

To Jeffrey Combs, thank you for graciously offering your beautiful memories of Stu, for the laughs and the tears, and for the tremendous love you shared.

To Dennis Paoli, thank you for your tireless insight and encouragement — and for finding those spectacular photos from your college days. Your friendship is endless.

To David George Gordon, thank you for the wonderful family photos and for taking charge as the resident "Gordon historian." Your love and support mean the world.

To Peter Jackson, Rick Baker, Rob Zombie, Mick Garris, and Joe Mantegna, thank you for sharing your kind words and heartfelt memories.

To Brandon Alinger and the Propstore team, thank you for helping to source, scan and provide some technical "heavy lifting" of photographs and archival material when needed. Papa Stu would be proud.

Thank you to Stuart Blatt, Duffy Hecht, Dean Schramm, Jesse Merlin, Jackson Stewart, Jessica Safavimehr, Robert Kurtzman, Thomas Hargis, and Paul Gentry for providing additional photos and loving support to help bring this book to fruition.

Most of all, we would like to thank Harvey Fenton, Gavin Baddeley, Jason Heeley and Francis Brewster at FAB Press for making this publication possible. The level of love and care you brought to this project far exceeded our expectations, and we could not have asked for a better home for this beloved memoir. Thank you for helping us fulfill one last dream.

Picture Credits

Except where indicated, all photos courtesy of the University of Wisconsin Madison Center for Film & Theater Research.

First Image Gallery
Page 97, 98: author's personal collection
Page 98 (lower left): UPI Telephoto
Page 99, 100, 101: Dennis Paoli
Page 102 (top): Danny Rest
Page 102 (bottom), 103, 104, 105, 106, 107, 108 (top right): author's personal collection
Page 108 (top left, bottom), 109, 110: Chicago Public Library
Page 111, 112: author's personal collection

Second Image Gallery
Page 162, 163, 164, 165 (center), 165 (lower right), 166: Brian Yuzna
Page 167 (top left): author's personal collection
Page 167 (all other images), 168: Brian Yuzna

Third Image Gallery
Page 218 (top), 220 (top right): Robert Kurtzman
Page 220 (top left): John Carl Buechler
Page 220 (all other images): Robert Kurtzman
Page 221: John Carl Buechler
Page 223 (top): Paul Gentry
Page 223 (bottom right): Kathie Clark
Page 224: author's personal collection

Fourth Image Gallery
Page 289, 290 (top), 292 (top, lower left), 293 (top left, top right), 294 (lower left): author's personal collection
Page 295: Stuart Blatt
Page 296 (lower left): author's personal collection

Fifth Image Gallery
Page 329 (background, lower right): Filmax
Page 329 (center left, lower left), 330, 331, 332 (lower right): author's personal collection
Page 332 (top): Brian Yuzna
Page 333 (center): author's personal collection
Page 335: Thomas Hargis
Page 335 (center right, lower right), 336: author's personal collection

Index